In memory of Arturo Toscanini

⇛ ACKNOWLEDGMENTS

I WISH to thank the conductors who took time from their busy schedules to talk with me. Most of them volunteered much more than the usual interview material. They gave me an insight into their craft. They discussed their special problems. They were individuals rather than public figures.

I am also indebted to the staff of the Newark (New Jersey) Public Library for their wholehearted cooperation. Through them I had access to innumerable periodicals. I consulted the following books: *Paul Paray, Nos Amis Les Musiciens* by W.-L. Landowski (Editions et Imprimeries du Sud-Est, 1956); *I Am a Conductor* by Charles Munch, translated by Leonard Burkat (Oxford University Press, 1955); *Great Conductors* by Kurt Blaukopf (Arco Publishers, Ltd., 1955); *Music and Maestros* by John K. Sherman (University of Minnesota Press, 1952); *The Musical Scene* and *The Art of Judging Music* by Virgil Thomson (Alfred A. Knopf, Inc., 1945, 1948); *Theme and Variations, an Autobiography* by Bruno Walter (Alfred A. Knopf, Inc., 1946); *Music for All of Us* by Leopold Stokowski (Simon and Schuster, Inc., 1943); *Gustav Mahler* by Bruno Walter (The Greystone Press, 1941).

Much of the material in this book was first published in the *International Musician*. I wish to thank its editor and publisher, Leo Cluesmann, for his kind permission to use it.

HOPE STODDARD

CONTENTS

PART II ⋙ Conductors at Large

PART III ⋙ Thumbnail Sketches

PART I

Conductors of Our
Major Symphony Orchestras

CHAPTER I

⋙ THE CONDUCTOR

THE symphony conductor stands with poised baton. The eighty or so members of the orchestra hold fingers over strings and keys, fix wind instruments to lips, lift bows, mallets, and cymbals. The ushers close the doors at the back of the hall. The rustle of programs, the coughs, and the whispers subside. Two thousand listeners wait for the opening note.

In the second before the music starts, let us take a look at this conductor, this typical conductor of a typical symphony orchestra in the United States, as he stands there, elegantly clothed, alert, dramatic.

What is his personality—this composite conductor? He may be shy or outgoing; genial or severe; carefree or solemn. He may be a man of the world or an ascetic. He may be tall or short, florid or pale. One thing certain, though—he is energetic. A lazy conductor is a contradiction in terms.

Another thing is equally certain. Whatever sort of personality his is—he definitely has one. He never is hidden in the background. He has characteristics that won't rub off. He is himself and only himself. The minute he appears on the platform the audience feels his presence.

It goes without saying he is musical. But his musicianship is particularly marked in four categories: he is extremely rhythm conscious; he is acutely aware of tone colors; he has an excellent musical memory; and he is highly sensitive to styles.

He is a leader but he is also able to subject himself and is constantly doing so. Of all artists he is the most channeled.

He is channeled by the audience. Though he chooses his own programs, he is under obligation to the people who pay to hear them. He must stimulate and inspire them. He must instruct them. He must please them.

He is channeled by the orchestra. As a violinist or flutist is conditioned to his instrument, so the conductor not only knows his orchestra's capabilities but has developed a technique for making fullest use of them. He is aware, of course, of the basic fact that the right hand gives the beat and the left indicates the nuances and the expression. But he also knows that the trumpet must have a different send-off from the oboe; that the violinists' phrasing depends on the bowings assigned them; that the brasses must be prevented from submerging the strings. He is aware of the lip tension and breathing of each woodwind and brass player, of temperature effects on oboes, drums, and harps, of the part played by a hall's acoustics in orchestral balance. He is aware of the human element—the players' varying responses.

Most of all, the conductor is channeled by the composers. Through the black notes on the page, they tell him what he is to do. He is their messenger, their spokesman, their connecting current with the world. Often the notation is inadequate to express the composer's full meaning and, even when it is a fair guide, it gets distorted through the years. The conductor, however, studies what the score offers and finds, beneath copyists' errors, editors' revisions, and tradition's stumblings, the original conception. To do this he has to have an enormous amount of knowledge of musical history, of the various schools of composition, of the idiosyncrasies of each composer—and, again, insight into human nature.

But the conductor is channeled not only by audience, orchestra, and composer. His activities are influenced by school boards, civic leaders, women's auxiliaries, PTA groups, mayors, recording technicians, and orchestra managements. Usually, since the final aims of all these people are at one with his, namely the expert performance of great music, differences can be ironed out. But sometimes to maintain his integrity, to fulfill his artistic duties, or just to express his own nature, he diverges, and there is a clash. Then he is labeled an egocentric, a show-off, or a tyrant.

Even in the best of times, the orchestra men may begrudge him his power, composers his direct communication with the public, soloists his lion's share in the drama of the symphony.

However, his worst critics must face the facts: the astonishing emergence of music throughout the United States in the last twenty-five years would have been impossible without the conductor. This is not only because of what he does on the podium. He has been trail blazer, missionary, crusader. He has addressed chambers of commerce and Rotary Clubs, has invented acoustical shells, trained apprentice conductors, loosened philanthropists' purse strings, launched American composers.

He has initiated starlight concerts in Colorado Springs; furthered plans for a community arts center in Abilene, Texas; started youth concerts in Montclair, New Jersey; given school demonstrations in Chattanooga, Tennessee; organized an opera company in Omaha; directed a summer music camp in Transylvania, North Carolina; and formed a chamber music center in Bennington, Vermont. He has actually founded the orchestras of Burbank, California; Savannah, Georgia; Youngstown, Ohio; Joliet, Illinois; Cheyenne, Wyoming; Worcester, Massachusetts; Columbus, Indiana; Roanoke, Virginia; Jacksonville, Florida; Shreveport, Louisiana; and scores of other communities. More than any other category of musician, he has made music come to life in America. He is a symbol of what has been happening here musically and a guarantee that it will go on happening.

Because of the vastness of the conductor's work, we have had difficulty in this volume in compressing our material. We have been able to discuss at length only a few of the many excellent conductors in America today. We have chosen those occupying the podiums of the twenty-eight major symphony orchestras in the United States. These are the orchestras whose musicians are engaged at regular weekly salaries (union scale) for a season of around twenty weeks. Besides these twenty-eight conductors, we have devoted a chapter each to four "conductors at large"—men who have proved their mettle, yet for one reason or another have chosen to remain in the "guest" category and occupy no permanent podiums.

At the back of the book is a biographical dictionary: sketches of more than four hundred conductors who lead amateur, semi-professional and professional symphonies, and in some cases opera orchestras, in the United States.

Here, then, we present them: the men who direct the orchestras of our nation.

CHAPTER II

⫸ MAURICE ABRAVANEL

MAURICE ABRAVANEL and the Utah Symphony of which he is the conductor form as integral a part of Salt Lake City as the Mormon Tabernacle. Abravanel constantly seeks to deepen the association not only with the city but with the whole state. Most satisfying of all his projects have been the orchestra's touring activities. On one occasion, for instance, the Utah Symphony visited the mining camp, Bingham Canyon. This locality, with its ninety-odd-year history of fire and avalanche, shootings and knifings, hardly seemed an appropriate spot for symphonic endeavor. Yet here came conductor Abravanel and his eighty-five musicians rolling up the canyon in a blizzard. Engineers, brakemen, boilermakers, miners, turned out to hear and applaud. At the end of the program, Mine Superintendent Pett told the musicians, "Please drive carefully on the canyon road going home. We want to make sure you'll come again!"

This sense of interaction with the community is something Abravanel has sought throughout his life. He was born on January 6, 1903, in Salonika, which then belonged to Turkey and now is a part of Greece. His ancestors came from Spain, where in fact one of his many-times-great grandparents had been chancellor to Ferdinand and Isabella. But in 1492 they had fled, first to Italy, then to Salonika. Turkey, therefore, had not been the land of his forefathers, and he never felt it to be his.

When Abravanel was six, the family moved to Lausanne, Switzerland. He remembers trying to overcome his feeling of isolation there. His naturally dark complexion, sunned even darker under the hot skies of the Mediterranean, and his foreign accent set him apart from his classmates. Just at that time the Lehár opera *The Merry Widow* was all the rage, and the boys were singing snatches of it. Whenever he was with them Maurice would hum it loudly, hoping thus to identify himself with them. But it didn't work. In those days the Turks were persecuting the Armenians, and the world had built up a wall of resentment against them. When one of his teachers, in a fit of irritation, shouted at him, "Why don't you go back to Turkey!" he was finished so far as the boys were concerned.

Partly to keep from brooding over his loneliness, the boy turned energetically to music. His older sister studied piano. As long as she would play minor scales—these seemed to strike a particularly responsive note in him—Maurice would stand quietly beside the instrument. A German governess encouraged him in his music, and when he started to study piano, minor scales were the first he picked out.

In his teens Maurice got a job through his music. A neighbor, who was manager at the Municipal Theater in Lausanne, hired him as performer and arranger of incidental music for the shows. His work there made him happier than he had ever been before. Maybe—maybe—he could take up music as a profession! About this time, too, he discovered the little yellow-covered booklets, which had just been put up for sale, containing complete scores of most of the important symphonies. Scanning them, he realized he could hear the complete orchestral texture with his inner ear and could retain much of the scores in his memory. After that he couldn't buy them fast enough.

His father, sure that a musical life would mean comparative poverty, made careful plans for his son to enter the medical profession. He even sent Maurice to Zurich, hoping that a change of scene might mean a change of heart. It had the opposite effect. He plunged into the musical life of Zurich, went to every rehearsal and every concert of the orchestra.

It was irritating to have to take time out to study medicine. Soon he ceased even to attend classes at the university. Finally, he put the whole thing before his father in a letter. "I have come to the conclusion," he wrote, "that I cannot live without music. I don't know now which way this will lead. But I shall be content even to be assistant second percussionist in an orchestra if only I can hear and make music."

His father was horrified. "Lack of ambition" was what he called it. But since he could do nothing about it, he sagely decided to send his son to Germany, where the inflation of the early twenties was at its height and money would go further.

This transplantation at first gave Abravanel a wonderful sense of freedom. In Berlin, where he settled, he secured an introduction to Kurt Weill, and was soon taking lessons in harmony and counterpoint from him. As time went on, however, he felt he was making no real headway. His success in turning out contrapuntal bits came, he felt, merely through his skill in mathematics.

Now Abravanel was twenty. He wanted nothing but music. But music, it seemed, wanted nothing of him. His father had by now cut off his allowance altogether. He couldn't get a foothold in Berlin. He had days when he skipped meals. It was a dark, hard time and he had dark, hard thoughts.

Then on a chance suggestion of Weill's—"You should get a job in an opera house"—Abravanel went around to the agencies. He dropped in on one just at an opportune time. An accompanist had failed to show up for a singer's audition at the Mecklenburg-Strelitz Theater, and Abravanel was asked to substitute. His job finished, the director told him to drop around again, perhaps he could use him. On this slender encouragement he became a volunteer coach. He received no regular pay but was happy at the chance

to work with the chorus and soloists, to conduct a Christmas pan-
tomime from the piano, and now and then to substitute for an
absent orchestra member.

Then one memorable day he landed an additional job, a well-
paid one at that, as pianist in a café. Again he enjoyed solid meals.
He sampled during this period a long array of wonderful new
dishes—lobster, anchovies, elaborate desserts!

At the Mecklenburg-Strelitz Theater, Abravanel had four directors above him, all standing firmly on their rights of priority.
Therefore he felt he had small chance of advancement. As luck
would have it, however, the theater burned to the ground in midseason. (Abravanel will assure you, a twinkle in his eyes, that he
didn't start the fire!) The four directors automatically lost their
positions. The orchestra men, however, were engaged for life by
the State and were expected to produce somehow. In a body they
came to Abravanel. "You are going to conduct us in popular concerts," they told him.

Abravanel had never before conducted a concert, or for that
matter any real orchestra. True, he had gathered an ensemble of
sorts at the University of Lausanne and had orchestrated and
conducted for them the Molière-Lully *Le Bourgeois Gentilhomme*
and an Offenbach operetta. But this had been just a college affair,
confessedly amateurish. However, he knew that he could train a
choir, that he had a good grasp of symphonic literature, and that
he was teeming with ideas. "All right," he told them, "I'll do it!"
Even today when he tells about it there is a jubilant ring in his
voice. "The first time I conducted them, I had a wonderful feeling
that it went!"

There was one drawback. The men were paid by the year and
feared that an inexperienced conductor would need a lot of rehearsals. So, once they had Abravanel's promise, they added
warningly, "But no nonsense about rehearsals!" To this Abravanel
responded loftily, "If you don't need rehearsals, then I don't

either!" He conducted, all told, twenty concerts without any rehearsals whatsoever. He maintains he learned much technically that way, finding out how to convey his intentions with clear, unmistakable gestures.

He learned another cardinal principle of conducting during these days—not to make long speeches to the men. "Conducting," he notes, "is a craft of gestures and signals. The conductor remains inaudible. The sooner this is brought home to the young baton wielder the better."

The work in Berlin was followed by a two-year stretch as chorus master and conductor in Zwickau, Germany. After that, Abravanel served as regular conductor, then after two years as musical director, in Altenburg. Next he went on to Cassel in the same capacity.

The general manager of the Berlin State Opera, Heinz Tietjen, heard his performance of *La Forza del Destino* in Cassel and gave him a chance to guest conduct in Berlin. That performance went so well—the orchestra members gave him an ovation—that he acted as guest conductor there several times more and then was slated for a permanent job. By then, however, he had made up his mind to leave for Paris.

In a craft as complex as conducting, the need for the mentor, the propeller, the inspirer, at the beginning of one's career, is urgent—someone to give shape to the project, solidity to the dream. It was lucky, therefore, that at this point Bruno Walter appeared on Abravanel's path. The great man had heard him conduct at the Berlin State Opera and had recommended him as guest conductor for the Paris Grand Opera, where he himself was to appear in the same role. In this new post Walter gave his disciple the opportunity to cast, rehearse, and conduct Mozart's *Don Giovanni* as an alternate to himself.

Abravanel began to get other engagements in the French capital. In 1933 and 1934 he guest conducted Pierre Monteux's Paris

Symphony Orchestra and was musical director of George Balanchine's *Ballets 1933* in both its Paris and London engagements.

In 1934 he had a call to Australia to conduct a season in Melbourne and Sydney with the British National Opera Company. He had no steady job in Paris. Moreover, he had begun to sense an antiforeign feeling in France. Refugees were pouring in from Germany. Frenchmen were becoming alarmed. "Of course we don't mind foreigners," some were saying. "But when they are foreigners without a country, we know they want to stay here. We don't like that."

As Abravanel sums it up, "There just weren't enough jobs to go around. A tiny cheese and a full table!" He decided to go to Australia.

The orchestra Abravanel faced when he arrived in that country was ill trained and amateurish. His first improvement was to audition and accept seven women instrumentalists—an innovation there. His efforts brought their reward. He came for thirteen weeks. He stayed for two years. Under contract with the Australian Broadcasting Company, he conducted some fifty operas and many concerts.

Early in 1936 Abravanel received a letter that set him in a new course. It asked, "Would you be willing to come to the Metropolitan Opera Company?" America and the Metropolitan! *Would he be willing!* Since his contract in Australia was just expiring, he was free. He cabled his acceptance, and by the fall of 1936 was at his post at the Metropolitan.

As soon as he set foot on American shores, Abravanel says, he felt that things were different. Here was a people whose ancestors, like his own, had sailed the seas to find a homeland. "America is not a nation primarily made up of people born on this or that side of the mountain, or on this or that side of the railroad tracks," he points out, "but of people who are citizens because they have pledged loyalty."

Abravanel immediately took out his first citizenship papers.

If from the start he knew that America was to be his home, he was not so sure about the Metropolitan Opera Company. It seemed to him a small Europe, with European cliques formed along national lines, as well as European high standards. There were other difficulties. In those days the singers often came only for performances and were rarely available for rehearsals. He never felt he was able to make up a good ensemble. Since that day, Director Rudolf Bing has laid down the law that "stars" as well as orchestra and chorus members are to be rehearsed; and this, Abravanel feels, has been one of Bing's great achievements.

Abravanel felt hampered in repertoire, too. He did not want to be forever conducting operas already long in the repertoire and rendered traditional down to the last trill and sostenuto. He wanted to help fashion new productions.

One day his old friend Kurt Weill, also recently arrived in America, invited him up to his place. He played *Knickerbocker Holiday* in its first draft for Abravanel, showing him how he blended his own idiom with those of American operetta. This set Abravanel to thinking. The result was that in 1938 he accepted, on Weill's invitation, the post of conductor for a series of Broadway hits—*Knickerbocker Holiday, Lady in the Dark, One Touch of Venus, Street Scene*. He also opened *Day Before Spring, Seven Lively Arts,* and Marc Blitzstein's *Regina*. For his conducting of the latter production he received the Antoinette Perry Award.

Drawing comparisons between conducting grand opera and Broadway musicals, Abravanel points out that "on Broadway you aim at a long run. You polish things and get them exactly as they should be to succeed. Trouble is the aim here isn't high. You have to cut if the phrase is not simple enough. The product often is artificial, fabricated. Standards are whittled down. Despite this tampering with quality, however, it is paradoxically the musicals, in contradistinction to grand opera, which are given all the staging advantages: the best sets, the best costuming, the best everything. Someone once said to me at the Metropolitan, 'Careful! Don't breathe! You'll knock over the set!' "

Between Broadway hits, Abravanel conducted one season of the Chicago Civic Opera; several concerts in Montreal, Chicago's Grant Park, and New York's Lewisohn Stadium; a season of opera in Mexico City; and a season of symphony concerts in Sydney, Australia. This globe-spanning activity did not come from any deep urge to be on the move. It was, rather, an unconscious search for a place where he could settle down and become an integral part of the community as a symphony conductor. Increasingly with the years this desire was motivating his gestures of acceptance.

Also his gestures of rejection!

One afternoon in 1947 he was brooding over his conductorial career when the telephone rang. "Mr. Abravanel," he heard his manager saying, "the Radio City people have been watching you and have now made their decision. They will engage you for five years, starting at $30,000."

"I don't think I want it," said Abravanel.

"You don't understand," returned his manager carefully. "It starts at $30,000 and is raised every year."

"Would this lead to the permanent conductorship of a symphony orchestra?" asked Abravanel.

"No, but it would lead to a higher salary. Maybe $200,000 in five years. And recordings and Hollywood!"

Abravanel says he did some quick thinking. Already he had been deflected from his course far too long. He couldn't risk another detour. If he took this post with its glitter and its rush, and with its lack of close contact with audience and community, he felt that within six months he would have to engage a psycho-analyst. And that, he figured, would cost him all the money he earned—maybe more. His answer was a brief "No!"

This decision made him all the more receptive when, shortly thereafter, he was invited to look over the symphony orchestra in Salt Lake City.

When he arrived there in June 1947, Ruth M. Cowan, the manager of the orchestra, did a very wise and a very tactful thing. Instead of sitting him down with the board members and spreading out charts and listings, she made up a party and drove him up the canyon trail just outside Salt Lake City. The conductor-to-be spent that first day looking over the great land that, given his acceptance, was to be his base of operations. Abravanel had viewed the mountains of Switzerland. But the mountains of the moon could not have fascinated him as did these. For here he saw his homeland—that long-sought portion of the earth's surface that he could call his own.

When he came back from the auto trip the piece of paper they placed before him seemed not a mere typed set of lines with stipulations set forth and signatures to be added, but a personal message from co-workers and co-citizens. Therefore he was careful to tell them, in signing it, that he would insist on maintaining the highest standards in program selection and in the caliber of the orchestra men. To this they heartily agreed.

If he made the board of directors aware of the situation they were to face, he was not left in the dark either. Salt Lake City was a good two days' journey by rail from New York, and a day and a night from Chicago. It could be made a center of music only in so far as it could make itself, through an inner force, the pivot for generating symphonic music. Moreover, conducting this orchestra, statewide in scope, would necessitate traveling three hundred miles south and almost a hundred miles north to reach all concert centers. Music had been largely an adjunct of the

Church. Almost the first act of the early settlers had been to form a choir. Two of Brigham Young's grandchildren, Emma Lucy Gates and B. Cecil Gates, had become famous as opera singers and music organizers. The concerts of the Utah Symphony are even today presented in the Salt Lake City Tabernacle.

When Abravanel signed the necessary documents, he was aware of all this. He was also sure he had signed himself into exactly the kind of situation he had long craved. In September of that year he married Lucy Carasso of Paris and prepared to establish a home in the new location.

With mutual understanding and wholehearted zeal on the part of both the orchestral administrators and Abravanel, his tenure as conductor of the Utah Symphony has been richly rewarding. Since 1947, when he first took over, the concerts per season have increased from nine to sixty-two. Utah residents have listened, and listened intelligently, to Stravinsky's *Sacre du Printemps,* Beethoven's Ninth and his *Missa Solemnis,* Mahler's *Das Lied von der Erde,* and Honegger's *King David.* Thousands of students have been brought into intimate contact with great music via his introduction of concerts in schools and choral works for university students.

His musical program continues on into the summer. At the Summer Festival each year a musical and an opera are performed. The opera (which is his real love) must be properly supported or the musical—an audience indulgence—will not be forthcoming the next season.

He watches like a father over the material welfare of the orchestra. When bankruptcy once threatened it, he knuckled down and saved it. The board told him, "We have tried everything. We have to fold!" Abravanel went to the orchestra men. "I don't know about your contracts," he told them, "whether they will be honored or not. But whatever happens, I suggest that you come to the next rehearsal. I shall be here as per schedule at nine-thirty." His word was enough. Not one member missed a rehearsal or a concert for the next two weeks. Then he went to the board. "I want a substantial gesture, and I want it right now," he said. One member dived into his personal resources and put up $10,000.

The fact that he can work with and for the community never ceases to delight Abravanel. He is finding here what not even the Paris Grand Opera nor the Metropolitan could give him. He is discovering brand-new combinations in the art-plus-human motif, is working with music in its direct bearing on individuals. He is being given the opportunity to produce music in a variety of contexts before audiences unspoiled and unsatiated. Most important—the place is home. He and his wife are house owners in Salt Lake City. His two sons are products of the public school system. Abravanel has found his homeland, and his homeland has found him.

CHAPTER III

⇒ VICTOR ALESSANDRO

"Music is the most democratic thing on earth. All people should be allowed to partake of it to the fullest extent and at their own choice. It is our job, the professional musicians' job, to bring it to all who will take it."

Victor Alessandro, conductor of the San Antonio Symphony Orchestra, backs his words with deeds. When he was conductor in Oklahoma City, he had a "Little Symphony" playing in center floor, with the listeners circling it. He encouraged them to ask questions. He prepared his audience in San Antonio for the local première of Berg's *Lulu* by inserting in the previous week's program notes the announcement: "Next week I am going to present a modern work written in the twelve-tone scale. Many are not sympathetic to this idiom. I shall therefore present it as the first number on the program. Those who do not care to hear it can wait in the vestibule until it is finished. I shall then have the house lights turned up, so that they can take their seats for the rest of the program."

Touched in their pride as well as in their curiosity, the audience members were in their seats to a man for the first chord of *Lulu*.

Texas-born and Texas-reared, Alessandro has no reason to believe making music is an ivory-tower pursuit. At his home, first in Waco, where he was born on November 27, 1915, and then in Houston where the family moved when he was three, it was music from morning to night both for him and for his younger sister

Josephine. His father taught most instruments and gave his son instruction in them. He was also musical director of orchestras and bands at the Waco Cotton Palace Exposition and stood host to numerous musical celebrities during their stop-offs in the city.

The child's first memories were thus mostly musical memories. The broad-shouldered Texan says with a twinkle in his eyes, "I was still in baby dresses when they took me for the first time to see my father conduct. He was home from World War I and rarin' to get his bandsmen back into their routines. As soon as the Cotton Palace concerts were resumed, my grandfather began to take me to them. He'd give me a pencil and I'd stand on the seat—he took seats in the back row as being less conspicuous—and wave it. It was the only way to keep me quiet. I couldn't have been more than three when I decided that when I grew up I was going to be a conductor like my father."

Alessandro was three also when he heard his first opera—not without taking a firm stand in the matter, however. In fact his parents, just off for the performance, could hear him screaming halfway down the block. For the peace of the neighborhood, they came back and got him. "On the way, my father took my hand and told me the story of the opera," Alessandro recalls. "It was *Tosca,* the very work which started me off on my opera conducting activities in San Antonio in 1951."

For a year or so after moving to Houston young Victor remained quite satisfied with his role of back-seat conductor. Then one morning his mother received a phone call. Would Victor Alessandro conduct a children's rhythm band that was being formed? When she answered that her husband was far too busy for any such side line, she was interrupted by the voice hastily assuring her that it was the *younger* Alessandro who was meant. They'd been watching him at the concerts. They knew he could do it.

Mrs. Alessandro, when she had recovered from her surprise, sensibly suggested that the music be sent around. Having ascertained that her son could really be taught score reading—he had already been taking solfeggio lessons from his father—she consented.

The four-year-old was to prove a forthright wielder of the baton. At the initial rehearsal of the First Methodist Church Baby Band he refused to conduct at floor level. He must have a "podium." A footstool was produced. Satisfied with this elevation, he mounted it, looked sharply over the thirty-five urchins aged three to six assembled with their triangles, wood blocks, cymbals, and rhythm sticks, and swung into Victor Herbert's *March of the Toys,* assisted by an adult at the piano.

Alessandro recalls that his mode of discipline was simplicity itself. When some sound-bemused infant let his eyes stray from the footstool occupant, Victor would jump down and rap him smartly over the head. He has retained from that period two batons, which stand in marked contrast one to the other. One, sleek, unmarred, and with a neatly inscribed date, is the ivory baton presented him as a memento of his two-year tenure. The other, the one he actually used, is begrimed where his chubby hand clutched it and splintered at the tip from many a disciplinary thwack on some downy pate.

During the several years of its existence, this band, uniformed in miniature white suits with blue braid and smart caps with blue visors, was taken on short tours, given rotogravure coverage in the papers, and filmed by Pathé. The most vivid recollection of these years for Alessandro, however, is his chase down the main street of Houston after John Philip Sousa.

The famous bandmaster was just coming from a concert. As he paused for the traffic lights to change, Victor, catching up with him, shouted, "I just listened to your band. Now you listen to mine!" The bandmaster glanced down at the excited youngster tugging at his cape, took his hand, and good-naturedly went along with him to sit in on one of the Baby Band's performances.

Another Sousa *motif* was to sound in Alessandro's life. Many years later, when he had become conductor of the San Antonio Symphony, a concert presented by the orchestra fell on November 6, 1954, the one hundredth anniversary of the birth of Sousa. Alessandro programed *The Stars and Stripes Forever*. When the time came for playing this number, he told the audience, "I am turning over the baton for this march to a man who for fifty years has given his time and energy to developing music in Texas, a man who has taught students unto the third generation in the public schools of this state. It makes me doubly happy to do this, in that it is one of those rare occasions when a son can do honor to his father." Then he called the elder Alessandro to the podium and handed him the baton. It brought down the house!

Victor Alessandro lived in Houston until he was seventeen, learning to play the orchestral instruments, attending public school, composing a bit. For a brief period he toyed with the idea of becoming a lawyer. He attended Allen Military Academy in Bryan, Texas, for one year. Then, in October 1932, through the solicitude of the late Cesare Sodero, at that time conductor with NBC, his *Impromptu for Woodwind Quintet* was played over this national network.

This airing of his music was not only "the biggest thrill of my young life," as Alessandro put it, but the final nudge that determined him on a musical career. That fall he entered the Eastman School of Music in Rochester as a composition major, though with a conducting career firmly etched in the back of his mind. His teachers, Howard Hanson, Bernard Rogers, Paul White, and Emanuel Balaban, gave him the inspiration and knowledge he needed. So did the members of the Rochester Philharmonic. "These orchestra men told me what *not* to do. You don't get such pointers in the classroom. Orchestra men have to be realistic. The key has to come down, the string to sound, at the proper time. They learn through sheer necessity. They learn right!"

Another good piece of advice came from Sodero. "When you stop the orchestra because something is wrong," he said, "think, before you light into the men, 'Was there a point I didn't explain?' See if it wasn't your fault, and see you don't do it again!"

Alessandro insists on the necessity for respect between orchestra men and leader. "The orchestra players should be given the courtesy of being regarded as ladies and gentlemen and as artists," he says. "We are all colleagues working together. In this country we live in a democratic way, where people have human rights. You can't suddenly switch around in the orchestra and become a dictator. They have more respect for you if they know you believe in music as a human expression and in them as coauthors in this expression."

After the years at Eastman, Alessandro won scholarships to do postgraduate work at the Mozarteum in Salzburg, at the St. Cecilia Academy in Rome (here his teacher was Ildebrando Pizzetti), and at the American Academy in Rome.

When Alessandro returned to this country in 1938, he faced a land simmering with musical activity. First performances were given that year to Virgil Thomson's *Filling Station,* the first symphonies of Quincy Porter and Walter Piston, Ernest Bloch's Violin Concerto, Aaron Copland's *Outdoor Overture,* and Menotti's *Amelia Goes to the Ball.* Moriz Rosenthal, Lotte Lehmann, and Emanuel Feuermann picked that year to come to the United States. The Henry Hadley Foundation for the Advancement of American Music was organized.

The twenty-two-year-old Alessandro coming down the gangplank sensed new developments in the air. He realized that through the years outstanding teachers had been developed in our great music schools. Now they in turn were teaching students in public schools and colleges the country over to hold key musical positions in their communities. Because Howard Hanson and others of his kind had had the vision and the courage to stay with it, musicians were now welcomed in places off the beaten track, and they in turn welcomed the chance to be there. It was a musically workable America that Victor Alessandro faced. He was ready to pitch in.

It didn't take him long.

In the late summer of 1938, while visiting his parents in Houston, he received a telegram asking him to come to Oklahoma City. Some of the board members of the Oklahoma orchestra had happened to be in the audience when, as a nineteen-year-old, he had guest conducted the New York (WPA) Civic Orchestra in New York City. Now Oklahoma City had a WPA orchestra. They wanted him to take it over.

In no time at all Alessandro was in Oklahoma City. He went right to work—got instrumentalists in trim, citizens interested, programs arranged. He put concert giving on a regular basis. In 1942, when the WPA project came to an end, five thousand citizens of Oklahoma City, their taste for good music developed and their civic pride aroused, joined in a campaign to keep the orchestra going.

Alessandro used every possible means to make the Oklahoma Symphony the business of everyone. Oklahomans weren't allowed to be just ticket buyers. There was indeed no box office where tickets could be bought. One earned the right to attend concerts by taking out a share in the orchestral project. Tickets were the reward of paid-up membership in the Oklahoma State Symphony Orchestra Association.

Alessandro's programs also testified to his ingenuity. For instance, when a circus was quartered in the vicinity, he quickly added Saint-Saëns' *Carnival of the Animals* to the forthcoming program and borrowed a small elephant from the circus. At the concert Tina, as she was called, performed the *Dance of the Elephants* from this suite—with "grace and perfect rhythm," as the critics next morning put it. Of this episode Alessandro comments, "Tina did more for our budget than a whole battery of college professors."

Next Alessandro formed his Little Symphony, a unit of twenty or so members from the orchestra. They held their concerts in the intimate Hall of Mirrors, grouped in the center of the floor space. The audience members coming in greeted first one, then another, of the players by their first names. Then, once they had been seated in circles around the group and on risers banked against the four walls, they heard not only Mozart and Haydn but works by resident composers. At the close of each of the latter compositions, the composer rose, told how he came to write the work, and gave particulars of its creation. Then the audience asked him questions. Thus did Alessandro deliberately tear down the barriers between the professional musicians and the listeners, make audience members participants in the music.

On December 15, 1950, when Max Reiter, conductor of the San Antonio Symphony, was warned by his physicians to take a rest, he recommended Alessandro as his substitute. (It was his last official act. He was dead within the week.) During the remaining months of the 1950–51 season, Alessandro flew the five hundred miles between the two cities four to six times a week. In April he was signed as the orchestra's regular conductor. By the next season he was settled in San Antonio.

In May of 1955 he married Ruth Drisko, a flutist in his orchestras in both Oklahoma City and San Antonio.

Alessandro has inherited the dark wavy hair, the rounded contours of face, the full sensitive lips of his Italian forebears. He has also inherited their fervent love of opera. The opera season, a week-long festival held in San Antonio in February and known as a Southern institution, is one of his happier responsibilities.

During this week opera lovers come from a dozen states and from Mexico to attend the performances given by the great stars of the day. Unlike European opera companies, which develop orchestras as an offshoot, this opera company sprouted (in 1945) from the main stem of the orchestra.

The San Antonio Symphony sends up other healthy shoots in the tough mesquite plains of Texas. A score of youth, "pop," and special concerts are given, as well as five concerts for the thousands of men at Lackland Air Force Base near San Antonio. The orchestra's tours take it through Arkansas, Oklahoma, Nebraska, Kansas, South Dakota, and neighboring states.

Alessandro believes that "one of the first duties of the conductor is to understand his city. The conductor should seek to adopt a musical program in relation to its needs. He should work closely with the board of directors, get a thorough insight into the educational facilities, learn how the young people are developing, give encouragement and help to the teachers by tying in programs with their courses." For his solicitude to community music, Alessandro in 1956 received the honorary degree of Doctor of Humanities from Southern Methodist University and the Alice M. Ditson Award, given for "distinguished service to American music."

Alessandro's approach to his profession is something more than thorough and sympathetic, though. On a Thursday in October, 1955, the Symphony of the Air telegraphed him from New York, asking him to be their conductor in a concert that very week end. They had been contracted to act as accompanying medium for the Russian pianist, Emil Gilels, in one of his Carnegie Hall appearances. Alessandro came, studying the scores as the airplane winged across the continent.

The handful of music lovers who had gained access to the rehearsals of this concert witnessed a moving spectacle. Relations between Russia and America were tense, and Gilels' coming had been heralded as the first sign of a thaw in the cold war. Test case as he was, the Russian pianist could be forgiven a slightly wary attitude as he walked across the stage where the one hundred members of the Symphony of the Air were assembled. He looked this way and that as he passed between the lines of violins; as he slipped off his jacket and placed it over a chair back; as he peered into the darkened hall with its scattering of listeners. Then he nodded briefly to Alessandro and flung himself into his music as into a rescuing element.

The rehearsal was an all but wordless one, since Gilels knew no English and Alessandro no Russian. The word "okay," being international currency, was often used and at crucial points Nicolas Moldavan, violist in the orchestra, helped out as interpreter. To indicate to Gilels where to pick up a cue, Alessandro used their one common medium of expression—he pointed to the place on the printed score. Now and then Gilels illustrated a passage on the piano and the orchestra copied him. Sign language and a sort of sixth sense did the rest.

The rehearsal progressed somehow. But for a while it seemed no more than the concentrated activity of a group of workmen with a job to finish at an appointed time. Then something happened to put it in a higher category. Gilels, alien in looks and in language, pursuing his calling under strange circumstances in a strange land, stood up and went to the conductor's stand to refer to the score. Alessandro moved it over so Gilels could see better. Then, as the two of them peered at it together, he placed his arm across Gilels' back in a comradely gesture. They stood there a few moments, absorbed in a common study, while a warm wind blew over the iceberg of international relations and Gilels was made to feel at home. After that the rehearsal became all of a piece—a group of artists working creatively toward the end of high expression.

Of such human stuff is conductor Alessandro made.

CHAPTER IV

⫸ LEONARD BERNSTEIN

LEONARD BERNSTEIN, co-conductor, beginning in the fall of 1957, with Dimitri Mitropoulos of the New York Philharmonic, is the only symphony conductor who is habitually called by his first name. To his many admirers he is "Lenny." They like his friendliness. "I love people; that's my weakness," he says. They like his versatility. He is a piano virtuoso of no mean ability; he has conducted most of the major orchestras in America and Europe. He has symphonies, ballets, Broadway musicals, operas, and numerous other successful works to his credit.

What probably appeals to his friends most, though, is his breezy self-assurance. You can't down Lenny. Lenny will always come out on top. As far back as 1939 a colleague, noting Bernstein's behavior one evening at a party, remarked, "Lenny is hopelessly fated for success."

Lenny didn't always have this confidence. He was a thin, pale, withdrawn child, troubled with bad colds and asthma. His parents used to discuss his appearance and he got to feeling self-conscious. He didn't mix easily. "I felt like an underdog," he says.

Neither of his parents was musical. His father who had emigrated from Russia as a young man, had gradually risen from working in a sweatshop to being a successful Boston jobber in beauty supplies. Lenny was born in his grandmother's home at Lawrence, Massachusetts, on August 25, 1918. Life was comfortable during his childhood, and there were no financial worries. Still Lenny did not thrive.

Then something happened to change all this. When he was ten years old, Lenny came home from school one day and discovered, standing in the living room, a heavy upright piano. His Aunt Clara was breaking up housekeeping, his mother told him, and had sent it there to be stored. Lenny walked over to it and put a finger down on a key. Then he put two fingers down. He climbed on the bench and began using both hands. He happened to strike two notes that reminded him of the beginning of a popular song. Pretty soon he was banging the tune out with one finger of his right hand and keeping time with any sort of note with his left. He kept it up the whole evening. They could scarcely drag him away to supper. His five-year-old sister Shirley went to sleep to the sound of his keyboard explorations. She was to go to sleep to this sound almost every night for the next ten years.

Before the month was over, Lenny was a changed person. He brought home the boys from school to show them the piano and have them listen to him play it. He played it for grown-up guests. He demanded lessons.

At first his parents said no. Then, thinking formal training might chill his ardor, they rounded up a neighborhood teacher. In course of time they rounded up several neighborhood teachers, as Lenny ran through each one's scanty store of knowledge.

By the time he was fourteen Lenny was demanding a really good teacher. Bernstein Senior argued against it. It was a waste of time. It would lead nowhere. Lenny was to carry on with the beauty supply business. But when Lenny started coming home evenings with his fingers bruised from playing jazz for money to pay for lessons, his father relented. They chose Helen Coates, an assistant to the famous Boston professor, Heinrich Gebhard, and one of the best-known teachers in the area.

Miss Coates remembers that young Bernstein covered three times the ground per lesson of any other of her pupils. Besides mastering his piano lessons, he borrowed opera scores from the public library, learned the bass and tenor parts, and set his sister to learning the soprano and contralto parts. Their voices drifted across the lawn to the neighbors' houses as they maneuvered their way through a good portion of opera literature. During their summers at Sharon, Massachusetts, Lenny rounded up the children for opera productions. When he was fourteen they gave a burlesque version of *Carmen*. Two years later it was *The Mikado* and *Pinafore*. His father good-naturedly supplied wigs, and his mother one summer supplied the Bernstein maid, Leila Gianpietro. "I gave her the lead in *Pinafore*," says Bernstein.

This was music for fun, and the Bernsteins went along with it. It was another matter when Leonard was ready for college and still persisted in his music studies. There were some bitter arguments. Finally he and his father reached an agreement. His father would finance him in four years at Harvard, but outside music lessons would have to be Leonard's own lookout.

Once at Harvard, Bernstein started piano lessons with Heinrich Gebhard as his teacher. To pay for them he himself gave piano lessons. Among all sorts of "arrangements" he made, one stands out: lessons for three children for two dollars, with supper thrown in.

At college Leonard helped direct school musicals and composed short works for the Greek Society. He composed on the side. His music study didn't make him one-sided, though. He was a good all-round student. He graduated *cum laude*. Today he counts his Harvard training as one of his best assets, because it "opened my mind to the world's work in different fields, to human thinking and feeling that go into poems and plays and science and invention."

Bernstein must have had his doubts about the efficacy of a

college education, however, during the months immediately following his graduation at the age of twenty. No more money was coming from home. In New York, where he had gone to make his start in music, he faced real hardships. He had to find a cheap place to live. He looked up Adolph Green, a friend of camp days, and found him living with another man in a dingy East Side apartment. The two were glad to take Bernstein in. Paying rent would be easier shared three ways.

Evenings he'd sometimes join Adolph and four others in a musical skit at a Greenwich Village night club, the Village Vanguard—five dollars per performance for the whole group. Daytimes he tramped around to publishers looking for arranging jobs. Among those who turned him down was Harms-Remick, the house that published his earlier works. His present publishers are G. Schirmer, Inc.

He kept up his composing. He got to know Aaron Copland and talked music with him. Toward the end of the summer, he also met Dimitri Mitropoulos. This idealistic, shrewd, knowing conductor lent the young man a sympathetic ear. To Bernstein's blunt question, "What can I do to make a living in music?" he answered briefly, "You can study conducting."

Such a solution had never entered Bernstein's head. Moreover, he hadn't the faintest idea how to go about becoming a conductor. However, he'd heard that Curtis Institute had a flourishing conducting department under Fritz Reiner. He made application and was summoned for an interview.

It was an interview to remember. Reiner opened a heavily marked score at the middle and said, "You recognize this?" Bernstein looked at it in a daze, brought on partly by bewilderment and partly by an attack of hay fever he'd had over the week end.

"So," drawled Reiner out of the blank silence, "suppose you start here."

Reading an orchestral score is like instantaneously grasping the contents of a whole printed page by casting one's eyes over fifteen or twenty lines. To add to the difficulty, some of the lines in a score are given on the treble staff and some on another (tenor, bass). Thus it is like reading lines written in several languages. Bernstein was being asked to play all this at sight on the piano!

Bernstein plowed along, sniffling lugubriously. Then he came to a portion that sounded like a song he'd heard in his childhood. Was it a folk tune, a school song, a college air? Suddenly he almost shouted, "It's Brahms' *Academic Overture!*" It was one of the scores he'd got from the public library in the early days, and his mind had stored it safely away through the years. After that the going was easy.

During the two years he attended Curtis (1939–41) he studied, besides conducting, orchestration with Randall Thompson and piano with Isabella Vengerova.

Beginning in 1940, his summers were taken up with work at the Berkshire Music Center in Tanglewood. His role there has been a career in itself. From the start, the school's founder, Serge Koussevitzky, looked on the young man as his pet discovery. By the second summer everybody considered him a "pocket-sized edition" of the maestro. During Koussevitzky's lifetime he was to continue successively as student and assistant director, and, after his death, as director of orchestral conducting.

But in the fall of 1941, Bernstein, still a novice, knew only that the Curtis years were behind him and a question mark was before him. Koussevitzky suggested that he come to Boston. Perhaps he'd have some "odd jobs" for him there.

So that winter Bernstein opened a studio on Huntington Avenue in Boston as teacher of piano. Not a single pupil showed up. The winter wasn't a dead loss, however. His Clarinet Sonata had its première. He organized some concerts for Boston's Institute of Modern Art. He worked on a symphony, the *Jeremiah*. It was finished just in time to be submitted in a contest sponsored in the spring of 1942 by the New England Conservatory of Music. It was rejected. Shortly after this he himself was rejected by the draft board, because of asthma. On the whole, not a spring to remember.

But it was heaven compared to what followed. In the fall of 1942, Bernstein again tried his luck in New York. He lived in an eight-dollar-a-week room. He played for dancing lessons. He gave lessons—even *voice* lessons! "Lord, was I miserable!" he reminisces. "Walking the streets, hanging around publishers."

This time was worse than the first. For now he was not only a Harvard graduate but a trained conductor. He had letters in his pocket to prove it: Reiner's "extraordinary gifts"; Koussevitzky's "a conductor of outstanding talents, in whose brilliant future I have great faith."

Then he landed a job—at Harms-Remick. It consisted of listening to recordings of the improvisations of jazz men like Earl Hines and Coleman Hawkins and then writing them down. His ear was good. It was easy. And he got $25 a week for it.

Because of World War II the Berkshire Music Center was closed during the summer of 1943. Koussevitzky, however, was staying at his summer home in nearby Stockbridge. One day he telephoned Bernstein that he was giving a lecture on music for the local Red Cross and would like to have Bernstein come up and illustrate it at the piano. Bernstein jumped at the chance. This was the next thing to a vacation!

As he flung his things into a suitcase and rushed for the station, no sixth sense told him that he was setting out on one of the most momentous trips of his whole life.

After Koussevitzky's Red Cross lecture, Bernstein stayed on for a couple of days. One afternoon Artur Rodzinski, then conductor of the New York Philharmonic and a summer resident in the Berkshires, telephoned Koussevitzky. Would he please send Leonard Bernstein over to hear about a plan he had? "We talked sitting on a kind of haystack," says Bernstein. "I didn't go through any scores, or even play for him. An hour later I was assistant conductor of the Philharmonic. Just like that!"

The season of 1943–44, which has gone down in musical annals as the Bernstein Bonanza, started, so far as its namesake was concerned, on November 14, 1943. On that Sunday Bruno Walter, scheduled to guest conduct the New York Philharmonic, suddenly fell ill. The assistant conductor was asked to substitute. There was just time for Bernstein to run through the scores briefly with Dr. Walter as he lay muffled up in blankets in his apartment, to telephone his father who happened to be in New York, and to head for Carnegie Hall.

The Sunday afternoon concert-goers who filled the hall saw a young man in a gray slack suit—Bernstein had no tail coat and no time to buy or rent one—swing across the platform and raise batonless hands over the orchestra. From the first he had the audiences, seen and unseen, with him. Koussevitzky telegraphed from his radio dials at Stockbridge, "Listening now. Wonderful!" At the end, the audience cheered its head off. Reporters crowded backstage for the story of the year. He "showed that he is one of the very few conductors of the rising generation who are indubitably to be reckoned with," wrote Olin Downes on the first page of *The New York Times.* "A shoestring catch in center field. Make it, and you're a hero. Muff it and you're a dope. He made it," said a New York *Daily News* reporter. But to Bernstein the most memorable incident of the day was his father coming backstage afterward and telling him he was convinced at last that his son had chosen the right career.

Then it happened again.

In December Howard Barlow, just before the dates of his guest conductorship with the New York Philharmonic, fell ill. Once more Bernstein stepped in. Another triumph.

With the dawn of 1944, events went into even higher gear. Fritz Reiner, who was now the conductor of the Pittsburgh Symphony, arranged for Bernstein to come there on January 28 and 30 and conduct the world première of his *Jeremiah Symphony.* (Bernstein early that year had taken this out of desk-drawer obscurity and sent it to his former teacher.) The *Jeremiah* was heard one month later in Boston, when Bernstein conducted it with the Boston Symphony on February 18 and 19.

On March 29 and 31 and April 1, Rodzinski let Bernstein take over the Philharmonic in a program of his own selections. The young man chose Mozart's Overture to *The Marriage of Figaro,* Mendelssohn's *Italian Symphony,* Tchaikovsky's *Romeo and Juliet,* Aaron Copland's *El Salón México,* and his own *Jeremiah Symphony* with Jennie Tourel as soloist in the third movement, "Lamentation." Sure-fire hits all of them. He had shown himself to be an astute program builder.

In April his ballet *Fancy Free,* about three sailors on leave in New York, had its première under his conductorship at the Metropolitan Opera House. It was danced 250 times by the Ballet Theatre the first year and has become one of the most popular ballets in the repertoire here and abroad.

In May he won the Music Critics Award with his *Jeremiah* as "the most outstanding orchestra work by an American composer introduced during the 1943–44 season."

Bernstein's early successes in conducting and his early successes in composing, it is to be noted, were gained almost simultaneously. He has kept up both activities. However, he claims that a musician gifted in several different directions has a far greater problem than a musician gifted in one. A conductor is an "extrovert," he explains, who feels impelled "to get out there in front and let it out," while a composer "is a whole other guy with a complex inner life. His big relationship is with himself, or his Muse, or his God, or his unconscious." But though he laments having "to live in a schizophrenic world," he has to date done little to alter the situation. Perhaps he can't.

After that first sensational season as assistant conductor of the New York Philharmonic, Bernstein resigned in order to fill a series of guest conductorships—with major orchestras of New York, Cincinnati, Boston, Pittsburgh, St. Louis, Montreal, and Vancouver. On December 28, 1944, he managed to be in New York, however, for the Broadway opening of *On the Town,* his score composed to a book by Adolph Green. It was a smash hit and went into a movie version. Bernstein's share was $100,000.

The money came in handy, because by 1945 Bernstein had taken over the New York (WPA) Symphony and for three years was to direct it without pay. He scoured the town for talented musicians. He led the orchestra in premières of stimulating modern works. He did more—and won thereby composers' everlasting gratitude. He gave these works the two or three performances it takes to get audiences acquainted with them. When he resigned in 1948 Virgil Thomson wrote in the *Herald Tribune,* "He has reviewed the twentieth century for us, combed it for worthy revivals . . . brought up a nugget practically every time . . . mobilized for music a public of intellectuals that the standard orchestral concerts do not in any regular way attract."

During these years Bernstein became a symbol of a genius who was also a "real guy." After his concerts he usually stopped in at one of the small restaurants near the hall, with whoever had waited around for him, and, after a highball, had a raw beef sandwich with a raw egg on top and a side dish of chopped onions; then went to a party, where he sat at a piano pounding out boogie-woogie. Finally, after his friends dragged him away, they all would head for Greenwich Village. He'd stop on the step of his apartment on Washington Square and talk on and on, as if trying to stave off the time when he'd have to mount the four flights to his room.

In the spring of 1946 he made his first trip to Europe as a representative of the United States government at the Prague International Festival. Before the musical elect of postwar Europe he led the Czech Philharmonic in music by Americans—Schuman, Barber, Roy Harris, Copland—and his own *Jeremiah*. That same year he conducted the London Philharmonic in a series of concerts and introduced his *Fancy Free* with the Ballet Theatre at Covent Garden.

Meanwhile he was working on another ballet, *Facsimile* (premièred October 1946) and was brooding over a second symphony.

This was *The Age of Anxiety*.

The idea for it came to him when he was sitting in a bar having a beer and reading W. H. Auden's poem of the same name. The symphony is descriptive of a girl and three young men who meet at a bar, talk and drink, go to a wild party, and end up feeling pretty disillusioned. He composed it over a period of two years on trains, on airplanes, backstage in concert halls, in hotel lobbies, in any place he could find elbow room all the way from Montreal to Tel Aviv. He completed it while he was on a tour with the Pittsburgh Symphony. On this tour he also conducted twenty-five concerts in twenty-eight days and played a piano concerto at twenty-two of the concerts!

The work, which includes the jazz idiom and the twelve-tone scale and all points in between, was introduced by the Boston Symphony on April 8, 1949, with Koussevitzky conducting and the composer at the piano. The college students in the matinee audience stomped their approval. It won for Bernstein the Boston Symphony merit award for 1949, with the prize of $1000 presented by Koussevitzky himself.

In 1949 it was guest conductorships for Bernstein in America from coast to coast, and in 1950 it was Europe again. Wherever he went he created a stir—a hurricane! Entirely apart from musical values, Leonard Bernstein on the podium is quite a show. He jabs, points, punches; he stands on one spot simply bobbing up and down; he throbs his left hand close to his heart; he clenches both fists high over his head.

In November 1953, in Milan, he agreed to conduct Cherubini's *Medea*—an opera new to him. The score from which he worked dated back to 1797 and gave off dust. Bernstein is allergic to dust. Still he blithely remarked through sneezes after the last rehearsal, "The orchestra and I learned the opera together." Sure enough, when the curtain went up, he was his usual bouncy self, and the orchestra—as orchestras commonly do with him—responded heartily. The Milanese called him back a dozen times.

By the fall of 1951, Bernstein was a world-traveled conductor, head of the conducting department of the Berkshire Music Center, and Director of the Creative Arts Festival at Brandeis University. He was also a married man. His wife is Felicia Montealegre, an actress. They have two children, a daughter, Jamie Ann Maria, born in 1952, and a son, Alexander Serge, born in 1955.

In their nine-room apartment in New York, one room has been reserved for the exclusive use of Leonard Bernstein. He calls it his "thinking room," and it is well supplied with tools of his trade: a grand piano; a large work table with pencils, papers and two telephones; a portable phonograph; a recording machine; a couch.

Several projects are under way simultaneously. But this doesn't confuse him. He gets to work on one or another by standing in the middle of the room and "letting my body decide for me." If it moves toward the piano, then he runs his fingers over the keys in search of a melody; if he finds himself sitting at his work table, he starts writing his next television skit or mulling over the score of a symphony. If it's to the couch he's propelled, then he knows it's time to dream up new plans.

From this room has emerged his one-act opera, *Trouble in Tahiti,* first performed at the Brandeis University Creative Arts Festival in June, 1952; his *Wonderful Town,* which ran a year and a half on Broadway and won the Drama Critics Award; a ballet version of his *Age of Anxiety;* the score of the moving picture *On the Waterfront;* the incidental music for Julie Harris' *The Lark,* television programs on *Omnibus;* the Violin Serenade premièred at the Venice Festival on September 12, 1954, with Bernstein on the podium and Isaac Stern the soloist; the musical version of Voltaire's *Candide;* and the musical *The West Side Story.* In this room also he has prepared hundreds of programs for his guest conductorships all over the world and for his regular programs with the New York Philharmonic.

One wonders in which direction he will go next. One thing certain, he will not stand still—not for long.

CHAPTER V

⪢ SAUL CASTON

SAUL CASTON, conductor of the Denver Symphony Orchestra, has a high place in the affections of Denver's citizenry. A judge of the juvenile court awarded him a plaque as the one "who had done the most for children." His relations with his orchestra men are good. His home life is happy. Yet he has a grave and solemn face, Lincolnesque in its long lines, in its deep-set eyes, in the weight of brow. Except for brief flashes of eye and slight changes of mouth line—when, for instance, he tells one of his many funny stories—it rests in deeply furrowed soberness.

Probably this is an inherited trait, along with his musicianship. One of his famous ancestors, Michael Gusikoff, was referred to by Felix Mendelssohn as "this Michael of the sad expressive features." And Mendelssohn added, "He is inferior to no player on earth in style and execution."

Michael was the greatest known master of that curious instrument the *Strohfiedel,* composed of strips of wood laid on a matting of straw. He made improvements in its tone and increased its compass, so that it finally developed into the modern xylophone. The hardships he encountered on his tours were said to have hastened his death in 1837.

It has been a long-standing tradition in the Gusikoff family—Caston's mother's side—for every child not only to study music but, in so far as possible, to devote his life to it. The family has in fact been producing musicians—in Poland, in England, and in America—for more than two centuries. Some dozen members of the American branch have joined major orchestras in this country. The Philadelphia Orchestra alone has had a violinist, two cellists, one trombonist, and one trumpet player.

Saul Caston, born August 22, 1901, in New York City, was brought up in the Gusikoff musical conservatory, so to speak. His parents, both professional musicians—his father a violinist-conductor, and his mother a pianist—arranged that their son should go directly from school each afternoon to Grandmother Gusikoff, who lived some ten blocks away from their own upper Manhattan flat. Here he spent the rest of the day sitting in on the practice sessions of his uncles—boys only a little older than he. In Michael's room he became acquainted with violin music; in Benjamin's room he familiarized himself with the cello literature; and in the parlor, where another uncle practiced the piano, he listened to keyboard masterworks. Meanwhile he plied them with questions about their instruments and, when they were in the mood, got permission to finger the violin or cello or try the piano.

In the midst of this busy, creative household he longed to participate in music making. His grandmother held "coffee evenings" where musicians gathered to talk music and play quartets, and the boy listened fascinated until all hours of the night. Then he walked home through the dark streets, let himself into the lonely apartment—his parents still were working—and got ready for bed, thinking of ways to obtain a musical instrument of his own. His parents were not making enough to pay for both an instrument *and* music lessons, and they knew the first would mean the second.

When he was nine his mother came up with an idea. An uncle, Irwin Caston, had an old cornet. Maybe he'd lend it to Saul. Irwin not only handed over the instrument but volunteered to give the boy lessons. So now Saul was assigned his own practice room at Grandmother Gusikoff's and spent endless absorbed hours there. One thing marred his happiness. Out of his instrument came only one tone at a time, while his uncles could produce two, three, four at once. "Just a piece of brass I'm blowing into!" he brooded.

Still he made rapid progress, and after a short time his Uncle Caston sent him to study with Max Schlossberg, trumpet player of the New York Philharmonic. One day he heard his famous teacher play. After that the boy didn't complain any more. "I listened to the quality of his tone—so lush and so golden, like a voice—and I felt better. I decided I had a real musical instrument after all." Caston is grateful to Schlossberg on another count. He taught him the two indispensables of musicianship: to be able to produce a beautiful sound, and to know and feel rhythm keenly.

Then, when he was about twelve, Saul made a discovery. He was allowed to conduct a little school ensemble. As he "went through motions and heard sounds," he felt, "here's the instrument for me! No one-tone-at-a-time here!"

From then on he looked on his cornet primarily as an entering wedge into the ranks of a symphony orchestra—the training ground for conductors.

He began looking around for an opening. One occurred in his fifteenth year. By then he was specializing in the trumpet and had mastered its parts in most of the classic symphonic works. The Russian Symphony in New York City—one of his uncles was already playing in this orchestra—needed a trumpet player. Conductor Modest Altschuler let Saul sit in the trumpet section for a few concerts, and the boy's hopes mounted high. But alas, when the orchestra went on tour he was left behind. "You're too thin," Altschuler commented. "Tell your mother to give you more milk."

To add to his chagrin, Ossip Gabrilówitsch, the conductor of the Detroit Symphony, a few months later rejected him for the same reason.

So Saul continued studying. Schlossberg began to teach him conducting, too. Then in 1918, while he was still practicing and drinking extra portions of milk, he heard of an opening in the trumpet section of the Philadelphia Orchestra. With little real hope he decided to try for the position. In a darkened Carnegie Hall he played for the great Stokowski. To his amazement he was accepted—with the one proviso that he study theory under a teacher of Stokowski's choice. That fall he went to Philadelphia. He was to remain with the orchestra twenty-seven years.

Caston remembers that he went through the first season in Philadelphia in a daze. He rehearsed with the orchestra. He played in concerts. But the experience of hearing those magnificent sounds was almost more than he could bear. He believed —and still believes—that Stokowski had some mesmeric means of calling forth superhuman efforts from his men. At any rate, caught up in the web of glowing sound, Caston could scarcely credit his good fortune in being a part of it. After the concerts he would sometimes wander about the streets for hours, listening to the music inside his head. He had rented a tiny room in High Street, but he spent most of his time at the concert hall—watching other members practice, inspecting their instruments, asking questions.

In 1923 Stokowski told him he had decided to make him first trumpet of the orchestra. Caston remembers that he was scared stiff at the announcement. "Do you think I can do it?" he asked.

"Have you any doubts?" asked Stokowski.

"There are a few parts that would frighten me—for instance, starting all alone on the A natural in the *Rienzi* Overture."

"Is that all?"

"The solo trumpet parts in the Brandenburg Concerto Number Two, and the *Domestica* and *Zarathustra*."

He remembers Stokowski nodded briefly and said he would try him out. He did. He selected the *Rienzi* Overture as the first work on the opening program of the 1923–24 season. Saul went into its terribly exposed A natural opening as into gunfire. Somehow he came out unscathed.

Now Caston moved into a bigger apartment, which he shared with an oboe player friend. He learned much about the oboe that year, its tonal possibilities, what progressions lay within its scope. Also he studied theory with André Marquarre, the first flute of the orchestra, and through him became familiar with the flute. In time he grew used to the intensity of the Stokowski rehearsals. "More was accomplished," he recalls, "than I could have thought possible in so short a time. He knew when to drive and when to be lenient."

Then began a period of rapid and rich development. Caston studied with Rosario Scalero, Ernest Zechiel, and Fritz Reiner. In the Philadelphia Orchestra concerts Caston absorbed the techniques of such great visiting conductors and composers as Toscanini, Walter, Enesco, Strauss, Stravinsky, Krauss, Respighi, and Ravel.

Philadelphia had become a vital artistic center in painting as well as in music. The Barnes Foundation with its impressive art collection had established a school where modern theories battled violently against established modes. Gertrude Stein's disciple, Lincoln Gillespie, had set up his Bohemian headquarters in a midtown hotel. (Caston was later to première a memorial work dedicated to Gillespie.) Painters did sketches of musicians at quartet practice. Heated discussions were held on impressionism, on the relation between the arts, on the works of the local composers George Antheil, Frances McCollin, Samuel Barber, and Vittorio Giannini. Every nook and corner of the city provided Caston with chances to observe, learn, experience.

In 1930 he married the dramatic soprano Selma Amansky,

a student at the Curtis Institute. Their daughter Marise was born two years later.

About this time Stokowski began to show interest in Caston as conductorial material. He often asked him to conduct while he went to the back of the auditorium to listen to the sound of the orchestra. In 1935 he chose him as one of six conductorial assistants. In 1936 he invited him to be his assistant conductor on the transcontinental tour of the orchestra. Then at last came the big day. At the end of the tour, in the spring of 1936, Stokowski appointed Caston associate conductor of the Philadelphia Orchestra. He held this post until his departure for Denver in 1945.

An associate conductor of a major symphony orchestra must be a hard worker as well as a capable director. Since the associate does much of the rehearsing, and since often on a moment's notice he must substitute at concerts, it is necessary to master every score in the season's repertoire. Caston's situation was even more difficult. From 1936 to 1940 the podium was shared by Stokowski and Eugene Ormandy; so he was assistant to two conductors. Also he conducted half of the children's concerts and several of the adult concerts each season. He conducted at the Ann Arbor and Worcester festivals and on tour. After 1941, he took on the conductorship of the Reading (Pennsylvania) Symphony. In addition he guest conducted the NBC Symphony and the National Symphony of Washington, D.C., and served one season as musical director of the Robin Hood Dell summer concerts. His career is but another proof that, though successful conductors are of many casts of mind and types of background, they all have one characteristic in common. They are indefatigable workers.

In 1944 Caston was invited to conduct two concerts of the Denver Symphony Orchestra.

The Denver Symphony was facing a crisis in its musical affairs. This city in the heart of the Rocky Mountain region had been

populated by that greatest of migrations in our history, when in
1859 the slogan "Pike's Peak or bust!" lured young America
westward. In 1866 Denver's first choral society was formed. In
1882 Frank Damrosch, brother of Walter, who had come to
Denver to seek his fortune, united the scattered members of that
and other small groups into the New Choral Union and made
oratorio presentations annual events in the city. This brought a
sufficient number of instrumentalists together to make up an
orchestra. The Viennese Orchestra, as it was called, gave concerts
at the Elitch Gardens within horse-and-buggy distance of Denver. Later the orchestra moved to the Broadway Theater, and by
1912 it had grown to nearly symphonic proportions.

This was the first form of the orchestra. Actually it was not until
November 6, 1922 that the Denver Civic Symphony gave its first
concert, Horace E. Tureman conducting. After 1934 it was called
the Denver Symphony.

In 1943, when ill health forced Tureman's retirement, Denver
decided the time had come to raise the orchestra to professional
status. It would make the orchestra "a seaport wharf for an in-
land city, bringing trade, good residents and prestige to its
boundaries." A series of guest conductors, it decided, would afford
the best way to compare techniques and points of view.

Caston was happily unaware of all this when he stood as one
of the guest conductors on the podium of the Denver Symphony
in early 1944. He was a success from the very start. They asked
him to stay on. He was torn between desires. During all his adult
life he had been associated with the Philadelphia Orchestra. To
go out to the West and begin to create something new . . . "The
challenge itself is what drew me," he explains.

It turned out to be a greater challenge than he had expected.
To raise an orchestra of some seventy-five musicians from ama-
teur status to a high level of musicianship was a study in finesse.
Caston took the hurdles—replacements, stiffer disciplines, more

rigid schedules—deftly and with tact. He had contracts made out based on the same rulings as those of the Boston and Philadelphia orchestras. He changed the rehearsal periods from the evening to the morning hours. He drew upon the finest graduates of such music schools as Juilliard and Curtis for replacements. He created a training orchestra for talented young instrumentalists. He extended the season. He extended the tours. (In the spring of 1953 he took the orchestra on a tour of forty-one cities in eight Midwestern states.) He inaugurated children's concerts; fifty thousand children soon were hearing the Symphony in nineteen youth concerts annually. Along with the orchestra, the townsfolk also underwent a reorientation. It was made plain to them that their orchestra was not only to be enjoyed; it was to be supported.

Psychological changes Caston managed as adroitly. When uninitiated children, strangers to concert hall decorum, whistled at the orchestra, he had the orchestra men whistle right back. He lured new listeners in by starting "the family plan," under which tickets for an entire family cost but $1.20. He interested the Student Council of the University of Denver in holding affairs, half concert and half dance. The students arranged the details —time and place, whether corsages were to be worn, the matter of escorts. From start to finish it was their event. They listened to the concerts seated on the floor, and danced between numbers.

Caston extended the orchestra's season into the summer months. Since 1947 the orchestra has played for the summer series of the Red Rocks Festival, where the seats and platform are hewn out of a gigantic rock formation. This conductor understands the problem of out-of-door concerts. Mildred Norton, critic of the Los Angeles *Daily News,* wrote after his guest conductorship in Hollywood Bowl, "He proved at once that he knows how to make music performed out-of-doors sound urgent and exciting without the sacrifice of finesse or musical definition."

Long seasons, intensive rehearsals, had their effect. Virgil

Thomson speaks of the orchestra's "fine solo work in the wind section," of its "delicacy and precision, sensitivity and fine discipline," and attributes it to "Caston's exceptional ability to create a fine symphonic group."

Denverites put forward all sorts of reasons for Caston's success in their city: he is a good family man; he is shy; he is patient; he is democratic; he likes young people. The explanation may include all these factors. But it lies chiefly in Saul Caston's attitude toward music. Quite simply, he believes in it and loves it. He looks at it not as a mere added luster to a town, not as an indulgence, but as a thing inherent in human beings, something without which they may exist but not in the fullest sense live. He has staked his career on this premise. The indications are that he is right.

CHAPTER VI

»» ANTAL DORATI

"EACH time you conduct, it is a spiritual rebirth," comments Antal Dorati, conductor of the Minneapolis Symphony Orchestra. "You unload your own strength, nerves, feelings, everything. You are permitted again and again to relive a great moment."

Dorati considers the role of the conductor a privilege. To him it is not an opportunity to assert oneself, to lay down the law to some one hundred musicians, have them as prisoners under one's baton. The idea that the orchestra is an instrument that the conductor plays draws forth strenuous "No's!" "I work with my orchestra. I do not play on it," he emphasizes. "It is when one realizes that the men are not keys to hammer or strings to strum that great music comes out."

This sensitivity of outlook shows in his face as he talks—in his quiet, almost meditative manner of speaking, in the way his eyes take on a distant focus midway in a conversation as he searches for right answers, for inner reasons.

Or, cocking his ear suddenly, he says, "Hear that?" (It may be a spoon clattering on the tray in a restaurant or an automobile honking outside.) "One is aware of sounds always. One is thinking always, 'How could this be reproduced by musical instruments?' That is being a musician. But a conductor? He learns certain rules and skills, of course, but so also does a plumber. What one really gives one's men is taste and insight into the works at hand. That is a matter for rehearsals. At a concert I keep as still as I can. If it is a concert of my own orchestra I scarcely gesture at all. I just remind the men now and then of things we arrived at at rehearsals."

Such an approach to the art of sound implies a musicality in-born—and so it was with Dorati. In the small apartment in Buda-pest that was his birthplace—the time, April 9, 1906—it was music making from morning to night. His father, Alexander, was a violinist in the Budapest Philharmonic. His mother, Margit (Kunwald), was a teacher of piano and violin. As soon as he and his younger sister learned enough to take their places in ensemble playing, the family engaged in every type of chamber music, changing instruments—violin, viola, cello, piano, flute, clarinet—and delving into all periods and styles. Musical friends dropped in to fill out the ensembles and to provide audiences. The boy lived in music as in a safe and secure shelter.

At this early age, too, he got his first initiation into the wonders of Béla Bartók's music. He studied his piano pieces for children at the age of five. Soon he was playing his quartets in the home ensembles. "I watched eagerly," he says, "for every new string quartet to come from Bartók's pen, and each made a deeper im-pression on me."

Besides being gifted in music, Antal was proficient in other fields. He mastered his school subjects with ease. He could draw well. His parents used to discuss which career he should pursue, and it annoyed him when they suggested he become a painter. He never had the least doubt himself that his career would be in music. Long before he reached his teens he was composing—chamber works, even "operas." When he told his father he would like to study theory, the elder Dorati said he was too young! To prove his aptitude, the eight-year-old wrote a full-length quintet for piano and strings. After that his father looked up the best teachers there were. During his formative years, Dorati studied under Leo Weiner in harmony and Zoltán Kodály in composition. Later he worked with Bartók in the latter's seminar in folklore.

Although he started early, Dorati's composing career progressed somewhat erratically. For twenty-five years after he finished school, he composed only at great intervals. Then in 1954, "I started off like mad to compose—big works—a symphony, an evening-filling choral work. I write with great rapidity, with flame. I do not know yet what will come of it, but I have great confidence in my new writings."

Dorati finished his courses at the Academy of Music in Budapest at the age of eighteen, the youngest graduate of his class. One of his teachers at the Academy was at that time named director of the Budapest Royal Opera. So it was a fairly easy transition that brought Dorati the post of assistant there. He also matriculated at the University of Vienna. From 1924 to 1926 he not only did arranging, coaching, and rehearsing chores at the Royal Opera but, in order to pursue a philosophy course at the University, covered the 150 miles between the two cites once and sometimes twice weekly. After two years he gave up the Vienna studies. He rounded out four years at the Budapest Opera.

In this period he began what was to be a lifelong mission, that is, revealing the genius of Bartók. In 1927 he conducted Bartók's orchestra work, *Deux Images*. ("The emotional context was clear, but how to balance it intellectually!") At the Opera he and Bartók played four-hand on the piano, for the manager and a select circle of guests, the whole of Bartók's ballet, *The Miraculous Mandarin*.

To picture the young Dorati jumping out of bed at the sound of an alarm clock, gulping down a cup of black coffee, tearing along the streets of Budapest and up the broad marble steps of the Opera—to see him there rehearsing a chorus or providing orchestral background for a ballet—is perhaps to get some sort of picture of his outside existence during this period. But it is to miss entirely his inner life. These were days of long, long thoughts and of high resolves. He lived in the airy spaces of idealism. As he remembers, the region backstage and onstage was to him a magical land. When ugly actuality obtruded, he shut himself off from it or just fled.

Even as a man, Dorati has retained an otherworldliness rare in a profession of split-second timing and bedrock budgeting. Ask him what the indispensable attribute of the conductor is, and he answers quietly, "Nobility." Ask him what he means by that, and he repeats, as quietly, "I mean—nobility." The conductor, he believes, must "have exquisite musicality instinctive and acquired, very great knowledge; be completely informed on at least one instrument; understand all instruments so as to be able to discuss them with the players; and have very fine taste. But most of all he must have nobility of concept. For in the end, the concept is all the conductor can pass on to the players, who, already excellent musicians, have technique at their finger tips."

After four years in the Budapest Opera, Dorati began to grow restless. He longed to see Europe—to see the world. In the spring of 1928 he went on a holiday jaunt. In Dresden Mussorgsky's *Khovantchina,* that opera of mysticism and struggle toward independence, was being given. He wanted to hear it. The house was sold out. He begged at the stage door to be allowed to come in—to sit, to stand anywhere. He was so insistent that word reached the director, Fritz Busch. "If he wants to come in that much, let the boy have my ticket!" he exclaimed genially. So Dorati got to sit in the best seat in the house—the director's box! He got more. Going around to thank Busch the next day, he fell into a conversation with him. The upshot of this was that Busch invited him to become his assistant. Dorati accepted on the spot. A door was opening into a wider world.

In Dresden he was allowed to conduct at public performances. From the start it was evident that he never resorted to imbalance to obtain effects, and that he intuitively realized the composer's intentions. Dorati feels, "Composers have always given interpreters credit for ordinary comprehension, and they should make themselves worthy of the compliment. Instead, interpreters often are too acute. They overthink. They do not deal with the simple terms in the simple way they are presented."

What came out of Dorati's common-sense analyses and his sensitivity to sound was opera with texture and pattern, each voice with its appropriate place, each passage, main or subsidiary, coming out clear and with the right emphasis.

The reputation Dorati earned that 1928–29 season secured him his first big job as conductor. In 1929 he was engaged as the chief conductor of the Municipal Opera at Münster, in Westphalia. When he presented himself there the first day as the new director—he looked even younger than his twenty-three years—the doorman laughed in his face and refused to let him in. He had to wait until an official who knew him came and identified him. However, it wasn't long before everyone connected with the opera had learned to know and respect their new director. When he passed through the door of the Municipal Opera at Münster, Dorati passed into his adult life.

A few months before coming to Münster he had married Klara Korody, also a native of Budapest. Now he established a home in Münster and began to branch out. During the next few years he filled guest engagements in Frankfurt, Düsseldorf, Dessau, and other German cities, as well as in the Czechoslovakian town of Brünn. In 1930 he started what were to be, for some dozen years, regular annual guest conductorships of the Budapest Philharmonic Orchestra.

His conductorship of this orchestra signaled his adulthood in another respect. His father was a violinist in its ranks. To him Dorati was still a child, at times in need of admonition. He aired his opinions freely at rehearsals. He was a disturbing element.

Dorati Junior acted quickly and decisively. Dorati Senior was excused from participation during the young man's guest conductorships.

Dorati gave up his post at Münster in favor of guest conducting. After a year during which he made his headquarters in Berlin and toured all over the country, he left Germany for Paris. This was in 1932, a little before the general exodus of conductors and other key musical figures from Germany. (Hitler became chancellor in 1933 and *Fuehrer* in 1934.) However, Dorati disclaims any particular discernment or gift of prophecy. "I didn't like the way things were going," he says. "I didn't know *what* I disliked. It was like taking a rotten orange. You taste it, then you just throw it away. From one day to another, I decided, 'We go!' "

The Paris to which he came was still the gay metropolis, willing to sample any new offerings in the way of entertainment. He went to the headquarters of the French National Radio. "I'll make opera such as you never have had before," he told them. They gave him the job.

Dorati kept his promise. That year over the radio he presented works by Mozart, Gluck, Grétry, and Handel, many of them broadcast for the first time.

But *Wanderlust* again attacked him. In December 1933, when an invitation came out of the blue for him to conduct the Ballet Russe de Monte Carlo—a contract that carried with it the irresistible lure of a visit to America—he signed up. Thus he began a ten-year period as conductor of ballet. When that troupe, which had risen from the ashes of Diaghilev's famous ballet company, split in 1938, he went with the half that named itself "The Original Ballet Russe de Monte Carlo." Finally in 1941 he joined the American Ballet Theatre.

Now for ten years, for as many as three hundred performances annually, he stood on the podiums of theaters from the Metropolitan Opera House in New York, Covent Garden Opera in

London, the Liceo in Barcelona, and Théâtre des Champs Elysées in Paris, down to the smallest theater in faraway Australia, and saw that his orchestra men bowed strings, beat drums, and blew horns in synchronization with the swirling figures on the stage. He acquired telepathic sensitivity to a dancer's capabilities, moods, and endurance. He became expert in gauging, on the instant of entering the new theater, the size of the stage and its slant and surfacing, and from that could make a fairly accurate estimate of the dancers' slight alterations in diminuendos and accelerandos. He went into huddles in four languages with choreographers, dancers, stage designers. He worked out orchestrations so that the nuclear twenty or so musicians that he faced in the small towns on the road and the forty or fifty he faced in the larger cities would both be served. He jumped on trains and planes and steamers on split-second notice. He traveled to Copenhagen, Barcelona, Valencia, London; to Australia, New Zealand, Mexico. He crisscrossed America dozens of times.

During this decade Dorati made arrangements of *Le Pavillon, Eternal Struggle, Esquisse, Icare, Mirages, Romantic Age,* and *Pictures of Goya.* The Ballet Theatre today uses his versions of *Graduation Ball* (J. Strauss), *Bluebeard* (Offenbach), *Helen of Troy* (Offenbach), *Fair of Sorochinsk* (Mussorgsky), and *A Village Romeo and Juliet* (Delius).

Dorati's tenure with the ballet world was not an easy period for the dancers. He insisted relentlessly on the reign of music over movement, maintaining that dance in its largest part is but another interpretation of music and has to follow the laws and comply with the nature of music. The sessions with choreographers and dancers (and managers!) were sometimes stormy. However, out of the turmoil came useful contributions to the evolution of modern ballet. Also through these years American audiences became acquainted with ballet and learned to love it.

There was a more practical outcome for Dorati himself.

Through a ballet tour, he was introduced to Minneapolis. Between 1937 and 1945 he appeared several times in Minneapolis' Northrop Auditorium, the city succumbing simultaneously to ballet and to his quickening personality. It remembered the experience when it came to choose a resident conductor some years later.

As for Dorati, it did not take cross-country tours to convince him America was for him. "I liked America—the electricity in the air, the independence of the people—from the very first time I set foot on its shores." He took out his first citizenship papers in 1936 and now is legally as well as temperamentally an American.

During his decade of ballet conducting, Dorati carried on with his symphonic and operatic work. His debut as symphony conductor in this country took place in December 1937, when he led the National Symphony of Washington, D.C., in an all-Beethoven concert. During his ballet tours of Australia (1939–40) he conducted symphony orchestras in Sydney, Brisbane, Melbourne, and other key cities. In 1941 and 1942 he served as director of the New Opera Company in New York. On July 21, 1944, he conducted his own arrangement of Corelli's Seventh Concerto Grosso at Lewisohn Stadium. Of this event, Louis Biancolli of the New York *World-Telegram* wrote, "Mr. Dorati's version was steeped in the style and delicacy of Corelli's period. No heavy overlarding, no melodic puffing. Like the best arrangements, it let Corelli speak for himself with a little helpful prompting."

As calls to conduct symphony orchestras became more and more frequent, Dorati decided to make a change. In the summer of 1945 he left the Ballet Theatre. That same summer he was engaged as conductor of the orchestras in Montreal, Toronto, Lima (Peru), Havana (Cuba), and the Hollywood Bowl. He also presented two concerts over the American Broadcasting Company network.

Then in mid-September 1945, just as he was about to take off for Havana to conduct the Philharmonic Orchestra there, he received a long-distance telephone call. Would he come to Dallas to talk over the possibilities of his conductorship of their newly revived orchestra? By rearranging plane flights, he managed to squeeze in a few hours in that Texas city. During this time, he presented to the hardheaded businessmen at the helm of the enterprise a budgeting plan he had worked out on the plane.

They saw it made sense, but they were still unconvinced. "How do we know you can give us a good orchestra?" they asked. "If I can't, I hang myself!" Dorati replied. Texans like a show of spirit. They engaged him.

Then began a period that music critics John Sherman and John Rosenfield respectively call a "four-year musical boom" and a "love affair of four breathless seasons." It may have been both boom and love affair. Certainly it was musical adventuring of a high order. When it came to auditioning instrumentalists, Dorati picked and chose from the whole country. ("I traveled six thousand miles to get that orchestra together and did it in six weeks!") In selecting scores, every library and publishing house in Europe and America was his rummaging place. In the 1946–47 season alone he gave world premières to a new violin concerto of George Antheil, a symphony by Morton Gould, and an orchestral work by Paul Hindemith. New works by Hindemith, William Schuman, and Walter Piston were commissioned.

Dorati's enthusiasm and zeal were infectious. Citizens of Dallas began arguing over musical scores almost as enthusiastically as they did over football scores. Boasts about the orchestra figured as a close second to boasts about the state. City officials campaigned for the orchestra. Postmaster J. H. Payne instructed all mailmen to distribute blanks for membership in the orchestral association. Mayor J. R. Temple in 1948 proclaimed a "Symphony Week."

Dallas was Dorati's first home in this country. There he met American business executives man to man. He rode horseback "out on the range." He made sketches of the cactus-covered terrain, thus exercising his favorite hobby. He gave talks to the school children at assemblies. His little daughter Tonina started school there.

When he was once asked what was the highest moment in his Dallas sojourn, he exclaimed explosively, "Every moment was the highest!" He remembers with particular fondness, though, the presentation he staged of Bartók's *Prince Bluebeard's Castle*. It was its first performance in the United States and was broadcast from coast to coast.

Then in the fall of 1949, Dorati accepted an invitation to become conductor of the Minneapolis Symphony.

To mount the podium of an orchestra from which an Ormandy and a Mitropoulos had both been graduated, the one to the Philadelphia Orchestra, the other to the New York Philharmonic-Symphony, was to evince confidence of a special sort. But Dorati has such confidence. He plunged into his new assignment with tempestuous zeal. That very December he presented, with the Minneapolis Symphony and soloist William Primrose, the world première of Bartók's Viola Concerto.

In Minneapolis he gives audiences two things they particularly relish: an "open" tone and well-rounded programs. Each element of the orchestra, each line of a composition, he brings out with purity, and the compositions on any one program are balanced as skillfully.

Citizens of Minneapolis like also the way he takes his popularity in stride. "I think too much is made today of conductors," he says. "They are not that important. The orchestra men and I, we work together, share experiences. If great music comes out, it is to their credit just as much as it is to mine."

CHAPTER VII

⋙ MASSIMO FRECCIA

"THE most important thing for a conductor is to have such power of conviction as to succeed in making each member of the orchestra willingly place his individual talents at the service of one idea—the conductor's conception of a work."

Massimo Freccia, conductor of the Baltimore Symphony, speaks in an easy, conversational voice. A Florentine by birth, gentleness in thought and motion is his natural heritage. And the events of his life have encouraged this trait. His development as a conductor has cost him, if much endeavor, little pain.

From his earliest years—he was born on September 19, 1906—his mother, an excellent amateur pianist, saw to it that music surrounded her son. Around the age of five or six he decided he would like to become a violinist, and she supported him in this. His father, not so enthusiastic, gave his consent only if his son promised to keep up his academic studies as well.

When he was sixteen Massimo became a student at the Royal Conservatory of Music in Florence. Quickly becoming acquainted with his colleagues, he organized a quartet. They met at his house and ran through great amounts of chamber music. Another and still another member were added to the group, until the contours of a small orchestra began to appear. In playing the more difficult works, they found it hard to keep together. One day at a crucial point Massimo stood up and waved his violin bow to get them in line. It helped, and they grew to expect it.

As the orchestra continued to grow both in size and sound, the Freccia family indicated that some place other than the house might be better for practicing. So the musicians moved to a spacious garage on the grounds. Now they attempted larger works, and Massimo stood on a crate to do his time beating. The bow proved unwieldy and he got a baton. He found he was becoming intensely interested in getting the instrumentalists to play the music the way he felt it should be played. The sound of the instruments en masse, their mobility, their breadth, their infinite capacity for shades of meaning, intrigued him. As his sensitivity increased, so did his usefulness to the group. In the four years he worked with them, getting acquainted with the works of the great masters through actually conducting them, his inclination grew into a firm conviction. He would be a conductor.

His father finally became alarmed at Massimo's persistence. It seemed to him only logical that his eldest son (a younger son had taken up art) should follow his own profession, that of the law. "You can be a poor lawyer," he kept repeating to him, "and still command respect. But you can't be a poor musician. Count off the good musicians"—and he checked on his fingers the leading ones of the day—"and what have you left?" A flip of the hand gave the answer.

His father's scorn only made Freccia resolve to be one of those *good* musicians. Here the brilliant family tradition served him well. For not only was his father fourth in a line of distinguished barristers, but his mother's family went back in a direct line to the poet Tasso.

"At this period," says Freccia, "it was not only my father's skepticism that made things a bit hard. My very setting, Florence—the town of Dante, Michelangelo, Donatello, and Savonarola, with its art treasures and its traditions—had a tendency to make a young artist overanalytical, to make him belittle what he did himself. Moreover, all the art around me was in the

Italian tradition, which, though noble, by its very nobility was apt to shut out other traditions. Take the field of music. A young conductor in Italy usually ran the mill of the opera houses— became familiar only with the melodic and sometimes saccharine dramatic works of the Italian school. This to a young conductor could be stultifying. Only a genius such as Toscanini could for years assimilate Italian opera—Verdi, Puccini, Leoncavallo—and then with the same thoroughness become a master of German literature."

Freccia sensed from the start the need for a broadening repertoire and obtained it as he could. As a boy he had come in contact with the folk music of his people through playing his violin for the dancing at the fall "gathering of the grapes" in Pistoia Candeglia, the country place of his family. With his little orchestra he later covered a considerable portion of symphonic literature. As a young man, however, he looked to Vienna for further expansion. There instrumental music took the foremost place, and masterpieces of Haydn, Brahms, Bach, Mozart, Wagner were common fare. In Italy at the time there was but one symphony orchestra, and it was in Rome!

So he kept insisting he be allowed to go to Vienna, and at last his father gave in.

If ever the young man came to a parting of the ways, it was at this point.

Behind him were the happy life in the family circle, his home orchestra, his meditative walks along the storied streets of Florence. Before him were hard study and rigorous living. Freccia did not hesitate. He believed then, as he believes now, that the career of the artist is one of dedication. "The goal is not present indulgence but the attainment of one's ideal. One does not perform for the success of the evening. Even if there is great applause, one is in despair if something one has striven for doesn't come out. This is the tragedy all artists have to face."

In Vienna, Freccia studied the structure of music and mastered its mechanics. He was accepted as an apprentice to the great Franz Schalk, head of the Vienna State Opera.

Orchestral conducting quickly publicizes itself. Immediately word got around of Freccia's work in Vienna. He was called to be one of the conductors of the Spanish Ballet that centered in Paris and in Vichy, France. Not long after this he appeared as guest conductor at the famous Pasdeloup and Lamoureux concert series in Paris, then with the Vienna Symphony Orchestra and those of Warsaw and Poznan in Poland. Finally in 1933 he conducted a long series of concerts with the Budapest Symphony Orchestra, and, when on tour with this ensemble, visited towns in his native Italy. He acted as guest conductor on Italian podiums.

It was pleasant to be home again. But Freccia couldn't help noticing it was not the same homeland he had left. Now, under the Fascists, one had to think what the government wanted one to think. For Freccia, regimentation has always been uncomfortable. At first he tried to minimize his annoyance. Finally, though, he decided to leave Italy.

For many years he guest conducted on European podiums. Then, in the summer of 1938, Freccia was invited to conduct the New York Philharmonic at its Stadium concerts. *The New York Times* spoke of "plasticity acquired only by those born with a gift for conducting," the New York *World-Telegram* of "tonal beauties neither exaggerated nor understated," and of the way the conductor had of "whipping things up dramatically." This successful appearance had much to do with his guest conducting, the same year, the orchestras of Cleveland, Philadelphia, and Montreal, and with his assuming the conductorship, in 1939, of the Havana (Cuba) Philharmonic. The Havana engagement lasted four years. The orchestra, at an amateur level when he took over, was built to professional status. The subscriptions jumped from 275 to 2500.

Freccia left Cuba in 1943 when he was drafted into the Army of the United States. But when he arrived in the United States to take up his army duties, the war was drawing to a close and his name was marked off the list.

In 1944 he was engaged as conductor of the New Orleans Symphony. Soon the orchestra was enlarged to seventy-six players, then to eighty. Its budget was tripled. From an average of ten concerts a year the list grew to twenty-six, plus a tour of the most important cities of the South. During this time he was guest conductor of the San Francisco, Chicago, Detroit and, for several consecutive years, the NBC Symphony.

Freccia learned American ways as he went along. "In Europe an instrumental player generally trains primarily as a soloist. I have found it refreshing that it is the pride of an American to be an orchestra man."

He revels in the tempo of this country. When the New Orleans Symphony was to make its first broadcast over the NBC network, in the Orchestras of the Nation program, New Orleans could at first offer it no sound studio big enough. "But in less than twenty-four hours they had built one!" Freccia exclaims happily.

By this time Freccia had decided that America was to be his home, and in 1948 he became a full-fledged citizen. Shortly afterward Tulane University bestowed on him the honorary degree of doctor of music. They cited him as "a musician and scholar of notable attainments, having won respect and acclaim, contributing abundantly to the enrichment and culture of this region."

In 1952 Freccia became conductor of the Baltimore Symphony. This orchestra had been a going concern since 1916. In the first twenty-six years of its existence it had been wholly under the sponsorship of the city—the first orchestra on record to have been financed by municipal funds. Unfortunately, though, it had come to be looked on as the municipality's concern—and no one else's!

This orchestra on the downgrade was taken in hand by a group of interested citizens in 1942, through a plan suggested by Reginald Stewart. By making the sponsorship more equable— roughly one-third of the money raised by the city, one-third by the Association members, and the remainder by ticket sales and radio broadcasts—it again became a community enterprise. Gradually through the years it expanded to major orchestra dimensions. Then, at the end of the 1951–52 season, conductor Stewart resigned to devote himself to his duties as director of the Peabody Conservatory of Music, and Freccia took over.

In the fall of 1952 Baltimoreans welcomed their new conductor at a luncheon to which 1500 leaders in all fields—artistic, educational, governmental, scientific, and business—were invited. They decided that here was a man who could properly represent the musical interests of the city of Baltimore. Time has proved them correct. During the 1955–56 season the organization was faced by one of those financial crises which now and then assail symphony orchestras all over the country. The citizens of Baltimore organized a hundred-dollar-a-plate dinner to raise $50,000. By the night of the dinner, they had raised $66,000. At the end of the season the State of Maryland passed a bill granting the Baltimore Symphony $50,000 for 1956–57. The city of Baltimore also contributes $80,000 annually.

Freccia has a gracious approach to living. After the last fall concert and a period of auditioning and guest conducting in Europe, he goes with his wife, the former María Luisa Aspiazu, of Havana, to their summer home. This is situated on eighty-eight acres of Connecticut countryside and offers a sweeping view of mountains, valleys, and fields in every direction.

Here at Arrowhill (so named because "Freccia" means "arrow") life is serene and leisurely. Breakfast is early. Then comes the work period. Freccia closes himself in the music room, or, on fair warm days, takes his scores to a secluded out-of-doors spot, and studies until lunchtime. After lunch there is a short siesta. Then he works outside, pruning the apple orchard, cutting the lawn, or driving the tractor. Some of the land is cultivated and the crops sold to the neighbors for use as fodder.

After dinner the Freccias have coffee in front of the fire and listen to recordings.

One whole day each week is kept entirely free from music. Then Freccia goes hunting or takes long walks or just relaxes with friends—the Horowitzes, the Brailowskys, the Milsteins, the Francescattis.

In the evenings, Mr. Freccia likes especially to have his wife read aloud to him. They usually work out a program for a season —Proust, Balzac, Stendhal, Shakespeare, and the Greek plays. Whenever there is a drama, they divide the parts, and, if Mrs. Freccia's daughter is at home, she is added to the cast. Clytemnestra is Mrs. Freccia's favorite role. Her husband thinks she makes a very good Lady Macbeth also. Freccia himself stars as Oedipus Rex (in a frank imitation of Olivier) while the daughter, also named María Luisa, makes a fine Ophelia.

Baltimoreans delight in their conductor. They believe he speaks better from the podium because his life is well rounded and rich, because even in relaxation he is creative.

CHAPTER VIII

⨠ VLADIMIR GOLSCHMANN

VLADIMIR GOLSCHMANN, who for over a quarter of a century has been conductor of the St. Louis Symphony, finds it impossible to get excited over this record. Mere continuity does not interest him. It is the variety in life that is intriguing: new compositions; new light shed on old ones; new friends made in and out of the musical world; new hobbies developed; new insights gained. He is a man who relishes life in all its aspects.

If this is due to French exuberance, Golschmann has come by it naturally. By birth and by training, he is a Frenchman. His father at twenty years of age came from Russia to Paris and gained recognition there as an author, mathematician, and physician. He translated some ninety books from Russian into French. His mother, a member of a highly musical family, came to Paris when she was fourteen, also from Russia. They met and were married in the French capital and brought up their family of four sons there. It was their dearest wish that their eldest son, Vladimir, born December 16, 1893, should adopt music as a profession.

As he recalls his early life Golschmann's mobile face almost tells the story for him. He was taking piano lessons at four. At seven he began the violin, and adored this instrument as any other child would a favorite toy. He studied under the best teachers and progressed rapidly. What interested his parents particularly was his way of knowing what he wanted and his resourcefulness in getting it. He had already decided on his career when as a boy of ten he wrote in his diary, "I love piano and I love violin but I want to become a conductor." When he told his parents this, they put before him the joys of being a violin virtuoso. He was not to be tempted. He would study the violin, yes, but in order to get into an orchestra and thus learn more about ensemble playing. Already in his violin practice he was supplying the missing parts in an imagined symphony. Already after every concert he was arranging chairs and "conducting" them through the program he had heard.

The boy did get into an orchestra when he was twelve. Vladimir's piano teacher, Paul de Saunières, was responsible for this. A conductor of a semi-professional orchestra that held its concerts in the Sorbonne church, he let the boy play in the last row of the second violins. Gradually Vladimir worked up to the first row, then over to the "firsts." As for the academic side of his career, he studied piano successively with Madame Sitri, de Saunières, and Braud at the Schola Cantorum; violin with Moller, Berthelier, Capet; harmony and counterpoint with Dumas, Caussade, Berthelin.

Paris was a good place for a budding conductor. Here, at cafés with their awnings extended over little round tables, students held forth in endless discussions of the relative merits of Debussy and Ravel; of cubism in painting; of theories of art in general. Vladimir also stood in line for concerts—one could buy a ticket for as little as twenty cents—and was a top-balcony participant on première nights when opposing groups of self-appointed "critics" sometimes went at each other with their fists.

From the age of fifteen Vladimir earned his way with his music. First it was in the Sechiari Orchestra. Then it was in the Concerts Rougé, an ensemble of nineteen members with the pianist filling in the missing parts, which played for the highly intellectual and discriminating coterie assembled in a hall in the

Rue de Tournon. Every member of this group was an expert. José Iturbi was then the pianist. Jacques Thibaud and Lucien Capet had been concertmasters. "You had to be a terrific sight reader!" Golschmann shakes his head and rolls his eyes as he tells about it. "Everything was played without rehearsals." At intermission they played poker with the same zest with which, during the program, they attacked the classics. The conductor warned them, thrusting his head through the door backstage just in time for them to scramble back into their seats.

Francis Touche, a famous cellist who had played at the Concerts Rougé, decided to form an orchestra of his own and move over to the Right Bank. Golschmann went along with him. Since Touche continued to play the cello, sitting on a raised platform center-front, the members took the opening beat from his bow descending on the strings. After that they followed his long black beard bobbing up and down.

Golschmann was enjoying life to the full, but he still dreamed of becoming a conductor. Though he spent all his spare time studying scores, he had little real hope of finding a podium. To hire an orchestra was too expensive, and in France then there was almost no other way to make oneself known.

However, his circle of friends was widening. He had been introduced to Ravel, and through Ravel he had met Erik Satie. This contact was to bring him unexpected returns.

Satie, a man of genius and so far away from anything academic that the thought of his devoting time to the severe task of teaching was fantastic, still had one pupil. This man, Albert Verley, who was a genius in science and had made a small fortune through his inventions, was also a gifted composer. One day he told Satie that he wanted to find someone to play over his compositions on the piano and on the violin. Did Satie know of anyone who could fill the requirements? Satie knew just the man— a fine sight reader and a very likable fellow. So started a professional relationship between Golschmann and Verley, which was to prove a turning point in the young man's career.

Golschmann had been playing over Verley's compositions for almost a year when one day in 1918, as he sounded the final chord of a Verley composition, his employer said, "You know, when I listen to you, I get an impression of an orchestra. Have you ever thought of becoming a conductor?"

"I've never thought of anything else!" Golschmann answered. "I've just never had the money to start!"

"Tell you what we'll do," said Verley, rubbing his hands. "We'll make a splash and have a lot of fun for ourselves. I'll put down 25,000 francs for an orchestra for you. You decide who's to be in it and where the concerts are to be given. Then let me know."

Before the next meeting Golschmann did some hard figuring. This amount was the equivalent in buying power of $5000 in those days, and would approximate $10,000 now. It was the chance of a lifetime. He dared not muff it. There was enough money to give three concerts with a large orchestra. But if these failed, then the whole project would fail. Just then was a bad time to start any musical enterprise. World War I was drawing to a close, and Paris, severely bombed, was not thinking of concerts.

Suddenly he had a plan. He would wait until the end of the war. Then he would get together, not a large orchestra—that would be too expensive—but a small one, thirty or so men, the best available. He'd manage to pick the best by holding the concerts on Saturday afternoons—an open time for most musicians. This way the money would do for ten concerts.

Verley approved the plan. The year 1919 dawned on a world at peace. Golschmann was ready to begin.

The Salle des Agriculteurs, which he chose for the concerts, was a lovely hall seating six hundred. The orchestra was hand picked. To stretch out those precious francs, Golschmann managed everything himself, from ordering the posters to selling the tickets. As he struggled through the two rehearsals before the first concert, he consoled himself with the thought that, whether the concert succeeded or not, at least he would know whether he had the makings of a conductor.

The concert, presented early in 1919, was a success. One prominent critic wrote, "Here is an unknown, who will soon be known all over the musical world." Recalling it, Golschmann says, with the nearest he ever comes to boasting, "Well, I never was clumsy with the stick!"

Things began to happen fast. For ten Saturday afternoons the public's attention was focused on the "Concerts Golschmann." Now Verley was ready to put more money down. (Later another sponsor was to appear—the Princess Edmond de Polignac.) They moved to the larger Salle Gaveau. By 1920 the Concerts Golschmann had become a part of Paris musical life.

Golschmann has always believed one should present works of one's own time. At that period, though, this was a more daring procedure than it is now. In the Paris of the 1920's, the fate of new composers was fought out right in the concert halls. One evening Golschmann included Four Studies for Piano and Orchestra by Darius Milhaud. "As soon as I started," he relates, "the audience began to riot. The pianist turned pale, turned white, turned green. I could not even hear the work myself, but I finished it. Then I turned to the audience and said, 'I think it is perfectly wonderful that there is so much life, so much artistic vitality, here. But may I suggest that you first listen to the work and then show your reactions? After the intermission we shall play it a second time and I expect you to hear it through!' They listened in absolute silence to the end. Then pandemonium broke loose!"

Verley next offered two prizes for compositions, one for voice and orchestra, one for orchestra alone. This contest unearthed much new talent. At Golschmann's suggestion, Honegger sent in *Pastorale d'Été,* which won the prize and which has since become famous. In the 1921–22 season Golschmann conducted seventeen new works with his group.

His activities were not limited to his own orchestra. Jean Cocteau, organized a "Spectacle of the Group," built about the works of six famous composers of the day, and asked Golschmann to conduct it. It took place at the Comédie des Champs-Élysées and included *Le Boeuf sur le Toit* (*The Nothing Doing Bar*) by Milhaud, "imagined and arranged" by Cocteau. Stravinsky attended and was impressed with the young conductor. He invited him to his home in Brittany, tested him out with various musical assignments, and, on his return to Paris, introduced him to the famous director of the Russian Ballet, Sergei Diaghilev.

Diaghilev engaged him as conductor of his ballet. One of his outstanding programs of this time was the revival in 1921 of Stravinsky's *Le Sacre du Printemps.* Years before, when it was first performed, the ballet had caused violent and contrary reactions. This time it was unanimously acclaimed. It was a personal triumph for Golschmann.

From the year 1923 he mounted podiums not only in Paris— the Symphony Orchestra of Paris, the Concerts Pasdeloup, the concerts of the Cercle Musical Universitaire at the Sorbonne, and the electrifying festivals of contemporary music—but also in other parts of France—Lyons, Marseilles, Nantes—and in other countries—Spain, Portugal, Belgium, Norway, and England.

The Diaghilev engagement had sent ballet companies begging to Golschmann's doorstep. He conducted for Anna Pavlova and for Loie Fuller both in Paris and on tour. Then Rolf de Maré, sponsor of the Swedish Ballet, asked him to conduct it in France and during its forthcoming American tour.

This was the candle flame to the moth, but with the difference that Golschmann knew caution. Ever since he had made a nation-wide tour of America as violinist of the Paris Conservatory Orchestra in 1918, he had dreamed ceaselessly of conducting a symphony orchestra in America. Many of his best friends in Paris—George Antheil, Aaron Copland, Virgil Thomson—were Americans. He had consistently championed their music. Gershwin's Piano Concerto had its Parisian première under his baton.

Now, however, he hesitated. "Ballet won't help me in America," he kept reminding himself. "I have to wait my chance to conduct a symphony orchestra there." Still—de Maré's offer was very tempting. Finally he gave in.

The tour started early in 1924, in the old Century Theater in New York City. The program was all modern ballet, and this before even classical ballet had caught on in America! Anyone with a finger to the wind of public opinion could have predicted the result. But, though the company suffered terribly at the hands of critics and public alike, Golschmann was singled out for praise. This brought him to public attention. Just before he sailed for France, Walter Damrosch asked him to be guest conductor of the New York Symphony. His reception was spectacular. He was recalled for fifteen minutes. He was invited again for the following season. At last—a toe hold in America!

However, it took four years (1926–30) for plans to mature. Meanwhile he conducted throughout Europe, and in Paris was musical director of the Theatre Beriza. He continued his encouragement of American works. At the performance of Antheil's *Ballet Mécanique* in 1926 in Paris, the faction in favor of it, led by Satie, James Joyce, and Ezra Pound, cheered lustily, while the "conservative" element threw things from the balcony and staged a couple of fist fights in the aisles.

Then in 1930 the man who had his finger on the pulse of most of the major orchestras in America, Arthur Judson, came to Paris with the New York Philharmonic on tour under Toscanini, and on arrival called Golschmann and said he would like to have a talk with him. The St. Louis Symphony was getting restive under its four-year diet of guest conductors, and Golschmann had been highly recommended for the post. Judson put it point-blank to him, "Are you a good conductor?"

"What's the use of answering that?" shrugged Golschmann. "Let the St. Louis people hear me and decide for themselves."

They did decide. At the concert he directed there, they clapped and stamped their approval. When Golschmann appeared in Judson's New York office some days later, he held a three-year contract.

In the fall of 1931 Golschmann brought his bride, Odette Le Cointe, from France and began a conductorship that was to prove one of the longest in the annals of American musical history. The same year he substituted for Toscanini on the podium of the New York Philharmonic. Francis Perkins of the New York *Herald Tribune* praised his "clearly outlined interpretative ideas," Grena Bennett of the New York *American* "his well-placed emphases," and Oscar Thompson of the *Evening Post* his "brilliant and exact" style.

As soon as Golschmann took over the conductorship in St. Louis, the musical atmosphere there underwent an invigorating change. There were, of course, the standard works. But what charged the cultural air and made it good to breathe were the stimulating contemporary compositions. And it was not only the works but the way they were played. Golschmann's brand of discipline generously sprinkled with humor seemed just the right prescription for the orchestra. "Let's see," he said of the Prokofiev *Alexander Nevsky*, "the Russians are supposed to win this battle. The way you play it, they are losing it"; and, during a play-through of Ravel's *Daphnis and Chloe*, "Chloe is supposed to throw herself into Daphnis' arms here. Now maybe these sounds coming to my ears are your idea of making love. Mine is different!"

Through the orchestra's tours, more than two hundred cities became acquainted with it. On March 8, 1950, midway in the seventieth anniversary tour, it played for the first time in New York's Carnegie Hall. "A tightly knit, unified interpretive medium," Howard Taubman wrote of it in *The New York Times.* "The orchestra played with lovely sculpturing of the melodic designs," said Olin Downes. Harriett Johnson commented, "Its string section is surprisingly full, warm and beautiful and there was an exuberance of mood throughout which was refreshing." When it went to Boston, Rudolph Elie wrote in the Boston *Herald,* "Mr. Golschmann's style is straightforward to a degree; his signals are always clear, his ideas lucid rather than emotional, his interpretative bent orderly and disciplined rather than informed with fervor or heat."

All through his St. Louis tenure Golschmann has kept busy guest conducting. In fact he has conducted practically every major orchestra on this and the European continents.

But to speak only of premières, tours, and tenures, however successful, seems to understate the case of Vladimir Golschmann. He is so much the human being in everything life offers that to picture him in his professional capacity alone is to give an incomplete portrait.

It is his outgoing quality that especially marks him. Just to give one of many examples: A soloist new to appearances with symphony orchestras felt unsure about her preparation of the Rachmaninoff Third. Golschmann went over it with her at the piano bar by bar, explaining exactly what the orchestra did, playing a facsimile of the orchestral score on a second piano.

Such an approach is not to be laid to kindness alone. Golschmann's chief joy is in encounters with human beings. He talks science with scientists, journalism with reporters, world affairs with politicians. He has ideas about art, city planning, sports, travel, engineering. He is an avid collector of modern paintings, of African and archaic Greek sculpture. He talks his head off and is glad to listen to anyone else talking *his* head off.

André Coeuroy, a Paris critic, described him as "the most complete conductor of our time." Certainly, though a member of a calling particularly conducive to one-sidedness, he has retained balance, breadth of outlook, a sense of humor, and an ever fresh taste for life.

CHAPTER IX

‹‹ GUY FRASER HARRISON

GUY FRASER HARRISON, conductor of the Oklahoma City Symphony, has dealt with all kinds of listeners, and no conductor has his thumb more firmly on their pulse. Through his experience he has evolved some quite definite ideas on program building. Harrison believes that "those who pay to hear an orchestra should be made to face something new once in a while—but the attitude some have of shoving it down their throats . . . !" He shakes his head briskly. "Better to open the minds gently!" he says.

From the very start of his career, Harrison looked at his music making in terms of service to his listeners. His father was the first to teach him this. An organist in the parish church near the town of Guildford in Surrey, England, Harrison Senior worked weekdays in the local bank. He had time, though, to watch for musical inclinations in his five children. It was his eldest son, Guy Fraser, who rewarded his search. The boy not only had a good singing voice, but, as soon as he could walk by himself, liked to stand listening beside the keyboard during his father's piano and organ practice.

Harrison started giving the child piano lessons at six, and shortly afterward put him under the instruction of a professional voice coach. Within two years Guy qualified as a boy soprano and became choir boy in Oxford's Christ Church Cathedral. Two years after that, he became a soloist in the choir.

America has nothing comparable to the routine of a student

enrolled in an English cathedral school. It is rugged in the extreme. The program of the Oxford Christ Church Cathedral, for example, brought the boys out of bed at seven in the morning for a cold dip. Piano practice, chapel service, and school lessons took up the morning hours. After the one large meal of the day, at noontime, they had choir rehearsal. Then, after a play period, there was another service at the cathedral, the boys filing over in their gowns and mortarboards. After the evening meal they had piano practice, an hour of lesson preparation, and evening prayers. Then a snack, and they were ready for bed.

Each night as he lay in bed, Guy heard the great bell in Tom Tower begin to toll its 101 times in memory of the first Fellows of Christ Church College, who numbered exactly 101. He seldom was able to count more than twenty strokes before he was off to sleep.

As Mr. Harrison points out, such a routine is conducive neither to mischief-making nor to dream-spinning. He did his work from day to day, ate well, slept well, played hard, and left it to others to formulate his more distant goals. "I simply felt," he says, "that I was doing what I was supposed to do. I had things cut out for me from the start. I don't think I chose consciously the conducting profession or even the musician's life. It was chosen for me."

Whatever its impetus, the choir singing in which he took part in his childhood has left its imprint. To this day Harrison's greatest thrill comes from interpreting great choral works—Beethoven's Ninth, the Berlioz Requiem, the Verdi Requiem.

Scholarships in pipe organ were being offered at the Royal College of Music in London. Guy studied assiduously; and at seventeen, competing with contestants from all parts of the United Kingdom, he came out a winner. During the three years he was a pupil at the college, he studied with some of the best teachers of England: organ under "the master of the King's

Music," Walter Parratt; conducting and choir training under Dr. Walford Davies; and piano under Herbert Sharpe.

At nineteen he graduated. But, though the world that then lay before him looked broad and open, it was really a carefully circumscribed one. His father had just died, and his family now looked to him as its chief support. He took his responsibilities seriously. Yet he wanted to get free of boyhood restraints.

A way opened. One morning in the spring of 1914, at the final sessions of the choir training class, Professor Davies made an announcement. Charles Henry Brent, Bishop of the Philippine Islands, was looking for a young man to take the dual position of personal secretary and of organist and choir director of the cathedral in Manila. The salary in this post would be far more than a student fresh from college could hope to be paid in the British Isles. Besides—a most attractive point to this rigorously brought up young man—one would get to see distant places and do new things.

He told Professor Davies he would like to apply for the position. He was accepted. He makes no bones of the fact that his being the only applicant might well have had something to do with it! Not long afterward he was on board a ship headed for the Philippines via Suez.

Harrison's duties in the Philippines were pleasant. He was organist and choir director at the Cathedral of St. Mary and St. John. He was conductor of an all-Filipino orchestra. He taught classes at the university. He directed and accompanied on the organ a choir of fifty voices (American and English) singing *The Messiah* and other oratorios.

However after six years of working in a post where newspapers arrived with month-old news and people basked in their very isolation, he forced himself to face the facts. Here, he was an important musician—a big duck in a little puddle. But was it leading anywhere? The American contingent in the Philippines had always attracted him. Their absence of cliquishness, their breadth, their democracy were appealing. So it was to America his thoughts turned.

Once he had made up his mind, it didn't take him long to act. Within a month he wound up his affairs in the Islands and got himself a job as checker of cargo on a transport. It was the USAT *Crook* and was, he believes, the longest and narrowest ship ever to ride the seas. Its cargo, which embarked at Vladivostok, was a whole army of Czechoslovakians who had traversed Europe and Russia on foot during World War I and were stranded in Siberia. The ship was to anchor at many ports before reaching Trieste, the disembarkation point for the soldiers.

One of these was Port Said, and there a message from Bishop Brent caught up with Harrison. There was a job open in Rochester, New York, for combined choir director and organist of St. Paul's Episcopal Church. There was a good chance of his getting it if he would apply immediately.

He arrived in Rochester in September of 1920, presented his credentials, demonstrated his skill on the pipe organ, and was accepted. When he unpacked the few articles from his one slim suitcase, he would have laughed away anyone's prophecy that this city would be his home for thirty years, that for twenty-six of them he would be conductor of the Rochester Civic Orchestra and for twenty-one associate conductor of the Rochester Philharmonic.

His arrival could not have been better timed. George Eastman of Kodak fame was just looking about for means to expand the musical life of the city. In 1919 he had announced the gift of $3,500,000 for the establishment of the Eastman School of Music, to be administered under the University of Rochester. In 1920, just before Harrison had arrived, he had made a further grant of $1,000,000. When the school opened in 1921, Mr. Harrison was appointed instructor in organ and piano.

The appointment was a "natural." Cheery, objective, likable, with a strong sense of responsibility, Harrison has the air of being prepared for anything but of expecting the best.

So when in March 1923 Eastman brought the Rochester Philharmonic to active life in a brand-new theater—the core of the orchestra was the pit ensemble at the theater—it was clear that Harrison would have some part in the project.

He had organized a Bach choir at St. Paul's Church, and at a performance of the *St. Matthew Passion,* Albert Coates, conductor of the Rochester Philharmonic, observed him and advised him to take up conducting seriously. Harrison's response was to study conducting under Coates himself. Soon he was accepted as one of the conductors of the Eastman Theater Orchestra.

With the advent of synchronized music, the pit orchestra, like so many other moving-picture ensembles, became unnecessary overnight. The Rochester Philharmonic depended on this pit unit as its main stem of support, and things looked bad. Finally a solution was reached. The pit men became members of a new orchestra, the Rochester Civic Orchestra, geared to give concerts out of the regular season. Mr. Harrison in 1929 was made conductor of this group. In 1930 he was also appointed associate conductor of the Rochester Philharmonic.

The ensuing twenty-odd years were a happy period in Harrison's life. He conducted the Rochester Civic Chorus. He was musical director of the Rochester Civic Opera Company. In 1929 he went on the air. He was heard on the famous *Treasury of Music* broadcast from coast to coast. His programs, of a high order, were popular when radio music of any kind was looked on as something freakish, and serious music was all but taboo. For a while, Harrison and Walter Damrosch were practically the only regular conductors of serious music on the air.

During those early years Harrison developed his knack for

planning programs of wide appeal. "In radio you must please. It is so easy to turn the dial to another station. The listeners must know that they will be satisfied in spending a half hour or an hour in listening to your broadcast."

What Harrison remembers most happily about his Rochester tenure, however, is the large choral works performed and the operas presented. As musical director of the Rochester Civic Music Association's grand opera productions, he conducted two works a season. "We would gear the whole season to these productions," he says. "That sense of all forces—choral, instrumental, dramatic, artistic—being united was something I shall never forget. It brought the whole community together."

By 1951 Harrison was an American citizen and married to an American wife, Cecile Becker. Rochester had been his home now for thirty-one years. It had been a stimulating tenure, but still a severely regularized job in a tightly knit organization. His spirit of adventure started working again. An opening appeared for the conductorship of the Oklahoma City Symphony. He was invited to fill this post—and accepted.

He couldn't have chosen a better place to become further identified with the American scene. From 1950 to 1955, 75,000 newcomers settled in Oklahoma County (in which Oklahoma City is centered). Harrison and his projects were accepted as one of the evidences of the new era.

Here, too, radio work is one of his specialities. His Oklahoma City Symphony gives weekly broadcasts over the Mutual Broadcasting System. They are heard in many parts of the world. In 1956 a minister in Durban, South Africa, wrote, "I make a point of being at home in order to hear your orchestra—which I consider to be an excellent one. Your idea of including contemporary composers is a good one. . . . I came to this country two years ago from Britain and find a lack of appreciation of the Arts. . . . I can only believe that these excellent concerts of yours will do much to stimulate interest. From my personal love of good music I thank you most sincerely."

On three occasions Harrison's young people's radio programs have won outstanding prizes.

Harrison also works with young groups at the annual Oklahoma All-State Symphony in Norman, seat of the state university. For eighteen years he has been going also to Akron, Ohio, directing its city schools' May Festival.

True to his training, Harrison derives his greatest satisfaction from the choral works. In 1953 he gave the United States première of Sir William Walton's Coronation *Te Deum* with the Oklahoma City Symphony and three choirs, obtained from three Oklahoma universities. Visiting music critic John Rosenfield wrote back to the Dallas *Morning News,* "The *Te Deum* reached 10,000 ears with expressive eloquence. . . . Guy Fraser Harrison, a handsome, agile figure in the maturity of threescore gentle years, is one of the most considerable conductors ever to make our region his residence. He has produced technically one of the most silken ensembles around here."

Harrison deprecates such praise. Then he forgets all about it and cheerily gives plans for the coming season. Always, as he plots it, it will be better than the current one—and always, given his contagious optimism and energy, it turns out so to be.

CHAPTER X

⇻ WALTER HENDL

WHEN Walter Hendl, conductor of the Dallas Symphony, received the honorary degree of Doctor of Music from the Cincinnati College of Music in June 1954, he gave a brief speech directed
to what he called the "triptych" of music—its creators, its performers, and its listeners. The creators, he said, should give unstinting and uncalculating effort to music, always remembering
"to thine own self be true." Listeners, he went on, since they
provide the stimulus for both composers and performers, have a
responsibility as great as the artists themselves.

When he spoke about the performers, however, a grim note
crept in. "Your world," he told the young instrumentalists, vo-
calists, and conductors gathered there for the commencement day
exercises, "is profoundly guided by the spirit of competition.
Those of you who win taste of a greater glory than is given to
most. To those who fall by the wayside, I would say music is a
hard and severe taskmaster and is better off without you."

Walter Hendl has reason to speak of the career of the performer in hard terms. The road he has had to follow as pianist
and conductor has not been an easy one.

As a boy, he was aware of no special musical inclination. In
the little town of West New York, New Jersey, where he was
born January 12, 1917, and in nearby Union City, where he
moved at the age of five, he was just an all-round boy who began
to specialize in chemistry when he got to the upper grades. He

took his piano lessons as a matter of course, like his swimming classes and his afternoons on the baseball team. Neither his mother, a German by birth, nor his father, an amateur violinist who had come from Vienna as a young man, had reason to believe that their son was musically gifted.

Then in his early teens Walter got to talking music with two boys in his class at school, and they began going on Saturdays to New York City, just across the river, to recitals and concerts. On the ferry coming home in the evenings, they discussed enthusiastically the programs they had heard.

One of the boys, Leonard Atkins, was taking music courses at New York University, and he kept talking about a teacher of his, Philip James. When in 1932 James won a prize of $5000 offered by NBC for his composition, *Station WGZBK,* Leonard and Walter listened to it over the radio. Walter was so intrigued by this orchestral work, which gave a tonal picture of the noises, absurdities, and confusions of radio, that he asked Leonard to introduce him to his teacher. So one night Leonard took him around to station WOR, where James had a second job—as conductor of the Bamberger Little Symphony. James invited the two boys to stay till after the evening's broadcast, when they could have more time to talk.

The feature that evening was the performance of Mozart's Double Concerto for Orchestra by pianist Clarence Adler and a pupil of his, Pauline Ruvinska. Confronted with some fine piano playing, young Hendl was deeply stirred. For the first time, as he puts it, "I *experienced* music." He begged Adler to take him as a pupil.

Adler remembers that his young student showed great musical and intellectual curiosity, that he was an excellent sight reader, and that he had an "insatiable craving to familiarize himself with the repertoire." He also remembers that "he didn't seem to be a particularly happy young fellow—gave the impression of being taunted by others—or by himself—to acquire always more skill and more knowledge."

Hendl revealed this intensity in the letters he sent to his teacher. In 1933 he wrote, "Notwithstanding a fever and a cold I am managing to do six hours a day. . . . I have been in such a state of discouragement for the past two weeks that it has made me mentally and physically exhausted. My mind is constantly mulling things over and over, and I have lost any feeling for relaxation that I ever had. I have developed a terrific amount of psychological hazards which make playing almost impossible. My head has become too critical for my hands to cope with."

About this time, Hendl happened to leave his music portfolio at Adler's studio, and he telephoned his teacher to look through it for a missing document. Adler discovered the scores of several Beethoven and Brahms symphonies and realized that the young man was reaching out to other fields of music.

When he was eighteen Hendl won the New Jersey State Music Contest sponsored by the Griffith Foundation. When he was nineteen he was awarded a piano scholarship at the Curtis Institute of Music. Here he studied piano with David Saperton, and, the year after, conducting with Fritz Reiner.

His scholarship at Curtis paid for his tuition but for little else. He supported himself by being piano entertainer in a hotel and by playing accompaniments in a vocal studio. This job required wide familiarity with vocal literature; so Hendl embarked on a memorizing drill. "I began by making myself memorize one bar of music a day for a week. The next week I increased the assignment to two bars; the next to four; then to eight. I began on song accompaniments, and went over to piano literature, then to orchestral scores."

During his second year at Curtis, Hendl developed a bad case of neuritis, which prohibited more than one or two hours a day at the piano. He trained himself to learn music away from the piano, and he turned his thoughts to conducting, since the required movements, broad in comparison to the pianist's, seemed to bother him less. He learned to master scores rapidly. "The trick of score reading," he says, "is to pick out the most important ideas, acquiring facility of detail as you go along. I always break down a new score in terms of its main thematic material, tracing this phrase through in its entirety. Then I go back to find secondary material. In the third place I add the subsidiary ideas, leaving details and embellishments for the end."

After his graduation from Curtis, Hendl taught piano from 1939 to 1942 at Sarah Lawrence College in Bronxville, New York, and tried at the same time to prepare himself for a concert career as pianist. "I can't go on like this," he wrote Adler during a difficult interval, "practicing one day, college the next, here and there. While memorizing—the essential qualification for developing a repertoire—comes easy to me, technic and facility don't. Work means nothing. If I had to practice five, ten years, ten hours per day, I would do it. But I must do something different than this petty way of working."

Hendl's summers included study with Koussevitzky in the Berkshires. His first actual conducting experience came with the New Jersey National Youth Association Orchestra, one of the training orchestras for the Stokowski All-American Youth Orchestra.

Then in 1942, as he was preparing for a tour as both pianist and conductor, he was called to the armed services as a member of the Air Force Ferry Command. At first this gave him a chance to branch out musically in still another direction. While stationed in Wilmington, Delaware, he organized an army dance band, "The Jive Bombers," and threw all his energies into making good band arrangements for the group.

Then came a setback. While still in training, he suffered a severe back injury and had to be hospitalized at Mitchell Field.

For months he lay flat on his back. He had grave doubts of ever being able to get about again.

As he lay in a state of near-despair, a Red Cross worker, Mrs. Francis McFarland, had a long talk with him. She found out what was at the root of his worries. Then she interested Captain Murray Ferderber, of the Army Convalescent Rehabilitation Service, in his case. Mrs. McFarland happened to be acquainted with one of the backers of the play *Dark of the Moon*. The book and the lyrics were ready, but difficulties had arisen about finding a composer. Yet the job had to be done in a month. The backer was willing to let Hendl have a try at it. Captain Ferderber obtained permission for him to accept a professional contract while still in the army hospital. He was given the play to read. "I had done no composing before," Hendl relates, "but after reading the play, I had some musical ideas which I jotted down as samples. They liked these, and I got the assignment. I was too eager to be scared and all went well."

Dark of the Moon was a Broadway hit and went into an eighteen-month run. It was the turning point in Hendl's career. Fritz Reiner saw his name on the Broadway marquee, remembered his former student's brilliant piano transcriptions of scores, and invited him to be soloist in a radio program he was conducting. A few years later he was to have him as guest conductor with his Pittsburgh Symphony.

Things didn't come Hendl's way all at once, however. By the summer of 1945 he was again unemployed. A letter he wrote to Richard Burgin, associate conductor of the Boston Symphony, brought an offer to tour as accompanist with violinist Ruth Posselt (Mrs. Burgin). While on the road he read in the papers that Ignace Strasfogel, assistant conductor of the New York Philharmonic, had resigned. He got off a letter to Rodzinski applying for the position. When next he arrived in New York, he was summoned for an interview, and that very day he was hired.

It wasn't so many weeks before he got his chance. Rodzinski fell ill, and at the concert of December 8, 1945, Hendl took over. The papers headlined another rising star. "Assistant Wins Plaudits" (*New York Times*); "Last Minute Sub Conducts Philharmonic in Triumph" (New York *Daily News*); "Hendl's Emergency Debut with Philharmonic Brilliant" (New York *World-Telegram*). Kolodin in the New York *Sun* spoke of his "easy affinity with the essence of the music."

Not long afterward, Oscar Levant, scheduled as soloist in Gershwin's Piano Concerto in F with the New York Philharmonic, had to cancel his engagements because of commitments in Hollywood, and Rodzinski asked Hendl to take his place. With two weeks to practice, Hendl rushed out to buy the score, never having played the work before. That evening, January 3, 1946, he registered another success, this time as a pianist.

In the three years Hendl served as assistant conductor of the Philharmonic, he was last-minute substitute for more senior conductors than any other assistant ever to sign up with that orchestra.

In spite of this luck, Hendl knew that appearances as substitute conductor and pianist were undependable at best. A permanent conductorship was what he wanted. So he looked more than favorably on the invitation in 1949 to become regular conductor of the Dallas Symphony. Following his first two concerts, the trustees of the orchestra authorized his engagement for three years. The contract has since been renewed regularly.

Since 1953, he has also been conductor of the (summer) Chautauqua Orchestra in New York State.

Walter Hendl is a handsome and dramatic figure on the podium. His movements are light and lithe. He seems to cover the whole orchestra with his sweeping gestures. His tactics in Dallas are both ingratiating and effective. He had the Dallas Symphony appear at the Palace Theater on the same program with a movie. (A local newspaper reported, "It opened new frontiers of thought.") He has taken the Dallas Symphony on tour of much of the midwestern and eastern portions of the United States. He engineered a musical rapprochement between Dallas and its onetime bitter rival, Fort Worth, thirty-five miles away. One afternoon he donned overalls and a farmer's straw hat and drove over with the orchestra to conduct a children's concert there. Since then he has annually conducted a series of six concerts in the neighbor city.

Hendl is a huge success with children. He has them come to the stage and "try out" on various musical instruments. He chats with them, takes them into his confidence, tells them tall tales. His compositions for children, commissioned by the Young People's Record Guild—*Neighbor's Band, Little Brass Band, Concerto for Toys and Orchestra*—are used in children's programs in schools throughout the country. Teachers report that "children ask for them first." His own small daughter, Susan, often travels with him on his guest conductorships and visits his rehearsals.

Hendl has gone on three cultural missions. In 1950 he went to South America for the Braniff International Airways. On this trip he conducted orchestras in Rio de Janeiro and Buenos Aires and collected compositions in eight Latin American countries for later performances with the Dallas Symphony. In 1953 he spent three weeks in the Philippines at the request of the United States Department of State, conducting orchestras and opera company there and lecturing in the universities. He was guest of President Quirino, and on his return was notified that he had been selected as the outstanding artist to visit them during 1953. In 1955 he and Thor Johnson, conductor of the Cincinnati Orchestra, traveled to the Orient as conductors of the Symphony of the Air. This trip was made under the auspices of ANTA International Exchange Program.

Successful as he is, Hendl remains restless and intense. But if to him music is a hard taskmaster, he is willingly goaded by her. His very impatience and dissatisfaction are qualities to which his audiences respond. He is always pushing ahead, and his orchestra —all Dallas, in fact—has the sense of pushing ahead with him.

CHAPTER XI

⇛ ALEXANDER HILSBERG

ALEXANDER HILSBERG could not have been happier with the New Orleans Philharmonic Symphony if it had been a Stradivarius violin presented to him at the height of his performing career. The orchestra even has an advantage over a Stradivarius, as he sees it. The "player" can actually improve it, make it more sensitive, more responsive. This, moreover, is done not by an arbitrary whittling or application of varnish, as with a Strad, but wholly by human means.

The humanness of it is what intrigues him most. "A good orchestra is not conducted," he says. "It is spoken to without words. The good orchestra player has his own individuality. One will have more warmth, one more vigor, one more lyricism. The good conductor sees that each one *keeps* this individuality. But at the same time he will see that they conform within the pattern. The men in turn, even while they subject themselves, will express themselves. They will understand (without words) tragedy, tenderness, brutality, love—all these conveyed by the conductor by means of something no one can define and no one can teach." Hilsberg pauses, his head on one side, as his eyes slant up and all but get lost in the crease of a sudden smile.

When Hilsberg talks, his face, his whole body enter into the conversation. He reaches a hand out; bends toward one; throws his head back. With his spare figure, his closely fitting suit, his cropped gray hair, "dapper" would be the word for him, if it were not for the way he takes fire suddenly. When he speaks of music and of conducting, he is the mobile, voluble artist.

"To interpret, to express yourself," he says, "this cannot be taught, and this is the main thing in conducting. For each conductor the frame is the same, but the painting is different.

"Not that there are not certain characteristics which make one a conductor. In my twenty-seven years as violinist in the Philadelphia Orchestra I became able to tell almost as soon as the conductor stepped on the podium whether he had these characteristics. At a maximum of one minute after he started conducting, my opinion was firmly established. What is it? A sense of authority? The ability to coordinate? A certain feeling? Anyway, I knew. And so does every good orchestra man."

To practice conducting as one practices scales may turn out conductors of a sort. But for Hilsberg, it has been rather the development through channels seemingly divorced from podium skills. True, he made his debut as a conductor at the Lewisohn Stadium as early as 1935, and he conducted a concert the same year at Robin Hood Dell. But these were exceptional instances. His concertmastership of the Philadelphia Orchestra and his teaching at the Curtis Institute took so much of his time that he almost gave up the idea of conducting. Then in 1945 he was engaged as associate conductor of the Philadelphia Orchestra and almost overnight became a high-level conductor, acting as guest on prominent podiums throughout the land.

Up to his forty-fifth year, Hilsberg's career was that of a violinist. It was a career pursued with such joy that several times it led him to out-of-the-way corners of the globe—Siberia, Outer Mongolia, China, Japan—where he was quite content to make beautiful music, oblivious to calls from the outside world.

Hilsberg was born in Warsaw (then Russian territory) on April 24, 1900. But it was in St. Petersburg he spent his childhood. His days were filled with violin study, helped by his father and his older brother. At nine he was touring as a violin prodigy. A brief encounter with Heifetz occurred in Vilna, when the elder Heifetz brought his eight-year-old son to the hotel and had the boy play for young Hilsberg, himself only nine years old. They struck up a boyish friendship until their ways parted.

At ten, Alexander entered the Imperial Conservatory of Music in St. Petersburg and came under the tutelage of the great master Leopold Auer. For seven years it was hard study and healthy companionship with other ardent young students. Then, in the fall of 1917, came the Revolution, splitting asunder almost every institution in Russia, the Conservatory included. Hilsberg was invited to join the faculty at a conservatory in Tomsk. So, packing his few belongings, he set out for this small city in western Siberia.

For about a year he taught while the Revolution spread. Before it could catch up with him, he was off again on a concert tour of Siberia. When he reached Harbin, a railway junction in Manchukuo, he came to a stop.

He couldn't have picked a less quiet spot. Displaced persons of every race and color thronged the narrow streets. The city changed hands with almost every round of the clock. All this mattered little to Hilsberg. For in the midst of this welter of intrigue and political upheaval there was an excellent string quartet. Chamber music was the pet project of Solomon Skidelsky, one of the richest men in the region, the owner of most of the railroads, land, and gold mines. His quartet had achieved a wide renown not only in Manchukuo but also in China and Japan.

When Skidelsky asked Hilsberg to become first violin in the quartet, he accepted happily and for four years remained in the post. They were not dull years. For one thing, he had his beloved music to engross him. For another, the quartet went on tours. In 1921, the famine year in China, the group devoted the proceeds of its concerts to the aid of starvation victims. In thanks, the president of the Chinese Republic, Sun Yat-sen, invited them to his palace in Pekin.

Hilsberg spent an entire day being coached in official etiquette. The quartet was driven to the palace in a white Pierce-Arrow car, preceded by a military escort. Before and after the performance Sun Yat-sen and his family rose and bowed low three times to the musicians. Each member of the quartet was then presented with a decoration by the president.

With the serenity of the life in Harbin, Hilsberg, like Haydn in his Esterhazy court, might have been content to live out his days there. But two events caused him to decide otherwise: a recording of the Philadelphia Orchestra fell into his hands, and his old friend Jascha Heifetz happened along.

After listening to the recording, *The Unfinished Symphony* by Schubert, Hilsberg went to the trouble of getting more records of the orchestra and of looking up the history of that organization with the peculiar-sounding name in far-off America. It is too much to say he set his sights for the concertmastership of the orchestra on the evidence of these slim discs. But their effect did stay with him—and the realization that great music was being superbly performed in a place called Philadelphia somewhere on the other side of the globe.

Then came Heifetz, on a concert tour, in the summer of 1923. "What are you doing here, when you could be making a name for yourself in the wide world?" he asked. "America is the place of great artistic life and opportunity. Go there!"

When Heifetz had left, Hilsberg was no longer the contented quartet member. He made inquiries and consulted other touring musicians. He kept on the lookout for openings. A professorship at the Tokyo Imperial Conservatory was offered him, and he accepted. But when a severe earthquake occurred that summer in Tokyo this enterprise fell through.

Finally he decided simply to start out for America and trust to luck. As the ship moored briefly in the harbor of the all-but-demolished Tokyo, its captain warned passengers against even setting foot in the ruined streets.

If Hilsberg had been fearful of landing in Tokyo, he wasn't at all so when the ship reached Vancouver. He stepped on shore with a great sense of exhilaration. At once he headed East to hear the Philadelphia Orchestra. The experience justified his dreams. Then and there he put in his bid to join it.

Turning down an offer to be concertmaster of another orchestra, he toured as violin soloist. At last he received word of an opening in the Philadelphia Orchestra. By 1926 he was sitting in the violin section of that great ensemble. Shortly thereafter he was admitted to the faculty of the Curtis Institute of Music.

As head of the string orchestra department at Curtis in 1927, he began conducting a group of string players. It was the first intimation he had of his real calling.

In 1931 he became concertmaster of the Philadelphia Orchestra and in 1945 the orchestra's associate conductor. In the same year he became conductor of the Reading (Pennsylvania) Symphony.

When one asks Mr. Hilsberg what he considers the most important event in his career, he answers, "There were two: one for my career as a violinist, and one for my career as a conductor. The first was when Toscanini came as guest conductor to Philadelphia, and I, as concertmaster, played Strauss's *Heldenleben,* the solo part, for the first time. I shall never forget it! The second was as a conductor, when I substituted for Ormandy in Carnegie Hall with Brahms' First Symphony.

"Carnegie Hall!" he breathes. "Yes, that was a great experience!"

It was a great experience for the audience, too. It was one of those occasions when the listeners come prepared to be disappointed and stay to be elated. Brahms can be made deadly dull in inexpert hands. He was not dull this time. The critics had a field day. Virgil Thomson in the New York *Herald-Tribune* described Hilsberg's brand of conducting as "power, penetrating and original." Olin Downes in *The New York Times* called his performance "sheer virtuosity," and added, "To play overfamiliar classics and bring to the performances an understanding and a spirit that were thrilling because of their integrity and conviction, is little less than a sensational achievement. Mr. Hilsberg accomplished as much. His modest but completely sincere and authoritative presentations have wholly vindicated his methods. To hear Brahms so communicated is to feel the pulses pounding."

This event made Hilsberg famous as a conductor. Before long he was leading the Philadelphia Orchestra, as associate conductor, and was guest conducting the Minneapolis, Pittsburgh, Seattle, Houston, and NBC orchestras, as well as at Robin Hood Dell and in Lewisohn Stadium.

Mr. Hilsberg does not regret the long waiting period before he actually assumed the baton. He thinks it did him good. Having sat under so many different conductors, he has come to learn the difference between easy "interpretations" and the hard struggle to give clean and powerful renderings of what the composer really wants.

Since assuming the conductorship of the New Orleans Philharmonic in 1952 he has built a chorus (135 voices) there; obtained a rehearsal hall, the old St. Charles Theater; increased the orchestral season from twenty to twenty-five weeks; raised the minimum pay of the men; widened the tours; and heightened the level of its players' skill. During these years he has also established twelve statewide broadcasts for children. These go directly to the schools, and the broadcast hour is included in the regular school curriculum. It is estimated that about sixty thousand children listen to these broadcasts. The schools receive the programs in advance and prepare the listeners. In the first year of its establishment, this system was sponsored by twenty-five big firms and corporations at $3000 each. In 1955 the state appropriated $70,000 for two years of these concerts.

Touring shows a healthy upward curve. Before Hilsberg came to New Orleans, the largest number of out-of-town concerts was in the 1945–46 season, when the orchestra played in seven cities. In the 1955–56 season it played twenty-five concerts in eighteen cities, including the symphony's first visit to Texas and Arkansas.

In April and May of 1956 the United States Department of State sponsored the New Orleans Philharmonic in a tour of fourteen Latin American countries. Specially chartered aircraft carried the entire membership and its instruments to twenty-six concerts in thirty days. In Mexico City people stood in the streets listening through open windows, and followed the orchestra men for blocks to their hotels. In Guayaquil in Ecuador, and Tegucigalpa in Honduras, the people had never seen or heard a symphony before. In Managua, Nicaragua, as soon as the concert was over they took up a collection and raised $3500 to go toward the establishment of an orchestra of their own.

Just after Hilsberg's return, Tulane University, according him an honorary doctorate of music, stressed his musical ambassadorship, "reminding our friends and neighbors—and, indeed, reminding us—that America has for export, not only products of industry, but also inspiring achievements of art." As for Hilsberg, he told newspaper reporters on landing again on the soil of the United States, "It was the most heart-warming and worthwhile thing I have done in my life." The conductor, he has found, has a power of projection—a power for good—beyond any dream of the lone instrumentalist.

CHAPTER XII

⇛ THOR JOHNSON

"WE musicians of America must make good our opportunity, or the cause of American music may be set back for years." Earnestly Thor Johnson, conductor of the Cincinnati Symphony Orchestra, reiterates this motif in his many contacts with his fellow citizens. He does not appear the zealot or the fanatic. A sturdy, brisk man with the concentrated look of a successful lawyer, his attitude is collected, his ideas composed. He simply insists on a recognition of the facts: a great country on the verge of artistic discovery, but hesitant, halting. The situation calls for more than absorption. It calls for dedication.

Mr. Johnson has never been without an orchestra. Always, everywhere he has gone he has got together an orchestra. If a full-fledged symphony orchestra has not been at hand, he has made one—gathered together his musical friends, instrument-playing school comrades, college classmates, fellows in the army, and welded them into orchestral shape.

With his philosophy, his vitality, and his well-ordered nervous system, Johnson has made his influence felt in practically all of the forty-eight states. It has meant economy of motion. It has meant economy of reaction even. That is why when a reporter once handed him the day's newspaper so that he could read a glowing account of his conducting at the Tanglewood Festival, there was a shake of the head and a gesture of withdrawal. There just wasn't time for gloating.

For one who must always have his orchestra, Johnson was lucky in the communities in which he was reared. The first four years of his life, spent in Wisconsin Springs, Wisconsin, though not actually orchestra producing, yet laid the groundwork well. From the day of his birth, June 10, 1913, his father, a Moravian minister of Norse stock, and his mother, a pianist and music teacher, taught him not only integrity but how to move in a world of high idealism and of music. His paternal grandmother married at thirteen and was widowed before she was twenty. She reared her three sons in a built-over apartment in an abandoned church, while she ran the town's general store. All three boys received college educations.

In Winston-Salem, North Carolina, where the family went in 1917 when Johnson Senior changed pastorates, Thor really began to awaken to music. Little wonder! This town lives, breathes, exudes music. Trombone choirs sing from balconies on an Easter morning; girls practice Bach in their little studio rooms at the seminaries. Choirs meet the year round in long rehearsal sessions. Choruses with instrumental accompaniment are rendered in memorial services at the graves of the dead. Bands and orchestras —excellent ones—are fixtures in every school.

By the time he was ten, Thor had learned violin well enough to make up a family chamber group with his parents and his sister Marian. When at thirteen he first went to the Richard J. Reynolds High School in Winston-Salem, he automatically became a violinist member of the symphony orchestra there. But this didn't satisfy him. He went into a huddle with some of his school friends, and had soon organized a seventeen-piece "Little Symphony." "It was lots of fun!" he recalls. "We played a Bach work, the Schubert *Rosamunde* Overture, movements of Haydn symphonies. Sometimes our relatives and friends came to hear us— and it turned into a concert!"

The school's orchestra head, Christian D. Kutschinski, wasn't one to let such talent go to waste—not in this community where every available musical skill was utilized. At the school's orchestra practice one day, he had Thor take over the baton for one of the numbers—*Connecticut March,* by Reeves. Then he led the boy aside and told him, "Neither I nor the assistant conductor will be able to be there for the chapel exercises tomorrow. You are to conduct."

"I was so excited," Mr. Johnson relates, "that I didn't know what to do. Excited—and scared! I didn't tell my parents. They guessed something was up, though—I went around with such an air. Then, when I polished my own shoes the next morning without being told, they knew it must be something special. Still I didn't say a word and they didn't question me. I thought, 'What if it's a flop! Better not say anything!' "

When Thor Johnson tells this story, his blue eyes shining, a shock of straw-colored hair above, the listener realizes that here, for all his dignity, is a boy still—a boy taking chances, savoring new situations, exulting in the results.

But he continues, "Morning came. The ninety-piece school orchestra was assembled. I raised my baton—and they wouldn't start! They couldn't see me! Someone had to get a chair to stand me on. I was so ashamed! There in that fine great auditorium with the seniors all ready to march down the aisle—and they had to hold up everything to get a chair for a kid in knee pants!" He shakes his great head and then smiles largely. "They *did* start when I stood on a chair, though! It was the most glorious feeling I've ever had!"

From then on Thor Johnson's orchestras, even the self-made ones, were serious affairs.

He continued to be lucky in his environment. At the University of North Carolina where he got his B.A. in music, he was assistant conductor of the North Carolina Symphony from 1932 to 1934.

Lamar Stringfield, winner of a Pulitzer prize for composition, was the conductor. Mr. Johnson speaks happily of the vast amount of literature he plowed through.

But this wasn't enough. He formed the Carolina Ensemble, which gave one hundred concerts in the years from 1929 to 1934 and also furnished the musical settings for the Carolina Play-makers.

At the University of Michigan School of Music, which Johnson entered after graduating from the University of North Carolina, he formed another orchestra. At first it was just a group of amateurs who held rehearsals in the local Congregational Church and performed sporadically in return for lavish helpings at church suppers. But Thor wasn't thinking in terms of handouts. He spent his Christmas holidays in North Carolina rounding up bookings for the group. The eighteen concerts obtained that first year brought the orchestra still more dates. Soon the ensemble reached such a status that the University of Michigan allowed it to use its name. In the seven years the U. of M. Little Symphony functioned, it presented over five hundred concerts in some twenty-eight states. From 1934 to 1936 and from 1938 to 1942 Johnson took it on two tours annually.

Thor Johnson's work with this Little Symphony brought rewards from unexpected quarters.

For one thing, it was the means of getting him in touch with Serge Koussevitzky, one of the greatest influences in his life. That conductor happened to hear the orchestra playing on the campus and had a talk with its conductor. "Some day I will teach," he told Johnson, "and you will come and study with me."

The Little Symphony also brought him a Beebe Scholarship. The year in Europe that it provided, from the middle of 1936 to the middle of 1937, gave him new experiences in coaching, in research, in contacts. He studied under Nicolai Malko at the

Salzburg Mozarteum, under Felix Weingartner, under Bruno Walter. He took a course in conducting under Hermann Abendroth at the Leipzig Conservatory.

A Mozart Festival he attended so impressed him that he came home with the determination to start one of his own. He got his chance when he was engaged to conduct the WPA Orchestra in Asheville, North Carolina. He turned the two-week assignment into a Mozart Festival. "We had our nerve to call it 'The First Annual Mozart Festival,'" he says. "We didn't know what would come of it. But we put all we had into it, and it caught on." The festival has become an annual event.

In 1937 Thor Johnson was appointed assistant professor of music at the University of Michigan. Meanwhile, he conducted the University of Michigan Symphony and his own University of Michigan Little Symphony, took over the direction of the University of Michigan May Festival and the Choral Union, and for two years (1939–41) conducted the Grand Rapids Symphony.

In the summers of 1940 and 1941 Koussevitzky started to teach in the Berkshire School and, true to his promise, accepted Johnson as his first-year student. This master served him as a model—a necessity, Johnson believes, for all conducting students.

During this period, Johnson's ideas on conducting took shape. The conductor's role, he feels, calls for three abilities. The first has to do with will power. "The conductor must make manifest his will. He has to lead. Conductors have many different ways of imparting their will: by absolute dictatorship, by mutual admiration, by cajolery. But somehow it must be done. Dr. Koussevitzky said often, 'The will must be ten times greater than that of the players.'"

The second necessity for the conductor, Johnson believes, is imagination, that is, the creative power. "The creation of a pattern from the woefully inadequate musical symbolism is his task. Notation has so little to tell us. Endless research is required, and the ability to adapt obsolete styles to current musical situations."

The third quality is inspiration—"that which gives the glow to the performance." Johnson believes that "when this is present, the conductor has the capacity of permitting music to pass through him. At such moments of inspiration, the composer, the conductor, and the audience become one."

In 1942 Thor Johnson enlisted in the army. At Fort Monmouth, New Jersey, he organized the first all-soldier symphony. For two years he gave concerts with it in the United States, while his reputation grew. On permission from the army, he led the New York Philharmonic Symphony at a Stadium concert, the Boston Symphony, the Chicago Symphony, and the Philadelphia Orchestra. Then he was sent (by the army) to England to conduct the American University Symphony Orchestra, organized at the United States base at Shrivenham.

Because of such assignments, Johnson left the army in 1946 actually better known than when he went in. Engagements came thick and fast. He was invited to conduct the New York Philharmonic Symphony again at its Stadium concerts. He was appointed director of the Juilliard School of Music Orchestra. During his year in this post, he led the group of 120 students in two concerts featuring modern music in Carnegie Hall and in a program highlighting Columbia University's third annual Festival of Contemporary Music.

The very year of his army discharge, he was engaged, on December 8, as guest conductor of the Cincinnati Symphony. (Eugene Goossens, the conductor, had just announced his resignation to go to Australia.) His obvious ability and the audience reaction impressed the board. In the course of their deliberations they telephoned Koussevitzky. "You need have no doubts," he told them. "In five years Thor Johnson will be among the great." Ten days after his first guest concert in Cincinnati he was appointed the orchestra's regular conductor. He was only thirty-four years old.

At the helm of a major orchestra, Thor Johnson might have turned into a maestro confined to score reading, social big-wigging and ovation acknowledging. He did nothing of the sort. More than ever he approached his work in terms of a mission. He went to Cincinnati that first season long before the concerts began and set about getting acquainted with the townsfolk. He spoke at civic clubs, board meetings, dinners, teas, radio forums, school assemblies, Boy Scout conclaves, church suppers, board of education meetings. He called upon teachers, doctors, politicians. He described possibilities, mapped out procedures, urged forward steps.

In his first season in Cincinnati he conducted 110 full-length concerts, organized two series each of young people's and junior high concerts, revived the "pop" concert series, and conducted four weeks of out-of-town concerts.

Johnson has sponsored the Cincinnati Music Drama Guild, which uses local singers and performs contemporary opera. He presents annually a Yuletide concert and a concert for the Girl Scouts. In 1952 he gave a performance of Arnold Schönberg's massive cantata, *Gurre-Lieder,* for which he marshaled an orchestra of 147 members, 6 soloists, and a chorus of several hundred voices.

He continued his practice of commissioning compositions. By July 1956, he had presented during his career as conductor 110 premières, half of them commissioned by himself. He studies yearly some 300 scores which ambitious composers send him for evaluation.

Though he is unstinting in his labors for Cincinnati, Johnson still considers the whole United States as his proper workshop. He has conducted annual intercollegiate band meetings and student-orchestra clinics in Michigan, Colorado, Ohio, Illinois, Utah, Washington, Kansas, Montana, Wisconsin, Indiana, North Carolina, Texas, and Kentucky. As for festivals—there isn't a one in the United States that he hasn't influenced through one channel or another. The Ann Arbor May Festival, Bethlehem's Moravian-American Festival, Cincinnati's May Music Festival, the Brevard Music Festival, the Salt Lake City annual *Messiah* performance, Tanglewood, Dumbarton Oaks, the Schubert Festival at Charlottesville, Virginia—all these have taken on new vitality through his endeavors. In 1949 alone, in addition to his schedule of over one hundred concerts with the Cincinnati Symphony, he was engaged for seven festivals.

Three festivals, now annual events, were actually created by him. He started the Mozart Festival in Asheville. He originated in 1949 the California Ojai Music Festival. In 1953 he founded the Peninsula Festival in Fish Creek, Door County, Wisconsin, "to give Wisconsin musicians a summer home." Its chamber orchestra is recruited from winter-season orchestras all over the United States.

It is apparent that this capacity for planning festivals goes along with Johnson's fervor for serving communities with music. Like the religious revival, the music festival is the quickest, the sharpest, way to achieve results. It reaches the most people in the shortest time, and its impact is felt throughout the year.

The most recent festival project has brought Johnson back to his native state—and he likes the idea. The white walls and brightly colored roofs of the cottages in the quaint villages built around Door County's many harbors, the clean, fresh air with its invigorating tang, all bring out the Norse adventurousness in him. The programs give evidence of his explorations. The new works, the new approaches to old works, challenge both the orchestra and the audiences. Johnson steers this latest project of his into further channels, widening music's scope and developing taste and perceptivity in all who hear it.

CHAPTER XIII

⇶ ENRIQUE JORDÁ

ENRIQUE JORDÁ, conductor of the San Francisco Symphony, is a searcher. His searching means delving into the period of the composer he interprets, getting at the spirit of the composition, looking behind the workings of the modern musical world for the emotions and thoughts that make it tick.

Jordá looks serene; talks softly; moves quietly; takes time to listen and to weigh statements; is equable, moderate, and many-sided in his approaches. He often speaks in mystical terms. "When a real conductor is on the podium a transference takes place. Players and conductor think together, feel together. It is like pigeons wheeling in flight. One does not point out the leader. There is an invisible leader, though. The one who propels them all is the composer. The conductor who can make himself the channel for the composer's thoughts and feelings is the great conductor."

Born March 24, 1911, in the Spanish seaside town of San Sebastián, Jordá spent his whole youth there. In this place he developed in music naturally. It was a world of folk-singing and guitars as well as of sophisticated concerts and of magnificent church music. He became immersed in church music especially during Holy Week. The great works of that sixteenth-century composer, Tomás Luis de Victoria, who had believed music was intended alone for the praise and glory of God and who therefore had refused to write secular music at all, particularly absorbed the boy. He remembers especially the Kyrie from Victoria's mass *Quarti Toni*—"Lord, have mercy on us"—rising through the incense-laden air and up into the dimly lit arches. Today Jordá's intense joy in preparing choral works—he has presented Handel's *Messiah,* Beethoven's *Missa Solemnis,* and Fauré's *Requiem* in San Francisco—partly stems from these boyhood initiations into Spanish church music.

But music in the Spain in which Jordá was brought up was also a very earthy expression. The villagers danced to the sounds of guitars and flutes. The peasants sang as they worked. Young lovers serenaded their ladies under flower-hung balconies. At every turn, Enrique's imagination was captivated.

Very early he started collecting the folk songs of his people. He wandered out into the country and lingered wherever men and women sang as they tilled their land or plodded beside their mules along the dusty roads. Then, at the right moment, he asked permission to take down the songs.

But this work had its difficulties. The folk singer cannot begin in the middle of a song. He remembers it as a whole. So, if Jordá missed a phrase, the singer would have to go back to the beginning and make a fresh start. He copied some ninety songs this way, and many of them formed the basis of his youthful compositions.

Musical activity was taken as a matter of course in Enrique's family. His father, who died when the boy was five, had been a violinist before he had joined the navy, and *his* father had been an opera singer. Enrique's mother was a pianist, and her father had been an organist in the village church. One of her more remote ancestors had been a court musician to the Emperor Charles V (1500–58).

Enrique was an only child, and the bond between him and his widowed mother was very strong. She not only gave him his first lessons but encouraged him at every step in his career until her death when he was twenty-three years old.

Some of his musical voyages of discovery, though, Enrique chose to go on by himself. In his teens he got to threading through orchestral scores, much as any other youngsters would work out the directions for a fascinating game. Whenever he found puzzling places in a score he discovered how they were actually executed by waiting until the town band or orchestra included them on their programs. Then he watched the conductor closely to see how he managed them.

When he was eight Enrique joined the choir of his school as boy soprano. At twelve he became assistant organist at his parish church, Santa María. This precocious appointment was really not so surprising. The boy's teacher was head organist at the church and needed a helping hand. During the four years Enrique presided in emergencies at the console, he not only widened his organ repertoire but began to study the voice and its production.

By the time he was sixteen Enrique was composing choral music, piano sketches, orchestral essays.

In 1929, when he was eighteen, Enrique Jordá left Spain to study in Paris. His mother knew he must have some guarantee of financial independence and felt music could not give it to him. Therefore she made it strictly understood that along with his musical education her son must pursue studies in a more stable profession. Enrique chose medicine and began the preliminary courses. It was only with the death of his mother in 1934 that he abandoned this project. As a gesture of respect to his mother's wishes, he did, however, follow lectures in "philosophy and letters" at the Sorbonne. He took all the courses in aesthetics and remembers being particularly absorbed in Immanuel Kant's *Critique of Aesthetic Judgment.*

Jordá spent eleven years in Paris. They were good years both in and out of the classroom. The improvisations of his organ teacher, Marcel Dupré, never ceased to delight him. The scintillating wit of Paul Le Flem—he was a music critic as well as Jordá's teacher in composition—was as invigorating as his brilliant counterpoint. He could also watch his teacher in conducting, Frans Rühlmann, put his classroom theories to work in his capacity as conductor at the Paris Opera.

Then there were the discussions with his fellow students, gathered in table foursome at the cafés. They engaged in endless arguments and broached every topic fearlessly, since they were all young and were all sure they had the answers.

Jordá's first chance to conduct came when, as a member of a student's orchestra in Paris, he was asked one day to take over in the conductor's absence. "In a matter of minutes," he says, "I realized that this was my medium of expression." As musical director of the Spanish Ballet for a short period, he had the pleasure of conducting several ballets he had composed.

He was twenty-seven when a major symphony orchestra first came under his baton, through his guest conductorship of the Symphony Orchestra of Paris, Pierre Monteux's orchestra. It was a situation that was to be repeated. The San Francisco Symphony was also to be delivered into Jordá's hands from those of Monteux.

Jordá's success with the Paris Symphony was immediate and unmistakable. But the favorable newspaper critiques and the audience demonstrations were not what convinced him. These are not what convince any real conductor, Jordá believes. It is the "feel" one gets that one is a medium for the composer's intentions—that one has the gift of clairvoyance in music, can by some mystic means reveal the spirit of the composer. This cannot be taught. But when one has it, one knows one has it.

From then on Jordá's life plan was clear.

Monteux figured again in its early stages. That conductor's rehearsals of the Paris Symphony were strictly closed to the public. But Jordá longed to watch the maestro at his preparations. Finally he found a way. In the twists and turns of the passageways leading to the concert hall, he discovered a small door that led into an anteroom of the foyer. Each rehearsal morning he used to fumble his way in the darkness, let himself into the auditorium, slump down low in one of the end seats, and spend an hour or two absorbing Monteux's signals, suggestions, and interpretations. Years later, when he took over the San Francisco Symphony from Monteux, he told the great conductor about his youthful forays in search of enlightenment. Monteux patted him on the shoulder. "You are absolved," he said.

Beginning with his twenty-ninth year—from 1940—Jordá enjoyed the regular conductorship of a symphony orchestra. This was the Madrid Symphony, an orchestra that had become famous through the thirty-five-year tenure (1904–39) of the great Spanish musician E. Fernández Arbós. He had used it to stimulate a taste for symphonic music throughout Spain.

Jordá led the orchestra from 1940 to 1945. It gave him just the training he needed. The seventy concerts he directed annually not only helped him build up a repertoire but taught him the knack of getting across to orchestra and audience the fine points in the scores. The fact that it was a cooperative orchestra, the members themselves electing the conductor, allowed him to emphasize from the start that he was a co-worker with his players, that they were all joined in a common task—to get across the concepts of the composers.

Jordá believes the conductor must not start by saying, "Now what shall I do with this Tchaikovsky work?" He will get nowhere that way. The question is, how will the Tchaikovsky work use the conductor? Jordá thinks that the medium through which this transference takes place is love. "I fervently believe," he says, "that life is love. If one acts through pure love one sees the most beautiful things. What one sees is much in the person who looks."

War years are always hard on an orchestra. The Madrid Symphony was handicapped by lack of new scores as well as restrictions on guest soloists. After his marriage on Jan. 21, 1944, Jordá felt he must look about for a conductorship that spelled reasonable permanency and stability. To this end he spent two years guest conducting in various foreign cities: London, Manchester, Liverpool, Edinburgh, Brussels, Paris, Zurich. In the four years following their marriage, the couple lived in three different countries. Of his wife, Audrey Blaes, Jordá speaks with gentle happiness. "She has been my mainstay, my great good. She never interferes but always gives support." Their two daughters are Karin and Tessa, and their names were chosen for a reason every conductor will understand—because they are pronounced the same in every country of the world.

In 1947 Jordá received word that Cape Town, South Africa, wanted to rebuild its orchestra and that it thought he was the man to do it. His six-year tenure at this tip-end of the African continent posed unusual problems. The audiences, made up of many different national groups with different cultural backgrounds, called for programing with wide appeal. Modern works, usually international in their characteristics, were well received. So Jordá often gave concerts dedicated exclusively to contemporary music.

On Jordá's arrival the orchestra had only forty-five players. He solved this predicament by adding the local radio orchestra to the symphony—though the former still carried on a separate existence in its broadcasting.

The Cape Town Symphony has one of the longest seasons of any orchestra in the world: eleven months including a yearly tour. Besides filling this schedule, Jordá guest conducted in Buenos Aires and Europe. The trip to Europe in 1951 was very fruitful. He rounded up many new players for his orchestra.

As the years went by Jordá began to be concerned over his little daughters. They were growing up, and he wanted them to have every advantage. He decided to make a change. At about the same time the San Francisco Symphony, on the retirement of Monteux, was looking about for a new conductor.

The history of the San Francisco Symphony is dramatic. The famous earthquake of 1906 started it, since in the course of rebuilding the town the citizens included an orchestra in their plans. The great depression of 1929–33 almost killed it. But in the end it helped, too. For, faced with the prospect of no symphony at all, the citizens in 1935 voted a civic symphony tax into the city charter. At the same time Monteux became the orchestra's conductor. In 1951 he announced his retirement, at the age of seventy-six.

In its manner of choosing Monteux's successor, the San Francisco Symphony lived up to its reputation for the dramatic. There was a "year of discovery" (1952–53), when a series of guests were put on display, and a "year of decision" (1953–54) when audience vote indicated to the Board of Directors which guest was best suited for the job.

The year of discovery was ushered in by Jordá, since he was the first of the nine conductors to mount the podium during that season. The audience, of which a large percentage were university students—eminently severe critics—gave him a tremendous ovation.

During the year of decision Jordá was invited back for a much longer stay. Another ovation! One critic reported, "Conducting without a score, sometimes with a baton and sometimes with the stick dangling between his fingers while he used both hands to sculpture the phrases, Mr. Jordá brought forth playing that had a beautiful free musical surge. Rarely did he indulge in distracting gyrations (although he was far more mobile than Pierre Monteux), but he was sufficiently animated and dynamic in his movements to fascinate."

Jordá was elected by an overwhelming majority.

As for the conductor himself—"From the first moment in San Francisco," he says, "I felt at home. I was impressed by the extreme warmth, hospitality, kindness, and gentleness of its people. Apart from this I enjoyed my collaboration with the orchestra, not only a remarkable group of artists but also a fine group of individuals. This, coupled with the beauty of the city, made it a most tempting invitation."

Jordá accepted. The battle of the batons was over.

What makes Jordá happiest with his present situation is the fact that he has received not only a highly trained orchestra but one tempered to justice and love. Monteux has given his successor as heritage a group who have been sympathetically dealt with and who respond in kind.

CHAPTER XIV

⇶ JOSEF KRIPS

In his appearance Josef Krips, conductor of the Buffalo Philharmonic Orchestra, suggests the solid citizen. Portly, substantial, deliberate as he moves in the moil of an airport, a ship's dock, or a train's platform, he would be taken for a successful executive on his way to a top-level board meeting. His attitude toward conducting is logical and thorough. Questioned about his calling, he looks steadily at the speaker. "To be a conductor is not just an eight-hour-a-day job," he says. "It is an inner vocation, or it is less than nothing."

Krips had to face early the fact that taking up music as a profession was a serious matter. He was born April 8, 1902, in that most musical of cities, Vienna, and into a music-loving family. But from the first he was discouraged from thinking of music in terms of a life calling. His father, a successful physician, believed that "in a career so difficult as that of the professional musician, everything should be done to prevent a child from adopting it. Then, if he still persists in spite of all obstacles, you know he really is fitted for it."

There were plenty of chances to have fun with music in the Krips household, however. As a five-year-old, Josef used to wheedle his mother, brother, sister, and the three servants into the garden for ensemble singing. Equipped with a good-sized twig for baton, he would "lead" them—which to him meant bringing them to time by flicking them with the switch. Each time his "orchestra" dispersed, he would burst into tears and beg them to reassemble.

He often provided keyboard accompaniment for his father, who had a fine tenor voice. From the age of six he went through Schubert works this way, and, at ten, began tackling Wagnerian operas. As he played, he imagined the parts being taken by the appropriate instruments. A sense of actual participation in ensemble was acquired through his role as choirboy in the Karmeliter Church in Vienna, where his father also served as choir member.

On his thirteenth Christmas, Josef received a violin. He paid for his lessons himself (part of his father's plan for making things hard) with money he took in from coaching neighborhood boys in Latin.

His violin was also an entering wedge into the orchestral field. When he was fifteen he became a substitute first violinist in the Vienna People's Opera orchestra. He went on brief tours with a small opera company in his late teens, acting not only as violinist but also, in crises, as stage manager, harmonium player, and singer. He once substituted for an ailing bass as Angelotti in *La Tosca*. He was on the chunky side even in those days, and the critics chuckled over so healthy a specimen taking the role of a long-confined prisoner.

At sixteen Josef enrolled at the Vienna Academy of Music and studied harmony under Eusebius Mandyczewski.

Young Krips' opening in the conducting field came through his study in the Classic repertoire with Felix Weingartner. Josef had been coaching singers on the side. One day he accompanied one of them to an audition with Weingartner who, besides teaching, was director of the People's Opera and conductor of the Vienna Philharmonic. When they arrived at the studio, auditionists were crowding the anteroom and Weingartner was striding excitedly up and down among them. The accompanist had failed to show up.

When Weingartner saw his pupil Krips, he asked him to substitute at the piano. Before the day was over the young man had accompanied forty singers through their selections without once having had to refer to the scores. Weingartner decided he could make use of this extraordinary memorizer. He engaged him as chorus master and assistant conductor of the People's Opera. That was in 1921, and Krips was nineteen years old.

In the first year of his work with Weingartner, Krips conducted Verdi's *A Masked Ball,* and the next, Bizet's *Carmen.* His initial appearance on the podium, he recalls, filled him with terror. How to make the musicians respond! Then suddenly it all seemed to come just right. "I swam into it like a fish in water."

Between 1924 and 1926 Krips made three forward moves: as music director of the opera in Aussig, Czechoslovakia; as music director in Dortmund, Germany; and as general music director in Karlsruhe, at the opera made famous by Felix Mottl's twenty-one-year tenure.

After seven years in Karlsruhe, Krips returned to his home town (in 1933) with a contract as principal conductor of the Vienna State Opera in his pocket and more than one hundred operas and symphonies in his head. He also became teacher at the Vienna Music Academy and conductor (in 1935) at the Salzburg Festival.

The most important single event of this period was his first encounter with Toscanini. "It changed the whole course of my life. Most conductors of the early days interpreted compositions in a very free way, with little regard for the composer's wishes. But through Toscanini I learned humility before the composer. Everything that I had done before then seemed to me not the right way. It took me a long time to restudy every score—to reorient my viewpoint—but I did it! I emerged with the scores in my very blood stream, in my nerves, in my heart."

As to the actual process of conducting, Krips has an almost mystic belief that "we do not make music with our hands. We make music with our breath. Until I see and feel that every musician takes breath at the same time, I do not start the composition. When they breathe with me, then I know it is time. Before many minutes the audience is breathing with us, too." Again, he says, "What should be taught is to feel the musical line of a piece. The orchestra does not play to your beat; the orchestra plays what you feel. Each member must read in my eyes what I expect."

Absolute knowledge of each work, unsparing pains at rehearsals, and unerring directions to his men won Krips a firm place in the Vienna of the mid-thirties. But World War II shook even that. Because of his political stand at the Nazi *Anschluss* in 1938, Krips was forced to give up both his positions, as conductor of the State Opera and as professor at the Academy. He left for Belgrade, but had to return when Yugoslavia also came under Nazi domination.

Then for seven years he was prevented from taking any public part in the musical life of Vienna. (Occasionally he did coach famous singers.) For several years he worked in a food-processing factory.

The war ended. Vienna was a black ruin. Streetcars, subways, taxis, were at a standstill. Food was scarce. The State Opera had been bombed and was a mass of rubble. This was the situation when Josef Krips and a small group of dedicated singers and instrumentalists gathered in the People's Opera House, its windows blown out, its heating facilities out of order, and started rehearsals on *The Marriage of Figaro*. The performance took place May 1, 1945. A month later the dusty, long-unused Theater an der Wien, scene of the world première of Mozart's *The Magic Flute* in 1791 and of Beethoven's *Fidelio* in 1805, was reopened as a stopgap home of the Vienna State Opera. In September of the same year Krips presided at the opening concert of the reconstructed Musik-verein. Preparations for these concerts and operas took on the guise of a sacred rite performed amid unbelievable difficulties. "Mozart and Schubert went through a great deal of suffering in Vienna," Krips reminisces. "They composed music in want and destitution. We who took part in those concerts felt the bond of misfortune."

Through such efforts, in Vienna and elsewhere, Krips helped bring about a Mozart renaissance. He became known as a Mozart specialist.

Krips now began a mode of life that has persisted through the years. Faced with a tired, horror-stricken Europe, he engaged in far-flung guest conductorships. From the years 1947 to 1950 he took the Vienna Opera and the Vienna Philharmonic on tour to Paris, Brussels, Amsterdam, Rotterdam, The Hague. He oc-cupied podiums in Moscow, in Leningrad, and at Covent Garden, London. In Florence at the Maggio Musicale he conducted a com-plete Mozart week with five operas, concluding with the Requiem in the cathedral.

His five years as conductor of the London Symphony began in 1949. "A wonderful period it was!" he exults. "I started an annual Beethoven cycle there and an annual Brahms cycle." He continued to guest conduct in many lands. He led the French Na-tional, the Conservatoire, and Lamoureux orchestras in Paris; the Concertgebouw and the Opera Orchestra in Amsterdam; the Residenzie Orchestra at The Hague; the Santa Cecilia in Rome; the Suisse Romande; the Zurich Philharmonic; the Royal and Radio orchestras in Copenhagen.

In 1953 he widened his radius to include the New World. He made a tour in Canada, the principal stop being the Montreal

Symphony. The Buffalo Philharmonic, which was that year looking for a conductor, invited him for a pair of concerts.

At the end of his first appearance in Buffalo's Kleinhans Music
Hall, listeners sprang to their feet and applauded wildly. They
repeated the demonstration at another set of concerts. Proved the
popular choice, he was given a contract—"with a free hand in
all artistic matters."

Heavily booked during the rest of 1953, Krips did not assume
his duties in Buffalo until the early part of 1954. Then for three
weeks in May he performed a Beethoven cycle.

In his first full season in Buffalo (1954–55), Krips presented a
Brahms cycle. He also took the orchestra on tour. Canada, New
England, and New York were its first stops. In the following
season, it toured from Canada to West Virginia. Subscriptions rose
from 2700 to 4600. Mr. Krips' feelings today about Buffalo are
summed up in the one happy statement: "It is a place where you
can get a standing ovation after you conduct the Bruckner Symphony!"

But this conductor has spread modern masterworks far beyond
the Buffalo radius. Through the Cincinnati May Festival, which
he directed in 1954 and 1956, through his Ravinia (Chicago) engagements, through his tours in Europe, he has introduced many
new works. Between the close of the Buffalo spring season in 1955
and the reopening in the fall, he appeared six times in Montreal;
twice in Mexico City; at the International Bruckner Festival in
Berne, Switzerland; at the London Festival; and at the June
Festival in Vienna. He also gave twenty-six concerts in Australia.

Touring conductors are lucky in having constantly fresh audiences and in being able to offer new music to many ears. But
there is also a side less pleasant and less publicized—the constant
packing and unpacking, the endless telephone calls, taxi runs
through heavy traffic, split-second timings, hectic airport clatter.

If ever Mr. Krips speaks of this side, however, it is to look gratefully at his wife, Maria, and say, "Marrying her was the most important event in my life. She holds me at an even keel. I could never go on tours without her!"

Mrs. Krips, whom he met when she was singing a cycle of Schubert songs in Vienna, has something to say herself about the tours. "I've learned to read time tables and order meals in many languages," she says, laughing. She has quick-moving, twinkling eyes. "I have learned to see people my husband hasn't time to see, travel by plane with two skirts—one to change to from the one mussed in travel—and to keep up with my husband's American speed." Of her husband, she explains, "He grew up to his profession. His system seems built for it. When people say to me, when he rehearses, 'Couldn't you hold him back, he gives so much!' I say, 'Impossible! He is building like an architect—balancing, shaping!' They say, 'But he must be exhausted!' I tell them, 'Ask the fish if he's tired of swimming!'"

This conductor is not tired. He feels, in fact, that he is just getting into his stride. For the first twenty-five years, he believes, one learns from the players. After that one is in a position to teach them something. That is his stimulus and his inspiration now—to initiate his players into the true spirit, the initial glory, of the compositions played.

CHAPTER XV

⇉ HOWARD MITCHELL

WHOEVER thinks one enters a special esoteric sphere when one crosses the threshold into the conductor's world must make a quick turnabout on meeting Howard Mitchell, conductor of the National Symphony Orchestra. Here is a clear-thinking, quick-answering, up-to-the-minute conversationalist. He looks outward. He deals in people. He is extremely happy in his family life, with the wife whom he married in his student days and his five children. His recreations are really re-creative. He is an expert golf player, who has within the past few years won prizes in this field in the District of Columbia. He deals with businessmen directly and with hard-hitting decisiveness. He is as aware of the world of supply and demand as he is of the world of Bach and Brahms.

He looks on orchestral situations not only as a musician but also as an economist—knows how competition among major orchestras can help and can harm, realizes the value of publicity, senses to the last decibel the volume of sound the box office gives off. He believes that hard work and enterprise get one where one wants to go. He knows that confidence breeds confidence and treats his men accordingly. His cause-to-result reasoning hits the nail squarely on the head. He has a serviceable amount of righteous indignation, knows a wrong when he sees it, and puts his finger on the culprit, be he visiting soloist, second violinist, or member of the board.

His life story refutes once and for all the idea that musicianship cannot thrive in a normal background and with a Middle Western accent. It also refutes the thought that conductors cannot rise from the orchestra ranks. He was chosen for his present job as conductor of the National Symphony after playing in the orchestra for sixteen years as cellist.

It is with a Middle Western heartiness that he speaks about his career. His face lights up as he recalls this and that incident. He is apt to jump up and walk back and forth as his energy overflows. His rich, full laugh, his quick repartee, his wholesome good sense, tell why he is the perfect choice for an orchestra called the National Symphony based in the nation's capital, Washington, D. C.

Mitchell tells his own story well; here it is, with only a bit of editorial framework.

"The first time I conducted an orchestra—a big orchestra—was in the fall of 1941 for some 'pop' concerts, when I was twenty-nine years old. It was about this time that the National Symphony wanted to expand its activities by having a series of pop concerts at Riverside Stadium. Even though those concerts didn't last— they made the indoor stadium into a roller-skating rink—it meant something. It started me in the conducting field. A little later in that same year another significant thing happened. The manager of the orchestra, Pat Hayes, was trying to discover a way to get the schools to become members of the Symphony Association at $25 per year a member. One night he and I happened to be traveling on the same bus. Pat was mulling over his worries. I said, 'Pat, I'll tell you what I'll do. I'll play in any school that will become a member of the association. Play for free. They must become a member, though. And you'll have to pay my accompanist.'

" 'You mean it?' asked Pat.

" 'Of course I mean it!'

"First year Pat booked me for twenty-four schools. Many of

them became members at $100. They could charge the children a small admission. That was up to them. But they got my cello recital free.

"It was a good thing all around. Many schools that became members wanted me back. Finally I could draw my own terms. A very wholesome thing—willingness to start something, willingness to throw yourself into life. Today there is too much feeling of getting out of things rather than of getting into things. Make your own way, I say.

"That's what I tell new orchestra players. 'You have to get yourself ahead. You have the gifts to become a fine trumpet player—or a great oboist, or an excellent harpist—to go as far as you wish. Throw yourself into it!'

"Anyway, it worked with me. I feel the success of those cello concerts had a direct relationship with my getting the assistant conductorship of the National Symphony in 1944. They put me right away to directing for young people's and neighborhood concerts."

If the listener asks at this point, "Weren't you in some doubt about your ability to conduct?" Mitchell comes back in a flash, "I never had any doubts about it in my life! I think I could almost lead an orchestra with my eyes!"

Then he launches into an explanation of what makes a conductor.

"The first requisite—he has to be a good musician. But he has to be more. He must not only be musician enough to know when a thing is not right, but to be able to tell *why* it is not right. He has to get it across to the players. He doesn't have to have instruments at his finger tips, but he must know how each instrument can be made to sound and tell the player, 'You can get it nearer than that.' Mind you, the men are skilled instrumentalists. You're not teaching them. You're showing them how the over-all effect has to sound and how they can help to make it sound that way."

Mitchell likes to recall his childhood, which was rich in music.

"I started studying piano on my sixth birthday. It was a ritual in our house. Every one of us—I had four brothers and one sister —started piano lessons on his sixth birthday. I had just moved with the family to Sioux City, Iowa, from Lyons, Nebraska, where I had been born in 1911. As for my brothers, one is a member of the San Francisco Symphony and one is dean of the music department of West Chester State Teachers College, in Pennsylvania. The others went into business."

At first young Mitchell's education wasn't all smooth sailing.

"I didn't like the piano. My parents told me any time I got another instrument I could give it up. I was nine when a man who worked for Father gave me a tenor tuba. That ended the piano for me. I took the tuba two years. At eleven I got a yen for the trumpet. I bought a trumpet and started playing dances at twelve. Made money. Was in demand.

"In my high school days I came in contact with Arthur Poister, an organist and a fine teacher as well as an inspiring conductor. I was first trumpet in his orchestra and band. He needed a cello, and persuaded me to take it up. I bought my first cello for thirty dollars when I was fifteen years old. Soon I was playing it in the orchestra. After six months I entered a cello contest. Came out third, although I could play only in the first position. After that I learned the higher finger-board positions quick enough!

"I was winning prizes with my golf, too. A well-known cellist out there, Lorenz De Minter, made me a proposition. He would teach me cello if I would teach him golf. It was a deal. For two years we exchanged lessons. At sixteen I won two contests: the state contest for cello and the city golf championship.

"In 1928, though, I got to thinking—it was shortly after I had graduated from Central High School—just what did I want to do? A brother of mine was studying at Peabody Conservatory in Baltimore. I decided to go there. At the school, I had my audition and won a scholarship. I studied there two and a half years.

"In 1930 I went to Curtis Institute in Philadelphia. There my teacher was the English cellist, Felix Salmond. He told me, 'You're too tight in the wrist. Are you a baseball player?' I told him 'No.'

" 'An American and not a baseball player?' he exclaimed. 'What do you play, then?' I told him 'Golf.' He couldn't wait to get me out on the golf course. We had a good relationship those years both in the studio and on the course. I was at Curtis, remember, in the golden days. I got $90 a month and free schooling. In my cello class were Frank Miller, Leonard Rose, Sammy Mayes, Orlando Cole, and Victor Gottlieb. Quite a class! They've all made their marks."

Mitchell was soon to make his mark, too. While still at Curtis, he became first cellist in the National Symphony, commuting between Washington and Philadelphia during the two years before his graduation in 1935. In 1944 Hans Kindler, the orchestra's conductor, felt the need of a helping hand with his heavy schedule. He asked Mitchell to take over the children's concerts and to become the orchestra's assistant conductor. Because of the frequent illnesses of Kindler, more and more responsibilities devolved on Mitchell. Many days, Mitchell relates, he would get scores at five o'clock and conduct them that same night. Then in February, 1948, just as the southern tour was to start, Kindler realized he was not up to it. Mitchell was asked to assume the touring responsibilities. In the 1948–49 season Mitchell was appointed associate conductor. With Kindler's death in August, 1949, he was appointed permanent conductor.

Mitchell believes his record on this podium speaks quite as eloquently in bare figures as in highflown phrases. Today, he points out, the number of people who give to the orchestra has doubled. The goals of the drives have increased from $165,000 (1948–49) to $300,000 and beyond; the season from twenty-four to thirty-one weeks; the minimum scale from $72 to $92. Seventy-seven concerts were presented in 1947–48 as against 145 concerts in 1955–56. Seven children's programs were played to 10,000 children in 1947; in the 1955–56 season, sixty young people's concerts were presented before 161,000 youthful listeners.

Mitchell expands the scope of the orchestra in its repertoire as in its membership and audiences. He commissioned two American works for the orchestra's twenty-fifth anniversary season, 1955–56 —one, Paul Creston's Fifth Symphony, paid for by the National Symphony itself; the other, Dello Joio's Piano Concerto, paid for by the Koussevitzky Foundation. The orchestra also gave a five-thousand-dollar prize for three compositions—a symphony, a tone poem, an overture—through the Filene Foundation.

That anniversary season went down on record, too, as fostering another of Mitchell's brain children. The season of the National Symphony was extended, as of April, 1956, five weeks in the spring. In these five weeks it plays annually a series of thirty concerts for the thousands of teen-age school children who make sightseeing pilgrimages to Washington at cherry blossom time. This "Music for Young America" series by the summer of 1956 had already attracted 61,266 young Americans from forty-three states.

As resident orchestra in our nation's capital, the National Symphony has developed a semiofficial status, a situation to which Mitchell responds with alacrity and resourcefulness. One concert will be a function for the foreign ministers of the American republics, their names on the program, their presence in the circle of boxes acknowledged by the evening's soloists. Another concert will be a welcoming gesture for a foreign head of state, with the appropriate national anthem preceding the regular program. Still another will be a Presidential affair such as an inauguration concert.

In one of these concerts, attended by President and Mrs. Eisenhower and many cabinet members, Mitchell had the foresight to inquire of the President what sort of music he liked. The answer was "bass singing." Mitchell was happy to oblige. He procured George London as soloist. The press reported that "the orchestra played brilliantly and produced impressive shadings of tonal color," and that everyone concerned, including the President, was very well satisfied.

The orchestra gives several "International Nights" each season, in which the programs are made up of works of particular nations—a French program, a German, an Italian.

Although the orchestra is semiofficial in its function and "national" in its name, it gets no financial support either from the national or the federally supported local government. Nor does it have any endowment fund. It is one of Mitchell's concerns—or he makes it his concern—to see that the $650,000 budget gets raised. More than half is realized through ticket sales and concerts for children which are sponsored by business firms and individuals. About $300,000 must be raised from scratch through the efforts of volunteer workers. Every kind of promotional scheme is used—fashion shows, guided tours of the embassies, and benefits of an extraordinarily wide appeal. A ball held every year, in the fall, where society dances to Strauss waltzes played by the symphony, raises around $70,000 annually. Summer concerts give entertainment for twelve weeks in the Carter-Barron Amphitheatre in Rock Creek Park, through the management of the Feld brothers, Irving and Isidor.

A heavy schedule and extracurricular duties that would floor a less energetic conductor are all in the order of things for Mr. Mitchell, who has never been one to avoid issues or to escape work. Today, as one of the most resourceful conductors on our podiums, he is still the Midwesterner making his own way with all available resources, inner and outer, and very glad to be able to carry along with him in his upward climb a symphony orchestra of some ninety members.

CHAPTER XVI

⇛ DIMITRI MITROPOULOS

"A GOOD musician should try also as much as possible to be a first-rate human being. Possessing a certain talent is no excuse for him to be arrogant and presumptuous." Dimitri Mitropoulos, conductor of the New York Philharmonic-Symphony, says this earnestly and simply. A man of convictions, he feels that the good way is the hard way.

This belief is evidenced not only in his strenuous wintertime schedule. Vacations, which most conductors find necessary for recouping their energies, he uses to expend his. He climbs mountains for the sense it gives him of battling with the elements. He serves his fellow men in direct and basic ways. One summer during World War II he traveled about Minnesota with a mobile blood-donating unit as a Red Cross worker. For twelve to fourteen hours a day he loaded and unloaded supplies and cleaned test tubes at grimy sinks in railroad stations. He did this not only with cheerfulness; he did it as a special sort of outlet into the larger life. A few years later he and his men of the New York Philharmonic paid for a Red Cross ambulance.

This man with a mission has a capacity for driving work that would kill a less hardy soul. He is up at five or six in the morning. After a sketchy breakfast he plunges into a minute analysis of the score at hand. "I take the score apart, just as a child takes a clock apart," is the way he describes his disentanglement of main themes, subthemes and counterthemes. "Then I put the pieces together again. Sometimes there will be a piece or two left over the first time—measure 157 or measure 233, say. So I start over again. If it takes two or three months, I still work at it. Finally, when everything fits, I know I have it."

At nine thirty, Mitropoulos finishes his morning study of scores. Then he goes to Carnegie Hall, a block away from his apartment, and begins a rehearsal session that lasts till noon. After dining in a small restaurant nearby, and perhaps again rehearsing, he goes home to the seclusion of his penthouse apartment. There religious symbols remind him that his personal life, quite as fully as his professional life, is a dedicated one. On the evenings when there are no concerts, he studies far into the night. Mitropoulos eats no supper. He is a one-meal-a-day man.

This conductor comes naturally by his view of life as a spiritual struggle. He was born in Athens, on February 18, 1896, into a deeply religious household. His two uncles were monks of the Greek Orthodox Church. One of his granduncles was an archbishop. His home was a regular meeting place for disciples of the Church. Dimitri's father considered entering the priesthood himself, but finally settled for a life of good works in the capacity of citizen and leather merchant. When the Turks expelled some two million Greeks from Asia Minor in 1921, he served as unofficial priest and comforter to his suffering countrymen who came as refugees from the ports of Smyrna. He was jailed for his work in their behalf and died in his prison cell of the plague.

It was this man whom Mitropoulos had as his example throughout his youth and early manhood.

The young Dimitri dreamed of leading the consecrated life of a monk. He often visited the nearby monasteries. He sought out distant chapels and stayed days and nights there, sleeping on the floor and eating the black bread and thick soup of the hermits. He sometimes got together an audience of the small boys in the village and delivered a sermon or had them act as acolytes to his own ritualistic devotions.

He prayed constantly for his fellow beings, for his own soul. But when the time came to decide on his life work, he realized that if he entered a monastery, they would not allow him even a little harmonium—the Greek Orthodox Church does not countenance musical instruments in its religious rituals. He knew then he could not do it.

Love of music had been as deeply instilled in Mitropoulos as love of religion. From the age of nine he had studied piano. One day Armand Marsick, a professor at the Odeion Conservatory in Athens as well as leader of the Athens Symphony, chancing to stroll by the boy's house, overheard strange and intriguing music. He made inquiries and discovered that the works were of the boy's own making. He suggested that he become his private pupil at the Conservatory. So at the age of twelve, Dimitri began studying composition with one of the best teachers in Greece.

As he had formerly sought out mountain chapels, the boy now sought out new forms in music. He was much interested in the theater and tried to compose brief dramatic works. His spiritual life gained new impetus. Marsick took Mitropoulos with him on his vacations in Italy (Marsick's wife was Italian), and the young man was thrilled with the religious history of Rome. He delved deeply into the mystical writings of St. Francis of Assisi. To do good to one's fellow men, to follow the path of humility, became the chief purpose of his existence.

When Dimitri was twenty-three, his opera *Sister Beatrice,* based on a text by Maeterlinck, was performed at the Conservatory. Camille Saint-Saëns, who happened to be in Athens, carried back to Paris a glowing account of it. This famous composer's recognition brought the city of Athens to a sense of responsibility for its talented son. Funds were provided to send Mitropoulos first to

Brussels to study under Paul Gilson, then, in 1921, to Berlin to study under Ferruccio Busoni.

Busoni, though he was touched by the thin, shy young man who played the piano so astoundingly, who composed so earnestly, who thought so deeply, did not let his feelings keep him from his usual brutal frankness. When Mitropoulos played for him a forty-five-minute-long sonata of his own, one into which he had "poured his whole soul," Busoni pulled it apart mercilessly. "Too much passion," he said. "Go back to Mozart for purity of form!"

Mitropoulos had looked on composing as his life work. From that moment he gave it up. "I listened to Busoni, absorbed his knowledge, and ended up as a re-creator instead of a creator," he says. Or he can be more abrupt: "Well—so I deteriorated into a conductor!"

Mitropoulos during this period acted as assistant at the Berlin State Opera, rehearsing, coaching, accompanying, conducting. Since the Berlin Theater was under the same general management as the Opera, he made himself useful there also, conducting and playing piano and organ for the incidental music in performances of Shakespeare and Ibsen.

When after four years Mitropoulos received an offer from Athens to lead the city orchestra, he accepted with alacrity. It was not only the conducting itself he enjoyed. He liked contributing money for instruments and music for the men. He liked hearing their problems and arriving at solutions together with them. He might well have concluded that here was to be his future. But destiny decided differently.

Mitropoulos' guest conducting assignments had taken him to many European cities outside Greece. In March, 1930, he was invited to conduct the Berlin Philharmonic. Shortly before the concert Egon Petri, who had been scheduled as soloist to play Prokofiev's Third Piano Concerto, fell ill. It was impossible at that late date to find a pianist who included this erratic and mechanistic concerto in his repertoire. So Mitropoulos offered to serve as both soloist and conductor. The management, doubting but desperate, agreed.

What happened that evening made Mitropoulos known all over Europe. With the piano lid removed to allow visibility both ways, he flayed the air orchestraward during the pianoless passages; then, precisely at the opening notes of the solo passages, plummeted hands to the keyboard, leaving it to his darting eyes and bobbing head to carry on the conductor's role. His amazingly quick reactions, his interplay of finger and mind, his split-second timings, his ability to project his intentions instantaneously to the orchestra men, made his performance something to talk about. Music critics didn't miss their chance. Word of the performance spread all over Europe.

All doors were now open to Mitropoulos. He made his Paris debut with this work. The composer himself was in the audience and declared that this amazing man could outstrip him as pianist-interpreter. News spread to the other side of the Atlantic, and Serge Koussevitzky invited him to be guest conductor of the Boston Symphony.

When Mitropoulos, at forty years of age, first set foot on American soil, he was no novice in the field of conducting. He had for years made an annual tour of the principal Italian cities. For years he had had a standing engagement to conduct an annual three-month season at Monte Carlo. For a dozen seasons he had been at the helm of the Athens Symphony. He had conducted most of the major orchestras of Europe.

For all this experience, he knew that to appear before one of the most famous orchestras of America was a challenge of a very special sort.

As usual, Mitropoulos met the challenge head on. Bostonians

came to startled attention as he lashed the orchestra men to fever heat, as he swooped earthward, clenched his fists, shook his body like a garment. Once their ears took over from their eyes, however, what they heard was pure, unimpeded music. At the close of the concert they gave him an ovation. More to the point, they asked him back.

When Mitropoulos returned to America the next year it was on a double invitation, from both the Boston and the Minneapolis orchestras. In Boston, his success was repeated. In Minneapolis, on January 29, 1937, "An audience that is considered one of the calmest and coldest-handed in the country," wrote John K. Sherman in his *Music and Maestros,* published by the University of Minnesota Press, 1952, "became an excited mob that staged the nearest thing to a riot ever seen in Twin Cities concert halls. Wild-eyed spectators cheered and shouted bravos, clapped strangers on the back, and otherwise acted as if they were under the influence of strong stimulants. . . . Mitropoulos appeared to be a fanatic who had sold his soul to music and conducted the orchestra like a man possessed."

The answer to such a triumph was a permanent conductorship. When this was announced from the platform of Northrop Auditorium, the audience stood up and cheered. Mitropoulos was to hold the post twelve years.

In welcoming Mitropoulos, America has had unexpected returns. His uncommon ability to adjust to our ways of life has led him to address Christian Endeavor societies, eat in one-arm joints, explore the mountains of the great West, and attend movies—"opening cans of life for one who has no time to cook," he calls this movie-going.

But it is Mitropoulos' attitude as conductor that particularly stamps him as American. "I do not want to be a dictator but a man who pleads for love, justice, and consideration both for the composers and for my colleagues in the orchestra," he says. "I could no more do without my colleagues than they could do without me." His feeling for the men is more than professional respect. On tours, he rides with them, carries on discussions with them, snatches cat naps as they do on the dusty plush seats of the day coaches.

In Minneapolis, Mitropoulos threw himself into civic enterprises. Northrop Auditorium needed a new shell for its stage. It got its shell—an excellent one—because Mitropoulos launched the project, going from house to house asking for contributions. In two days he had $5000 in his pocket for the cause.

In Minneapolis, too, he became famous for his "firsts." Composers far and near blessed his presence on the podium, as he launched premières one after another. "If we do not face and listen to the spirit of our time," he pleaded, "we shall not be able to resolve its frustrations and confusions"; and again, "The next Bach or Beethoven will be born in America. We want to be in on the birth."

Mitropoulos began to take regular guest conductorships in the East. In 1938 he conducted the NBC Symphony. In 1940 he guest conducted the New York Philharmonic-Symphony. In 1945 and 1946 he was conductor at Robin Hood Dell. The latter year was a big one for him. He became a citizen of the United States—for him a deeply symbolic act.

As a result of a series of successful guest conductorships with the New York Philharmonic, Mitropoulos was asked in 1949 to become the orchestra's regular conductor. He accepted. It must have been stimulating to this scaler of mountain peaks to take over a podium whose record of casualties among conductors quite equals Mount Everest's among climbers.

A farewell talk Mitropoulos gave at Northrop Auditorium at the end of the last concert there eased hurt feelings. "My friends," he said in part, "you helped me grow and you did grow with me. . . . So I am going someplace where I don't know if I am going to be happy. But I have to go. I have to climb the mountain that is expected from me. . . . If I have sometimes been harsh, please forgive me, and if I have ever hurt you with some modern compositions, I hope you will not keep it in mind . . . because I had some duties also toward your education and also to serve my art. . . . So I tell you—so long! And God be always with you!"

For the first season the New York conductorship was a shared one: Mitropoulos and Leopold Stokowski were podium colleagues. But, beginning with the 1950–51 season, until 1957, the whole task devolved on Mitropoulos. He gave his whole self to it.

In September 1950, Mitropoulos took the Philharmonic into Manhattan's Roxy Theatre as the stage attraction—brought fine music to those who could not afford to pay the high prices at Carnegie Hall. He answered the hesitant who disliked having the impeccable Philharmonic play in a Broadway theater with, "Art is pure no matter where it goes. Art cannot be brought down. . . . People can only be brought up."

He sent shivers up the spines of Carnegie Hall habitués with his concert presentations of Strauss's *Elektra* and Berg's *Wozzeck*.

Unorthodox in his ideas, Mitropoulos is also unorthodox in his podium methods. Brenda Ueland's vivid description of his practice sessions is quoted by John K. Sherman in his *Music and Maestros:* "His face is lighted with joyful excitement; he springs down among the violins, pulling out their theme, bounds to point with a fierce index finger into the horns. To whip the rhythm, he leaps high, stamps his heels in pistol shots." Meanwhile, pulling at the collar of his turtle-neck sweater, he shouts in a raw, dramatic voice, "Don't act Hamlet! *Be* Hamlet! Don't act the music. *Be* the music!"

When he takes time out for a recess, the orchestra men crowd around him, to discuss, to hear his remarks about the work, or to offer him a cigarette and solicitously light it for him. At such times his craggy features shadow into a smile.

Mitropoulos' individualistic approach has not always met with approval. Music critic Virgil Thomson wrote, "Mitropoulos has taken over the Philharmonic-Symphony concerts like an occupying army. . . . Panzer division tactics . . . all is discipline, machine finish, tension and power. . . . He makes every piece sound nervous and violent." Another New York critic, B. H. Haggin, mourned the gentle renditions of former conductors and added, "To allow a passage of music to take its natural course is precisely the thing Mitropoulos cannot do. For that he is too unrelaxed; and when his tenseness doesn't produce explosive violence it shows itself in the manipulation that breaks the flow of the music."

In 1954, Mitropoulos, along with his Philharmonic duties, became guest conductor at the Metropolitan Opera House. He has since conducted *Salome*, *The Masked Ball*, *Boris Godunov*, *Tosca*, and *Manon Lescaut*.

With the increase in his activities, Mitropoulos has had regretfully to forego his hobby of mountain climbing. (Earlier he had climbed the West Coast Sierra, the Tetons, and many high mountains in Colorado.) His whole concern now is "instead of struggle for the high peaks, struggle for the heights in music."

Many honors have come his way. King Paul and Queen Frederika of Greece personally presented to him the decoration of Commander of the Order of the Phoenix. He was named Chevalier of the French Legion of Honor for his services to France in playing contemporary French music. He was awarded the "San Luca 1954 for Music," the Florentine equivalent of Hollywood's "Oscar."

His New York podium occupancy has set Mitropoulos' characteristics in sharp relief. In the midst of devotees of Freud and

Adler, he holds to his simplicity; with anti-atonalists to the left and right of him, he continues to encourage modern composers; with unlimited opportunity to dictate, he remains humble. The struggle to maintain these values has been unrelenting. But to one who believes "only life suffered can transform a symphony from a collection of notes into a message for humanity," this is all as it should be.

CHAPTER XVII

⇶ CHARLES MUNCH

"Like all sacred callings, that of conductor supposes a total self-renunciation and a profound humility." *

When one realizes this attitude on the part of Charles Munch, conductor of the Boston Symphony Orchestra, one understands his relish of the fact that he was forty-one years old before he became a conductor. He is thankful he worked out so long an apprenticeship as a student and as a member of the orchestra. He even seeks to extend it. In the early 1950's he attended Passerone's percussion classes and Sabaritch's trumpet course at the Paris Conservatory. Shortly before that, when Toscanini was guest conducting in France, Munch played in the second violin section, last row, in order to profit from this great maestro's leadership. His respect for the orchestra men and their "splendid anonymity" continues today. He always steps from the podium to acknowledge applause and always gestures the orchestra men to stand and share it with him.

Mr. Munch avoids both lionizing and publicizing. He is either indifferent to statements of the press or has learned to rise above them. "I have been assassinated many times," he says with a whimsical smile, "but I am still among the living." He is one of

* This quotation and several others in this chapter are from Charles Munch's book, *I Am a Conductor,* first published in France, then, in a translation by Leonard Burkat, in this country, in 1955, by the Oxford University Press.

the very few conductors who can be heard to say, even in earshot of music critics, "How do you suppose Conductor X manages that passage? *I* can't do it, no matter how I try!"

What he has to give to a piece of music, Munch gives frankly and with joy. He is not a conductor to work up a set interpretation of a composition, to standardize it down to the last bow stroke and triangle tinkle. If his Brahms' Second one year is different from his Brahms' Second of another year, well, it is live music that is being projected, and live things never reach the stage of crystallization.

Munch certainly has never reached that stage. For, though the pattern of his personality was set early, it is a pattern that allows for infinite development.

In Strasbourg, from his birth on September 26, 1891, up to 1912 when he went to Paris, he drew in music as he drew in the tangy air of that Alsatian town. As a boy he used to sit spellbound while his father, Ernst Munch, and Albert Schweitzer, the famous Bach exponent, organist, and philosopher, discussed how to play a particular phrase in a Bach chorale-prelude. He remembers that sometimes they would get so excited that they would whack the furniture until it trembled. Then, after they had brought up authorities galore and presented interpretations hours on end, each, weary with reasoning, would speak from the heart, tell how he felt it *must* be played. "This is how I learned to love music," says Munch.

Strasbourg, where old palaces and ancient quays lie in the shadow of the cathedral spire, is the evangelical center of Alsace. For generations the members of the Munch family have been musicians affiliated with the church. Most of Charles' paternal ancestors were organists. His father, besides being organist at St. William's Church in Strasbourg, founded its choir, formed and led an orchestra, and organized a school of music. During Charles' early years his father was dubbed "the cantata man" by the villagers, through his feat of presenting with his choir all 198 of the sacred cantatas of Bach.

Musical get-togethers at the Munch home were as set a custom as attendance at church. Each of the six children—two daughters, four sons—was taught to play the piano and one stringed instrument. Every Sunday afternoon there were family concerts. During the summers they visited at the rectory of their maternal grandfather, Frederic Simon, at Neiderbroon-les-Bains in the Vosges mountains. Here they kept at their chamber music so continually that the neighbors nicknamed the house "the music box."

Eminent musicians often stayed at the Munches' when they were in town. The boy thus came to know such visiting conductors and composers as Artur Nikisch, Edouard Colonne, Gabriel Pierné, and Vincent d'Indy. He acted as guide for d'Indy on a sight-seeing tour of the city and remembers he felt well compensated for his services by being allowed to carry the composer's scores to the hall on concert night.

During this period young Charles took lessons on the violin and the organ, and in harmony and counterpoint. He was allowed to join his father's chorus and to play at the last stand of the second violins in his father's orchestra. From the age of fourteen he was occasional substitute at the console. He thinks of the organ as his first orchestra. "Before those keyboards and pedals and the palette of stops," he says, "I felt almost like a demigod, holding in my hands the reins that controlled the musical universe."

Charles also composed, much as youngsters today scribble verses during algebra class. Those youthful efforts, he believes, have given him an insight into the composer's urges and problems that has proved helpful to him as a conductor.

It was as a violinist, though, that Munch filed up to receive his diploma at the Strasbourg Conservatory in 1912, and it was as a violinist that he headed for Paris to study under Lucien Capet. Here he took on a gloss of sophistication and acquired the Parisian's ability to take life as one finds it. But the essential pattern remained unchanged.

He was still in doubt as to which course his musical career was to take. The decision was further delayed by the outbreak of World War I in 1914. Since Alsace was then German territory and Munch, for all his French leanings, officially a German citizen, he had no choice but to return to his home and in due course be conscripted into the German army. The four years he spent as sergeant of artillery were not entirely wasted, however. Between intervals of being gassed before Peronne and wounded at Verdun, he had a chance to ponder the trend of his life. When he was demobilized at Cologne in 1918, he had come to the conclusion that conducting was to be his career and that he would pursue it as a Frenchman. He returned to Strasbourg, which had by then become French territory, and took out French citizenship papers.

Now to school himself in the art of conducting! As concertmaster of the Strasbourg orchestra, he had two examples to profit from: Guy Ropartz, who was director of the orchestra and of the Strasbourg Conservatory, and Paul Bastide, who was director of the Opera. He scrutinized both "as an entomologist watches insects." All their gestures soon became so familiar to him that he could execute them in his sleep. When he did not have to play, he sat in a back row with a score, followed the parts of the other instruments, and tried to discover how they were manipulated.

In Leipzig, where he went in 1926 as concertmaster of the Leipzig Philharmonic under Wilhelm Furtwängler, he had actual chances to conduct. On Sunday mornings he played violin in the small orchestra that accompanied Bach cantatas in the *Thomaskirche* in Leipzig. One Saturday afternoon the cantor sprained his ankle. The assistant conductor was not available. Munch was asked to fill in. He accepted with alacrity, studied the score through the night, and conducted the program the next day. ("It went splendidly," he wrote home.) His second chance came when, at a historical concert of the Leipzig orchestra, he was asked to assume the role that concertmasters of the early nineteenth century used to take, namely to stand in his place in the orchestra and lead the performance by means of his violin.

So stimulating were these experiences that Munch knew the time had come to try his luck as a conductor. He would begin his career, he decided, in Paris.

In 1932, when Munch headed again for the capital of France, he possessed one vast advantage over the green youth who twenty years before had timidly rung the doorbell of Monsieur Capet to inquire about violin lessons. He had a firm belief in his destiny as a conductor and was determined to make the world share this belief.

Luckily for him, at least one other person did share it. His fiancée, Geneviève Maury, daughter of one of the most prominent families of Switzerland and then living in Paris, was confident that conducting was his field. They decided to pool their resources and thus make it possible for him to get a start. They hired the Straram Orchestra (of full symphonic proportions) and rented a hall. The introductory concert, which took place on November 1, 1932, made Munch's name known throughout Paris. Shortly thereafter Mademoiselle Maury and Charles Munch pooled their plans for the future also. Their marriage of twenty-four years was brought to an end by Mrs. Munch's death in 1956.

The success of Munch's first concert led to his conducting the Concerts Siohan and the Sunday afternoon concerts of the Associations Symphoniques. A season with the Biarritz Orchestra was followed by guest conductorships with the Lamoureux Orchestra. Then Munch assembled his own orchestra. He called it the Paris Philharmonic, and he made a point of playing works of men then living in Paris, such as Honegger, Roussel, and Poulenc. He allowed the International Society for Contemporary Music to use his orchestra for concerts during their Paris Festival.

Munch had become thoroughly affiliated with Paris, and his orchestra a Parisian ensemble. But he wasn't forgetting the universal aspects of music, either. He engaged his brother Fritz to bring his Strasbourg chorus to Paris to sing with the orchestra. It was Bach they sang—the very cantatas that their father had helped to bring back into popularity fifty years before.

In this period also, Charles Munch's reputation as a Berlioz interpreter got its start. It has grown steadily. On November 19, 1955, he was awarded the Grand Prix du Disque from the French government—this the equivalent of the "Oscar" bestowed on movie stars in this country—for his recording of Berlioz' *Romeo and Juliet*. "A Berlioz interpreter of uncommon gifts," Roland Gelatt calls him in the *Saturday Review*—"a conductor extraordinarily responsive to the rise and fall of this composer's unique rhetoric and possessed of an unerring ear for his kaleidoscopic scoring." Harry Shapiro, French horn in the Boston Symphony, says in awed tones, "In Berlioz works, you could swear it was Berlioz himself conducting!"

In 1937 came Munch's appointment to one of the most important conducting posts in France, the directorship of the Paris Conservatory Orchestra. For eight years, from 1938 to 1946, he conducted this orchestra, striving "to bring to each concert still more thought, more care, more passion to bear on the practice of my art."

Perhaps in no country, with the possible exception of the United States, do people flare into prominence as quickly as they do in France. This now happened to Charles Munch. Clubs of bobby-soxers called "les Munchettes" jammed front rows to admire "le beau Charles"; questionnaires run in the daily papers found him heading the popularity lists; autograph seekers and camera fans dogged his steps.

In this period Munch developed a strict work schedule, to which he still adheres. "In the morning my mind is fresh," he says, "and everything seems to come easily and quickly. This is the best time to rehearse. Afternoons must be kept free. This is the time for receiving young composers looking for sponsors, soloists come for advice, and the time for reading new scores and making programs. For careful study of scores I am performing, I prefer the silence of the night, when I get my second wind and the music engraves itself more quickly on my memory. The senses are sharpened by the day's excitement, and, most important, I know that nothing will disturb the solitude, peace and silence which are so rare and precious these days."

Throughout the years of German occupation (1940–44) Munch kept to his conducting at the Conservatory, while managing to avoid—by pleading indisposition or previous commitments—official concerts of the Nazis. Every franc of his earnings he turned over to the French underground movement. His country house was a station in the "underground railway." For his services to France he was given the red ribbon of the Legion of Honor in 1945 and was made a Commander in 1952. In these bitter days he read Schweitzer's books, and the latter's philosophy of living to do good to others became his inspiration. Later on, when Munch had assumed the conductorship of the Boston Symphony, he showed his gratitude by presenting a concert for the benefit of Schweitzer's hospital in Lambaréné, Africa.

After the war Munch conducted in Israel and at the festivals of Prague and Edinburgh. Wherever he went, he presented new, often controversial works. "I like all music," he says, "no matter from what country or what composer; but I do like to interpret music in which something is happening all the time!"

The tradition-bound Paris Conservatory became alarmed at the array of moderns Munch called up. It instructed him to play better-known compositions. As an answer, Munch handed in his resignation.

On December 27, 1946, Munch guest conducted the Boston Symphony. He returned for a fortnight in 1947–48, and the Boston press delicately hinted that, in view of Koussevitzky's recent announcement of retirement, listeners might be observing in Munch their next conductor. (In the case of the Boston Symphony and in fact of practically all major symphony orchestras, the choice of a conductor is left almost entirely with the board of directors, as the ones who manage the orchestra and foot the bills.)

In the 1947–48 season Munch also conducted the New York Philharmonic. The then music critic of *The New York Times,* the late Olin Downes, wrote of "his masterly treatment of phrase, his exceptional range of sonorities, from the nearly inaudible *pianissimo* to the *fortissimo* . . . the complete flexibility of beat and capacity, when that is desirable, for romantic rhetoric."

In 1948 Munch and the French (government) National Radio Orchestra traveled by bus across the American continent. It was a successful tour. But it took conviction beyond the line of duty to sustain these troupers, who often arrived at the night's destination tired, cold, and dirty after some three hundred miles on the road. Again and again they came so near missing their schedule that they hadn't time even for a change of clothes or a cup of coffee before going on the platform. "We shall never forget," relates Munch, "the kindness of the good people of Montreal, who, hearing of our miseries and knowing that we had arrived hungry and thirsty, immediately ordered fifty roast chickens for an after-concert supper. The concert was a good one, the chickens delicious."

On October 7, 1949, Bostonians, assembled in their low, oblong red-brick Symphony Hall for the first concert of the season, had three reasons for a show of excitement: it was a celebration of the fiftieth anniversary of the Hall; a dedicatory ceremony for their magnificent new pipe organ; and a welcoming of the conductor who was to succeed the retiring Serge Koussevitzky, Charles Munch.

The tall, dignified figure with the thick mop of silvery hair came on the platform accompanied by President Henry B. Cabot, who briefly introduced him. Bostonians rose en masse in greeting. Munch smiled his thanks, then turned and faced the hundred musicians under his care.

Already, via rehearsals, conductor and members of the orchestra had become friends. It is a friendship that has been strengthened through the years. The members agree that their leader is not only the most economical rehearser they have ever had, but also the most sympathetic. His directions are vivid: *"Glisse-glisse* like a snake! . . . Float in the air like smoke. . . . Breathe the music!" His gestures are amazingly articulate: his drawing the men toward him as if on reins of persuasion; a sudden plummeting of the hand for silence; a solicitous pointing; an urging inward sweep of the arm. Everything is of an appealing rather than a dictatorial nature. "The orchestra," according to him, "is not a docile or mechanical instrument. It is a social body, a collection of human beings. It has a psychology and reflexes. It can be guided but it must not be offended."

That Munch likes the men is obvious. He meets them in their homes and he meets them at their sports. America has introduced him to the pleasures of golf. Often he approaches one of the golf-playing members—perhaps James Stagliano, solo French horn and a golfer of no mean pretensions—with a tentative, "You play golf with me this afternoon after you teach your lessons?" Munch has invested in two sets of clubs, one for America, one for France. He plays a good deal of golf during his summers at the Berkshires.

An orchestra member will sometimes accompany Munch on his tours of the Boston antique shops. An avid art collector, he initiates his companion into the special signs to look for in tracking originals. During his sojourns in his Paris home each year, he makes the rounds of the Parisian shops in the same way.

It does not take the orchestra men's say-so to establish the fact of Munch's comradeliness, however. Members of his audiences who sit in side boxes at his concerts become aware that he is smiling as he gestures to the cellos, as he lulls the basses, as he beckons the clarinets. "You'll get this. You're doing better than you know! A bit softer there, my friend!"

The same spirit of kindliness and mutual helpfulness obtains among his "orchestral family," in fact, as existed in his family circle in Strasbourg in his boyhood days.

Munch took the Boston Symphony on the first European tour in its seventy-one-year history. In four weeks in 1952 they went to England, France, Holland, Belgium, Germany. A gala concert at the Paris Opera was attended by President Vincent Auriol and by foreign dignitaries. But what Munch remembers most lovingly in the whole tour was the concert given in his home town. "When the capacity audience in Strasbourg's Salle de Palais des Fêtes let loose with a storm of applause," wrote Cyrus Durgin of the Boston *Globe,* "that moment was perhaps the culmination of a lifetime of music-making for Charles Munch. I was able to see him, from a vantage point backstage, as he conducted the final number, Brahms' great and noble Fourth Symphony. There was something almost transfigured in the expression upon his face." A home-town critic wrote in *Les Dernières Nouvelles d'Alsace,* "After the concert it looked as though the whole audience, trembling with joy after what they had heard, would strew his path homeward with roses."

So the conductor, with world fame won, had returned home. What passed through Munch's mind after the concert that night, after he had withdrawn from his cocitizens, his friends, his family? Perhaps as he walked under the shadow of the Cathedral, he recalled his credo, the parting advice he used to give his students at the Conservatory: "If you interpret music as you feel it, with ardor and faith, with all your heart and with complete conviction, I am certain that even if the critics attack you, God will forgive you!"

CHAPTER XVIII

≫ EUGENE ORMANDY

"My career could have happened only in America."

It is true America has offered just the right ingredients for this combination of human dynamo, hail-fellow-well-met, fiery disciplinarian, and consummate artist which, rolled into one, make Eugene Ormandy, conductor of the Philadelphia Orchestra. Yet the whole course of Ormandy's life—the twenty-one early years spent in Europe as well as the years spent in America—show an intensity of purpose transcending environment. Just as he interprets a composition so that every element in it seems to fall into a pattern—draws detail, broad line, mass, and shadings into a single canvas of tone—so in his life every word spoken, every action engaged in, has been controlled, aimed. Nothing with Ormandy is casual. Nothing is inadvertent. The man who stands on the podium of the Philadelphia Orchestra, leading the players in 120 concerts a year, is a goal-directed individual. That the goal happens to be the masterly interpretation of music is our good luck.

The goal was set for him before he himself arrived at deciding age.

It is hard for Americans to understand the rigor with which Ormandy's early path was plotted. Freedom of choice, unmolested playtime, and study made easy, were concepts unknown to him in his youth. From the day he was born his life was planned toward a single end—not quite the one he was to select later himself, but one bearing in the same general direction.

Ormandy's father had made up his mind that his son was to be a great violin virtuoso. His childhood bears an interesting similarity to that of Mozart. Both boys were dedicated to music from the cradle. Both were piloted along its path with none-too-gentle insistence by forceful fathers, and both later veered from the path their fathers wished for them. Mozart's father complained bitterly of what seemed to him dilettantism in his son, and Ormandy's father grieved at his son's change from the violinist's to the conductor's career.

Even after he had become a famous conductor, Ormandy received repercussions of his father's disappointment. In 1935–36 a great international concert was given at the Eucharistic Congress in Budapest. Some of the world's greatest artists were there. Ormandy was asked to conduct, and Joseph Szigeti was invited, to give an aura to the affair. The great violinist Jenö Hubay was the host. Hubay chose to walk into the hall with Ormandy's mother on his arm and to let Ormandy's family use his personal car. It was a dignified and grand affair.

On the way home, however, Ormandy noticed that his father looked unhappy, and asked him why. The elder Ormandy burst into tears. "If I had only disciplined you more severely," he said, "you might have been in Szigeti's place tonight!"

Ormandy's father came naturally by his fixation. In his youth he had had an intense longing to become a violinist, but had had to stifle it for practical reasons. He took up dentistry as a profession. However, his hopes were not shattered—only deferred. He made a vow when he was twenty that his first-born—who of course would be a boy!—would become a great violinist. He harbored this dream through the ten years that elapsed before his marriage. Then, when the hoped-for son was born in Budapest on November 18, 1899, he felt that now at last he could carry out his plan. He named the boy after his idol, Jenö Hubay. "Eugene" is but the American version of "Jenö."

Two other sons were also trained for careers in music. Martin Ormandy is a cellist in the New York Philharmonic, and Laslo Ormandy is a harpist, as well as a physician in Washington, D. C. It was on the first-born, Jenö, however, that the father focused his dreams.

Everything worked out as planned. Jenö proved a *Wunderkind*. At one and a half he could identify in baby jargon many different tunes. At three, before he had mastered his A B C's, he was reading music. At four he was playing a pint-sized violin—in perfect tune. His sense of pitch was something to marvel at. He could tell what tones his father's dental instruments were buzzing on, what note of the scale his mother's pots and pans clattered on, what note was being sounded by the rag peddler in the street.

Besides having absolute pitch, Ormandy has "absolute timing" —a clock, so to speak, inside his head. At any hour of the day he can tell to the minute what time it is. Several years ago he confounded the technicians at a recording session by finishing a four-minute, thirty-second side in four minutes and twenty-nine and a half seconds. One can imagine how this time sense serves him in giving finish to such devices in music as accelerandos and crescendos, and in interpretations of rhythmically complex modern works.

At the age of five and a half the young Jenö was admitted to the Royal State Academy of Music, a chubby youngster among gangling youths. At nine he was taken by his father—and a proud day it was for both of them—to begin study with Hubay. After that it was practice from morning to night: Kreutzer and Cramer, Cramer and Kreutzer—scales, scales, scales! *Spiccato, martellato, détaché, pizzicato, col legno!* Harmonics and double-stops! Practice until his fingers were numb and sore.

Unrelenting goading was Hubay's method. "Smooth on the string crossing there." . . . "Take that in the seventh position, Lazy!" . . . or, sarcastically, "My dear namesake is playing out of tune!" Tongue-lashings did not crush the boy. He had his innings, too. Once when he was directed to play a phrase with all but impossible fingerings, Hubay illustrating the passage himself, the boy queried gently, "Do you want me to miss as many notes as you did just now, Herr Professor?"

He got no respite at home. His father's office was right in the house, and the boy put in his three and four hours a day of exercises in a small room adjoining it. If he so much as missed a note or blurred a trill, the elder Ormandy flung open the door and exploded in wrath. "I got more whippings than I got meals," says Ormandy ruefully. But he adds, "Sometimes when my father had a particularly serious case, I sneaked out and played soccer with the boys." Mostly, though, Jenö was at one with his father in realizing that, if he was to excel, this was the way things had to be.

The work-packed years passed swiftly. At the age of fourteen— six years younger than any of his colleagues—Jenö received his diploma from the Royal Academy of Budapest. Two years later he got his state diploma and the title "artist violinist." At seventeen—again the youngest recipient—he obtained a certificate to teach violin at the Royal Academy. A year after that he matriculated at the University of Budapest. (He graduated in philosophy after three years there.) Also, in 1917, he made a short tour of Germany and Hungary as soloist and concertmaster with the Blüthner Orchestra. In 1920 he toured Austria and France.

By this time impresarios were becoming interested in this fair-haired young violinist who phrased so impeccably and who always won over his audiences. At a concert in Vienna two men bubbling with ideas came backstage. They would guarantee him, they said, 300 concerts in America at a total fee of $30,000. It was sure-fire!

For all the adult concentration and adult accomplishment of his years, Jenö in some ways was still a child, with a child's dreams of miraculous openings to fame. Also, like most Europeans, he

believed the streets of America shone, if not with gold, with unlimited opportunity. Had not Jascha Heifetz and Toscha Seidel,
in 1917 and 1918 respectively, reaped American fame, and wasn't
the prodigy Erica Morini even then preparing to make her American debut? To Jenö's ears the men's proposition seemed logical
and sound. Yes, he would be glad to go to America.

With the blessings of his family, he started out.

On the voyage over, one of rosy anticipation, he played a benefit concert for seamen. The lady who volunteered as his accompanist read palms as a hobby. She asked permission to read his.
"You will have a hard time in America at first," she told him.
"But your energy, determination and honesty will see you
through. You will not marry the girl you are now engaged to [he
was affianced to a Viennese at the time] but to a young lady you
will meet the first week you are in New York City. You will have
two children, both of whom will die in infancy. You will have a
spectacular career, but not in the field you are now pursuing."

On December 2, 1921, the boat docked in New York. The
promoters trudged with their charge first jubilantly, then un-
easily, from one manager's office to another. They visited, all told,
eighteen executives of the music business. At last the truth hit
home. Nothing could be done without money. If $1500 were put
up for a Carnegie Hall recital, with a promise of another $3000
for two additional recitals, then and only then could Ormandy be
taken on.

Bleakly, two insolvent backers and one insolvent virtuoso faced
the facts of musical life in America. In some cases misery does
not love company. The farewells were brief. Ormandy has never
seen his "promoters" since.

December is a cold month in New York, and it becomes still
colder when one is alone and with no money for food or rent.
But Ormandy was used to having things hard. It never once
occurred to him to telegraph home for funds. Instead he set

himself to find a way out of his predicament. Racking his brains as he walked the floor in the barely furnished room he had taken for the week, he recalled meeting, in one manager's office, a former acquaintance of his in Budapest. Maybe that man could give him a tip. He clutched his beloved Balestrieri violin and headed downtown. He refers to this moment of decision as "the time I was born in New York City at the age of twenty-two."

Ormandy got the man's address from the manager and looked him up. The man gave him a valuable suggestion. "Go to Erno Rapee, conductor of the Capitol Theatre Orchestra," he said, "and audition with him."

Before the day was over, Ormandy had landed a job. True, he was put in the very last row of the violin section of the theater orchestra, but that didn't keep him from enjoying the first hot meal he had had in days.

Ormandy wasn't to stay in the end seat for long. Within a week, he had been advanced to the concertmaster's desk. A few days later Times Square resounded with welcoming celebration for the year 1922. The joyous ring of the bells, the exultant shouts seemed to this young man at least partly for him.

In the first week of 1922 Ormandy took two significant steps: he applied for his first citizenship papers, and he fell in love with a harpist colleague in the Capitol Theatre Orchestra, Stephanie Goldner. They were married soon afterward. Later she was to become harpist in the New York Philharmonic.

For two and a half years, seven days a week, four times a day, Ormandy filled his post as concertmaster of the Capitol Theatre Orchestra. He memorized his parts. He also memorized the parts of the other instrumentalists. In the back of his mind—though he had no conscious idea of becoming a conductor—he already was cuing the instruments.

Then one day late in September, 1924, Lady Luck turned a new page in his career. When he arrived at the theater for the afternoon's performance, the doorman, a former pugilist not given to pleasantries, said to him, "Hey, Ormandy—you have to take the two o'clock show."

"What kind of a joke is that?" asked Ormandy.

"No joke at all. The conductor's sick. You have to take the show."

This report from the tag end of the grapevine proved true. In the fifteen minutes allotted him for struggling into his cutaway and threading the path between the orchestra men up to the podium, Ormandy scanned, in the recesses of his mind, page after page of the work to be played that day, Tchaikovsky's Fourth. When he reached the podium, he gave one glance at the spread-out score, then closed it. He conducted the whole from memory. After that, even the doorman knew he was to be a "regular" on the podium.

For a year Ormandy was engaged as alternate assistant conductor and concertmaster at the Capitol. Then, in late 1925, when two of the conductors left to take over at the newly erected Roxy movie palace, he became full-time associate director of the orchestra.

In 1927 came another big chance.

Anna Duncan, the adopted daughter of Isadora, saw him conduct at the Capitol, and engaged him and about half of the New York Philharmonic for a dance recital in Carnegie Hall. Arthur Judson, her concert manager, was a member of the audience. By the time Ormandy had finished the Schubert *Rosamunde* Overture (played for latecomers) Judson had arrived at a conclusion. "I came to see a dancer and instead I heard a conductor," he said afterward. He made Ormandy a proposition. The result was that the young man resigned from the Capitol, and Judson became his manager.

So ended Ormandy's career as a theater conductor. Ruminating over those days, he shakes his head. "It was a hard time. They almost broke me. But I don't regret the struggle. It brought me up the American way. I just knew I had to work harder than anyone else and wait my chance. And at last it came!"

In the summer of 1929, Ormandy directed the New York Philharmonic at Lewisohn Stadium, New York City. In 1930 the engagement was renewed, and in addition he appeared with the Robin Hood Dell Orchestra in Philadelphia. During this period he was also one of the leading conductors on the Columbia Broadcasting network. Then, in 1931, came the biggest opportunity of all—an opportunity to substitute for Toscanini! As Ormandy sees it, this was "the most important moment of my life."

To understand this statement one must understand the place Toscanini then held in the American musical scene. From the time he took over the conductorship of the New York Philharmonic in 1928—not to speak of the years from 1908 to 1915 when he was conductor at the Metropolitan Opera—Toscanini was the musical god of America. Not only the public but instrumentalists, and above all conductors, worshiped him. Ormandy himself went to every rehearsal, absorbed every remark, every baton-flick of the master. When Toscanini resigned from the New York Philharmonic in 1936, every seat in the house was sold months in advance of his final concert. The morning of his concert 5000 music lovers lined up for the 190 standing room places.

In 1931, when Ormandy's big chance came, Toscanini was at the height of his career. Judson, then manager of the Philadelphia Orchestra, had obtained the maestro's services for two pairs of concerts in the fall. But the week before the first concert Toscanini had cabled from Italy, where he was spending the summer, that a severe attack of neuritis made it impossible for him to come.

On receiving the news Judson immediately approached most of the major symphony conductors in America. Some may have had previous commitments. Some may not have cared to face the double responsibility of replacing Toscanini and following Stokowski, who was then the Philadelphia Orchestra's conductor. Whatever the reasons, not one of the conductors appealed to availed himself of the opportunity.

As the process of elimination continued, Judson from his New York office frantically rang telephones and dispatched telegrams. "At last he called me in," Ormandy relates gleefully. "He had decided here was a chance to discover someone. It was just three days ahead of the first rehearsal. He told me the situation. 'You are the only one left. Here's the opportunity to start your career or break your neck. Before you say "yes" or "no," think it over.' To which I replied, 'Mr. Judson, I will take the chance!' "

Ormandy was given a difficult program—Brahms' Fourth Symphony, Weinberger's Polka and Fugue from *Schwanda*, R. Strauss's *Till Eulenspiegel and his Merry Pranks*, and the same composer's *Rosenkavalier* waltzes. Over the week end he memorized them all. On Monday morning he took the seven o'clock train to Philadelphia and started rehearsing the orchestra. The following Friday, October 30, 1931, he conducted the program.

The story of this young man (he was thirty-one but looked twenty) conducting from the podium of the Philadelphia Orchestra and making a triumph out of it was front-page news all over the country. Aspects most commented on were his power to vitalize every phrase, his ability to electrify his hearers, his capacity to draw through sheer artistry.

But Ormandy was to be even further tested. That same week the aged conductor of the Minneapolis Symphony, Henri Verbrugghen, suffered a stroke, and his son, a brain specialist, said he would never be able to conduct again. Mrs. Carlyle Scott, the Minneapolis Orchestra's manager, had heard of young Ormandy, who, according to newspaper reports, was good enough to substitute for Toscanini. She put through a frantic telephone call to Willis I. Norton, Minnesota legislator, who at the time happened to be on business in Philadelphia, and told him to listen to an Ormandy concert.

Norton got to the one on October 31. At its close he rang up Mrs. Scott. "You couldn't do better than take him," he announced excitedly. "They're still applauding and shouting in the auditorium. He's a wonder!"

When Mrs. Scott called Judson's office the next day, to tell him to send this young magician right out to Minnesota, he had to tell her there were still two concerts to go. (Ormandy had been held over for a second pair.) However, after the next Saturday night concert, while Philadelphians were still frantically clapping and calling, Ormandy, in full dress and swinging a suitcase, boarded a train at the Philadelphia station bound for Minneapolis.

After the first rehearsal in the Twin City, the orchestra members stood and applauded. After the second rehearsal and before Ormandy had appeared in a single concert in Minneapolis, the board had signed him as the orchestra's regular conductor.

If those first rehearsals had been exciting, the first concert was, as John Sherman of the Minneapolis *Star-Tribune* described it * "an explosion that operated in reverse, consolidating rather than shattering like one seen in a motion picture film run backward. The pieces not only fell in place, but were pulled and magnetized into the lightest, most effective and dynamic entity the orchestra, its backers and its hearers had so far known. . . . The tone had come alive, the phrases had grown sharp and purposeful, the climaxes made the blood pound. Overnight the ensemble had acquired a youthful vigor, flexibility and unanimity, with compelling rhythmic impulse."

What the orchestra acquired on that night in November, 1931, it was to hold through Ormandy's five-year tenure. Now that the

* *Music and Maestros* by John K. Sherman, University of Minnesota Press, 1952.

young man had found his real instrument, no discipline, no rigor, no industry, was too extreme for him. That his "instrument" happened to be ninety men instead of a violin and bow made the stint only the more challenging. Infinitely resourceful, he persuaded, exhorted, disciplined the men. He also got them a raise before many weeks rolled around. Through all this activity the end in view was utter, unqualified perfection.

Ormandy's experiences had helped him to realize this aim. At the Capitol Theatre he had conducted the same works some twenty-eight times a week. Thus, through selection and rejection, he had arrived at the purest interpretations possible. His memory, in a class with Toscanini's, had been further developed. He had, in short, become a virtuoso of the baton. It is little wonder that, during his stay in Minneapolis, the orchestra became one of our country's famous groups, with international standing.

Ormandy's scope of endeavor extended far beyond the regular subscription concerts. The stock market crash in 1929 had submerged the orchestra in debt. Ormandy initiated "Viennese Afternoons," and his Johann Strauss programs became famous. His Victor recordings with the orchestra, begun in 1934, proved a bonanza. He was on constant call for social functions, lecture courses, campaign rallies, anything that the orchestra backers thought might benefit by his presence. For the extra pennies it would earn, he led the orchestra on tours during the darkest days of the depression, taking in stride icicle-hung railroad cars, frigid auditoriums, transportation hazards. As one prominent music lover of St. Paul put it, "Ormandy would have turned handsprings on the stage if that would have helped the orchestra."

As the Minneapolis Symphony rose, so did Ormandy. When in the winter of 1935–36 Stokowski announced his intention of withdrawing as full-time director of the Philadelphia Orchestra, it was Ormandy who was thought of—this time first, not last. Because he had done so much for the Minneapolis orchestra, the board released him with the quiet announcement, "We have realized for some time that we could not retain his services permanently."

So on January 2, 1936, Ormandy was appointed musical director of the Philadelphia Orchestra. (Stokowski remained as co-conductor for three more seasons.) His position on a podium occupied through the previous quarter of a century by that very special conductor could not have been an easy one. But he not only won over Stokowski devotees through his initial impact. He has kept his hold on them and through the years has strengthened it.

One of the reasons for Ormandy's staying powers has been his knack of never letting his audiences down. On February 21, 1956, a world-famous violinist was prevented by sudden illness from appearing in Carnegie Hall with the Philadelphia Orchestra. The audience, however, got a treat of another sort. Ormandy outdid himself in his re-creation of works by Handel, Beethoven, and Brahms. It was a performance that no violin soloist, with whatever special skills or gifts, could have equaled for purity, for artistry, for virtuosity. When he responded to the applause—he and his men—at the end of the program, there was a sense of almost verbal communication between him and the audience. "You see," he seemed to be saying, "I gave you full value after all."

During Ormandy's tenure on the podium of the Philadelphia Orchestra, it has made history through its touring. In 1936 it went on its first transcontinental tour, with repeats in 1937, 1946, and 1948. In 1949 it made its first foreign pilgrimage—to Britain, playing twenty-eight concerts in ten cities. London reviewers dwelt on the orchestra's uncanny precision, tone quality, and balance of ensemble. In the spring of 1955 it flew to Europe, to give concerts in France, the Netherlands, Spain, Portugal, Italy, Switzerland, Austria, Germany, Sweden, and Finland.

With the accession of Ormandy, the Philadelphia Orchestra increased its radio scope and entered the field of television. It was, in fact, one of the first orchestras to be heard over a nation-wide hookup and to be televised. Since 1943 it has been under contract to Columbia Records. It has one of the largest recorded repertoires among major orchestras.

Since being in Philadelphia, Ormandy has received six honorary doctorates of music and the Order of Merit of Juan Pablo Duarte from the Dominican Republic (1945), and has become an officer of the French Legion of Honor (1952), a Knight of the Order of Dannebrog, first class (1952), and a Knight of the Order of the White Rose of Finland (1955).

It is evident that Ormandy has accepted Philadelphia as his home as well as his professional headquarters. On April 27, 1952, when the last train pulled slowly out of Broad Street Station just before that ancient landmark was torn down, he led the orchestra's brass in the strains of *Auld Lang Syne* from the train's platform, while some 5000 onlookers joined in the refrain, many of them with tears in their eyes. Symbolic also is the fact that he has made the orchestra a present of his Balestrieri violin and Tourte bow, and that they are now being used by the men. In 1950 he married Vienna-born Margaret Frances Hitsch—his first marriage ended in divorce in 1947—a naturalized American who had served in the navy during World War II.

Ormandy is completely aware of the great good fortune his tenure in Philadelphia has spelled for him. He is deeply grateful to those who made and still make it possible, including every member of his orchestra. "My wish," he says, "is to give as many years as the Philadelphia Orchestra Association wishes me to give. The men in the orchestra had confidence in me, a young, little-tried conductor from the Middle West. Mr. Stokowski decided to retire from Philadelphia. The honor fell on me to be chosen as his successor. Because of this honor, I must do everything to keep this orchestra as great as I found it. That is my aim. That is my success."

CHAPTER XIX

⫸ PAUL PARAY

PAUL PARAY, conductor of the Detroit Symphony, for all his seventy-odd years, is young of heart. He has instantaneous and violent reactions. He is wholly loyal, wholly convinced, wholly enthusiastic. He loves or he hates. His intense blue eyes under his sandy eyebrows are alive, alert. He throws his hands, his arms, about when speaking. He looks intently at his listener, as though he expected strong reactions in response.

Irving Sablosky, reporting on Paray's conducting in the Chicago *Daily News,* said he was struck by its "honesty and clarity and forthrightness." His French compatriots—musicians and critics—have cited him repeatedly as a citizen who cannot compromise with evil, bad taste, or mediocrity.

When the Detroit Symphony was reorganized in 1951, those in charge had the good sense to give Paray full authority in all artistic matters. It wouldn't have worked any other way. Paray can function only in an atmosphere of freedom.

From his earliest childhood Paray was allowed full scope in his musical development.

In the early 1880's Auguste Paray, ivory carver and amateur musician, set up shop in the little town of Le Tréport, about a hundred miles northwest of Paris. Here he made small *objets d'art,* catering especially to summer visitors. Soon he struck up a friendship with the Abbé Lesergeant, an intelligent and widely

read man, and through him found an outlet for his hobby—
music. He became organist and choirmaster of Lesergeant's
church, the Saint Jacques. By the time his son Paul, born May 24,
1886, could walk, Auguste was presenting, with the Abbé's encouragement, Haydn's *Creation,* Gounod's *Redemption,* and
Berlioz' *The Childhood of Christ.*

Eminent artists, guests in this resort town during the summer,
were glad to act as soloists in these fervent if not wholly finished
performances. Somehow Auguste instilled in the chorus, made
up of sailors, clerks, and artisans, and their wives and daughters,
a feeling for beauty. Paul was in time to acquire this same knack
in training both amateur and professional choruses.

Young Paul used to go with his father to rehearsals. He always
made a beeline for the seat nearest the percussion and sat there
throughout the program, listening to the drums' reverberations.
When he got home, he poked about the kitchen until he found a
big kettle or a pan, on which he imitated the rolls.

When he was four his parents provided him with a real drum.
His father noticed that with the simple rhythm of the drum, Paul
could reproduce whole compositions complete with effects and
embellishments.

Before long Paul had a place in his father's band. When the
ensemble went to nearby Beauvais for a contest, the judges were
so taken with this youngster, gravely executing flams and drags,
that on the spot they created a first prize for drums. Of course
he won it, hands down.

At nine Paul was sent to the choir school at Rouen, some forty
miles from Le Tréport. He studied solfeggio, piano, and the cello
with the Abbés Bourgeois and Bourdon, and organ with Jules
Haelling. But he did not give up the drums. In fact, he was percussionist at the performance of Beethoven's Mass in D at the
cathedral at Easter.

In school and in the community, Paul filled in in a variety of capacities: as piano accompanist for visiting soloists; as cellist in a small chamber ensemble; as stopgap organist.

His first paid job was as an organist, also in Rouen. He was seventeen years old. One of the vacationers there was Henri Dallier, then presiding at the great organ of the Church of St. Eustache in Paris. He heard the lad, became interested in him, and accepted him as his pupil. The enthusiasm of this great musician convinced Paul's parents that a musical career was the logical choice for their son. They gave him their permission to go to Paris.

So in October of 1904 this eighteen-year-old, taking with him his cello, his drums, and a sheaf of music he had composed, started for Paris. The first person to whom Dallier introduced him was Xavier Leroux, already famous as a composer of operas. ("You can send me a whole chestful like this!" Leroux told Dallier after the audition.) At the Paris Conservatory Paray studied composition with Leroux and counterpoint with Georges Caussade. He made ends meet by getting a job as cellist in the pit orchestra at the Sarah Bernhardt Theatre.

Bernhardt, one of the world's greatest actresses and known as "The Divine Sarah," was then acting there. Paray's encounters with her pointed up his own individuality rather than any special divinity on her part. One day she needed an accompanist and summoned Paray by telegram on ten minutes' notice. He took a cab—against his better judgment since his funds were low—but even so arrived at her house five minutes late. "Madame could not wait," the butler told him. "The rehearsal is over." A month later she called him again. This time he arrived ten minutes early. He waited. She did not appear. At precisely five minutes after the time set for the appointment, Paray, with all the dignity of his eighteen years, told the butler, "You will say to Madame Sarah that the pianist cannot wait," and so left the house and Madame Sarah's circle forever.

In his early twenties, during his year of military service, Paray got his first chance to conduct. The 128th Infantry Regiment, of which he was a member, gave a concert. He was bandmaster. The next day the local paper described him as "very blond, svelt, with blue eyes, a sharp glance, an elegant silhouette. His gestures were lively and precise, and his smile indulgent." Paray remembers he did not feel too elated either over the notice or the podium experience. At that time his main interest was composing.

Paray's fame as a composer started with his winning the Prix de Rome with his cantata *Janitza* in 1911. Paray recalls with enthusiasm the excitement of the première in Paris, but he recalls with even more enthusiasm the three wonderful years the composition gave him, as prize winner, in Italy. Here, living at the sumptuous Villa de Medici, the residence of all Prix de Rome students, without financial worries, surrounded by works of art, he was imbued with a sense of this world's goodness and beauty that has never since left him.

It was just as well he was granted this experience before World War I. He had need of it during the war years.

He was called up at the very start of the war—August 2, 1914. He saw several months of active duty. Then he was captured and for two years was interned in a German prison camp at Darmstadt. Thanks to his resourcefulness, the period was not a total blank. He played at occasional concerts allowed the prisoners. He practiced on a silent keyboard sent him from home. He composed a quartet for strings, a nocturne, and a serenade. He refused, however, to play for the Germans.

At the end of the first year his name was high up on the list for exchange of prisoners. But a comrade of his was in a state of precarious health, could not have endured another year of captivity. Paray put his friend's name in place of his own.

Then, after another year of confinement, came the end of the war and his release in 1918.

The Armistice had made a free man of Paray but had not given him any answer to his career problems. Among a variety of suggestions made by his friends, the best came from Suzanne Cesbron, who had sung the leading part in the première of his *Janitza*. Her husband, Monsieur Viseur, was director of the Casino de Cauterets, and the orchestra of this vacation resort in the Pyrenees stood in need of a conductor. It was a forty-member ensemble made up of musicians who in the winter season belonged to some of the best orchestras of France. Paray was offered the position. He accepted gladly.

The orchestra men liked this dynamic young conductor who could make even rehearsals fresh and interesting and who, knowing the hazards of composing himself, could lead them through the labyrinth of a new work as though he himself had fashioned it. A group of them, members of the Lamoureux Orchestra in Paris, took Paray into their confidence. "Our leader, Camille Chevillard," they told him, "is getting old and tired. He is going to use guest conductors more and more. Why don't you put in your bid?"

In the summer of 1919, Paray wrote a letter of application to Chevillard. He received the answer that for the next season the concert schedule was completely filled.

So that was that! Their summer engagements over, the men returned to their various orchestras, and Paray went to Paris to look around. He attended every concert he could of the Lamoureux Orchestra and admired immensely the strong, precise gestures of Chevillard.

Then in early 1920 the composer André Caplet, engaged as one of the season's guest conductors for two concerts in February, fell ill and had to cancel his dates. Chevillard remembered the young conductor who had applied to him at the beginning of the season. He decided to give him a chance. Thus, with only fifteen days' notice, Paray was contracted to conduct one of the most important orchestras of all France.

He was given his own choice of program. He selected the Overture to *The Flying Dutchman* because it was vigorous and instantaneous in its appeal; the *Symphonie Fantastique* because Chevillard had never done it and therefore he did not run the risk of invidious comparisons; *The Afternoon of a Faun* because everybody liked it; and other shorter works that would bring out his own particular qualities as a conductor.

These two concerts at the Salle Gaveau on February 24 and 29, 1920, brought Paray his first fame as a conductor. Such was his success that three days later he was unanimously elected assistant conductor of the Lamoureux Orchestra.

Paray's father and mother had come to Paris for the concerts and now invited the great Chevillard and his wife to a family celebration in Le Tréport. The sumptuous dinner was followed by Paray's brother, his sister, his father, and himself playing quartets for the guests.

Now based in Paris, Paray busied himself both as conductor and as composer. As Chevillard became less active, Paray's podium engagements increased. Besides, he was building up a reputation as a composer. In 1922 his *Adonis Perturbed* was presented at the Paris Opera, performed by the famous dancer Ida Rubinstein.

In 1923 Chevillard died, and Paray was advanced to the conductorship of the Lamoureux Orchestra. During the five years he led it, critics noted that he had adopted some of Chevillard's mannerisms—his forthright, clear-cut stick work, his direct appeal by glance or nod to the individual players.

In 1927 Paray's *Joan of Arc Mass* was first presented. This, the most often performed of his works, gives "an impression of an intense life illuminated by hope," and thus is a portrayal of Paul Paray's own individuality as well as the subject's.

Eager for wider experiences, Paray in 1928 became conductor of the Municipal Orchestra of the Casino of Monte Carlo. Then in 1931 Gabriel Pierné, the conductor of the Colonne Orchestra and the direct successor of its founder, came to see Paray at Monte Carlo. He told him, "I feel I must give up soon, and for my personal peace of mind before I die, I want to find a successor who has the ability to fill the position. I have decided you are the man." Paray was not sure that the members of the orchestra would accept him. (It was a self-governing body.) However, on Pierné's insistence, he took the chance, and again he was elected unanimously.

For a while he held both the Monte Carlo and the Paris conductorships, something of a feat. Every week he conducted the rehearsals and concerts at Monte Carlo, then took an overnight train to Paris (sleeping en route) where he directed the Colonne rehearsals and concerts at the Châtelet.

World War II dealt with Paray almost as harshly as World War I. In late 1940 the Germans changed the name of the Colonne Orchestra because its founder, Edouard Colonne, was a Jew. Paray, infuriated, resigned. He went to Marseilles, which was then a part of unoccupied France, and conducted radio concerts. Soon, the Nazi radius widening, this orchestra, too, came under the ban. He was asked to give the names of the Jewish members of the orchestra. He refused. However, the names were obtained through other channels and the men forbidden to appear. At the last concert before the edict took effect, Paray told his men, "You are all my children, and I cannot bear to have some of you treated with such cruel injustice. I can only join you in your misfortune. If it is your last concert, then it is my last concert, too!"

In 1942 Paray defied the Germans a third time. On May 16 a propaganda concert of German music was presented at Lyons. The following day the French resistance movement, of which Paray and his wife Yolande were members, organized a concert in the same hall—with French musicians. Paray was chosen to conduct. He included on the program *The Sorcerer's Apprentice* by the Jewish composer, Paul Dukas. At the end of the concert he asked the audience to join the orchestra in the *Marseillaise*. They sang it with tears streaming down their faces.

Now a main target for the Nazis, Paray went into voluntary exile. On the invitation of Prince Louis II, he settled in Monte Carlo and directed the opera there until the liberation. When he returned to the Colonne Orchestra on October 22, 1944, it was again operating under its rightful title, and Paray was the hero of the day. In 1950 the French government honored him for his contributions by electing him "Membre de l'Institut" (a sort of hall of fame), thus making him one of the few living "immortals" of France.

Paray's long tenure as head of the Colonne ended officially in 1955, but has never come to an end in the sentiments of Frenchmen. When he handed in his formal resignation, his colleagues of the orchestra wrote him, "The musicians of the Colonne Orchestra do not forget the creative talent of their President. They are now happy that the great French artists are honored in the United States, thanks to this great conductor who brings the breath of pure air from Paris to the industrial city of Detroit."

Detroit was not Paray's first stop in America, however. Thirteen years before his Detroit engagement, in the summer of 1939, he had made his American debut. He had conducted an all-French program at the Lewisohn Stadium as representative of France in the World's Fair year in New York City. Then the war had called him home.

After the war, Paray began extensive guest conducting in the United States: with the Boston Symphony, with the Pittsburgh Symphony on tour, with the Philadelphia Orchestra, with the New York Philharmonic.

In 1952 he took over the conductorship of the Detroit Symphony.

The Detroit Symphony has arrived at its present eminence after taking just about every turn possible for an orchestra to take. Its beginning in 1914 was little more than an invitation to Detroiters to a series of concerts by musicians who wanted to be heard so badly that they were willing to pay expenses. The experiment jogged along in this fashion until 1919. Then Ossip Gabrilówitsch took over as conductor.

For seventeen years the Detroit Symphony was Gabrilówitsch's orchestra—his, and the upper stratum of Detroit society. After his death in 1935, with only society to support it, it gradually went into a decline. By the early forties its members had begun to scatter to other cities or to be absorbed into other professions.

Then in the late summer of 1943, through the ministrations of Henry H. Reichhold, president of the worldwide Reichhold Chemical Company, the orchestra was brought back to life. He signed Karl Krueger as conductor and started to put into practice his theories. They included mass audiences, development of side lines, and good public relations. He got industrialists to buy up tickets to distribute to their employees as a goodwill gesture. He bought the Wilson Theatre to provide a hall and office space for the musicians. He established youth series and "pops" concerts.

Still the orchestra was not paying for itself.

Reichhold next allowed it to become a sort of pool of musicians available for "jobbing out"—with units employable in various combinations for single dates. One of the split-up units was Jean Goldkette and his "Music in the Jazz Manner." Valter Poole, the orchestra's assistant conductor, performed with a chamber group over radio beamed to South America and Canada. A "folks-at-home" hour of music was purchased as a Sunday evening broadcast by Henry Ford.

Still the orchestra wasn't making ends meet. Reichhold began running side enterprises, among them a glossy-paged music magazine with very specialized appeal. Paradoxically, as his side lines increased, Detroit Symphony audiences dwindled. Newspaper reviews took on an acid tone. The question seemed to be, "Is a symphony orchestra a symphony orchestra or is it not?" At last Reichhold confessed himself beaten and closed up shop. The Wilson Theatre was leased for wrestling bouts.

A group of staunch survivors banded together as the Detroit Little Symphony, but after a time they were forced to give up, too.

After two and a half years Detroit music lovers became desperate. John B. Ford (no relation to Henry Ford) came forward with the suggestion that a plan that had recently raised twenty million dollars for hospitals could also be applied to the orchestra. The plan involved thirty-four large organizations—businesses, industries, banks, foundations, labor unions—joining with hundreds of smaller organizations and individuals and making three-year pledges of sufficient size to build a great orchestra. The governing board of the orchestra included representatives from all contributing sources. Within the space of twelve days in 1951 guarantees were raised to the amount of $260,000 a year for three years.

Then they looked around for a conductor.

Paul Paray was just the man to lead such an orchestra. He had respect for democratic enterprise. He was entirely free from snobbery. He had the enthusiasm and the resourcefulness of youth.

The orchestra showed the effects of his stimulation from the very start. When in 1954 Paray took it to the "testing ground," Carnegie Hall, Virgil Thomson wrote in the New York *Herald Tribune,* "He never forced his orchestra's sound or strained its balances. He never sacrificed a work's grand line to momentary emotivity. Like a great actor, he 'threw away' small effects to make each piece monumental and shapely. He did no special pleading, paraded no personal weaknesses, distorted no classical communication, played no games. He read familiar masterpieces with all the straightforwardness and all the subtlety of a master musician."

On October 18, 1956, the new Detroit music hall, the Ford Auditorium (named in memory of Henry and Edsel Ford) was dedicated. The dedication program consisted of a performance of Paray's *Joan of Arc Mass*—that expression of "an intense life illuminated by hope." The work and the conducting of it did justice to the great and beautiful hall. It seemed that Paul Paray and his music had indeed brought a breath of a purer realm to the industrial city of Detroit.

CHAPTER XX

⨠ FRITZ REINER

FRITZ REINER, conductor of the Chicago Symphony Orchestra, is convinced that, whatever else the conductor possesses, he must have the quality of leadership. He used to tell his students at the Curtis Institute of Music, "The point is to make the orchestra men accept you as the foremost authority. This, of course, involves a tremendous amount of knowledge—infallible knowledge. If a conductor makes a mistake, it is held against him immediately. You can't fool an orchestra. Most of the men are excellent musicians, and most have a secret desire to be conductors themselves."

Because he holds that years of study are necessary, he does not believe in prodigy conductors. True, he himself, as a twelve-year-old in Budapest—he was born there December 19, 1888—led the high school orchestra in Beethoven's First. He shakes his head tolerantly, though, when he tells about this.

His initiation into music came at an even earlier date. "We had a wonderful musical clock," he reminisces. "It played excerpts from *Lucia:* the sextet and the tenor aria of the last act." His absorption in this clock caused his father to take him, at the age of six, to his first opera. The spellbound attention that he gave to the goings-on on the stage convinced his parents that he should take piano lessons. Soon he was playing four-hand arrangements of the operas with his mother. At the age of nine, he could play the *Tannhäuser* Overture from memory.

This feat led, as a matter of fact, to his lifelong friendship with the famous composer Leo Weiner. The latter, then a lad of twelve, happened to be strolling past the Reiner cottage in Budakesz, a country village near Budapest where both families were vacationing. He heard strains of the overture floating from an open window. Here was a chance to have a partner for piano duets! He went in and asked the young Fritz if he would be interested in playing, "besides Wagner, some Beethoven and Schumann." The boy joyfully accepted.

At ten, Reiner was admitted to the Academy of Music in Budapest. At thirteen, he played in his first public concert.

For a child of a family without particular musical pretensions, Fritz was doing pretty well. He continued to do well. He progressed in his piano studies under Toman and Bartók. Since there were no conducting courses at the Academy in those days, one had to struggle along on one's own. It was lucky, therefore, that Reiner's gifts as a conductor were discovered and developed by his professor in composition, Hans Koessler. Reiner even had occasional chances to conduct. At the city's high school he led his classmates in annual concerts.

Reiner is one of the few conductors who has not started out as an orchestral instrumentalist and worked up through the ranks. True, he played the kettledrums in the Academy orchestra from his fourteenth to his nineteenth year. All pupils were required to be members of the orchestra, and he chose percussion as being the "heartbeat" of the ensemble. But aside from this period in the percussion section, he has never been aligned with any one orchestral instrument.

During these years of musical training, Reiner was planning to become a lawyer—to satisfy his father, who considered the musical profession a bad financial risk. With his father's death, however, the boy's legal studies at the university came to an end. Now young Reiner, sure of his goal, looked about for toe holds in the conducting profession.

The obvious place in the Europe of the day was the opera house. Having made a name for himself as accompanist for various soloists in their public performances, he got a position as a coach with the Comic Opera in Budapest. But, far from becoming a hunched figure over a piano keyboard sounding "A's" for frustrated sopranos, he began to familiarize himself with operatic endeavor in every aspect—pit, proscenium, auditorium, backstage. The management, confronted with his musical gifts, his immense vitality, and his power of projecting personality, decided here was someone worth "discovering." In one of those emergencies blessed by new batonists the world over, he was asked to take the place of an ailing conductor. The opera was *Carmen*. He had no time to rehearse. "It was sink or swim," he says; and adds dryly, "I swam." No wonder he used to tell his Curtis students, "Watch out for emergencies. They are your big chance!"

This one proved so to him. As a result of his success that evening, he became at twenty-one a full-fledged conductor at the opera house in Laibach (today the Yugoslav city of Ljubljana).

Although Reiner can take full advantage of happy circumstances, he never whittles down standards nor skimps on assignments to do so. Mastery, utter and unequivocal, is the keynote of his approach to conducting. Many a conductor occupying an important podium today has ringing in his ears from his student days Reiner's words, "The profession of conducting takes a great many qualities, musical and otherwise. You have to have executive ability. You have to be a diplomat with an eye to the box office. You have to have a wide education. You have to be thoroughly conversant with the sister arts—painting, sculpture, poetry. You have to know world literature. You have to have an infallible ear, a strong sense of rhythm, a sympathetic personality. You must know the use and nature of the various instruments. You must know the technique of scoring like a composer. You must have a knowledge of languages. You must possess genuine musicianship. Finally, you must be of such a character that, come hurricane or flood, influenza or train wreck, you will be standing on the podium precisely at eight fifteen."

Reiner knows what he says. He has had hurricanes—or their equivalent—to weather throughout his career. The Laibach post, for instance, required, besides the ability to conduct musical productions ranging from *La Bohème* to *The Merry Widow* with only a twenty-five-piece orchestra, an almost instantaneous mastery of the Slovenian tongue. He managed it somehow. The head of the Budapest People's Opera, hearing of his success, came to witness a performance. Reiner was signed up for three years in his home town.

Clearly the conductor was getting into his stride. He was also developing that knack, for which he has since become famous, of making the most of opportunities. The very moment it became legal to produce *Parsifal* in Europe outside Bayreuth, he staged it. This calls for a bit of explanation. Wagner intended that his "Sacred Festival Play," as he called it, should be reserved for Bayreuth. However, according to European copyright law, it became legal to produce it thirty full calendar years after the year of Wagner's death. (Wagner died in 1883.) Reiner stole a march on all other conductors in Europe by performing it in Budapest on December 31, 1913—or rather in the early morning hours of January 1, 1914, since he sounded the first note *just one minute after the stroke of midnight.*

He scored again during his Budapest tenure with the local première of Wolf-Ferrari's *The Jewels of the Madonna.* The fact that he starred three members of the Dresden Opera in it didn't do him any harm. They went home singing his praises. Shortly thereafter he was in Dresden as Royal Court Conductor, one of the most important posts in Europe. In the eight years that he stayed there (1914–22) he not only rounded out his operatic repertoire, but also guest conducted orchestras in Berlin, Hamburg, Vienna, and Rome. Meanwhile he shared direction of the symphony concerts of the Saxon State Orchestra in Dresden.

He made the most of his Dresden appointment in other ways. Dresden is fairly near both Berlin and Leipzig. Artur Nikisch, one of the greatest conductors of the day, was concurrently occupying podiums in these two cities. Whenever his schedule permitted, Reiner scurried off to watch Nikisch in action—to note how he achieved clarity of line, transparency of sound. Reiner believes imitation is impossible in conducting, but that seeking after the effects achieved by another through one's own individual paths is one of the surest means toward development. He became Nikisch's protégé. It was at this stage that Reiner developed his characteristic skills—his persistent right-hand beat; his economy of motion; his directive ability via eyes, eyebrows, tilt of head, set of shoulders, line of body.

In Dresden, too, Reiner came in contact with Richard Strauss, to a vast widening of the young conductor's horizon. Strauss was then, and later in America, to entrust Reiner with interpretations of many of his works. When Reiner went to the Metropolitan Opera House in 1948, Strauss wrote to him, "That is good news. Opera needs men like you!"

Through the reverberations of these achievements and successes there sounded a persistently foreboding note. Even before leaving his native town for Laibach, Reiner had become aware of it. It had been heard one day when he had approached a great man of the then Royal Opera House—an "aristocrat" who made much of titles and lineage. Reiner had begged to be engaged as a coach at the opera house. "Young man," he had been told, "the best thing for you to do is to get out of Hungary and learn your profession elsewhere."

In Dresden, it seemed to Reiner, he had much the same problem to face. The Dresden Opera House was run on a high artistic level. It respected ability. But as time went on, decisions were being made more and more on bases other than musicianship. The *Deutschland über Alles* motif was drowning out far worthier themes. Narrow nationalism was rampant. The feeling haunted Reiner that one could never really succeed unless one belonged to an old family—had a "von" in front of one's name. The very fact of his having a stable position—it was a life tenure—increased rather than decreased his uneasiness.

About that time—in December 1921—he got a chance to conduct *Die Meistersinger* at the Rome Opera House. He put in a request for a leave of absence. It was not granted. Government orders! Final! Reiner decided to go anyway. He conducted that year and the following year not only in Rome but also in Barcelona, Spain.

He tells it today with gruff satisfaction. "I was so fed up with conditions that I decided, 'This is the thing!' I gave up a life contract. . . . America came a few months later. Evidently I had done the right thing and it just worked out." Then he adds quietly, "It took a certain amount of courage."

He sums up. "I don't like the kowtowing system of aristocracies. I am all American. I am democratically minded. I like this kind of government."

Democratic—and yet aloof. Any instrumentalist who has ever played under him, any audience member who has ever sat behind his eloquently motioning figure, gets this impression. The man who gave up a life contract in Dresden because he did not like its emphasis on titles is an aristocrat himself—the one kind Americans tolerate, an aristocrat of the mind.

The call to America was another of those lucky breaks with which Reiner's life has been punctuated. The Cincinnati Orchestra happened to be in a dilemma. Eugène Ysaÿe, as its conductor from 1915 to 1919, had let it wander loose-reined. The ensuing guest conductors had not directed it toward any specific goal. It would require a firm hand to get it into shape.

Reiner's reputation had traveled the waters. Word was passed to his wife, then visiting in Italy, that Cincinnati wanted him. She wired him the message to Spain. But, by the time it had reached the island of Mallorca where he was guest conducting, it had become so garbled that he could not make it out. It was evident, though, that it was an invitation to conduct in America. That was enough. He cabled back to his wife, "Trust your decision. Happy to accept."

The nine years Reiner spent in Cincinnati were years of discipline for the orchestra. It was here, too, that Reiner crystallized his own ideas of work. "I spend 80 per cent of my time planning programs," he says, "and 20 per cent transferring my ideas to musicians." His programs are not only excellently balanced, but range through as wide a field of musical literature as any being performed in concert halls today. And they come through. In his conducting of Bartók, to name one of the moderns whom he interprets with skill, the percussive and wind contributions are welded into a concept entirely understandable and entirely palatable.

In Cincinnati, Reiner began to see the conductor's role as a community one. To him it holds a twofold responsibility—"First, to transfer to the musician the clear meaning of a piece of music the way I understand it; and secondly, to act as an authority, as a guide, and as an informant in musical matters for the community."

In 1929 Reiner became a citizen of the United States.

In 1930 he remarried (his previous marriage had ended in divorce)—his wife the former Carlotta Irwin, a Midwestern woman exactly suited to be his partner in his American career.

In 1931 a change came in his career.

The Curtis Institute of Philadelphia had come into existence some ten years before. Heavily endowed, with vast new projects, it now wished to expand its orchestral department. Since Reiner was famous as a master of explicit gesturing as well as for deep musical knowledge, it was logical that he should be asked to head the orchestral department and to teach conducting. Reiner in his turn was glad of a chance to pay his debt to America. He resigned his post in Cincinnati and went to Philadelphia.

There are persons who advance far in their chosen field through an inner drive and an outer sensitivity, but who are totally unable to tell how they do it. Reiner is not one of these. Never was mind more aware of every step, and of just why it was made. Reiner's fame as a teacher equals his fame as a conductor. It is his boast that pupils who have finished his courses "can stand up before an orchestra they have never seen before and conduct correctly a new piece at first sight without verbal explanation and by means only of manual technique."

While in Philadelphia, Reiner guest conducted the Philadelphia Orchestra, the Chicago Orchestra, the New York Philharmonic-Symphony. In the operatic world his work was even more productive. Philadelphia hungered for opera. Reiner gave them opera. During the 1934-35 season, with the backing of the Philadelphia Orchestral Association, he helped organize an opera company and put on, as one novelty, Strauss's *Elektra*. It was a period of trail blazing that Philadelphians still look back on with pride.

Reiner gave other cities a sample of his operatic initiative. In New York on November 8, 1932, he led the Musicians' Symphony Orchestra in concert excerpts from *Salome*. In 1937 he introduced New York to Menotti's *Amelia Goes to the Ball* with a student cast from the Curtis Institute of Music. In 1936, 1937, and 1938, he conducted opera in San Francisco, to the loud acclaim of press and patrons. He had only one clash—with the stage director who insisted on using a time-honored steam apparatus to hail the demolition of the gods in *Götterdämmerung*. Reiner barred the steam because it hissed.

"But Maestro," said the nervous stage director, "there will be a scandal if we don't have the steam. The audience expects it."

"There will be another scandal if we *do* have it," said Reiner. "Because the conductor will leave the pit." Valhalla got along without its steam.

During these years, Reiner began his regular guest conductorships abroad. In 1936 and 1937 he was invited to London. In subsequent years, he was guest conductor in most of the capitals of Europe. As his successes multiplied, it was inevitable that he should be considered as material for a permanent conductorship in the United States.

The Pittsburgh Symphony was first to put in its bid. This orchestra had fallen on hard times. Formed in 1927, it had jogged along at a half-professional gait for ten years. Then the citizenry had decided to bring it to major status. In 1937 Otto Klemperer had taken eight weeks off from conducting the Los Angeles Philharmonic to reorganize it. Once it was in shape, the management had engaged a number of guest conductors, Reiner among them.

His enthusiastic reception convinced them, and he was engaged. During the subsequent decade, 1938–48, he made the ensemble of ninety players into one of the outstanding orchestras of the nation.

While he held this conductorship Reiner was crisscrossing America and Europe, making guest appearances in their chief cities. From 1941 on he guest conducted the NBC Symphony annually. In 1940 and 1941 he received honorary degrees, respectively from the University of Pennsylvania and the University of Pittsburgh.

Then, in 1948, an economy-minded management decided to curtail both season and personnel of the Pittsburgh Orchestra. They came square up against the artistic integrity of Reiner. "They told me," he relates, "that they would have to cut the season from twenty-eight to twenty-five weeks, and the number of musicians from ninety to eighty-five. I told them I would take a salary cut, but I would not have the number of my musicians cut down. They did it anyway. There was nothing for me to do but resign."

Resign he did. But that summer of 1948 was scarcely over before he was snapped up by the Metropolitan Opera Company. On February 4, 1949, he made his debut there in a historic performance of Strauss's *Salome*. Virgil Thomson called it "one of the great musico-dramatic performances of our century." He remained with the company until the end of the 1952–53 season.

New Yorkers will not soon forget him in the role of opera conductor. It was part of the show at the "Met" to watch this stocky man stride through the crowded pit with head thrust forward, to see him give brief acknowledgment to the loud applause from the darkened auditorium, then fix himself deliberately in the high swivel chair, put on a pair of crescent-shaped glasses, and flick his baton into place. Word soon got around that Reiner's performances were always a success.

He himself makes no such blanket statement. "One strives for the fresh approach, the vitality of the work in question," he says. "But it is an almost unattainable ideal. Conducting is so much more than the creation of a single performance. So much depends on how you feel at the moment. One is not the same every day. It is not always possible to maintain that necessary freshness."

In any case, his audiences got to expecting perfection from him. After almost every performance at the Metropolitan at which he presided, the standees would run toward the stage, to direct their *bravos* to this gray-haired man, obscured in the darkened pit in one of the oldest of America's music halls.

Then, in 1953, another hall received him—a hall also time-honored and yet symbolic of an entirely different field of music. The occasion was the fiftieth anniversary of the dedication of blue-domed Orchestra Hall in Chicago. Reiner, as the newly appointed conductor of its symphony, had just completed a program in which two numbers were duplicates of the concert given half a century before, under the direction of Theodore Thomas: Strauss's *Death and Transfiguration* and Wagner's *Tannhäuser* Overture. Then something happened that was deeply moving, and, to those who know the lives of both of these conductors, deeply symbolic. The baton with which Thomas conducted that first concert was laid on the desk of Fritz Reiner, and Eric Oldberg, President of the Orchestral Association, said, "Mr. Reiner, I know you feel as I do that it is a great honor to stand here in the place first occupied by Theodore Thomas . . . and to be the conductor and director of music of the great orchestra founded by him. . . . You and I and all of us mortals can be humble as we contemplate our task, and forever remember that this building does in truth harbor a living soul, which has existed in it for fifty years and will live on to immortality."

Thomas, the son of a poor immigrant from Essen, came to America in 1845 as a boy of nine; Reiner, son of a prosperous Budapest merchant, came to America as a mature and successful conductor in 1922. Yet here are two of a kind—both intolerant of mediocrity, both inflexible in their insistence on the best, both loyal to and ambitious for their adopted country. The baton of the Chicago Symphony Orchestra had passed into the right hands.

CHAPTER XXI

⇛ HANS SCHWIEGER

THE podium Schwieger is intense. In preparing a concert for the Kansas City Philharmonic, of which he is the conductor, he marks the scores painstakingly. When occasion warrants, he gives separate section rehearsals. He rehearses with the whole group four or five times. A fervent worker, he explains each step meticulously to his men. Every motion has meaning; every direction is pertinent.

An instance of Schwieger's thoroughness occurred in 1947 when he was developing the Philharmonic Orchestra in Fort Wayne, Indiana. He presented Gabriel Pierné's *Children's Crusade,* which has a score so complex that it is seldom given even by major orchestras. For this project, he had to deal with a semiamateur orchestra, an adult chorus of more than 200, a children's chorus of more than 180, and soloists. With the limited budget, only one full rehearsal was possible.

So one day Schwieger went to a grade school, the next to a factory, the next to a ladies' club, the next to the church of an Amish colony in nearby Berne, coaching children, teachers, factory workers, salesmen, engineers, bank clerks, and housewives to as near perfection as isolated group practice permitted. Every page of music of every single instrumentalist he marked for fingerings, for positions, for up- and down-bowings, for crescendos and diminuendos, for tempo variations. At the end of the sessions, he told the performers, "Go home and practice."

Later he got them together by sections and went from one room to another, listening, criticizing, explaining, clarifying—to the strings, then to the woodwinds, and then to the brasses. When everything possible had been done in sectional rehearsals, he struggled through the one full rehearsal allowed him, fitting the pieces together with infinite care. At the concert the next two nights, the audiences in sold-out Quimby Hall rose as one man and cheered.

Far from being elated with this reaction, Schwieger told reporters, when they asked him if he were satisfied, "No! But I'll do it better another time. If not here, in another city!"

The mixture of professional thoroughness and youthful exuberance that is Schwieger on the podium—the drive, the confidence, the ability to instill faith and to generate energy—shows qualities formed through a series of life struggles certain either to bring out the best in a man or to subdue him completely.

Up to the age of twenty-five, Schwieger's might have been the life of any promising conductor. Born in Cologne, Germany, in 1906, he was reared by an aunt, for his mother died when he was three and a half years old. He began the study of music at five and pursued it even in the face of his father's opposition. He traveled all over Germany as a boy soprano, taking the "female" lead in Haydn's *Der Apotheker*. He remembers enjoying especially the curtain calls at the end, when he could remove his wig and take the bows in his real character.

There were certain trying episodes of his early life—the scene, for instance, when his father tore to bits concert tickets the boy had purchased, furious at his son's persistence in following music. It only made Hans stouter in his purpose. Attending a Wagnerian opera, *Tristan,* with his aunt when he was twelve, he conceived the notion of how grand it would be to conduct one's *own* compositions, as Wagner did. A composer-conductor—that was what he would be! As soon as he got home he started composing little pieces, all of which have since been lost to fame. The ambition to become a conductor, however, persisted.

He entered the University of Cologne in line with his father's wish that he study law, but graduated instead with a degree in philosophy. Then came his engagement to Elsbeth Bloemendal, daughter of a Dutch Jew who was head of a manufacturing concern in Cologne. At nineteen he began to study for his doctorate in philosophy at the University in Bonn. There, at a Beethoven Festival, he met Erich Kleiber, conductor of the Berlin State Opera. To his joy, Kleiber invited him to come to Berlin as his assistant at the State Opera House. He held the post for two and a half years.

Successively he was appointed conductor at the opera house in Cassel, then at the opera house in Augsburg. In Augsburg was produced for the first time, under his conductorship, the Augsburg Festival Play, *Am Roten Tor* (*At the Red Gate*) which utilizes the wall and portals of that ancient city as stage sets.

At the age of twenty-five, he got his lucky break. He was chosen out of 135 candidates—many older and better known than he—for the job of director of opera and symphony in Mainz. He became also director of the Mainz Choral Society, one of the more important choirs in Germany.

Now he was so sure of his future that he married Elsbeth Bloemendal. Certain facts were thus to be faced: her Jewish descent and Hitler's growing power.

As Schwieger had expected, he was summoned before the city authorities—in his position he was a civic employee—to establish his "racial purity." He accomplished this, but was not yet to be left in peace. In what seemed to be casual conversations, he caught mysterious references. He was the recipient of anonymous warnings. Finally came his abrupt dismissal from his conductorships in Mainz.

For two and a half years Schwieger was without a regular job.

Isolated guest engagements were only stopgaps. Furtwängler, for one, tried to help him with a guest conductorship of the Berlin Philharmonic. But finally even the guest conductorships stopped. At the last one—he was directing an orchestra at Krefeld—a mutter in the audience rose to a howl. The police filed in and formed a cordon through which Schwieger passed to the relative safety of the street.

Not long after this his wife told him that she would divorce him, for the sake of his career; and that they would be reunited only when the persecution was at an end. Soon she disappeared, leaving a note saying she was going to Holland, and would have arrived there before he had read her message. For two years he could communicate with her only through friends.

There were no jobs even outside of Germany for him now.

By 1936 the Nazis had become fairly tolerant of him, though his attitude toward them had operated in reverse. He got the position of general music director of opera and concerts in Danzig. (It was then the Free State of Danzig, without Nazi control.) In 1937, he was offered a three-year contract to succeed Leo Blech as leading conductor of the Berlin State Opera House. While he was pondering his answer, he received an offer to conduct in Japan. Elsbeth, hearing of it too, managed to get through the message: "By all means accept the Japanese offer."

Now the story becomes even more melodramatic.

Schwieger, leaving most of his belongings and practically all of his money behind, to make it appear as though he were only off on a concert tour, started for Japan. After six months' time there he had made enough money teaching at the Ueno Academy in Tokyo and conducting the Imperial Orchestra to get him to America. The United States Consul in Tokyo expedited matters, and, on March 4, 1938, as a young man of thirty-two, he arrived in California. He had no prospects, but he had a boundless sense of freedom.

After miles of red tape and months of waiting in New York City, he got Elsbeth over. As soon as the necessary legalities were gone through, they were remarried, in New York's City Hall. Then they went to Columbia, South Carolina, where he had rounded up a job as choral director and where, as music director of the Columbia Music Festivals, he organized the Southern Symphony Orchestra and directed the Symphony Orchestral School.

In course of time the couple bought themselves a house in Columbia and began to breathe easier. It was too soon to relax. December 7, 1941, came—and Pearl Harbor. Overnight Schwieger, as a German newly arrived in this country—and via Japan —was listed as suspect and was interned. For 401 days he remained in custody. His wife found work as an assistant manager of a resort hotel in Georgia. Finally, through the intercession of friends, his case was reviewed and the charges found false. On his release he hurried to rejoin his wife. After a rest period in Savannah they moved to New York. Then, on July 5, 1944—it was still wartime—he became an American citizen.

It was something for this maestro to be a full-fledged American and to be walking down Fifth Avenue with his wife on a bright day in July. For such a special occasion, they would have to have a special celebration!

The celebration never came off. As they stopped at a friend's apartment on their way home to plan it, Schwieger's wife suddenly threw up her hands. "Oh, my head!" she cried, and slumped to the floor. In five minutes she was dead, a victim of an unsuspected brain tumor.

Olga Samaroff-Stokowski, a guiding star to many young musicians, led the dazed Schwieger away to her New York apartment. Later she took him to spend a recuperatory month at her summer home in Connecticut. Returning to New York, Schwieger joined the staff of the New York City Center of Music and Drama. In the fall of 1944 he became conductor of the Fort Wayne Philharmonic.

Citizens of Fort Wayne still remember how avidly Schwieger took up his task there, how it became for him the way back. They remember how he wrestled to make the orchestra a workable, proficient unit. They remember to what an astonishing degree he succeeded. They felt from the start, though, that his tenure would be brief. He had other fields to conquer.

Schwieger did not leave the town, however, without realizing in a very personal way his desire for fuller Americanization: in 1947 he married a Fort Wayne girl, an alumna of the University of Michigan, Mary Fitzpatrick Shields.

Meanwhile he had become one of this country's and Europe's regularly heard guest conductors. In the late 1940's he appeared with the NBC Symphony for three successive seasons, with the New York Philharmonic at Lewisohn Stadium, with the Chicago Orchestra in Grant Park and Orchestra Hall. He returned for guest conductorships in Germany, appearing twice in the spring of 1950 on the podium of the Berlin Philharmonic.

Then, in 1948, he became conductor of the Kansas City Philharmonic.

This orchestra, it would appear, is one cut out for Mr. Schwieger. It, too, has weathered economic squalls, and passed through wars, recessions, political upheavals, and changes in popularity.

Its history traces back to 1938, when a committee composed of members of Local 34 of the American Federation of Musicians met to consider giving a pair of concerts, as a "feeler" and stimulator to the people of Kansas City. After six weeks of rehearsals (with no pay) under the leadership of Arnold Volpe, sixty members of the local played two concerts to a large audience at the old Convention Hall. The following year Karl Krueger, in Chicago at the time, read the newspaper reports, returned to Kansas City, his home town, and paid a call on the president of the Chamber of Commerce. So successful was the interview that this civic body voted a fund for the orchestra. As concerts got under way, further sponsors materialized. When in 1943 Krueger left to mount the Detroit podium, Efrem Kurtz took over. On Kurtz' departure five years later, the baton went to Schwieger.

Schwieger hasn't been one to let down either the orchestra or the community. In 1949 he started the Philharmonic Chorus because he felt "it is just as important to hear the great choral works as it is to hear the symphonies," and that "the linking of the two great media is natural and essential for complete musical expression."

This choral organization was the basis for the next step, namely, to present opera with its full accoutrements. By 1952, Schwieger had given Kansas City an opera festival—one which has become an annual spring affair, performing works like *Traviata, Butterfly, La Bohème, Faust,* and *The Marriage of Figaro.*

In March 1954, he launched—on the invitation of NBC—the first nationwide broadcast of grand opera ever made from any stage other than the Metropolitan in New York City.

Other developments in the broadcasting world: On the invitation of the State Department, Kansas City saluted France by broadcasting a performance to Strasbourg in February 1952; Japan, by broadcasting to Osaka in 1953—this latter, according to the State Department report, heard by some 15,000,000 people; and Germany, by broadcasting to Munich in 1954.

Schwieger, moreover, has a broadcast called "The Composer's Workshop," in which each week a composition is analyzed, with the motifs and the instrumental lines brought out with an explanatory narrative. He also has had a televised musical quiz for children.

In spite of all his activity, the years that Schwieger has spent in Kansas City are without a doubt the most serene as well as the most productive of his life. He and his wife have bought a home there. His cocitizen friends know him as an alive and zestful person, endlessly intrigued by human relationships, deeply interested in civic doings. They note his absorption in politics, in current events. His outstanding characteristic, they agree, is his youthfulness of spirit—an attribute that points to the future rather than to the past. This, combined with his experience of men and his exceptional abilities, should take him far indeed.

CHAPTER XXII

⇛ IZLER SOLOMON

IN conversation Izler Solomon is friendly but restrained. One senses his mind is running in two channels at once—the topic under discussion and the score he is currently studying. In his walk, too, he appears preoccupied—shoulders a bit hunched, head forward, eyes focused in the distance.

The podium Solomon, however, is an entirely different being. There his face glows, becomes tragic, is tender, is elated. As his eyes widen or close, as his brow becomes furrowed or smooth, as his jaw muscles tense or relax, they tell a tale to which every orchestra member must listen. Critics time and again have noted his "aura of magnetism." "The orchestra hadn't played a dozen bars before that mysterious magnetic power, which is exercised only by authoritative conductors, had taken hold of the man" (Michel Mok, New York *Post*); "He has power to get an electrifying response from his players" (Frank Morriss, Winnipeg *Free Press*); "He makes music sound as if it were being newly created in the white hot crucible of his own genius" (Mildred Norton, Los Angeles *Daily News*).

The fact that he is still in process of being discovered by many Americans does not disturb Solomon at all. He remembers it took him a long time to discover his own bent as a conductor.

As a six-year-old in his home town, St. Paul, Minnesota, he was devoted to his violin. Through his boyhood years in Kansas City, Missouri, where his family moved in 1919 when he was nine years old, he continued to practice. The customers in his father's grocery got used to hearing violin sounds drift in on their talk of the price of eggs and the new miracle of radio broadcasting.

Solomon remembers that none of his boy friends teased him about his devotion to the violin. They accepted him, violin and all. In fact, after baseball games on the corner lot, the team trooped up to his house and sat with him while he did his practice.

As soon as Izler's violin teacher let him play in recitals in and around Kansas City, the townsfolk became aware they had a prodigy in their midst. They were particularly happy about this in 1924. That year, Omaha, 150 miles up the Missouri River, a town only two-thirds the size of Kansas City, had formed its own symphony orchestra. If Kansas City couldn't tie Omaha on this score, it would, it decided, do something else. A group of businessmen banded together, called themselves the Kansas City Educational Art Society, and picked two young artists—a boy and a girl—for launching on musical careers. The boy was Izler Solomon; the girl was Marion Talley.

Izler luckily escaped the high-pressuring that finally ended Marion Talley's career at the Metropolitan Opera. Miss Talley had a "triumphant" Metropolitan Opera debut in 1926, and remained a member of the cast four seasons before returning to the West. It was said her voice was not yet ready for a Metropolitan career, and that it was ruined through being forced. The fourteen-year-old violinist Izler Solomon, on the other hand, was sent to the East for four years of intensive study. Funds for this were raised by a benefit concert, but his parents, too proud to accept more than the tuition money, paid his traveling and living expenses during the time he spent on the Atlantic coast.

Izler studied first in Philadelphia. It was exhilarating to be taking lessons with the famous teacher, Myron Poliakin, and to attend the concerts of the great Philadelphia Orchestra under

Leopold Stokowski. He was one of a group of students who pooled their resources and bought scores of the compositions to be played by the Philadelphia Orchestra on Saturday nights. Each student was assigned one composition for study each week. Then, while they stood in line waiting for the doors to the upper balcony to open, they hummed themes, analyzed the compositions, and discussed the historical backgrounds.

Finally came the rush for seats. Izler was the quickest runner; so he dashed up the stairs four at a time, scurried down to the first row, threw his hat on one seat, his coat on another, sat on one himself, put hands down on two others, and waited for his friends. One of the standees in these line-ups was a young piano student, Sevi Sorelle, who was later to become Mrs. Solomon.

When Solomon went to New York the following year to round out his Eastern training (for a while he commuted regularly between the two cities) more excitement awaited him. He was introduced to the violin virtuoso Michael Press, who had come to America three years before after a highly successful career in Europe. This great violinist and conductor, one of the earliest podium guests of the Koussevitzky regime in Boston, was drawn to the intent, eager youth. He took him into his home. "He was like a father to me," recalls Solomon. "We'd discuss music by the hour. I learned then for the first time what it was to live the life of a musician."

Press prepared Izler for a Midwestern tour, which was undertaken successfully in 1926. During this period Izler also won the Gold Medal of the five (New York) boroughs. In the summer of 1928, he went with his mentor to Germany. There an invitation came for Press to head the music department of Michigan Agricultural College (now Michigan State) and to bring an assistant with him. He chose Izler Solomon to be that assistant.

At Michigan, Solomon immediately plunged into a full schedule. He taught sometimes as many as forty violin students a week. Here, too, came his first chance to conduct. In 1929 the students played a concert for the faculty, and he was chosen to lead their thirty-five-member chamber orchestra.

Though this was a pleasant interlude, his concern just then was with other matters. His pupils were graduating and taking positions in the public schools of Lansing. It didn't take a sleuth to discover that they stood only a slim chance of holding these jobs as teachers of violin. Because of the growing popularity of school bands, school orchestras were deteriorating and violin study with them. To halt this trend, Izler presented a plan to John W. Stevens, the supervisor of music and conductor of school orchestras in Lansing. The main part of the plan was to make the violin a curricular study five days a week.

Stevens liked Solomon's plan, adopted it, and gave Solomon the post of violin teacher in the schools. Then he made a suggestion. "Let's get together a symphony orchestra in Lansing," he told Solomon. "I'll conduct. You be the concertmaster. Then I know we can make a go of it."

The search for talent began. Factory workers, teachers, clerks, salesmen—everyone within a sixty-mile radius who had the requisite skills and gifts—were approached. Before long the outlines of an orchestra emerged. The first concert of the Lansing Civic Orchestra was announced.

When all was in readiness, however, Stevens fell ill, and before the orchestra had achieved a single public concert, he died. Rather than abandon all the work done, Solomon quietly stepped onto the podium that night, March 17, 1932, and conducted the concert as a memorial to his friend. It went so well that his colleagues asked him to continue as their conductor.

Solomon considers the fate that so put him in charge of a large orchestra at a formative period in his development the decisive factor in his career. About that time he received a badge as the violin winner in a nationwide contest of the Federation of Music

Clubs, Young Artists' Division. He put it away in his desk drawer, together with all thoughts of a violin career. At twenty-two he had decided to become a conductor.

During the next four years Solomon not only led this orchestra of seventy members but was its manager, librarian, and publicity man as well. When expenses had to be met for the rental of scores or for new music stands, pie plates were passed around at intermission.

As the orchestra improved and its reputation grew, Solomon was able to obtain the services of eminent guest artists, and this in turn brought new developments. Ossip Gabrilówitsch, acting as piano soloist, was so impressed with the orchestra's caliber that he donated $300 to its upkeep. Eric De Lamarter, associate conductor of the Chicago Symphony, after guest conducting, persuaded Solomon to help him out with the Chicago Civic Orchestra, a training group for the Chicago Symphony. This meant traveling the two hundred miles between Chicago and Lansing once a week, but Solomon did it.

In July 1935, the Federal Music Project came into being, its purpose to help musicians who were out of work because of the depression. Pianist Guy Maier, assistant to the national director of the FMP, began frantically searching for good conductors. He attended a concert of the Lansing Civic Symphony and discovered Solomon. "I won't let you stay in Lansing," he told him. "I want you to come to live in Chicago and conduct for WPA there."

So Solomon and his wife—he had married Sevi Sorelle in November 1931—pulled up stakes and moved to Chicago. He was given a "beautiful little chamber orchestra" of thirty-five pieces, the American Concert Orchestra. He was a happy man.

This wasn't all. Chicago had a WPA orchestra of full symphonic proportions, the Illinois Symphony. Nikolai Sokoloff, the national director of the Federal Music Project, chose Solomon to work it into shape. "I conducted 125 concerts a year for six years with the Illinois Symphony," Solomon says. "It gave me a golden opportunity."

It gave Chicago musicians and composers a golden opportunity, too. From the Sunday afternoon in 1936 when he first stepped onto the podium, "things began to happen—such things as capacity audiences and a reputation for interesting concerts," Claudia Cassidy says in a later article in the Chicago *Sun*. "Poised over his orchestra, beckoning, persuading and shaping the music, he reminded me of a snake charmer, and the music coiled and uncoiled as if it understood and swayed to his spell. This was a superb exhibition of orchestral control in the finest sense of complete freedom within correct boundaries. It was as distinguished as it was hypnotic."

During his half dozen years as conductor of the Illinois Symphony, Solomon built it from the ground up. He made history with it. This orchestra gave the first performances of some 150 American works.

There was method in Solomon's mad passion for premières. "I realized," he says, "that with the artistic and financial limitations of the WPA it would be suicide to try to compete with the Chicago Symphony, that I had to do something different. Besides, since it was the American people's money that was being used, I felt it was my duty to foster new music, particularly to give new American compositions a break. Public performance was impossible for all the compositions submitted. So once a week we'd hold reading rehearsals—to let the composer hear his work and spot the weaknesses in material or orchestration."

Soon critics were calling the Illinois Symphony "the finest WPA orchestra in the United States." Solomon's success was the measure not only of his musicianship but also of his understanding of human beings. When he first took over the orchestra, he saw that dissatisfaction was rampant. So he told the men and women, "We have to put in our time here. It's ridiculous to believe that we are getting paid in proportion to our real value. Let's forget about the money. Let's play for ourselves. Let's see how good an orchestra we can develop—for our own personal pleasure and joy." The musicians responded beautifully, he says. "They used to run to me outside the concert hall with the latest editions in their hands. 'See what Claudia writes about us today!' or 'Look what Cecil Smith says about the Hindemith work!'"

In the fall of 1939 Solomon also took over the leadership of the Woman's Symphony of Chicago, till then eking out an existence in the obscurity of no money, no great conductor, and almost no prestige. It had the one element that Solomon craved, however—seasoned and well-trained musicians. Within a year he had so developed it that it was selected for the radio program, "Design for Happiness," broadcast weekly from coast to coast.

That year, 1939, was a big one in other ways, too. Music editor Winthrop Sargent happened in on one of the concerts of the Illinois Symphony and spread the news of its conductor across a full page of *Time* magazine. Then Samuel Chotzinoff telephoned Solomon to conduct four weeks with the NBC Orchestra (Toscanini's own). He was also engaged as guest conductor of the Philadelphia Orchestra, the Chicago Symphony, the Buffalo Philharmonic, and Les Concerts Symphoniques de Montreal.

Early in 1941 Solomon had another offer. Columbus, Ohio, wanted an orchestra. Spread over forty square miles of Scioto valley, this city had centered its activities, as does many a capital, around governmental doings. Its orchestral life had been spasmodic at best. Now, with a feeble WPA unit as nucleus, it wished to expand to symphonic proportions.

Solomon couldn't resist the temptation. But he couldn't think of leaving the orchestras in Chicago, either. He solved the problem characteristically. He shuttled the three hundred miles between Chicago and Columbus thirty times during the 1941–42 season. But in 1942, when the WPA came to an end and with it the Illinois Symphony, he moved with his family to Columbus.

Columbus saw much of him. He and his wife kept open house every Friday night, when guests came to listen to a string quartet play new compositions. Then over sandwiches and coffee they discussed the works. At the children's concerts the youngsters were encouraged to write reviews of the programs. After each concert the winning criticism was published in the leading newspapers. The National School of the Air presented Solomon with an Award of Honor for the broadcast concerts over which he presided in the schools.

Other honors came his way. In 1946 Solomon received the Award of Honor of the National Music Council. In 1947 the National Association of American Conductors and Composers cited him for "combining understanding and intelligent interpretations of contemporary American composers with persuasive readings of the classics." In 1950 he was recipient of the Alice M. Ditson Award.

Solomon's musical radius widened during his Columbus sojourn. In 1943 he began five seasons as conductor of the New Orleans Summer Symphony. He conducted in the Grant Park Concerts in Chicago, and in 1946 began to conduct at Hollywood Bowl. In 1948 he was appointed guest conductor of the Israel Philharmonic. When he and his wife left the United States by plane for Palestine on May 16, the day after the British relinquished their hold over that country, Mr. Solomon carried Visa No. 1 for the new state of Israel. In spite of stifling heat, air raids, and black-outs, his concerts there were sellouts. He conducted there again in 1949.

One concert was held at an army camp outside Tel Aviv. Israeli troops were fighting Arabs at Lydda airport, only an eight-minute jeep ride away. Yet the audience listened in utter concentration and at the end of the program fervidly recalled him. After the concert he returned to his barracks room to find a letter from the Columbus Philharmonic. They had discontinued, due to "difficulty in meeting the costs." He would not be required to return. He put the letter back into the envelope, feeling "as though I had lost a child." It made even the turmoil around him seem unreal.

Seven years after his departure from Columbus, music critic and onetime member of the orchestra Norman Nadel wrote in the Columbus *Citizen,* "Many of us still have a warm satisfaction in claiming this genius as our own. . . . He was always in intimate communication with his players and gave us a security such as I rarely had encountered with other conductors."

Solomon's attitude toward members of an orchestra he conducts is a nice blend of affection and respect. "I don't drive the men, but I do everything within the realm of persuasion to get the results," he says. "An orchestra is like a democracy; the proper relationship between all members is the thing. Not that the individual may not stand out at times. An oboe has a solo in a Brahms symphony. I let him interpret it first in his own way. If his interpretation fits my over-all conception of the symphony—fine! If not, I will discuss this with him either during the rehearsal if his solo affects other solo instruments, or if not, after the rehearsal when we are alone. In either case I make it plain it is his solo. I build the orchestra around him. All of us know the final concept must be the whole picture—the ensemble must be one—as in chamber music. It is like bringing up my son the democratic way: it is harder during the process but it brings results. It's a wonderful thing to come onto a platform and have the orchestra glad you came!"

For a while Solomon's guest conductorships filled his schedule. He labored over these as devotedly as over a home orchestra: in 1950 the CBS in New York City; in 1951 the coast-to-coast tour of the Israel Philharmonic, which he shared with Serge Koussevitzky and Leonard Bernstein. One of the cities he visited, Indianapolis, was not to forget this man who "permitted the music to move under its own impetus in the most logical manner, while always molding the long-spun phrases in a plastic, expressive style that is distinctly his own." In 1952–53 he was resident conductor of the Buffalo Philharmonic. In 1953 he guest conducted the Hollywood Bowl Symphony, the NBC, the Miami University Orchestra, and the St. Louis Little Symphony. In 1955, as musical director of the Annual Festival of Creative Arts at Brandeis University, "he propelled the performance like a demon, or several demons, producing a performance of almost shattering emotional force." (Cyrus Durgin in the Boston *Daily Globe*.)

For two concerts in November 1955, and again for two in February 1956, he stood before the Indianapolis Symphony as one of six guests chosen to appear as candidates for a permanent conductorship. On April 14, 1956, word was passed out of the board room that he was the one chosen. At the age of forty-six Solomon was to have the opportunity of becoming the permanent guardian and developer of a major symphony orchestra.

Solomon does not elaborate on his good fortune. When asked about his reactions, he gives one of his rare chuckles. "The best thing was the way my friends reacted," he says. "About then the American Telegraph and Telephone Company split their stock. I decided it was because I got so many long-distance telephone calls."

CHAPTER XXIII

⇻ HENRY SOPKIN

HENRY SOPKIN, conductor of the Atlanta Symphony, deals in facts. He speaks quietly and impressively when he says, "We are the youngest major symphony in the United States, and we are never in the red. We figure how much we are going to spend for the next season and collect it at the beginning of the year. Last year we auctioned off a Cadillac; in 1956 Cinerama gave us the proceeds of its opening night in Atlanta. We average 4200 at a concert. [The capacity of Carnegie Hall is about 2700.] Every seat goes for a low price. No, it's not a beautiful hall. It's a barn, and the acoustics are awful.

"That's the next thing I'm going to do—have them build a new hall," he says. "Oh, we'll do it! Think—this orchestra has had a remarkable rise. The budget was $5000 in the 1945–46 season. In the 1956–57 season it was $225,000." He pauses, then adds, "Let me tell you, I've had the most exciting years of my life down there in Atlanta!"

Formed in 1945, the Atlanta Symphony sprang from a juvenile orchestra that had its source in the public school system. A youth orchestra that just grew up! Sopkin was chosen as its conductor because of his success in the educational field. Since music in America more and more revolves around the educational system, the emergence of this orchestra under Sopkin is a pattern well worth examining.

Mr. Sopkin is Chicago bred. Born in Brooklyn on October 20,

1903, he was three years old when his family moved to that bustling Midwestern city. In their white frame house in West Chicago's suburbs he and his two younger sisters took music lessons. (His cellist brother, George, of the Fine Arts Quartet, had not yet been born.) Like other boys, he skated and played ball and fought imaginary Indians in vacant lots. He made weekly trips to Hull House for violin lessons with Wilfred Woolett, a member of the Chicago Symphony. He sometimes got free tickets to the concerts and sometimes went to the home of his cousin, Stephan Sopkin, also a violinist, to listen to quartet practice.

It was not until Henry was fourteen and had entered high school that he began to think that music might be something more than a pleasant interlude between school and the baseball field. Before long he was playing the violin in the high school orchestra and in a quartet at Hull House. The same year he entered the American Conservatory and became a member of its orchestra. He studied violin under Leon Samatini and composition and orchestration under Arthur Olaf Andersen. Paul Held and Albert Noelte, his teachers in harmony and counterpoint, helped him launch a side line career as arranger, particularly for high school and college orchestras.

Henry began to teach a few neighborhood youngsters violin. He and his pianist sister got occasional dates playing at dances, and he was sometimes lucky enough to land jobs in restaurants and pit orchestras. From the age of sixteen, he earned through music enough to support himself.

He was determined to be a great violinist. His father, Isidor Sopkin, a manufacturer of dresses, put no obstacles in his path. He told his son quietly, "I want you to do what you want to do most. The manufacturing business is ready if you want to step into it. If it's music you want, I'll back you all I can."

From this time on, Henry took his career in dead earnest. At sixteen he formed and directed the American Conservatory Junior

Orchestra of forty-five members. When he was seventeen he won the commencement contest at the Conservatory. The reward was an appearance as soloist with the Chicago Symphony in the commencement concert. At twenty-one he received his bachelor's degree from the Conservatory and was immediately engaged as a member of the faculty. When he was twenty-seven he became head of the instrumental department, teaching orchestration and conducting. By this time he had studied and could teach all the instruments.

But his responsibilities were expanding faster than his salary. Two years before, he had married Sylvia Millman of Louisville, and they now had a young son, Charles. With the introduction of synchronized music in the movie theaters, pit orchestras were disappearing. Dance dates were not dependable. He had toured one season with a string quartet throughout the West and Canada, but had gained only a bare living and no security for the future. Besides, it allowed him little time at home. There seemed but one outlet for a musician head of a family in the Chicago of his day: to affiliate with the public school system.

Sopkin's subsequent record shows that his choice was sound. From 1931 to 1937 he taught in the high schools of Chicago. Then he was appointed director of music at the Woodrow Wilson College in that city. He taught in summers at the Universities of Wisconsin and Michigan. He conducted campus festivals where he made use of his ability as an arranger. He was a speaker at musical educators' conventions.

The twenty-year span, 1925 to 1945, saw a phenomenal rise in school music. In the teens of our century, music in public schools could be summed up as group singing periods, one or two a month, led by a visiting "superintendent of music." Today many schools have their own high-quality orchestras and bands. In western Colorado alone, some thousand young people gather yearly to participate in band tournaments. In Wrangell, Alaska, about 46 per cent of all public school pupils play an instrument under school instruction.

At an Oklahoma City Southwestern Music Educators' Conference in 1954, 165 boys and girls were welded into a first-rate ensemble, culled from 3500 students picked from 1100 high school orchestras. In April 1956, at the celebration of the Music Educators' fiftieth anniversary in St. Louis, one item on the program was Wagner's *Parsifal,* presented by the Indiana University School of Music with an orchestra of 63. At least 75,000 bands and orchestras—full-sized, trained, coordinated—exist in our schools and colleges today.

In 1943 Sopkin was asked to speak and conduct at a Music Educators' convention, held in Atlanta, Georgia. That year a youth orchestra had been formed in Atlanta, and in his speech before the convention Mr. Sopkin stressed the importance of forming not only orchestras integrated with the schools but general youth orchestras in which all qualified young people, in and out of schools, could take part.

This advice simmered in the minds of the people of Atlanta. Then in 1944 Sopkin was again invited to Atlanta, especially to conduct the Youth Symphony. The young people did so well that his services were sought the next year, too—this time to conduct a newly organized Atlanta Youth Symphony, representing not just the school students but the town's whole youthful population.

Atlanta music lovers knew exactly what they wanted to do: bring serious music to the younger generation; give professional opportunity to young Georgia musicians; and, within a reasonable period of time, develop a native and professional Atlanta symphony orchestra. At the orchestra's first concert, free to the public, a capacity audience of 1700 applauded the work of 100 young musicians.

In September of 1945, the organizers underwrote Sopkin's salary for a full eight-months' season of four concerts. At the end of that summer he had severed his connections with the Woodrow Wilson College and the American Conservatory in Chicago, turned down a bid to take a permanent post with the Corpus Christi College Symphony, and moved to Atlanta. "It took a lot of crust!" he says of the step. "At the age of forty you don't pull up stakes and take your wife and sons [another son, Elliot, had been born a few years before] to a new locality. Not unless you have faith in yourself—and in the community you settle in!"

The community has justified Sopkin's faith in it, but not without a bit of prodding on his part. "I love these Southerners, and I like to hear their sweet talk," says Sopkin, "but there's a job to be done. We all just had to pitch in and do it."

By 1946 the orchestra had begun to grow up. In the 1946–47 season fifteen first-chair men were engaged, and, for the 1947–48 season, fifteen more. In the 1948–49 season the professionals numbered forty-five, and in two more years made up the entire membership. These players, whether they were outsiders or members of the original youth orchestra, tended to remain in Atlanta to put down roots and to affiliate themselves with its life. Most of them became music teachers or filled positions in the churches, to the further enrichment of the community.

As a means of stretching the income of the members of the Atlanta Symphony, Sopkin has seen to the formation of groups within it—a string quartet, a woodwind quintet, the Atlanta Little Symphony of twenty-five picked members—flexible and portable enough to play at educational series and in small towns around Atlanta.

The step from occasional get-togethers of an amateur orchestra to supporting a professional symphony with hard cash is a difficult one for any community to take. In spite of all of Sopkin's ingenious measures, the Symphony, in the spring of 1949, found itself several thousand dollars in debt. Then the Women's Committee of the Guild was formed. In one of the hottest summers on record, the ladies went to work. It is estimated that 150 women made 15,000 telephone calls, enlisting contributions and selling season tickets. The week from September 18 through 25 the Mayor designated as "Symphony Week," a proclamation that has since been annually repeated. The campaign netted the orchestra more than 4000 season tickets. The youth concerts were sold out within two days of their announcement, leaving 400 children on the waiting list. Since then, 70,000 children have heard the concerts yearly.

Sopkin keeps thinking up new ideas for these youth concerts. To help the children prepare for them, he had their tickets printed in special booklets containing program notes. Once at a concert he stopped the players suddenly in the midst of the slow movement of Brahms' Third Symphony. "I'm going to play the first eight bars again," he told his audience. "Listen very carefully, because when it's done, I want you to hum it." Relating the incident, he says, "I had an anxious moment there. They might have failed me. As a matter of fact the melody came out strong."

When Sopkin received an award from the Juvenile Court for his work with children, the judge told him, "The week you have children's concerts there are fewer arrests among juveniles."

Sopkin has taken great pains to train young people for ultimate membership in the adult orchestra. For two summers he acted as head of a symphony school operated eight weeks in July and August by the Symphony Orchestra Guild. In this work, with an assistant and four staff teachers, he trained two groups, one of children from seven and a half to thirteen, the other of children from thirteen to seventeen. He also supervised a training orchestra of his school students throughout the regular public school terms. No student was eligible for the training orchestra, no matter how talented, unless his or her talent was offered also to the school orchestra.

Sopkin's success with young people is explained easily by those who have seen him at work with them. He is competent and knowing, and has a quiet sort of confidence that draws out the best in everyone.

By 1955 the Atlanta Symphony was giving fifty concerts a season, the budget had multiplied many times over, and the personnel was derived from the best instrumentalists in the nation. Since 1952–53, Colonial Stores, Inc., has presented a series of five Sunday afternoon Family Concerts. Each spring the orchestra puts on a festival of American music. Throughout the season it fills one-day engagements (by bus) in smaller towns in the five surrounding states. On February 6, 1955, when the orchestra's tenth birthday was celebrated, NBC carried the broadcast to the whole nation.

Behind all this there is a very quiet and a very determined man. There are no letdowns in standards. The way the composer meant the music to be—that is the way it is to be. As to the methods— any method is right, Sopkin believes, that will produce these results and still keep the good will of the orchestra. The whole project in Atlanta is characterized by good will—his and the people's.

CHAPTER XXIV

⇒ WILLIAM STEINBERG

IT means everything to William Steinberg, conductor of the Pittsburgh Symphony, that there is perfect understanding between him and his orchestra men. For he believes that, as the violinist's concern is with strings and bow, so the conductor's concern is with the emotions, impulses, and instincts of his men.

For the development of this emphasis on human relations, one looks back to Steinberg's early home life. His mother was herself adept at the psychological approach. The son learned to read notes before he could read the letters of the alphabet, and she taught him by such natural means that he has always remembered it as a stimulating game.

He was born August 1, 1899, in Cologne, Germany. At five, he began piano lessons. He did not like the Czerny exercises; so his mother encouraged him to write his own. He started violin lessons at nine and was rewarded with a chance to play in the family chamber music sessions. At ten his mother told him, "Now we are going to play four-hand the G minor Symphony of Mozart." He says he would never have thought of doing this on his own, but "at her suggestion, I sat down at the piano and played the work with her." Other symphonies followed. He became familiar with a good part of the symphonic literature this way.

It was William's mother, too, who took him to hear his first Wagnerian *Ring*. He was so impressed that, in all the brashness of his fourteen years, he decided he would compose a trilogy of his own, libretto and all. He based it on the Gudrun saga and performed it before a devoted if small audience of family members. He took most of the singing parts as well as playing one of the two pianos. His mother played the other.

It was not all praise and easy sailing in those days, though. In his late teens his mother told him, "You have a great talent for composing, but it is not an original one," and advised him against taking it up as a profession.

Giving it up wasn't such a wrench after all. His composing had already served its purpose. It had introduced him to the baton. When he was thirteen, he had led the school orchestra in a composition of his own—a setting of the opening passage from Ovid's *Metamorphoses* for men's chorus and orchestra—and had realized that here on the podium was his real place. From then on, though he continued to study counterpoint with Franz Bölsche and piano with Lazzaro Uzielli, and even became a concert pianist for a brief period, conducting claimed his particular attention.

Not that his teacher, Hermann Abendroth, gave him "conducting lessons." "In those days they knew conducting could not be taught," Steinberg emphasizes. "Teaching conducting is like trying to teach someone to be general director of a great business house. Either you can do it or you cannot. The most that can be done is to expose you to it."

Abendroth exposed the boy to conducting in the most practical way possible. He was conductor of the Cologne Municipal Orchestra. Like other orchestras in Germany, this had been reduced by World War I to a mere skeleton. Abendroth took in young Steinberg as a member of the violin section. There he watched every move, absorbed every direction, of the master. He was amazed when he was given three marks (the equivalent of one dollar) for each concert. It hadn't entered his head that he would be paid for what he enjoyed so much.

Steinberg must have convinced his teachers of his ability as conductor. On graduating from the Cologne Conservatory in 1920, he received the Wüllner prize for conducting. It was the first-edition score of *Die Meistersinger,* and it was presented to him by the City of Cologne. It was the first time an award had gone to a conducting student.

Steinberg immediately began an active career. He became assistant to Otto Klemperer, head of the opera in Cologne. Four years later he was made first conductor there. Since the opera house was very near his home, he ran in and out at all hours, taking part in every stage of the preparations. And since, as in all German opera houses, some fifty to sixty different operas were presented a season, he quickly mastered a wide repertoire.

In 1925, at the request of Alexander von Zemlinsky, director of the Prague Opera, he transferred to Prague. First he acted solely as a conductor, then, after two years, became director. He was also his own stage director here, and could work at the visual aspects of opera production.

In 1927 he married Susanne Jicha, prima donna of the Prague Opera.

In 1929 he went to Frankfurt to take the job of general music director at the opera house and conductor of the museum concerts.

The years from 1927 to 1932 were the most productive and the happiest in Steinberg's whole European period. He was moving about and liked "living in a suitcase"; he was conducting in two of the outstanding opera houses in Germany (he had also become guest conductor at the Berlin State Opera); and he was making a name for himself as a symphony conductor.

In 1932, with the death of his wife and constant interference from the Hitler government, both his personal life and his public career became overcast. Steinberg had become known as protagonist of the moderns. He had conducted the first performance, after the Berlin première, of Alban Berg's *Wozzeck,* and also

Krenek's *Jonny spielt auf;* had presented world premières of Schönberg's *Von Heute bis Morgen* and Antheil's *Transatlantic.* Now political pressure was put on him to make him choose compositions along Nazi party lines. He resisted. The expected happened. One morning in 1933 he arrived at the Frankfurt Opera House to find a notice of his dismissal posted on the bulletin board. No explanations—and he required none. He turned around and left the building, never to return.

He was not to remain long without a job, however.

In the early part of their regime, the Nazis planned to slash a dividing line between Jewish and "Aryan" cultures. Key Jewish musicians were directed to form organizations made up exclusively of their own people. Steinberg, as one of the most prominent Jews in musical life in Germany at the time, was appointed head of the "Jewish Culture Association," first in Frankfurt and later in Berlin. Under the watchful eyes of the Nazis, he organized orchestras of all-Jewish membership and presented concerts to audiences officially at least all Jewish.

The project did not work out as anticipated by the Nazis. Not only were the concerts a source of great inspiration and comfort to the Jews, but the musical standards of the group were so high as to make many an "Aryan" orchestra suffer by comparison. The Nazis therefore issued another proclamation: henceforth Jewish orchestras were to perform only in secluded synagogues.

Steinberg realized this new command would spell death to the projects. He struck out in a new direction. The Polish violinist, Bronislav Huberman, planned to form an orchestra in Palestine and asked him to be its conductor. Steinberg told the better musicians in both his Frankfurt and Berlin orchestras that they would be welcomed as members of the Palestine Orchestra. A few weeks later, he and his second wife, the former Lotti Stern, left Germany.

After a year and a half of traveling with Huberman, selecting musicians from various European cities and even from the United States, they headed for Palestine. There they formed the Palestine Orchestra, now famous as the Israel Philharmonic.

In late 1936 Toscanini was invited to conduct the first series. To ready the men for the grand opening concert, Steinberg conducted them in fifty-five rehearsals in four weeks. The orchestra Toscanini found on his arrival there drew a *molto bene!* from this hard-to-please conductor. And he didn't forget the man who was responsible for it, either. In 1937, when he became conductor of the NBC Symphony, he invited Steinberg to come to America as his associate.

By early 1938 Steinberg was settled in New York City, rehearsing the NBC Symphony and conducting some of its concerts. He found this work delightful. "An orchestra," he insists, "is always eager to enter into a relationship of mutual respect and comradeship, if only the conductor will make this possible. Genuine encouragement and cooperative facing of the difficulties involved, as well as full appreciation of the interest and willingness of the members of the orchestra, bring the musicians to a point at which they can surpass themselves."

Steinberg is an explicit conductor as well as a sympathetic one. "His beat, his cuing, his whole signal system, is planned, dependable, complete, virtually foolproof," says Virgil Thomson. "His tempos are reflected, his pacings impeccable; pleasing balances of tone and a true rhythmic animation are ever present."

Through these years Steinberg directed from many guest podiums—among them the Los Angeles Philharmonic, the Philadelphia Orchestra, the Chicago Symphony, the Cleveland Orchestra, the Minneapolis Symphony, the New York Philharmonic, the San Francisco Opera. He conducted in South and Central America and in Canada.

Then in May 1945, Cameron Baird, later head of the music department of the University of Buffalo, came to him with the suggestion that he take over the conductorship of the Buffalo Philharmonic. This orchestra, started as a WPA unit, had improved steadily through the years. After the WPA funds were withdrawn, the Buffalo Philharmonic Orchestra Society sponsored it. In 1940 the Kleinhans Music Hall was opened. Franco Autori, through his years of conductorship (1936 to 1945), had raised its musical standards. By 1945 large endowments had made possible another step forward.

Steinberg was invited to look over the orchestra. He says that when he stepped into the beautiful hall and saw the members of the orchestra waiting there on the platform, he knew he would have to accept. During seven seasons there, he increased the personnel from seventy to eighty-two members, brought up the weekly minimum from $45 to $85, and extended the season. The group made its first recordings and first tours and had its first commercial broadcast. With the Schola Cantorum (directed by Mr. Baird) Steinberg performed the *St. Matthew Passion,* the Bach B minor Mass, the Verdi Requiem and other important choral works and operas. Youth concerts were expanded: 40,000 children from public, private, and parochial schools filled the Music Hall to hear programs. These were also broadcast directly to classrooms of the majority of Western New York schools. Public rehearsals were held for students in various city and suburban high schools.

These years in Buffalo were years of widened guest conductorships for Steinberg: six concerts in Rio de Janeiro's Municipal Theater, four performances of *Tristan* and *Die Walküre* at the National Opera of Mexico, appearances with the San Francisco Opera, at the Ojai Festival, at Robin Hood Dell, in Ravinia Park. Reporting on a concert of his given by the Los Angeles Woodwinds in October 1951, music critic Pauline Alderman spoke of "an effortless grace which is present only when infinite time has been spent and exhaustive pains have been taken. . . . Steinberg is sure yet daring; full of power which is never too heavy and playfulness which is never insignificant."

Then came his conductorship of the Pittsburgh Symphony in the fall of 1952. This orchestra had been assembled sixteen years before by his friend of Cologne days, Otto Klemperer: the Symphony Society had found the means to raise the orchestra to major status, and Dr. Klemperer had been engaged to reorganize it. Fritz Reiner during his conductorship there (1938–48) had improved it still further. When Steinberg mounted the podium, however, there had been a four-year period without a permanent conductor.

Steinberg soon had the orchestra back in stride. Its pace since has been steadily upward. During his second season, a cooperative arrangement was instituted between the United Steel Workers of America and the orchestra for "industrial concerts," something new in symphony orchestra sponsorship. The Pittsburgh Symphony was engaged by the USWA to play to workers in steel towns and on tour. Wherever the orchestra played, civic organizations were asked to help publicize the event, and where possible to buy up blocks of seats. In the 1952–53 season Steinberg played industrial concerts in North Braddock, Johnstown, and McKeesport, Pennsylvania; in Canton, Ohio; and in Weirton, West Virginia. Since then the radius of these concerts has been continually expanding. Additional sponsors have appeared: the National Steel Company and the Manufacturers Light and Heat Company.

Another innovation: in November of 1952 Steinberg was the conductor of the Pittsburgh International Contemporary Festival. Its effect has been not only to offer a welcome outlet to creative musicians but also to make Pittsburgh audiences more receptive to the new and the different.

On March 6, 1953, the Pittsburgh Symphony appeared for the first time in Carnegie Hall, a visit that was repeated on November 16, 1956. Jay S. Harrison wrote in the New York *Herald*

Tribune, "The Pittsburgh Symphony is a swashbuckling, virtuoso group. . . . Its combined timbre is powerful, lovely, ideally balanced and shot with color."

Steinberg is glad of the improvement in the Pittsburgh Symphony, but he is still gladder that this goal has been achieved through a natural and ever growing understanding between him and his orchestra players—artists responding to another artist through mutual regard.

CHAPTER XXV

≫ LEOPOLD STOKOWSKI

SINCE the fall of 1955, when Stokowski mounted the podium of the Houston Symphony as its permanent conductor, both box-office receipts and the number of modern works performed have soared. His ideas of equipping the hall with acoustical devices, of introducing new lighting and staging arrangements, and of increasing the orchestra to 104 members, the size of the "Big Three," are all being considered favorably by the board.

Leopold Stokowski was born, built, and bred for musical venturing, and he has always managed to get into a situation that requires it. When he took over the conductorship of the Cincinnati orchestra in 1909, he was one of the first to consider developing an orchestra outside the New York–Boston–Chicago radius. These three areas had been tended respectively by the late Walter Damrosch, Karl Muck, and Theodore Thomas. Other centers could boast orchestras consisting of little more than a number of folksy fellows in their fifties and sixties plugging conscientiously through standard works and presenting three or four concerts a year.

Stokowski has the qualities needed to initiate new trends. From the first, even in the staid London where he was born—on April 18, 1882—he showed a tendency toward independence. His Polish father and his Irish mother were neither of them musical. But the child was talented and he was persistent. His father, a skilled but not very prosperous cabinetmaker, managed to budget his resources to include piano and violin lessons for him, and Leopold himself found ways to study the pipe organ. One of the boys with whom he played ball was the son of a clergyman, and Leopold wheedled him into letting him practice on the organ in his father's church.

When he first tried Bach—his favorite composer from the start—Stokowski recalls that he could use only the four manuals of the organ. As his legs grew longer he was able to reach the middle pedals and then, as the months and years passed, the next and the next. By the time he had reached the lowest C pedal he had found his way through all the organ music of Bach.

A sponsor—a member of the congregation, who had happened to witness his struggles with Bach—appeared on the scene in the boy's fifteenth year. Through his help the young Stokowski was soon deep in studies under Stevenson Hoyte (organ), Walford Davies (counterpoint), and Sir Charles Stanford (composition) at the Royal College of Music. In 1900 he became organist at St. James, Piccadilly. During the five years he held this position—studying during brief vacation periods in Paris and Munich—he explored, mostly through piano and organ arrangements made by himself, works of Beethoven, Mozart, Schubert, Brahms, Chopin, Debussy.

His intensive study of Bach bore results beyond his immediate pleasure. Today even Stokowski's most carping critics admit that Bach's organ music, transcribed for the modern symphony orchestra by this conductor, has become a definite part of our symphonic literature.

When Stokowski sailed for America in 1905, to take up duties as organist at St. Bartholomew's in New York City, he already had a firm grounding in orchestral as well as organ literature. During the next three years, he had a chance to hear some very good orchestra concerts. The New York Philharmonic, in a sort of relay race of guest conductors, was led in rapid succession by

Colonne, Henry Wood, Weingartner, Safonoff, Richard Strauss, and Mengelberg. Walter Damrosch was both conducting his own New York Symphony and, as a foreshadowing of the two orchestras' final merger, guest conducting the Philharmonic.

Maybe this experience helped bring about the typically Stokowskian "irrevocable decision" that came in the summer of 1908. He was on a visit to London and had found himself some conducting jobs. As he led the orchestra men through their paces there came the realization that the assembly of buttons, stops, levers, and pedals he had been manipulating in the obscurity of cathedral alcoves was as nothing compared to this instrument of human beings. For not only could the orchestra produce in endless variety dynamics, tempos, tones, nuances, timbres; not only was it endlessly replenished by new compositions; but also it led to opportunities utterly beyond the scope of the churchbound organist.

About that time Cincinnati, hearing of Stokowski's conducting activities abroad and already aware of his excellent work at St. Bartholomew's, invited him to come to the podium of its orchestra. He accepted with alacrity.

The Cincinnati Symphony that he conducted in that year 1909 was no "dream orchestra." It had been near disintegration only the year before when its conductor, Van der Stucken, had departed for greener fields. Now, with its financial fissures patched up, it welcomed Stokowski. He went right to work on it. He culled expert instrumentalists from New York and across the ocean. He raised the membership to seventy-seven. He began routines for which he has since become famous: built dramatic programs; sensitized each member of the orchestra to full participation; reminded audiences of their responsibilities via curtain speeches.

He was accepted enthusiastically. His tenure, however, was brief. "Lack of cooperation" was his complaint when, in March

1912, he made a formal request to be relieved. Contributory circumstances may have been Cincinnati's tendency to keep its gigantic May Festival in the hands of outside orchestras and conductors, and the desire of his bride, Olga Samaroff—concert pianist and later famous educator—to be in the East, where most of her concerts were booked. There were also mutterings in Cincinnati circles of secret understandings with an Eastern orchestra, and these became louder when Stokowski that very fall took up his conductorship with the Philadelphia Orchestra.

When on October 12, 1912, Stokowski first faced the Philadelphia Orchestra as its permanent conductor, few could have predicted the future of this "surprisingly boyish but thoroughly businesslike" figure, nor the future of the Philadelphia Orchestra under his direction.

Even discounting his own immaturity, the situation was not particularly promising. Music was regarded with something near suspicion in this city of churchmen and lawyers. It usually was presented in the guise of good works. In order to be palatable to the residents, the very first public performance of the Philadelphia Orchestra, in March 1900, had to be advertised as a benefit "for the relief of families of the nation's heroes killed in the Philippines."

The orchestra's two previous conductors had failed to come to grips with the situation. Fritz Scheel, who had wielded the baton from 1900 to 1907, often had remarked he was thankful that he turned his back on the audience so that he could forget its diminishing size. Karl Pohlig, who had led it from 1907 to 1912, kept to so dull a course that the only rifts had been periodic complaints of his playing too much Wagner.

Stokowski won his way by a system of contrasts and balances. On his orchestra men he visited both paternal solicitude and searing sarcasm. Audiences were alternately lectured and subtly complimented. The board members got both promises and dire threats.

Whatever inconsistencies were apparent in Stokowski's attitude, the improvements in the musical situation itself came steadily and surely. He replaced the old and stiff orchestra members with men flexible in both muscle and will. He increased the personnel to 104. He inaugurated Tuesday night concerts in New York City. He started children's concerts. He obtained solid financial backing for the orchestra. Lawrence Gilman in the New York *Herald Tribune* wrote in the 1930's that the orchestra "needed his indomitability, his unslakable passion for perfection, his magnetizing contact, his adventurousness, his superb dissatisfactions." He added, "No other conductor of his time, so far as we are aware, could have brought to the enterprise just that particular fusion of traits."

From the very start Stokowski favored contemporary works. The 1912–13 season, according to a local newspaper, was filled with "an embarrassing number of novelties." In his fourth season he really got into his stride. He had heard the world première of Mahler's *Symphony of a Thousand Voices* in Munich in the summer of 1910 ("I felt like the first white man to view the Niagara Falls") and had been obsessed ever since with a desire to put it on in America. This he accomplished in nine performances in Philadelphia in March and April of 1916. What with the specially erected stage, salaries, and overhead, it cost the board $15,000. They agreed, however, that they more than broke even in the publicity gained. The thousand voices entrained to New York City, together with the dismantled stage. The concert in New York on April 10 marked the beginning of the international reputation of the Philadelphia Orchestra.

In 1917 Stokowski brought about the first complete symphonic recording made by an orchestra under its own name and conductor. That today the Philadelphia Orchestra has the largest recorded repertoire of any existing orchestra is due in considerable part to the enterprise of this man.

Recording was but one of many expansions Stokowski instituted for the Philadelphia Orchestra. An experimenter and an inventor, he looks on the orchestra as an instrument that one can improve as one would improve a working tool. As the flutist Theobald Böhm a century earlier struggled to better the flute in tone and controllability, so Stokowski works to extend the scope and increase the responsiveness of the orchestra.

Among his experiments have been simple platform rearrangements toward the end of better distribution of sound. In 1921 he reseated the string choirs of the Philadelphia Orchestra, putting the cellos at the front on his right and placing the second violins behind the firsts. In the string section he allowed the matter of up-and-down bowings to be decided by the individual players, instead of insisting on uniformity as do most conductors. (Uniform bowing, he feels, is an unnecessary cramping of the player's style.) He invented an acoustical reflector which has been widely copied.

Several of his experiments have been less happy. Of very short duration was his attempt to have the winds seated at the front of the platform, thus obscuring the more active strings. His idea of rotating the first violins—each one taking for a single concert the position and duties of concertmaster—was likewise discarded. Then there was the short-lived experiment in which he had the orchestra operate in complete darkness, save for tiny desk-lights and a strong beam playing on himself to make his gestures visible to his men.

His employment of Javanese gongs, Indian temple bells, and other exotic instruments in works in which the scores do not indicate them has made for the liveliest controversy.

Conductors are divided on the question of whether a composition should be played exactly as the composer conceived it, or with such alterations as new needs and resources indicate. Advocates of the former theory weigh suspiciously Stokowski's statement that "instrumentation should not be regarded as fixed and crystallized." Irving Kolodin tells of a conversation he had with Stokowski while they were going over some of his (Stokowski's) recordings.

Kolodin: "There is no tam-tam in the score of Dvořák's *New World Symphony* at this point."

Stokowski: "No tam-tam."

Kolodin: "Why do you put it in?"

Stokowski: "I feel the need for a new color, a climax."

The only answer to that, Kolodin sums up, is to go have a beer at the nearest bar.

For his research into recorded and broadcast music Stokowski has won the respect of many experts. His study has been intensive. He has gone into control rooms, talked with engineers, sat in radio reception rooms, noted defects, delved into the science of sound under noted physicists. He has experimented with the sound-absorbing potentials of drapes and the stuff of seats, with the placement of microphones and backdrops. He believes, "The first step is to make recorded music exactly like the original. The next is to surpass the original and, through future possibilities of recording, to achieve the dreams of musicians—of making music still more beautiful and eloquent—music they heard within themselves but which was unattainable in the past." *

Philadelphians never ceased to marvel at this boldness in Stokowski. They drank in such statements as, ". . . when we act spontaneously from the dictates of our heart, we may break the conventions. Those who are always correct and conventional are sometimes lacking in generosity—they are seldom impulsive,

* This and the following quotation are from Leopold Stokowski's book, *Music for All of Us*, Simon & Schuster, Inc., 1943.

natural, simple, expressive. In music, feeling and intuition are more important than accuracy—expressiveness is more important than literal correctness—more important than the intellect are the heart and soul of music."

Back in the twenties and early thirties, Philadelphians could not find enough ways of showing their admiration for their conductor. The ten-year contract Stokowski signed in 1922 for ninety annual concerts at $800 apiece was each year altered by a clause raising the fee per concert and lowering the number of concerts. By 1929 he was conducting fifty concerts and receiving $2000 for each. Huge smokers attended by over a thousand prominent persons were held annually for him. At Horticulture Hall on these occasions one saw members of "the clergy, the bench and the bar, the financial world, bank presidents and trust company heads galore, business folk and manufacturers, literary and musical circles and the men in society and public life."

These smokers were sponsored by Alexander Van Rensselaer. Another of Stokowski's patrons was Edward Bok, head of the Curtis Publishing Company. Through his personal enthusiasm for Stokowski this influential executive—admittedly nonmusical —put in motion and carried to completion a campaign to raise one million dollars for the orchestra. Stokowski was the first to get the Bok Award ($10,000) given to "the person who has done the most for Philadelphia." He was made honorary director of practically every musical organization in the city. He received an honorary doctorate from the University of Pennsylvania.

As for the orchestra members, for all they made fun of his chopped vegetable diet, for all they suffered under his periods of icy aloofness and burning reproof, they knew him for a genius at getting the best out of them. Under him they made superb music. They were correspondingly grateful.

But it was the youth of the city who gave him their all. Young standees for the Saturday evening concerts cued up at four in the afternoon and by eight o'clock had reached halfway around the block. Groups of them lingered after the concerts just to be able to brush his coat sleeve as he hurried to the taxi, and perhaps to receive a nod from him. At his special teen-age concerts he allowed the young people complete charge of the arrangements. They printed the programs, designed the covers, made the posters, and even chose their own programs by vote. The concerts, interspersed with short talks, quips, and special offerings, were deliriously applauded.

Stokowski enjoyed the young people as much as they enjoyed him. He egged them on. "I want to see that chandelier agitated by your emotions." . . . "I prefer a Bronx cheer to apathy."

For all his success and for all his achievement, the year 1932 saw the first ruffles in the smooth flow of Stokowski's Philadelphia career. The board renewed his contract; but, its left hand evidently not knowing what its right was doing, it also sent out a prospectus announcing it would present "known and accepted music and avoid modern compositions." Stokowski flared up. He made it clear that he would conduct what he pleased.

In 1934 he preferred not to sign himself to a long-term contract, but said he would agree to conduct a certain number of concerts a year. The board saw that this plan, if continued, would not be to the best interests of the orchestra, and engaged a co-conductor, Eugene Ormandy, to ease the load for Stokowski.

But it was not ease that Stokowski wanted. It was wider fields. In 1936 he took the Philadelphia Orchestra on its first transcontinental tour—thirty-six concerts in twenty-seven cities. The "standing room only" sign was out at every stop. Many of the audiences, introduced to the Philadelphia Orchestra by radio, had never seen a symphony orchestra perform before.

Stokowski closed the tour with a triumphant display in Madison Square Garden, where he conducted the orchestra before 12,000 persons.

After that he headed for Hollywood and the movies. "I go to answer a great spiritual challenge," he told reporters somewhat mysteriously on his departure.

In 1938 Ormandy was given the title of "musical director" of the Philadelphia Orchestra. Stokowski's regime was virtually at an end. He conducted a series of concerts each season until 1941, but some audience members remarked his heart did not seem to be in it.

Maybe his heart was in Hollywood, intent on answering that "challenge."

Besides acting in the films *The Great Broadcast of 1937* and *One Hundred Men and a Girl,* he contracted under Walt Disney to have complete authority over the music of *Fantasia.* This took three years to stage and cost two million dollars. If the movie people themselves were any judge, Stokowski met the "great spiritual challenge." In 1940 he received a special award of the Academy of Motion Picture Arts and Sciences for his work on *Fantasia.*

Of all the enterprises in the years that elapsed between Stokowski's relinquishment of the full-time Philadelphia podium in 1938 and his assumption of the conductorship in Houston in 1955—the Youth Orchestra, co-conductorships of the NBC Symphony and the New York Philharmonic, direction of the (WPA) New York City Symphony, leadership of the Hollywood Bowl Symphony—the one that lay nearest his heart was undoubtedly the Youth Orchestra.

If Stokowski is a bit vague about religion, family ties, tradition, and social obligations, he is not at all so about youth. He is drawn to it, stirred by it, believes in it. Youth's constant change, its charm, its wild imaginings, its forward look, its emotionalism are his own.

He has done much to further youth's musical opportunities. Stokowski's All-American Youth Orchestra, composed of twenty girls and sixty-some boys, was during its existence (1940–42) acknowledged as fairly near the top among symphony orchestras of the decade. Chosen via state and national contests, it represented every section of the country. Some 10,000 boys and girls competed for places in it.

Once it had been formed, and about twenty Philadelphia Orchestra members added for stability, Stokowski spent three weeks rehearsing it day and night. The members earned $50 a week each. Then in July 1940 they departed on a tour of South America, Cuba, Haiti, Puerto Rico, and the Virgin Islands. The next year the group, reorganized, toured the United States, Canada, and Mexico.

Stokowski wound up the enterprise with a concert in Carnegie Hall at which "the entire quota of violin players stood and played en masse the first movement of one of the Bach sonatas."

Youth had its say if not its way in another "affair Stokowski." In 1941 he severed all connections with the Philadelphia Orchestra. The reason he gave was failure of the board to approve his musical enterprises. The reaction among his young followers was vehement. The members of his youth concert audiences in Philadelphia voted unanimously the immediate resignation of the entire board.

Neither of Stokowski's co-conductorships—with Toscanini on the NBC Symphony podium (1942–43) and with Mitropoulos on that of the New York Philharmonic (1949–50)—was entirely successful. Stokowski's habits of reseating orchestras and of adjusting acoustics, not to speak of his almost mesmeric powers over orchestra members, bode ill for any such cooperative arrangement.

In 1945 Stokowski became director of musical activities of the Hollywood Bowl. At the opening concert on July 11, the 14,000 persons who saw him lift his famous hands in the initial blessing of Bach's Passacaglia and Fugue, sumptuously arranged for orchestra by himself, might well have concluded that here this

Barrymore of the baton had found his place. It didn't turn out that way. At the end of his second season there, Stokowski made another of his "irrevocable decisions" and abruptly departed.

During these years he guest conducted in practically every city that had an adequate orchestra. Always on his programs he featured compositions by young moderns. He invited composers to send him their works. "We are looking for two kinds of music," he told radio audiences in his 1953–54 "Twentieth Century Concert Hall" broadcasts, "the kind that reacts to the crude life around us and the kind that creates a remote world that is far from everyday life."

Now that the Philadelphia mantle had fallen from him, critics and audiences were able to judge Stokowski on his musical merits alone. He bore up extremely well under the test. Virgil Thomson wrote in the New York *Herald Tribune,* after a New York Philharmonic concert, "As for Mr. Stokowski's conducting, it was pure miracle from beginning to end. Often in the past critics, the present one included, have protested at errors of taste on this conductor's part. Last night there were none. Everything was played with a wondrous beauty of sound, with the noblest proportions, with the utmost grandeur of expression. The perfection of tonal rendering for which Stokowski and his Philadelphia Orchestra were so long famous was revived last night with the Philharmonic men in a performance of Debussy's *Afternoon of a Faun* that for both beauty and poetry has been unmatched for many years, if ever, in my experience."

Then in 1955, when it seemed that Stokowski would become permanently identified as conductor-at-large, came another surprise. He had accepted the position of conductor of the Houston Symphony.

Houston is the nation's fourteenth largest city. It is a city of youth. The average age of musicians in the Houston Symphony is thirty. Youth is the primary interest of its Symphony Society.

They are happy that Stokowski is developing special concerts for children from four to nine, in addition to the sixteen already being presented for older children.

What makes Houstonians happiest, though, is Stokowski's blunt query, "Do you want the Houston Symphony to be good, very good, or equal to any in the world?" There can be only one answer to that question—when directed to a Texan by a conductor of Stokowski's stature. Houstonians are answering it characteristically—with action.

CHAPTER XXVI

➤➤ BENJAMIN SWALIN

"Many people take symphony music as a kind of plaything—to amuse, to pass the time. It is not so at all. Great symphonic music, well performed, is one of the greatest achievements of the human mind."

How many times Benjamin Swalin has repeated this message, leaning forward, drawing all eyes to focus on him at Rotary and Kiwanis clubs, at conventions, and at PTA meetings. How many times he has poured out persuasive phrases, standing on senate floors, lecture platforms, pulpits, and the plush carpets of the wealthy. For Swalin believes we have the task, we here in America, not only of appreciating great music but also of making it available to all of our citizenry, regardless of how remote or humble they are.

"In our development as a people," he emphasizes, "we have not yet reached a full understanding of the significance of music. So the music lover must not only be an appreciator but a worker for the community. He must be a missionary, a crusader. Music—live music—must be made to reach out to the rural communities, to service vast numbers of people. Especially young people. For they are America's future!"

Sandy-haired, broad-faced Swalin is a crusader. He has about him something of the air of Carl Sandburg, the same love of people, the same zeal for cutting away demarcation lines where the cultural arts are concerned. Europe, with its magnificent opera houses, its long-standing orchestras, its traditions, could not have produced him. Unthinkable in Europe would be his concerts presented for a statewide rural audience, with an orchestra whose home is two buses and a truck, whose concert halls are gymnasiums, ball parks, libraries, auditoriums, schoolhouses, museums, evangelists' tents, and moving picture theaters. Unthinkable in Europe would be the role of the conductor's wife as Benjamin Swalin's wife carries it out: as narrator in the children's concerts; celesta and cembalo player; pianist; promoter; campaigner; interviewer. She takes along on the trips a medicine kit—her late father was a physician—and prescribes for the colds and other ills the members are apt to suffer as the winter winds whistle around the mountain-climbing buses.

Let us look at this orchestra-on-wheels, the North Carolina Symphony, which is so clearly a projection of Mr. Swalin.

This orchestra gives between 104 and 130 concerts in 127 days. They are heard wherever mountaineers, seafolk, or valley dwellers congregate in North Carolina settlements of from 344 to 150,-000 inhabitants. From January through March, twenty-five members of the orchestra tour as the "Little Symphony." In April and May all sixty-five members are on the road. The orchestra's arrival is perhaps the most exciting event of the year for many rural communities. Certainly it is the most culturally stimulating. At the Outer Band of Cape Hatteras the entire fishing community turns out to hear the concerts and afterward holds a square dance in the players' honor. When the buses climb into Banner Elk (elevation 4000 feet) the whole population of 344 pours into the street, waving greetings. In village after village the musicians are hurried away to farmers' or fishermen's homes to be fed fried chicken, home-cured ham, corn pone, sweet potatoes, greens, apple cider, jams, jellies. "Symphony Day" is like Christmas Day for these villagers.

Never does Swalin veer from his major tenet, namely that the youth must be served first. In many of the communities concerts are given especially for the young. Charts, booklets, discussions gauged exactly to their age level, prepare the children weeks in advance for the music. It is organized as *their* occasion—and they respond in kind. Before and after the concerts youngsters wearing overalls and gingham dresses swarm onto the stage. They inspect tubas, kettledrums, harp; ask questions; get autographs; beg (and are given) the chance to touch violin strings or press down celesta keys. Then, full of the knowledge that the concert is for them, they find their places and are sitting still as mice by the time the first note sounds.

Mr. Swalin did not actually organize the North Carolina Symphony. It was formed before he came on the scene. Lamar Stringfield officiated at its birth in 1932. It was a Federal Emergency Relief Administration project until 1935. Then Mr. Stringfield left and the orchestra gradually dissolved. Swalin took up its cause in 1939.

What in Swalin's life led up to this career of such varied activities and such undeviating aim?

He was born on March 30, 1901, in Minneapolis, Minnesota, the son of Benjamin and Augusta Swalin. It was a musical family. Benjamin Senior had brought his violin from Sweden when he came to America in 1880. He practiced it off and on, even while providing for a growing family of three girls and three boys. The father's two fields of operation—working as blacksmith in the "old days" in Minneapolis and later as a real estate agent —weren't allowed to dim his love for music. In his household, violin and piano duets—all the children could play—sounded forth at all hours. Benjamin Junior and one of his sisters, as they grew more expert respectively on the violin and piano, played at churches, lodges, dance halls, and socials.

Young Benjamin's first memorable musical experience came on his graduation from high school. He auditioned with Emil

Oberhoffer, then conductor of the Minneapolis Symphony, and was accepted as violinist—the youngest musician ever to play with the orchestra. This meant more to him than the chance to learn the repertoire, rich as this was. It meant touring and new outlooks.

The Minneapolis Symphony was one of the most traveled orchestras of the day. Come snow, come high water, come railroad wreck, it kept on its way. In many centers it served as a feature in the spring festival. In many, it *was* the spring festival. All this was excellent training for a young and impressionable musical missionary.

It was also an opening of doors. In the stopovers in college communities and in the larger towns, he became acquainted with distinguished musicians of the day. Conversations with them caused him to adjust his sights. He decided to pick out "the greatest violin teacher in the United States" and study under him. The violinists of the Minneapolis Symphony spoke of Franz Kneisel with bated breath. "If you can study with him, you will have the finest!" So Swalin wrote to Kneisel. He got an answer that lessons were $15 for a half hour—a steep price in those days. But this didn't stop him. He made an appointment with him in New York early in 1921 and was accepted.

Swalin studied with Kneisel from 1921 to 1926, privately the first two years and after that at the Institute of Musical Art. (This later became the Juilliard School of Music.) He earned the money to pay for his lessons by playing in the orchestra at the Capitol Theatre and in musical shows on Broadway. After Kneisel's death in 1926 he studied with Leopold Auer, also at the Institute of Musical Art. He graduated from Columbia University in 1928. In 1929 he became concertmaster of the WOR Concert Orchestra. That eased his financial situation a bit. In 1930 he received his M.A. degree in English from Columbia.

About this time he applied for a European fellowship, and,

to his surprise, won it. But his feelings were mixed. He had a good position in the WOR Orchestra, and had started working for his doctorate in English at Columbia. It seemed a pity to pull up stakes. On the other hand, he had always wanted to conduct. He consulted Carl Van Doren, who was one of his English professors. "Always do the hard thing," Van Doren advised him. "Don't get in a rut. Make new contacts. Go abroad!"

So Swalin went to Vienna and through two and a half years, that is, from 1930 until early 1933, studied conducting in the Hochschule für Musik and completed his Ph.D. in the University of Vienna.

When he came back to America the depression was at its darkest and deepest. People just scowled when asked about a job. Then Swalin recalled the advice of his former teacher, Auer: "Don't stay in New York. Go West or South—go where people are starved for good music." In 1933 he assumed the post of Professor of Violin and Theory at DePauw University, in Greencastle, Indiana. For two years he taught violin and theory there and conducted the university orchestra.

The year 1935 was one of transition for him both outwardly and inwardly. The United States was slowly recovering from its worst depression in years. Swalin was reaching out for fuller means of realizing his conviction, "It is everyone's duty to serve his fellow man—to give more to society than he takes from it."

An opening occurred on the faculty of the University of North Carolina at Chapel Hill and Swalin went there with his bride, Maxine, a graduate of Radcliffe. As soon as he was settled in his new post he began to study the orchestral situation. He noted that the North Carolina Symphony was gradually being liquidated as a federal music project. The musicians were scattering.

To Swalin it was deplorable to see an orchestra lost completely. He decided to do something about it. At first he appealed to this and that committee. Then in 1938 he began coaching instrumentalists with a view to working up the needed membership for an orchestra. "I'd rehearse two hornists and one violist together in Asheville, take the train or bus to get there. Then I'd rehearse a tympanist and a cellist in High Point. I used to spend my week ends doing this work. Transportation wasn't what it is now. One Friday afternoon I drove my car about thirty-five miles to a small town on a bus route to Charlotte. As I entered the town, I saw a bus just ready to start for Charlotte and shouted to a garage mechanic—I'd never seen him before in my life—that I had to catch that bus and that I'd pick up my car Sunday night when I returned. Then I threw the keys to him and hopped the bus— just as it pulled out. The car was safe all right when I returned."

During this period, Mr. Swalin was not only teaching full time in the music department of the university but was also writing a book. His *The Violin Concerto: A Study in German Romanticism,* was published by the University of North Carolina Press in 1941.

Finally Swalin assembled a sufficient number of players to make up a good orchestra. For the first few years, they jogged along with "hello" concerts in halls in the environs of Chapel Hill. Then the state became aware of its crusading conductor, and of musicians who seemed to materialize out of the mists of the mountains, and voted it an appropriation.

The $4000 which the state legislature first set aside for the orchestra for the two-year period 1943–45, however, was not enough to put its members on regular salaries. Since they had therefore to keep their outside jobs, it was a case of the butcher, the baker, and the banker sitting down in their spare time and doing the best they could with Bach, Brahms, and Beethoven. It didn't work out too well. The first cellist would send in word at the last minute that he had to audit the company's books. The oboist would write that her sister was ill. The tuba would telephone, "It's mother's first visit in two years!" A tympanist once wired collect, "Can't make the concert tomorrow. Hope you have nice concert! Regards!"

By 1946, however, the members had become salaried and were placed under regular contracts. Then it became possible not only to schedule a season's itinerary and plan its programs in advance, but also to insure the quality of music the listeners had a right to expect.

It is a point of particular pride with Swalin that never before in America had a state recognized a symphony orchestra as a fundamental educational institution. So that the senators and representatives may get a taste of "what they are paying for," a concert is presented every other year on the floor of the state legislature.

Though the state did successively raise its biennial allocations, in 1949 to $30,000 and in 1953 to $40,000, the amount by no means covers the expenditures of the orchestra. Necessary also are the contributions of members of the Symphony Society and other individuals. The latter range from the crumpled dollar bill the small mountain boy drew out of his faded overalls pocket and presented to a symphony chairman at the end of a concert in Hickory, to a check for $10,000 sent from the Burlington Mills.

The North Carolina Symphony travels some 8000 miles by bus per season and plays to around 50,000 adults and 140,000 children in some 56 communities. As the years pass there are fewer and fewer large places claiming four walls and a roof in the whole state of North Carolina that have not resounded to Beethoven and Wagner, to Debussy and Sibelius and American composers.

With the same energy that Swalin puts into his hobby of mountain climbing—he has scaled rugged heights in the Alps, the Green and White mountains of New England, and the Great Smokies of western North Carolina—he undertakes his orchestral duties. He fills so many extracurricular roles that to call him a "conductor" is to widen considerably the meaning of the word.

To him, this is as it should be. "The conductor," he is never tired of reiterating, "isn't a space man, isn't a strange bird from another planet. He is part of the local scene. He must be well equipped in his special field, just as is the businessman or the scientist in his. It is not true that he lives in a place apart or thinks differently from other human beings."

Whatever Swalin's tactics, it is a fact that each year sees new communities and new people won to music. The grownups who as children listened to master works in symphonic literature would feel lost without them. Adult audiences in the mountains and along the coast of North Carolina consider great music to be their right and heritage.

CHAPTER XXVII

➤➤ GEORGE SZELL

"I AM a musician who loves music. I want to make music to the best of my ability. My happiest moments have been those in which I have succeeded in doing some justice to the great works I am permitted to perform." As George Szell, conductor of the Cleveland Orchestra, says this in his low, even voice, one realizes that here is a conductor who is the very symbol of his profession, one wholly conditioned to, focused on, his craft. In his quick sensing of situations; in his careful planning of work schedules; in his ability to "interpret" people instantly, to realize their bent and their disposition; in his tendency to become involved only in such experiences as further musical ends—he is the conductor off the podium as well as on it.

When one first sees Mr. Szell, one thinks of the college professor—one whose campus could be any country, one doing research on the whole world. Not that he has the professorial stoop or the absent-minded stare. He stands straight and tall, moves with deliberate swiftness, and looks out keenly through his thick-lensed glasses. Still, those eyes he turns on the world are the searching eyes of the student and the teacher.

Though George Szell was born in Budapest on June 7, 1897, and though he spent his boyhood and young manhood in Vienna, it is Czechoslovakia he thinks of as his homeland. His mother's ancestors came from there. He spent many happy years conducting there. He is married to a Czechoslovak, Helen Schultz. However, it is Szell's internationality rather than his nationality that impresses one. He handles five or six languages as though they were his mother tongue. He is absolutely impartial in his orchestral repertoire. Since 1939 he has accepted the United States unequivocally as his home.

The roads of Szell's life began early to converge on music. At the age of three—the year the family moved to Vienna—he learned to sing forty different folk songs. From the age of four he "superintended" his mother's piano practice, standing at her side and tapping her wrist with a pencil when she hit wrong notes. At six he wrote down from memory thirty measures of a composition he had heard the day before. These and other feats convinced his parents that their only child should be given every musical advantage. When he was seven, therefore, they put him in the charge of Richard Robert, whom Szell describes as "not only a great teacher but a great musician and a great person." He was to be the boy's teacher for ten years.

At the age of eleven George Szell made his debut as a composer-pianist with the Vienna Symphony, in the Grosse Musikverein-saal, the Carnegie Hall of that city. Besides Mendelssohn and Mozart concertos, he played his own Rondo for Piano and Orchestra. The program was topped off with an overture, also of his workmanship. In his adult life he has made a hobby of composing and has had a number of works published. His transcriptions for orchestra, especially of Smetana works, are well known.

Vienna was just the city for an impressionable and musically gifted youth. Gustav Mahler, at the helm of the Vienna Imperial Opera House from 1897 to 1907, had made that famous old institution the center of the European musical world. Young George's teacher in composition, Joseph Bohuslav Foerster, who was a close friend of Mahler's, never tired of relating instances of the great man's musical prowess. Szell remembers being taken, when he was eight years old, to see the new mountings of Mozart's *Don*

Giovanni and of being particularly impressed by the two gray towers that stood as a frame to the stage. He watched with fascination the way Mahler let his baton shoot forward like an arrow out of a bow. The boy was also taken to hear a succession of Richard Strauss works, as well as the innovations of the much-hissed Schönberg. He also became familiar with the baton tactics of Bruno Walter and Felix Weingartner.

At intervals, in the role of child prodigy, he visited other cities —Prague, Dresden, London. In the last named he played as piano soloist four times under the batons of such masters as Sir Landon Ronald and Fernández Arbós.

His veering finally toward conducting was a case of the conducting profession choosing him rather than of his choosing conducting. "It might have been those four or five hours a day I had to put in on piano practice that made conducting seem so alluring," he says, but adds ruefully, "Little did I know that in the end conducting would exact even more hours a day of study!"

He was given a chance to try his luck with that "complex human instrument," the symphony orchestra, during a series of concerts the Vienna Symphony gave in Bad Kissingen in the summer of 1913. Its conductor had injured his arm. The sixteen-year-old Szell, vacationing there, was asked to substitute. Without having rehearsed the orchestra, without having ever rehearsed or directed any orchestra in his whole life, he took over the baton. The concert was a success. Having discovered the miraculous potentialities of the small white stick, he was never again to relinquish it.

As a composer-pianist already known to the public, George Szell had an advantage over most aspiring conductors of his age. Thus, when he was only seventeen, he appeared with the Berlin Philharmonic, in the triple capacity of conductor, pianist, and composer. The program, he remembers, consisted of Beethoven's *Emperor* Concerto, Richard Strauss's *Till Eulenspiegel,* and a symphony of his own composition.

Soon after this concert, Szell met Leo Blech, a director at the Berlin State Opera, and through him got the post of coach in that famous house. No sooner had he started his work than Richard Strauss, who was the ranking general music director there, recognized his ability and took him under his wing. It was a particularly copious wing to be taken under. Strauss, for instance, gave the first performance of Szell's *Variations for Orchestra,* which subsequently had over eighty performances all over the world.

In 1917 Strauss gave the young man another boost. He recommended him for the conductorship of the State Theater in Strasbourg. Szell remained there only one season, however, before seeking wider experiences. For the next six years he was successively principal conductor in the German Opera House in Prague, in the Court Theater in Darmstadt, and in the Municipal Theater in Düsseldorf. By 1924 he was back at the Berlin State Opera, but now as its principal conductor.

Szell stayed in this post five years. In Berlin he also taught at the State Academy of Music. From the start he liked teaching. He was to enter this field again and again.

Then for eight years, beginning in 1929, Szell transferred his activities to his "home city," Prague, as General Music Director of the Philharmonic Concerts and the German Opera House, and as teacher at the Academy of Music and Dramatic Arts. He guest conducted widely during these years—in Vienna, Berlin, London, Leningrad, Amsterdam, The Hague, Brussels, Stockholm, and Copenhagen. In 1930 and 1931 he filled engagements with the St. Louis Symphony.

Then in 1937 a visit to Glasgow to conduct the Scottish Orchestra turned into a resident conductorship. For a part of the 1937–38 and the 1938–39 seasons, he also conducted the Residentie Orchestra in The Hague.

At this point any crystal-gazer would have predicted for Szell a future mainly in the European arena. However, wars have a way of upsetting predictions. During the years 1938 and 1939, Szell had carried his summer conducting assignments as far as Australia, flying from England to direct the Celebrity Concerts of the Australian Broadcasting Commission in Sydney, Melbourne, and other cities. As he was returning through the United States to Scotland in 1939, he was halted by news of the outbreak of World War II. About the same time he received notification that the Scottish Orchestra would be suspended for the duration.

America had always seemed to him a likely place for conductorial enterprise. Now that he had no commitments to call him elsewhere, he decided to stay in this country.

This forty-two-year-old man in the hotel room in New York City scanning a new world and a new turn in his career—what were his thoughts? If these elude us, his activities are more traceable. After taking the routine steps toward making his presence in this country known, he no doubt filled in any free time he had in much the same way he fills in his vacations—in brushing up his piano technique and freshening his score interpretations.

The violinist Henri Temianka describes, for instance, a vacation they spent together on the Italian Lake Como. "There was little to do on those quiet summer evenings," he relates in an article in *Etude* for May 1953. "A game of bridge or a stroll along the lake would terminate in a glass of *grappa* on the terrace of a café. Soon we were spending our evenings, and many of our days, making music on the hotel lounge piano for our own amusement and that of any guest who happened by. It was a typical busman's holiday. We went through practically every violin concerto or sonata I had ever heard, Szell helping me out when my memory failed. He never skipped a bar of a *tutti*. We played everything (even *God Save the Queen*) in variations. . . . The next evening Szell started out playing the Overture of Mozart's *Don Giovanni*. But he did not stop after the Overture. He stopped three hours later, having played Strauss's *Till Eulen-*

spiegel as an encore. Everything from Beethoven's Opus 131 to Schubert's Two Cello Quintet emerged from Szell's infallible mental filing system."

By 1940 Szell was in harness again. He secured a teaching job in the newly organized opera workshop at the New School for Social Research in New York, and became head of the theory department at the Mannes College of Music. In his instruction he emphasized again and again, "A conductor must have not only a good memory, a faultless sense of rhythm and, preferably, absolute pitch, but also a thorough training in all the disciplines of music such as harmony, counterpoint, form, orchestration, scorereading. He should also have the insight and imagination which will enable him to slip into the skin, as it were, of each composer he interprets, in order to transmit the composer's message to his listeners. Above all, he must have that not easily defined power of communication which will carry through to the orchestra men as well as to his listeners."

In 1941 Toscanini invited him to conduct the NBC Symphony, and he made his formal debut as conductor in this country. The orchestra men, used to the rigors of Toscanini's rehearsals, noted the exacting approach of this conductor, his capacity for infinite pains in preparation, his inability to compromise where music was concerned. They noted also his erudition—his ability, as his friend, the violin virtuoso Joseph Szigeti, puts it, "to meet the whole violin section of an orchestra on common ground and suggest ingenious fingerings and bowings that would never have occurred to that body of experts." *

Szell's guest conductorships multiplied. He led the Boston, Philadelphia, Chicago, Detroit, and Los Angeles orchestras. In 1942 and 1943 he was guest conductor at the Metropolitan Opera House. In the 1944–45 season he became regular conductor there,

* From *With Strings Attached,* by Joseph Szigeti, Alfred A. Knopf, 1947.

terminating his connections with that organization in 1954. He also directed four performances of the New York Philharmonic-Symphony, an engagement that has since been repeated.

Early in 1945, among his other guest conductorships, Szell went to the Cleveland Orchestra for a two-week engagement. In December he repeated the visit. The house was jammed. The audience thundered applause. In January 1946 Cleveland signed him to a three-year contract on his own terms—no less than "complete authority in all artistic matters" and the means, as he put it, "of making the orchestra second to none." Even before the opening of his first season there, the Thursday and Saturday evening series were completely sold out.

Szell fully appreciates his position as musical director of an orchestra (with a $6,000,000 endowment) entirely at his disposal. "We aim," he says, "at combining the virtuosity and polish that are characteristic of top-ranking American orchestras with the expressive warmth of typically European orchestras in their best days"; and he adds dryly, as reporters lean forward to catch any slightest overtones of dissatisfaction, "If you give me a week, I might think of a gripe."

In January 1955 Szell received the Laurel Leaf Award of the American Composers Alliance "for distinguished service to contemporary music." He has also received the National Music Council Award for distinguished service to American music.

Szell continues to be in demand as a guest conductor on podiums in Europe. The closest ties seem to be those with the Salzburg Festival. In 1953 he was entrusted with the world première of Rolf Liebermann's *Penelope* and in 1954 with the world première of Werner Egk's *The Irish Legend*. In the Mozart year of 1956 he did the new production of *The Abduction from the Seraglio*.

With all his conducting responsibilities, George Szell is still the teacher. When the Conductors' Workshop, a school for young conductors under the auspices of the American Symphony Orchestra League, is held in Cleveland, Szell not only allows the twenty or so young conductors who assemble at these sessions full use of his experience but also full use of his treasured Cleveland Orchestra. At the close of each composition he goes to the point of the difficulty with the unerring precision of a surgeon. He discusses which kind of beat is demanded by the character of the composition, how one knits together soloist and orchestra into an integrated whole, how one helps orchestral choirs with their intricate and varying rhythmic patterns while conveying a single musical idea to the listener.

Hear about Szell's hobbies—stirring up delectable dishes in the streamlined kitchen of his Cleveland home, playing bridge, collecting odd journalistic misprints—and one still does not know the man. Nor do audiences become acquainted with him. He is not one to give heart-to-heart pre-concert talks to his assembled listeners or to wax eloquent before radio loudspeakers.

It is the students perhaps who know him best. Watching his blue eyes kindle, becoming aware of the intensity of his thought and of the concentration in every move and gesture, listening to his low, sustained voice, they get to the very heart of his credo, namely that the conductor's task is to absorb in one's very bloodstream the structure of the work, to go the same path the composer went in the process of creation.

CHAPTER XXVIII

⇶ EDUARD VAN BEINUM

ALTHOUGH Eduard van Beinum, conductor of the Los Angeles
Philharmonic, has held a long-term conductorship in London and
been guest conductor on the principal podiums of Europe and
America, his home base throughout his career has been Holland.
He was born there, in Arnhem, on September 3, 1900; he studied
there; and since 1931 he has been conductor of Holland's principal orchestra, the Amsterdam Concertgebouw.

Holland, for all its diversified artistic life, is a small and closely
knit country. Its inhabitants are noted for their sturdiness and
their thoroughness. Van Beinum shows these qualities in his
conducting. He gives balanced performances with minute attention to detail. He directs his men with no show and fuss, but
with extreme clarity.

When he toured the United States with the Concertgebouw
Orchestra in 1954, the critics marked the lack of "excessive ges-
ticulation," of "frills and monkeyshines," of "theatricalities."
Kenneth Gill, music critic of Buffalo, noted that this feeling
carried over to the orchestra. "No tension obviously grips the
players, or such tonal excellence from strings, woodwinds and
brass could not have been accomplished." The least enthusiastic
of the critics, Kurt Blaukopf, remarked in *Great Conductors,**
"a cautious thoroughness, at times a purposeful aridity in his
music-making," but added that this was "a clear and distinct con-

---

* Arco Publishers, Ltd., 1955.

fession of his musical creed," and that "the aim was to reveal the substance of the music."

Music has always been a family affair with Eduard van Beinum. His ancestors for centuries have supplied the town of Arnhem with chorus masters and military band leaders. Eduard's elder brother gave him his first lessons on the piano and the violin. The boy also studied the viola. He became a member of the Arnhem Orchestra when he was seventeen and won a scholarship to the Amsterdam Conservatory at eighteen. Here he concentrated on the piano.

After his graduation Van Beinum appeared as piano soloist with various Dutch orchestras. As chorus master in Zutfen and Schiedam he sometimes conducted an orchestral work included on the programs—and thus came into the profession, as he says, "somewhat by accident."

However he entered the field of conducting, he took to it and it took to him. With crisp and clear cues, firm beat, and absolute authority he gives orchestra men a feeling of security.

Van Beinum played several times as soloist with the Haarlem Orchestra. In 1927 its conductor resigned. Van Beinum wrote inquiring about the possibility of getting the job. He was asked to come to Haarlem for an audition.

The audition was carried out with Dutch thoroughness. The nine applicants were tested before a commission consisting of Cornelis Dopper, Peter van Anrooy and Professor Stronk. One test was to conduct the orchestra and soloist in portions of three concertos in one hour. Another was to rehearse Beethoven's Seventh Symphony during one hour. As a final test, Van Beinum had to choose between Wagner's *Meistersinger* Prelude, Berlioz' *Roman Carnival Overture* and Dukas' *The Sorcerer's Apprentice*. Van Beinum chose the last, came out number one and was engaged.

During his four years in Haarlem, he conducted the Haarlem

Roman Catholic Choral Society as well as the orchestra. This period also saw his marriage to Sepha Jansen, an accomplished violinist. The couple have two sons, both of whom, in the family tradition, are musicians, one an organist, the other a symphony orchestra violinist.

In 1931 an opening occurred in the Concertgebouw Orchestra of Amsterdam for an assistant conductor. Its conductor, Willem Mengelberg had heard about Van Beinum's success in Haarlem and got in touch with him. Van Beinum on his part was eager to be associated with one of the greatest orchestras of Europe— for even then the Concertgebouw was famous for its musicianship and its enterprise. It gave eighty to ninety concerts annually in Amsterdam, besides regular subscription concerts in other Dutch cities—The Hague, Rotterdam, Utrecht, Arnhem, Nijmegen, and Haarlem. Mengelberg, who had conducted it since 1895, was noted for the refinement of his technique. A young conductor could learn much from him. Van Beinum gladly accepted the assistant conductorship.

Even during the early years there, he conducted actively. By 1937 he had gained a reputation not only for his excellent work with the Concertgebouw, but also for his work on an extensive tour made throughout Russia with the Leningrad Philharmonic. In 1938 he received the title of "first conductor," while Mengelberg remained as "music director."

World War II brought a curtailment of the orchestra's activities. After 1945, however, musical life was liberated along with the country. Mengelberg was declared by Dutch authorities to be "guilty of unpermissible dealings with the Nazis in direct opposition to national honor" and to be undeserving of "ever again raising a baton in the Netherlands." He never did.

Van Beinum, now the Concertgebouw's regular conductor, began taking the orchestra on extensive tours—to France, Belgium, Scotland, Denmark, Sweden, and Switzerland. In 1953 it made its first postwar tour to Germany. The success of these visits drew attention to his growing powers and led to his appointment as conductor of the London Philharmonic. He appeared there annually from 1949 to 1952, holding the post along with his Concertgebouw conductorship.

In 1954 he made his United States debut, conducting the Philadelphia Orchestra. The same year he toured America with the Concertgebouw.

From the start he was enthusiastically received. "A leader possessing cogent ideas in the matters of tonal quality and balance," said Felix Borowski in the Chicago *Daily Sun-Times*. "His music is warm and persuasive, solid in its tempos and not perverse in its dynamics," said Day Thorpe in the Washington *Evening Star*. "The high musicianship and evident idealism of Mr. Van Beinum made the occasion a triumph of art," said *The New York Times*.

In the summer of 1955 he spent several weeks in the United States as guest conductor with the Chicago Symphony at Ravinia; with the Symphony of the Air at Ellenville, New York; with the Los Angeles Philharmonic at Hollywood Bowl. Despite the vagaries of out-of-door conducting, he made the Philharmonic sound homogeneous and rich-toned. In the winter season he returned to guest conduct the orchestra. In January 1956, he was appointed its musical director.

His schedule with the Los Angeles Philharmonic consists of two months annually, January and February, a period coinciding with his yearly leave of absence from the Concertgebouw. Thus he is one of a very few conductors heading two major orchestras at once.

The Los Angeles tenure has meant profit on both sides. Van Beinum finds the colorful pattern of California life stimulating, and Californians feel rested and secure in this conductor's music of simple and sound texture.

CHAPTER XXIX

⇛ ROBERT WHITNEY

"GENTLEMEN, we are not the Brooklyn Dodgers!" A slight, dark-haired man with a toothbrush mustache and keen eyes set deep under a high forehead gets to his feet in Columbia Auditorium in Louisville, Kentucky, and swings around to face the audience. It is an audience assembled for a panel discussion on "art versus entertainment" at the third Annual Music Critics Workshop held in Louisville in October 1955. The question has been raised whether modern music is good "box office." The man who has somewhat testily stated his opinion is Robert Whitney, conductor of the Louisville Orchestra.

Not that Whitney, born and bred American, has anything against the Dodgers. His belief, to which he has consistently adhered during his twenty years of conductorship of the Louisville Orchestra, is that the role of the symphony orchestra is not merely to draw audiences but to play the music that is being written today and that expresses today's world. "People must catch up with the idea," he says, "that they have to live in the contemporary musical scene—appreciate music as it is now being made, listen to it, judge it. It is only by persistent exposure to this music that they can come to know new serious compositions."

It is because of his determination that the Louisville Plan—a policy resting on the annual commissioning of a certain number of newly created compositions by the world's foremost composers —has today become famous throughout the world.

Robert Whitney is not the virtuoso conductor. He holds to the exact boundaries of his calling as he sees it: to act as the intermediary between composer and public. His greatest joy is in being able to play middleman to contemporary works—to get them on the market and display them in a sympathetic manner. He couldn't be in a better position for carrying out this purpose. For from 1948 through 1956, to name just nine years in his tenure in Louisville, he personally conducted eighty-four premières of contemporary works.

Whitney's good luck in having such a job might be attributed to his having something of the adventurer as well as something of the crusader in him. He blithely admits he just "blundered into" this position in Louisville, which he calls "the most enviable one for any musician in the world."

His adventuring started early. American from birth, he happened to be born in England. His father was on a two-year tour there as tuba player in the Cowboy Band, a unit of a Buffalo Bill Wild West Show. He met and married an English girl, and on July 6, 1904, the couple had their first child—young Robert.

The baby's birth, in midseason, was cause for general rejoicing by the members of the band. Gifts were showered on him—a miniature saddle, chaps, spurs. However, Robert was not to be a trouper long. When he was eight months old, his parents, deciding that now they had started a family, circus life was no longer for them, headed for America and settled in Chicago. His father got a job as double-bass at the old Olympic Theatre. Young Robert used to like to sit beside him in the pit, not only because the orchestra members gave him chewing gum and candy but also because he enjoyed listening to the blended sounds of the instruments.

As he grew older he kept pestering his father to let him study music. The elder Whitney at first refused. With two generations behind him of ardent but often financially embarrassed musicians, he thought the profession a poor business risk. By the time Robert was eleven, however, he was taking lessons. He studied first with Marx Oberndorfer, then at eighteen matriculated at the American Conservatory of Music, where Rudolph Reuter was his piano teacher and Arthur Olaf Andersen and Leo Sowerby his teachers in theory and composition.

Meanwhile he had been playing in a family trio (Robert, piano; Grace, cello; Noreen, violin) and, as two other sisters grew up, in a quintet. In the late twenties they all toured the country one month out of every year, and for nine years broadcast successively over WMAQ and NBC in Chicago.

In the depression of 1931, Whitney found himself out of a job. Eric De Lamarter, conductor of the Chicago Civic Orchestra, was making up a class in conducting, and young Whitney was accepted for it. At this time he came under the influence of Frederick Stock, conductor of the Chicago Symphony. Stock encouraged Whitney in his composing—in fact, premièred his *Concerto Grosso* with the great Chicago Symphony.

In 1932 De Lamarter let Whitney have a try at leading the Chicago Civic Orchestra. To really feel at home on the podium, though, the young man knew he would have to follow De Lamarter's advice: "Get an orchestra of your own. Learn from experience!"

Whitney kept on the lookout, and when he heard the Louisville was in need of a conductor, put in his bid and was engaged. In the fall of 1937 he and his bride, Margaret Gilbert, who had to give up her teaching position in Chicago to go with him, headed for Louisville. He shrugs off any implications of special foresight in taking the step. "I didn't have any feeling of fate guiding my footsteps. When you're young you don't think about those things. Just about then there was a real dearth of musical opportunities. The bottom had fallen out of everything. It was the right time to make a fresh start."

The Louisville Philharmonic, which Whitney faced on his arrival in this town famous for Bourbon whisky and the Kentucky Derby, lacked a full complement of players. Skilled instrumentalists, especially in the wind section, had to be imported for concerts. Many a time Whitney had occasion to bless the presence of the army bandsmen at nearby Fort Knox.

However, musicians brought in from outside for concerts are a little like borrowed silverware at a family party. They'll serve the purpose, but it's awkward having to explain their presence. As long as the tuba, the bassoon, or the French horn players are strangers, the orchestra isn't yet part of the community.

Then, too, in the early days, the concerts were held in the huge Memorial Hall, which no amount of ingenuity could fill. Empty seats in a concert hall are always disheartening. Finally, hiring expensive big-name soloists—the usual procedure to boost ticket sales—drained the resources of the orchestra.

Season by season the Louisville Philharmonic found itself deeper in debt. Just as things looked very black indeed, a savior appeared on the scene. In 1948 the board of aldermen of Louisville appointed Charles Rowland Peaslee Farnsley to the post of mayor. He proved to be the conductor's dream of what a city administrator ought to be. In fact, he was the means of launching a government-in-culture program unmatched in the history of that or any other American city.

He wasn't in office ten days before he and Robert Whitney had gone into a huddle. The result was the formation of the "Louisville Plan." It was threefold in scope: (1) The size of the orchestra was reduced to fifty members and "Philharmonic" dropped from the title. (2) The orchestra was moved to a smaller hall. (3) The orchestra became a channel for introducing modern compositions.

Time has proved these changes to have been practical as well as artistically sound. At its reduced size, the Louisville Orchestra can be made up entirely of professional musicians commanding professional fees. The players are encouraged in other ways. Since rehearsals and performances are fixed for evenings, Saturdays, and other out-of-work-schedule hours, the players are able to hold full-time positions in a variety of capacities. Some are clerks, jewelers, chemists, salesmen. The great majority, however, have taken teaching jobs, not only in the elementary schools and the high schools but also at the university. This has meant an enrichment not only to them but to the community at large.

Another advantage of the reduced size: the orchestra is convenient for recording and radio sessions and for making one-day bus tours through Kentucky.

The small Columbia Hall, besides being both acoustically and aesthetically satisfying, is as a rule sold out for each performance.

It is the orchestra's emphasis on modern composers, however, that has reaped for it the richest rewards. From the start it was Mayor Farnsley's idea to present one new composition at every regular subscription concert of the orchestra—a composition, moreover, especially ordered, composed, and purchased for the occasion. This system has been in effect since 1948. The scope of the project was further extended in April 1953, when the Rockefeller Foundation awarded a grant of $400,000 to the Louisville Orchestra "to encourage and foster the creation, performance and recording of new musical works by living composers."

Naturally this plan has helped the composers. Twelve hundred dollars is paid for each symphonic work, $4000 for each opera. And not only have the composers been well paid; their works have been widely publicized. Each composition is performed by the orchestra at least three times publicly and is recorded on LP discs which are offered for sale. The two series released in 1955 and 1956 have found listeners all over the world. The reports have been illuminating. Francis A. Klein wrote in the St. Louis *Globe,* "All [the recorded works] are expertly performed by the

Louisville Orchestra under the vital and inspiring leadership of Robert Whitney, who evinces an innate feeling for these untried works which presents them with their best foot forward. His orchestra is keenly alert and shows amazing flexibility in coping adequately with the diverse styling. The reproductions are a model of clarity."

Many of the works have been broadcast over the Columbia network in foreign lands through Radio Free Europe.

Student composers are encouraged, too. Awards of $500 each are offered annually for orchestra compositions by students. These works are given at least one performance and are tape-recorded for the composers' private use.

The orchestra has reaped gains from the project. The composers are contracted to compose works for a fifty-member group and with the precise instrumentation of the Louisville Orchestra in mind. The orchestra is thus provided with compositions tailored to fit its needs. Also, the audiences receive the challenge of new contemporary works at every sitting.

A most happy by-product of this system of commissioning compositions has been the appearance at the concerts of the composers themselves. It is exciting to have, say, Virgil Thomson or William Schuman or Roy Harris or Robert Russell Bennett stand up in the audience and perhaps give a few words of explanation. In some instances the composer actually conducts his work. This personal contact gives to symphony music the same composed-on-the-spot aura that makes name-band music so stimulating.

With this new arrangement at his command, Whitney came into his full powers. The Louisville Orchestra became world famous. From the years 1948 to 1956 it presented 117 world premières, and by the end of the 1955–56 season nearly 200 subsequent performances of these new works had been given by orchestras throughout the world.

In December 1950 the orchestra was flown to New York to

perform some of these commissioned works. The audience in Carnegie Hall got a new slant on musical pioneering. "New Yorkers who think that everything exciting in the artistic world originates on their side of the Hudson had a valuable object lesson to the contrary with this first visit of the Louisville Orchestra," said "R.S." in *Musical America*. Said Paul Affelder in the Brooklyn *Eagle,* "New York likes to pride itself on being the music capital of the nation—perhaps the world. But two weeks ago last Friday, a complacent segment of the city's music-loving public, assembled in Carnegie Hall, had a rude awakening. . . . The startling fact is that all six compositions were specially commissioned by the Louisville group." "A program of daring and novelty put New York's own name bands to shame," said Louis Biancolli of the New York *World-Telegram and Sun*.

As for Whitney's conducting, the reviews mostly stressed his extreme conscientiousness in carrying out the composer's intentions. "Mr. Whitney caught something of the individual character of each composition," said R.S. in *Musical America*. Harold C. Schonberg in *The New York Times* called him "a precise craftsman who has thoroughly learned the scores and has decisive ideas about how they should be played."

Mr. Whitney's preparation of new compositions for their public hearings shows a man doing what he was meant to do. "I approach a new score," he says, "via the keyboard. I sing and play it straight through as a piano score and after that combine it all into structural patterns or phrases. In course of doing this, I am careful to check if the tempo markings the composer gives are the ones he really wants. The transfer from the desk to the podium involves new conditions which he sometimes cannot foretell. Of course, with us the composer usually comes down for the first performance and we can then get together to make the necessary adjustments.

"My next move is to pass out the parts to the orchestra, so

that they can work out the difficult passages. At the first rehearsals we usually have a quick run-through and then attack
the rough spots, correcting as we go along the mistakes in the
orchestral parts, and coming to the necessary agreements regarding the balance between various sections of the orchestra."

Once the regular rehearsals are begun, the idea is to get the
orchestra in the spirit of the thing—play it so that it gives the
composer's meaning. Whitney believes that his experience as
composer—he has many published works to his credit—helps
him to conduct. "You have to conduct from the inside—you have
to know the compositions as though you had written them." To
get this inside knowledge of the composition across to the orchestra requires, he believes, "a communication which is practically
telepathic. The conductor in a sense sings with the orchestra. His
eyes and facial expressions convey as much as his gestures."

Mr. Whitney finds the preparation of every one of the commissioned works interesting. As a sort of symbol of the creative
aspect of his calling, he conducts with batons he has made himself. Original sticks for original works!

Whitney has many off-podium duties. The tables in his office
are stacked with mimeographed releases. Telephones ring and
typewriters tattoo messages for all parts of the world. Since the
terms of the Rockefeller grant specify that one-third of the composer output must come from outside the United States, Mr.
Whitney has latterly been going on scouting trips to Europe.
While there he often conducts. For instance in the summer of
1956 he was the means of shifting first-performance procedure
from East-West to West-East when he conducted the European
premières of two works commissioned by the Louisville Orchestra after they had received their world premières in America.

Whitney serves as musical adviser to F.M. Station WFPL of
the Louisville Public Library. He is a director of Artists of Louisville, Inc., an organization that makes soloists of outstanding

ability available to the community. He is also dean of the School of Music of the University of Louisville.

His varied activities have brought him varied honors. Radio Station WHAS in Louisville gave him a citation for "introducing tens of thousands of children to the magic of music" and for "encouraging new compositions and helping make the orchestra's music known across the nation." In 1951 the Alice M. Ditson Fund named him recipient of its seventh annual award of $1000 for "distinguished service to American music." The University of Louisville in bestowing on him an honorary doctorate of music (June 2, 1952) stated, "You have brought distinction and renown to this city, this state, and this country by the musical integrity that has governed your direction for fifteen years of the Louisville Orchestra." On May 22, 1956, he received the Laurel Leaf Award, presented each year by the American Composers Alliance, for "distinguished service to contemporary music."

All these honors emphasize Whitney's contribution to contemporary music. This is altogether fitting. For it is due in good part to him—his critical powers, his interpretative skill, his untiring enthusiasm—that the Louisville Orchestra has become one of the richest sources of encouragement to the contemporary composer anywhere in the world.

PART II

Conductors at Large

CHAPTER XXX

❧ ERICH LEINSDORF

A CHARACTERISTIC gesture of Erich Leinsdorf, as he sits at table or desk, is to edge out with his elbows—as if he were resolved to get the maximum of comfort and freedom out of every inch of space. Such is his gesture toward life. He refuses to become tense and nerve-ridden, self-centered, or occupation-obsessed. His duties as widely traveled guest conductor and as conductor of opera at the Metropolitan and elsewhere are accomplished with sanity and balance. He enjoys his home life, talks and writes on a variety of subjects, and seeks success consistently, but never at the cost of distorting his personality. "It is less important to make a great career than it is to make it on one's own terms," he says.

Leinsdorf was born in Vienna on February 4, 1912. At seven he was taking lessons on the piano, but he was ten before, as he put it, he "saw any meaning in music." About that time he began browsing through the music left by his father, an out-of-office-hours pianist of some attainment, who had died when Erich was under three. The volumes—he remembers they were hand-bound in rough paper—contained many pieces that the boy tried over on the piano. His method from the first was more the interpreter's, less the technician's. He quickly absorbed one and then passed on to the next. His aim was to get a sense of the different approaches and developments, the "feel" of the composition. This, he holds, was a useful preliminary to his career as conductor.

By the time he was seventeen Leinsdorf had stopped practicing altogether in the usual sense. When his teacher said something about his never becoming a pianist if he didn't keep at his scales, he flung back, "Who wants to be a pianist anyway!" At that very instant, he says, "The idea of becoming a conductor first entered my head."

Later, feeling "a conductor who cannot play the piano well has two strikes against him, it is his first line of defense," he took up the piano again, but under another teacher, Hedwig Kanner-Rosenthal, the wife of Moriz Rosenthal. She taught him with a conductor's career in view, so that he might play with the instrumentalists at rehearsals, or, in oratorio presentation, coach the singers from the keyboard.

Leinsdorf had to get his higher education—musical and otherwise—on a scholarship basis. His mother was willing to give him every educational advantage possible, but she hadn't enough money to pay for his tuition.

Being a scholarship student amounted to working his way through school, since he was expected to run errands for his teacher, copy music and make himself generally useful. Far from finding the routine distasteful, he looks back on this period with satisfaction. To his way of thinking, more bad repute has been brought to the profession of music by a mistaken sense of dignity than by any other one thing. "If I were thrown back to the point where I was twenty years ago," he says, "I would feel no qualms whatever at starting again. I'd fill in. I'd somehow make the grade."

When Leinsdorf was eighteen he attended the University of Vienna—in the department of music, which was a division of the School of Philosophy. He soon discovered, however, that none of the other students could play an instrument, that they were all of them rank amateurs or mere theoreticians. That was enough for him. He left after the first year. Leinsdorf's real alma mater was the State Academy of Music in Vienna. Here he studied composition, theory, piano, cello—all subjects that might possibly be of assistance to him in his conducting career.

That this career would have to be pursued outside his native country became apparent to Leinsdorf by the time he was twenty-two. For even then, in 1934, the shadow of Hitler was beginning to loom not only over musical Germany but over musical Austria as well. Salzburg was still artistically free, however; and to the Salzburg Festival, where Bruno Walter was conducting that season, Leinsdorf determined to go. Salzburg was 155 miles away and money for the train ticket was lacking, so he hitchhiked.

When he arrived at the Festspielhaus he was tired and dusty. No matter. He walked right into the building. Walter happened to be at the piano, rehearsing *Don Giovanni*. When the maestro left off for a moment to cross the stage and advise an artist, Leinsdorf decided, "Now or never!" He slipped to the keyboard and took up the phrase just where it had been interrupted—from memory. Walter was impressed, and after a talk with the young man made him coach for the preliminary period of the festival.

As for the festival itself, he got in on it through a curious set of circumstances. The Italian singers were in desperate straits. Unlike the German and Austrian contingents, they were used to being prompted by singing cues rather than merely spoken ones. The prompter, however, was a retired actor of the Vienna Opera and could only speak the lines. Leinsdorf noticed one of the distraught Italians—his name was Ezio Pinza—frantically trying to explain their predicament to the prompter and getting nowhere, since the prompter spoke no Italian and Pinza no German. Leinsdorf, since he knew both languages, helpfully translated for the singer and illustrated by singing the cues.

"That's it! That's how it must be done!" shouted Pinza. Later he drew Leinsdorf aside and begged him to help with the prompting, telling him he would intercede with the management. As a result Leinsdorf was hired—and for the whole festival! "You see," Leinsdorf grins, "I really learned the opera business from the bottom up!"

This would seem just a lucky break. But there's the fact that Leinsdorf had learned Italian. Asked why he had bothered to do this, he shrugs, "A musician who is interested in opera should know Italian. Back there in my conservatory days, I decided German translations of opera were so terribly stupid. If I knew Italian I could do a better job. So I just learned it."

The festival over, Leinsdorf went back to Vienna. Toscanini was conducting a series of symphony concerts there that winter. They were looking for a rehearsal pianist for Kodály's *Psalmus Hungaricus,* one who would suit the maestro's exacting tastes. Leinsdorf knew he could do it. He went to the first rehearsal, asked for a tryout, landed the job. Toscanini's praise encouraged him to apply for an assistant conductorship the next summer in Salzburg. The maestro accepted him for that, too.

This time he worked in Salzburg as assistant to both Walter and Toscanini. It kept him busy—practicing with the orchestra, directing the chorus, coaching soloists, carrying on discussions with stage directors. During three seasons there, he prepared the artists and chorus practically alone for *Falstaff, Fidelio, Meistersinger,* and *The Magic Flute,* as well as for Beethoven's Ninth Symphony and the Verdi and Brahms Requiems. Meanwhile, in winters he was a guest conductor in Italy, Belgium, and France.

Leinsdorf discounts the idea, however, that at this or any other time in his career he was overworked. "I happen to be able to learn quickly," he says. "I never feel that I am working hard. I enjoy it. A cocktail party tires me more than four opera rehearsals."

The months between late 1935 and early 1937 were restless ones, with the spread of Hitler's doctrines and the lessening of opportunities in Austria. Leinsdorf spent most of the time in Italy, where he conducted in Bologna, Trieste, and San Remo. The summers he spent in Salzburg. But 1937 was the last, not only for him but for Toscanini and Walter. Austria's great musicians were scattering.

It was natural that Leinsdorf should turn toward America at this point. A chance finally came to go there. In 1937 Edward Johnson, the manager of the Metropolitan Opera Company, was looking about for an assistant for his overworked chief conductor, Artur Bodanzky. Toscanini put in a good word for Leinsdorf, and the young man was engaged sight unseen. His duties, it was presumed, were to consist largely of piano rehearsals with the singers. They did not know their Leinsdorf.

Before many months had gone by he had convinced them that, in his case at least, the assistant conductor should be actively conducting. Experimentally, he was asked to direct one act of *Die Walküre* in full dress rehearsal. With the final chord, the Metropolitan orchestra—a hard-to-please group if ever there was one—and the artists on the stage all rose and applauded. On the strength of this and of his obvious ability in all aspects of opera conducting, Leinsdorf was assigned to conduct the actual *Die Walküre* performance the following week.

Lawrence Gilman said in the New York *Herald Tribune* of this debut of January 21, 1938, "They saw an astonishingly boyish figure, short, small of build, graceful, with one or two of the familiar gestures of his great master, Toscanini. Though he wiped his brow occasionally with his handkerchief, he soon made it evident that he was entirely at home." Gilman spoke also of Leinsdorf's "remarkable musical memory," his "clear and intelligible beat," and his "music feeling, taste and authority."

In 1938 he also began his conductorships of the San Francisco Opera, starting, as chance would have it, with his favorite opera, *Pelleas and Melisande*.

Then came the illness of Artur Bodanzky, and more and more work devolved on Leinsdorf. On November 23, 1939, Bodanzky died. Soon after, Leinsdorf was given the directorship of the entire Metropolitan German opera repertoire.

To have this twenty-seven-year-old man suddenly fall heir to the principal conducting post at the Metropolitan and acquit himself with honor was quite as spectacular an achievement in the world of music as the feat of Lindbergh spanning the ocean in solo flight twelve years before had been in the field of aviation. Curiously, both these men were born on February 4; both married wives named Anne at the climax of their early careers (Leinsdorf in August 1939); and both have been particularly happy in their home life. Leinsdorf's wife, his three sons, and two daughters are his pride and delight.

Through all the excitement of success the young conductor remained calm, collected, and philosophical. He became the butt of adverse criticism as well as the subject for exaggerated praise. "No one in public life can escape unpleasantness," he said. "It's as much a part of the profession as a full-dress suit. . . . I have no intention of becoming a nervous wreck." In the spring of 1956 he faced with the same equanimity both the praise and blame given him as director of the New York City Opera.

So he conducted, and conducted with sense and insight, while music critics argued, while letters from Metropolitan subscribers stuffed the mailboxes and arguments flared in foyers and dressing rooms. Both the box-office and artistic standards held their own at the Metropolitan, and before the 1939-40 season ended, it was evident that the young man had made good. As time went on— he was there during seven separate seasons all told—the furor died down. It looked as though Leinsdorf were to become a fixture at the Metropolitan.

But the prophets again reckoned without their man. With that characteristic "give me room" gesture of his, Leinsdorf was yearning for a wider variety of musical experiences. He disliked being typed as a "Wagnerian specialist." Besides, there was the vast symphonic literature that he longed to explore. "In symphony conducting," he explains, "the conductor is a larger percentage of the show than in opera. There is not the visual to fall back on, and therefore one's resources must be richer, bigger."

So when in 1943 the Cleveland Orchestra invited him to be their conductor, Leinsdorf lent a willing ear. But it was not destined for him to establish himself in that city. In the fall of that year he was inducted into the United States Army. When a medical discharge came a year later, Cleveland had already lined up guest conductors for the 1944–45 season.

During this and subsequent seasons, "emergency" remained Leinsdorf's steadfast friend. He guest conducted with the orchestras of Havana, St. Louis, Chicago, and Minneapolis, and at the Metropolitan Opera. In the summer of 1946 he went to England to conduct the London Philharmonic. The regular conductor was suddenly taken ill. The result: instead of conducting the scheduled eight concerts, he conducted twenty, touring with the orchestra through England, Scotland, and Ireland.

Such roaming has never ceased to be part of Leinsdorf's annual program and, given his special cast of mind, probably never will cease to be. In 1947, the year he became conductor of the Rochester Philharmonic, he made a European tour that included sixteen appearances with the Vienna State Opera and the Vienna Philharmonic Orchestra, as well as concerts at The Hague, with the Dutch Radio in Hilversum, and with the Royal Orchestra in Copenhagen.

In the 1952–53 season, in addition to fourteen regular concerts with the Rochester Philharmonic and touring with the orchestra, he globe-trotted by land, sea, and air to conduct thirty concerts in Asia, Europe, and America. He appeared with the Tel Aviv Philharmonic, the Philharmonic Orkest of Radio Netherlands, the Philadelphia Orchestra in Robin Hood Dell, the Concertgebouw in Amsterdam. Besides, he conducted a series of eight concerts and radio broadcasts with the San Francisco Symphony.

The 1952–53 season was a rich one in other respects, too. He was given an honorary degree of doctor of music by Rutgers University and was elected president of the International Music Institute, succeeding Dimitri Mitropoulos.

Leinsdorf's tenure with the Rochester Philharmonic (1947–56) proved his marked gift for coordinating various groups concerned in the musical life of that city: the Eastman School of Music, which provides many of the orchestral players; the orchestra, which provides teachers from among its first-desk players; the annual Festival of American Music, which uses musicians from both school and orchestra.

Leinsdorf constantly underlines the need of coordinating a career with one's own development. "Survival is one question," he wrote in the *National Music Council Bulletin* of May 1954, "but another, just as important, is the state in which one manages to survive. Musical organizations which want to survive must find wide popular support. How wide? The measurements of this 'width' are the most important figures we would want to get. If we make it too wide, we'll be vulgarizing ourselves. If we don't make it wide enough, we'll go broke."

Leinsdorf has some very definite ideas, too, about the role of the conductor. He believes it is a job that should be free of business and administrative details; free of worries of promotion, publicity, box office; unhampered by luncheons, dinners, meetings. The present tendency, he fears, is to make the conductor an executive with a side endeavor of conducting.

He confesses the virtual impossibility of achieving his ideal in the present age. However, even in his 1956 season as director of the New York City Opera Company, a job carrying with it as many peripheral duties as any in the field of conducting, he maintained an equilibrium and sanity that mark him as the philosopher among conductors.

CHAPTER XXXI

⇒ PIERRE MONTEUX

PIERRE MONTEUX is a conductor so natural and so sane that it has taken the public, attracted by the spectacular, a long time to appreciate him. He simply directs: no flourishes, no play acting. In his study of scores he tries solely to discover what the composer wants. When he guest conducts orchestras, he has them play accurate interpretations. "Do you want me to play that trill?" asked a violinist, after executing a trill the regular conductor had written in. "Trill?" Monteux questioned. "Did you play a trill? I thought it was just a rather conspicuous vibrato. No—no trill!"

Monteux knows the bounds of his profession. Thus he can step outside them with perfect safety. He makes a marvelous fourth in quartet playing. At the Ravinia summer season in Chicago a few years ago, he filled in when the violist of the Budapest Quartet was unexpectedly delayed. He found a viola—"not *my* viola," he says, "but *a* viola"—took his place in the quartet, and played with such security as to effect a completely smooth ensemble.

This rotund little man, with black curly hair brushed straight back and enormous walrus mustaches, cracks jokes and appreciates jokes others make about him. His wife says, "It amuses Pierre to see younger conductors eye him appraisingly, saying to themselves, 'When is that old bozo going to give up?' But he insists, 'I shall conduct till I'm ninety. I shall die holding a baton.'" At this point, his black eyes twinkling, Monteux interrupts, "I didn't say ninety. I said a hundred and nine."

He can step outside the bounds of his profession in still another way. He can teach. He has been doing this at his summer school in Hancock, Maine, since 1941.

During the month of August in two daily sessions of three hours each he and his assistant, Joseph Barone, bring fifty students through the various stages of baton development. These fifty students are obtained after screening some five hundred. First the student, whether he has a voice or not, must learn to sight-sing along every line in the score—oboe, clarinet, violin, French horn. Then he must analyze the composition harmonically and structurally—point out main and subsidiary themes, show the modulatory developments, gain insight into the composition in its parts and as a whole. Next comes an intensive drill in baton technique. Every variety of rhythmic pattern is studied. Motions must be both adequate and economical. The student is taught to indicate bow pressure for each string section, to "breathe" for the wind players, to prepare the percussion section for a clean attack. No bluffing, no faking, is allowed. Meaningless gestures are taboo.

The student stands on a podium before an actual orchestra. This orchestra is made of the student conductors playing their own instruments. One summer the ensemble included two flutes, two oboes, five clarinets, five horns, "plenty of trumpets," a trombone, two bassoons, timpani, and all the strings.

While the lessons are in progress, Monteux, chubby and cheery in his loud-checked lumberjack shirt, but very businesslike too, sits in the midst of the orchestra. Nothing gets past him. "The clarinet owes you two notes," he says. "Collect them." Or he points out, "The percussion cannot read your beat." Or "The violins are not sustaining well. Give them a better bowing for the passage." Or, "You are conducting the instruments that do not play in this passage and not conducting the ones that do." Or, "You may give a divided or an undivided beat but not both. Make up your mind."

The end in view is to make every note an integral part of a phrase, and every phrase a living part of the composition. The conductor must learn to "read between the lines." Monteux himself is a master at this. Prokofiev always wanted him to do his premières "not because he thought I was the greatest conductor, but because he knew I would correct all the mistakes in his manuscripts." Monteux's advice on modern composers' styles is invaluable, since he has been able to consult personally with many of them. Richard Strauss, he recalls, was very explicit, very precise in explaining his wishes. Debussy left more to the conductor.

This is the teacher, Pierre Monteux. Never once does he bother to notice how the conductor looks from behind. He teaches his students to communicate with an orchestra and to convey the conception of the composer. These he considers the conductor's true concerns.

Monteux's whole career has been marked by this unpretentious attitude.

He was born in Paris, April 4, 1875, the son of Gustave and Clémence (Brisac) Monteux. At six years of age he demanded a violin and entered the National Conservatory of Paris at nine. He studied there with Maurin and Berthelier in violin, with Lavignac in solfeggio and harmony and with Lenepveu in counterpoint and fugue. He later trained himself to play the viola. At the age of twelve he conducted café concerts and at fifteen took a French orchestra on a tour of the provinces with Cortot as pianist.

At eighteen Monteux became first violist of the Concerts Colonne. During the next fourteen years he advanced to the assistant conductorship. In 1911, when he was thirty-six, he organized his own Concerts Berlioz in Paris, as well as his Concerts d'Avant Garde. His conducting of these orchestras attracted the attention of Sergei Diaghilev, who made him principal conductor of the Ballet Russe.

Diaghilev was famous for his ability to choose wisely. This

time he certainly made no mistake. From the start Monteux was the aware, sensitive conductor. Stravinsky said of his work in *Le Sacre du Printemps,* "He was able to achieve a very clean and finished execution of my score. I ask no more of a conductor, for any other attitude on his part turns into interpretation, a thing I have a horror of."

The conducting of *Le Sacre* at the première on May 29, 1913, was carried on in such a din—the audience staged a riot—that no one could hear it after the first few bars. However, Monteux was able to give it another "première" as a concert work on April 5, 1914. It was well received this time, and thereafter became a stable part of the symphonic literature.

Then came World War I. On becoming a member of the French infantry in August 1914, Monteux had to give up both the Ballet Russe conductorship and an orchestra of his own which he had formed. He participated in the battles of Verdun, Rheims, Soissons, and the Argonne. After two years he was released, the French government deciding he was of more value to them conducting a Russian Ballet tour in the United States than sloughing through mud in the trenches. This tour, undertaken in the 1916–17 season, was his introduction to America. From then on, he was closely identified with this country.

Monteux's work with the Ballet Russe won him a Metropolitan Opera contract, leading the French operas. Then, in 1919, he became conductor of the Boston Symphony.

During his five years in Boston, Monteux established his reputation as a builder of orchestras. On his arrival there he found the symphony reduced to almost half its size. The orchestra had contained many German nationals, who because of the war had been called home. He left it a distinguished body of some eighty fine musicians. On his departure, critic Philip Hale said of him, "He formed and moulded the orchestra in the face of obstacles that would have daunted a man of less patience, courage and artistic enthusiasm. To that well-equipped body he gave life and beauty by his skill and taste as an interpreter of ancient, modern and ultra-modern music."

He introduced Griffes' *The Pleasure Dome of Kubla Khan;* Stravinsky's *Petrouchka;* Respighi's *The Pines of Rome;* Schönberg's *Verklärte Nacht* (this work revealed the vitalized string section); and Stravinsky's *Le Sacre*. He played the latter, not knowing how staid Bostonians would receive it, because through the years he had continued to believe in it. It was a great success. As the audience called and re-called him, he gestured to the orchestra to rise. But when they did, they turned and applauded him. Years later, in 1950, when Monteux again conducted *Le Sacre* in Paris, that audience also received the once bitterly abused music with tremendous enthusiasm. Stravinsky, then nearly seventy, appeared on the stage, tears running down his cheeks, and kissed Monteux.

In 1924 Koussevitzky took over the Boston Symphony, and the same fall, Monteux began an annual guest conducting series with the Concertgebouw Orchestra of Amsterdam. Again he proved his ability. In 1950, when he received the decoration of Commander of the Order of Orange-Nassau from the Dutch government, the speaker told him, "In the ten years you were conductor of the Concertgebouw Orchestra, you not only revised and improved its repertoire in many respects but, although you do not possess Netherlands nationality, it was your endeavor to give Netherlands creative music the place to which it has a right. You were always willing to help young talent." To which Monteux replied simply, "I have great affection for Holland and its people. I know that love is mutual, and I am proud of that."

On September 26, 1928, during his tenure in Amsterdam, he married the vivacious Doris Hodgkins. Her home town is Hancock, Maine, and they spend their summers there. This was the reason Monteux selected Hancock as the site for his conducting school.

In 1929, along with his Concertgebouw work, Monteux became conductor of the Paris Symphony. About this time a group of young conductors sought his advice on performing difficult modern works, and he began teaching orchestral conducting.

Then in the fall of 1935 Monteux was called to San Francisco to rebuild the orchestra there.

The year before, concerts had been suspended because of lack of funds. However, in May 1935, the San Francisco Symphony had been given renewed hope through a civic statute that allowed a half-cent tax to be levied for its benefit. This yielded about $40,000 annually and has ever since been the means of at least partly supporting the symphony. The War Memorial Opera House, municipally owned and acoustically superb, had recently been dedicated. So the San Francisco Symphony had a home.

Even with its financial and housing problems solved, however, the orchestra would have succumbed had not the new conductor stirred the citizens' affections as well as their pride. From the start Monteux was "an extraordinarily likable guy," was "Frisco's Frenchman," was "our Pierre." Rehearsal by rehearsal, concert by concert, with geniality, humor, and firmness, he raised the level of the orchestra. By 1942 it was a major orchestra, and he was an American citizen.

Especially illuminating was his eleventh season with the orchestra, 1946–47. Of the 117 concerts given, Monteux conducted all but two. On March 15, at the close of its home season, the orchestra set out on a tour that covered fifty-three cities and made the whole United States aware of its fine musicianship. The tour included a celebration in Norfolk, Virginia, on Monteux's seventy-second birthday. A huge cake was brought onstage at intermission, and *Happy Birthday* was sung by the orchestra and audience.

That year Monteux included on his programs eighteen contemporary works (eleven American, seven foreign), with four world premières. On May 15 he was awarded the Henry Hadley gold medal by the National Association of American Composers and Conductors, as "a great conductor, an imaginative and forceful interpreter of classic and modern repertoire, a friend and protagonist of the best in American music."

When in 1952 Monteux resigned his conductorship of the San Francisco Symphony, five gala farewell parties were held in his honor. At the final banquet he was called on for a speech. He complied with a few well-chosen words. "I make you a solemn declaration," he said. "My hair is not dyed."

Since leaving the San Francisco area, Monteux has become the property of the whole United States as well as its emissary abroad. In 1955, at the age of eighty, he conducted ten Boston Symphony concerts and one Metropolitan Opera performance. He took four American singers to Brussels to perform in a spring festival of two operas, *Orpheus* and *Pelleas and Melisande,* and conducted five performances there under the patronage of the American ambassador. He conducted two concerts with the London Philharmonic. In Paris he conducted a gala program of the most famous "firsts" that he had launched in his lifetime: Debussy's *Jeux,* Ravel's *Daphnis and Chloe* and Stravinsky's *Petrouchka* and again *Le Sacre du Printemps*. He directed four concerts for the Holland Music Festival. Then, returning to the United States in July, he conducted at the New York Stadium, at Tanglewood, and at Ravinia.

Monteux is a much-sought-after guest conductor, not only because he presents works as the composers meant them to be, but also because he is always *there*. "In sixty-five years of conducting he has not missed a rehearsal or a performance," Olin Downes pointed out in Monteux's eightieth year. This is due not only to his physical stamina but also to his courage. A few years ago, on a short tour with the Boston Symphony, he was in an automobile accident that cracked four of his ribs. He conducted that night, after the doctor had taped and strapped him, and he went through the remaining four concerts of the itinerary.

Though he is the guest conductor par excellence, he is also very much the small-town American. On a summer day in Hancock, Maine, the whole village turned out to paint and dedicate a new flagpole erected in front of his house. Each resident gave one stroke of the paint brush so that all could say they had a part in the gift. In a radio broadcast on the spot, Mrs. Monteux spoke about her husband's feelings regarding this town in Maine. She had thought he might like to return to his homeland to end his days. But he emphatically vetoed the idea. He was going to stay right here in Hancock. This was his home. This was where he wanted to live his life among his friends.

CHAPTER XXXII

⇒ ALFRED WALLENSTEIN

"THE conductor is not a star, is not Beethoven, is not the orchestra expressed in one man. He is only a tool." Talking with extreme rapidity, in clipped, incisive phrases, Alfred Wallenstein compresses into a few words an attitude developed over a lifetime. "Humility before a great work of art—that is the first thing in conducting. If the orchestra men must follow a conductor arbitrarily sometimes, it is because deadlines must be met. Really the men and the conductor have the same task—to get at the composer's intentions."

Mr. Wallenstein shows disciplined movements off as well as on the podium. As he talks he scarcely moves hands or head. His facial expression, save for his eyes which shine with inner excitement, is equable, masklike.

His mind, however, is quick and precise. He finds satisfaction in dealing with numbers. It gives him pleasure to note that his career seems to progress in terms of the number seven.

His life has presented a different scene each seven years, as if manipulated like a vast revolving stage; the transition years have been 1908, 1915, 1922, 1929, 1936, and 1943.

The first turn of the stage occurred when, at the age of ten, he began to play the cello professionally. The place was Los Angeles, where the family had moved from Chicago shortly after Alfred's birth on October 7, 1898.

During this period he played in a cafeteria orchestra from five to seven in the evening, then at the movies from seven-thirty to eleven. On the sets, that is. For this was Los Angeles of the silent movie era, when "mood music" was a part of the film-making process.

He remembers once he was engaged to play on Mary Pickford's set. He had been instructed to produce a sad mood through his music, but he found this difficult. Douglas Fairbanks was courting Mary, and that evening he was trying to further his suit by jumping over barrels, boxes, chairs, everything.

Another time young Wallenstein was cellist in a theater pit in Los Angeles when Pavlova was on the stage. He was playing *The Swan,* and the stage was bombarded with bouquets. She picked one up and threw it toward the boy cellist, thus focusing the audience's attention on him. After the show, he went around to thank her. That contact brought him an engagement later on.

What got Wallenstein out of the pit and onto the stage was the great flood that occurred in the winter of 1914 between San Francisco and Los Angeles. Troupes in both towns were stranded and had to make up impromptu acts to keep the audiences interested. The Los Angeles troupe asked Wallenstein to help out. Agents for Keith and Orpheum circuits happened to be in the audience and signed Wallenstein up as a "boy wonder." Boy or no, he got a man's wages from then on.

In the second seven-year cycle of his career (1915–22) Wallenstein not only continued barnstorming as in vaudeville, but also became cellist in the San Francisco Symphony, toured South and Central America and the West Indies with Pavlova, played a brief season with the Los Angeles Philharmonic, and again toured South America, this time in joint recitals with the dancer Maud Allen. This brought him enough money to pay for a trip to Europe.

Embarking directly from South America, Wallenstein arrived in Europe on Christmas Day in 1920. In Leipzig he studied cello under Julius Klengel.

He also studied medicine at the University of Leipzig, at the wish of his father—who, as a member of the old Austrian aristocracy, thought his son should go into one of the professions. Dissecting, analyzing—he was in his element. He believes there is a close affinity between medicine and music. "Look at all the doctors' orchestras! There's much that they do both in their practice and in their benefactions that parallels the musician's career."

He liked medicine, but he gave it up without a tussle. "Music just began to absorb all my time," he says.

In 1922 the stage was due for another revolution. Klengel sent Wallenstein back to America, telling him he had taught him all he could. The days of memorizing three new concertos a week for the master were over.

Through the next seven years Wallenstein was first cellist in the Chicago Symphony under Frederick Stock and solo cellist with that and other groups. (Stock dedicated his own Cello Concerto to him.) He taught at the Chicago Musical College. In 1924 he married Virginia Wilson, a student-pianist at the College. They visited Europe in 1927 and while in Italy attended a La Scala performance of *Ariane et Barbe-Bleu* by Dukas. Wallenstein had always wanted to hear it. But, once there, he was so fascinated watching the conductor that he didn't listen to the opera at all. This conductor was Arturo Toscanini, who was to exert great influence on his later career.

Shortly after Wallenstein's return from Europe he obtained an audition with Toscanini and, in 1929, was summoned to be first-chair cellist with the New York Philharmonic. Toscanini was its conductor.

In the seven years 1929–36, Wallenstein worked as principal cellist under Toscanini. He was his pupil—by observation. And a good chance he had to observe, sitting there, first row, first chair, under the great maestro.

Besides filling a heavy schedule as a member of the New York

Philharmonic, Wallenstein made guest artist appearances with that and other orchestras. Then, in 1931, he began trying his hand at conducting. His first chance came, in the great tradition of almost all conductors, through a last-minute indisposition of the regular conductor. It was a WOR radio program, and it attracted the company's attention to him. In 1933 he inaugurated the Wallenstein Sinfonietta over WOR.

He kept his New York Philharmonic position along with this assignment until 1936, when Toscanini resigned his conductorship. Then Wallenstein left too, and became WOR's full-time musical director.

It is indicative of Wallenstein's high standards that he started his series with an all-Bach program. "One must be careful not to make mediocrity the standard," he explains. "Besides, success has never impressed me. Applause is nice, but it is nicer to feel yourself that what you have done is good."

During the seven years he was musical director of WOR, Wallenstein brought more good music to more people than probably any other conductor of the decade. Hundreds of first performances of both new and classical works were presented by him. He gave a series of Bach cantatas, scheduled on the Sundays for which they were composed; the first presentation in America of the twenty-six Mozart piano concertos complete; a series of Mozart operas; and the first American Opera Festival. The Peabody award that was given him in 1942 for "pioneering for good music in a quiet way" was just the sort of recognition he treasures.

The call to conduct the Los Angeles Philharmonic came in 1943. It was a call not only to his childhood city but to a city that was growing rapidly. The salary offered was one-third that of his radio posts. However, he was to have a free hand with the management of the orchestra. He accepted without a moment's hesitation.

He was well aware of the problems involved. The orchestra he was to take over, while it had reached major proportions and was a stable body of twenty-three years' standing, had been handled for several years by a variety of guest conductors. It would take discipline to get it into line.

Discipline Wallenstein had. He drilled the orchestra as only an artist convinced he is dealing with artists dares to drill. Virgil Thomson, hearing it a few years later, said of it: "Woodwinds and brasses, which are likely to be good in all American orchestras, are no less excellent here than elsewhere; but a string section at once so live in sound and so homogeneous in color, so sensitive, so silken, so handsomely drilled and blended for beauty, is not to be encountered in more than five or six of our cities."

From a season of less than fifty concerts Wallenstein set up schedules totaling as many as ninety, including broadcasts over the Pacific network and the NBC, and a series of fifteen concerts known as "Symphonies for Youth," for which he was both conductor and commentator. "Hundreds of thousands of moppets," wrote one critic, "deserted their sandlots and Hopalong's gunplay to tune in their radios to the unpatronizing program of Wagner, Berlioz, Dvořák and David Diamond."

In 1951, when Hollywood Bowl broke up in midseason, Wallenstein, being at the helm of the home orchestra, was approached in hopes that he could save some of the pieces—see at least that the orchestra men had their contracts honored. Within forty-eight hours he had set up virtually the entire season and single-handedly contracted noted conductors and soloists who gave their services for the revived series. In 1952 he was music director of the Bowl.

Wallenstein assumed the conductorship of the Los Angeles Philharmonic in 1943. The seven-year mark saw him still there. But with another seven years covered, the stage swung to another scene. In the spring of 1956 Wallenstein took the orchestra on a ten-week tour of the Orient sponsored by the State Department agency, the American National Theater and Academy. The good will won abroad through this extensive trip was one of the reasons for the passage on July 23, 1956, by the Eighty-fourth Congress, of the International Cultural Exchange and Trade Fair Participation Act, committing the federal government to other such tour sponsorships.

Music lovers expect much from Wallenstein in the next turn of his career. The five concerts he conducted in Carnegie Hall in early 1956, with Artur Rubinstein the soloist, have awakened New Yorkers anew to his sensitivity and skill. But whatever the developments are, music lovers everywhere know that here is a conductor who, come what may, will not let down his musical standards.

CHAPTER XXXIII

⇶ BRUNO WALTER

IN conversation, in casual encounters, on the podium, Bruno Walter is serene. His movements are measured and coordinated; his speech is slow and modulated; his podium attitude is quiet. In his music he inclines toward moderate tempos and gradual tonal transitions. Under his direction the orchestra does not merely phrase. It sings.

The quirk in history that made Bruno Walter, like Albert Einstein, a celebrated victim of Hitler Germany is not the great drama of his career. The real milestones in his life have been his struggle toward fuller expression in music, his learning not to compromise in matters of art, his passing new frontiers with courage, his development of "the wide heart."

Walter's early surroundings in a middle-class, highly musical family in Berlin, where he was born on September 15, 1876, were just right for a boy who was "every inch of him music." Piano lessons with his mother were started at the same time that he started school—at the age of five. A few years later he was enrolled at the Stern Conservatory of Music.

Music absorbed his life. The difficult three-against-two rhythm —in which the pianist's right hand plays two beats to a measure while his left plays three beats, and, in an orchestra, one section beats three times to another's two—was mastered in his walks to school. First he counted to three while he stepped two steps, his feet going "left-right, left-right," in exact time to the words "one-two-three, one-two-three." Then he reversed the process. Stepping in the three rhythm: "left-right-left, right-left-right," he said aloud "one-two, one-two," so that the "one" came first on the left foot and then on the right.

When his family took him to the temple, the majestic sounds of the organ affected him powerfully.

His teachers, his parents, and he himself had decided that he should prepare for a pianist's career. But when the boy, aged thirteen, attended a Berlin Philharmonic concert directed by the famous conductor, Hans von Bülow, all this was changed. "I felt the compelling force of his gestures," Walter recalls. "I noticed the attention and devotion of the players, and was conscious of the expressiveness and precision of their playing. It became at once clear to me that it was that one man who was producing the music, that he had transformed those hundred performers into his instrument, and that he was playing it as a pianist played the piano. Now I knew what I was meant for. No musical activity but that of an orchestral conductor could any longer be considered by me." *

Before he went to bed that night he told his father that while he would be glad to continue his piano studies and act as soloist later, just as Bülow had, it was a conductor he had decided to be.

When Walter was seventeen, one of his teachers at the Stern Conservatory, who had previously been a conductor at the Municipal Opera in Cologne, found a place for him there as coach. He began work on September 1, 1893, at a monthly salary of one hundred marks (about $25).

The thrill at entering a theater for the first time by the stage door was quickly dispelled in the rush of work. In *Theme and Variations,* Walter relates that on arriving at the Opera in

* This and several subsequent quotations in this chapter are from *Theme and Variations,* an autobiography by Bruno Walter, Alfred A. Knopf, Inc., 1946.

the morning he was given an ensemble to rehearse for *Il Trovatore*. In the midst of the rehearsal he was summoned by the stage manager to conduct the backstage trumpets for a *Lohengrin* rehearsal. In the afternoon he rehearsed a soprano cast for the Forest Bird in *Siegfried*. Then he took over a rehearsal of Agathe and Ännchen in *Der Freischütz*. After this he tested the voice of a young woman for the shepherd's part in *Tannhäuser*. He was hurriedly called to play the organ in a performance of *Cavalleria*. He was told to be ready on the dot to signal a chorus member standing in the wings for her scream announcing the death of Turridu. All this while, he was carrying under his arm the score of an opera that the directors said had to be reported on within a week.

Before the year was out he was allowed to conduct Lortzing's *Der Waffenschmied,* a light but charming work. His hand knew automatically what to do. It was wonderful to be able to unleash forces by a gesture, a look. Then as now, he found his deepest satisfaction in getting at the spirit of the work.

By the end of the year at the Cologne Opera, Walter realized that he would not be advanced to any important post there. So he took the job of assistant conductor at the Hamburg Stadttheater. Here he came in contact with the person who was to exert the greatest influence in his life—Gustav Mahler. On first meeting this great conductor and composer, who was at the time the general director of the Hamburg Stadttheater, Walter felt, he says, "as though a higher realm had been opened to me. In his aspect and manner Mahler appeared to me both a genius and a demon. Life had all of a sudden become romantic." *

He learned much from Mahler: how to get to the very core of a work; how to "participate in the creation"; how to express the spiritual element in music and yet attend to the technical aspects.

---

* From *Gustav Mahler,* by Bruno Walter, The Greystone Press, 1941.

After two years in Hamburg, Mahler advised Walter to go out into the world. The young man seconded the idea. Worship of Mahler could develop into slavish imitation. He needed to be on his own.

The next season (1896–97), he was second conductor at the small Stadttheater in Breslau. Unfortunately it was a place of slipshod methods. Practical jokes, wisecracks, slaps on the back were the way to popularity. But there was a favorable side to this. Since Bruno Walter was the only one who really worked at the job, he was in demand when a stage director wanted a day off, a chorus leader failed to put in an appearance, or a conductor took sick leave. In the rush, Walter was afraid he might let down his standards. At the end of the year he resigned.

At his next place, the Stadttheater at Pressburg, just over the border from Germany in Hungary, he was chief conductor. He hurled himself into the task of getting the best out of the amateurish cast and the meager orchestra. To some extent he succeeded. But he needed better material. Soon he found it. In the fall of 1898 he became chief conductor at the Stadttheater in Riga. The capital of Latvia, Riga was then in Russian territory. But the Stadttheater was German in its administration, in its audiences, and in the language of the operas presented.

Here, with a good singing cast and a fine orchestra, Walter could prepare and produce great operas artistically. He impressed on the cast his motto, to "live resolutely." A week before a première they were told to refrain from parties and sprees. The rehearsals were thorough down to the least detail. Always, though, he stressed the importance of bringing out the spirit of the work.

At the end of two years in Riga, Walter received an offer astonishing for a conductor in only his twenty-fifth year. He was asked to become "Royal Prussian Conductor" at the Berlin Opera. Berlin was his childhood home. His father, mother, brother, and sister still lived there. At the Berlin Opera he had heard his first performances. The offer was irresistible. By the fall of 1900 he had entered on his duties in Berlin.

He was soon wishing he had never taken the step. At the Berlin Opera, bureaucracy prevailed. Every detail had to be referred to a higher-up. Everything was subject to censorship. It was "Pegasus harried by a Spanish riding master and unable either to be ridden or to fly." *

All this was intolerable to Walter, who believed one could not obtain artistic results if the relation of superior and subordinate prevailed. "No oboist obedient to a master's command is able to play a solo beautifully. His soul must lend charm to his playing and the conductor, respecting its freedom, must influence it by methods more subtle than a superior's paralyzing command."

Walter tried to get an annulment of his five-year contract. He redoubled his efforts when Mahler sent him an invitation to be his assistant at his new post as director of the Vienna Opera. He felt now that he could work with Mahler and yet be independent of him. At last he was released.

In May 1901 he married Elsa Korneck, a lyric-dramatic soprano of the Riga Opera, and by the end of the summer the couple were on their way to Austria.

Walter describes this period with Mahler in Vienna as a "ten-year feast to which the great artist invited co-workers and devotees." Unfortunately, though, he was not always in a condition to enjoy the feast.

Before Walter had been in Vienna one month he was assigned to conduct *Tannhäuser*. The performance went well. But the next morning he was shocked to read a furious attack on himself in the papers. He was "inept." He was "a blunderer." He "would not do as the leader even of a riflemen's band." Mahler explained

* From *Theme and Variations* by Bruno Walter, Alfred A. Knopf, Inc., 1946.

to him that the attack was really meant for him, but that the critics dared not stage an outright assault on the general director and therefore were using his protégé as a target.

Walter, however, was deeply hurt. His confidence was shaken. As the attacks grew even more bitter, he began to be uncertain of his mission as a conductor.

Performances became nightmares. He looked forward to every pizzicato, to every chord in the strings, with apprehension. No matter how he beat, it would seem to lack precision. "Slow six-eight measures became inexact when I beat them in two," he recalls, "and stiff when I beat them in six. . . . My excessive watchfulness of details interfered when I had to plan a longer phrase. I felt as if I had happened into a bog and was sinking lower and lower."

The strain told on him. He developed an arm paralysis and was forced to take sick leave. He consulted Sigmund Freud, who was already a famous practitioner in Vienna. Freud advised him to go on conducting. Then, as related in *Theme and Variations,*

"But I can't move my arm," Walter told him.

"Try it at any rate."

"And what if I should have to stop?"

"You won't have to stop."

"Can I take upon myself the responsibility of possibly upsetting a performance?"

"I'll take the responsibility," said Freud.

So Walter went at it again. He found that he was able to conduct without interference from his arm; only then did he realize that, during the previous weeks, he had been *willing* the paralysis, in hopes of being forced to abandon his career.

Finally the critics subsided. Walter had won a high place by that time in the regard of the Viennese.

In December 1907 Mahler left the Vienna Opera. He was

found to be suffering from a heart ailment and was advised to take up less strenuous duties. Bruno Walter stayed on for four more years. The two succeeding directors were not congenial to him, however, and he kept on the lookout for another job.

Meanwhile he became a regular guest conductor in England, and in Vienna led orchestral concerts besides operatic performances.

In July 1911, on the death of Felix Mottl, artistic head of the Munich Court Opera, Bruno Walter was asked to take his place. A whole year elapsed before he could get his release from the Vienna Opera, but they waited for him and at last he was free to go.

Before he left the city he conducted the première of Mahler's posthumous Ninth Symphony. This performance took place on June 26, 1912, a little more than a year after its composer's death. It was Walter's letter of thanks to that great man.

The ten years Walter spent at the Munich Court Opera were the most prolific and the happiest of his European phase. He expanded the general repertoire, engaged valuable new players for the orchestra, heightened the standards of production. He considers the single great development of these years "the increased depth of my relation to Mozart," and his single great mistake his performing Bach's *St. Matthew Passion* with cuts. This he regards as unjustifiable. "The work is an organic whole and he who meddles with it violates it as well as the fundamental of art."

After ten years in Munich, he felt he had rounded out the artistic circle there. He left in the fall of 1922.

Now began his guest conductorships in America. As the ship left the dock at Cuxhaven late that year, he had an oppressive sense of leaving behind not only a country but an era.

For two years he guest conducted alternately in America and in Europe. On January 1925, when he was on his way to America for the third time, a telegram reached him from the Berlin Municipal Opera asking whether he would resume duties there as general musical director. Again the lure was strong. His aged parents as well as his wife's family were there. He was assured full scope in all artistic matters.

He accepted. On September 18, 1925, the Opera opened its season with a performance of *Die Meistersinger* under his baton.

During his four-year stay in Berlin, the Municipal Opera had a brief flowering. Walter also branched out. He conducted in America and England, in Paris and Russia. He was a motivating spirit in the newly organized Salzburg Festivals.

Then Berlin officialdom began to irk him again. He had been a frequent guest conductor at the Gewandhaus Concerts in Leipzig and had enjoyed his relationship with this famous orchestra. So in 1929 he resigned his Berlin post and became the regular conductor of the Leipzig organization. He kept his apartment in Berlin, however. His "Bruno Walter Concerts," which had been started there some ten years before, had become an integral part of Berlin's musical life and were continued.

Now began a turn in Walter's career that he himself had no part in bringing about nor any power to direct. On the night of September 14, 1930, he was enjoying a quiet evening at his apartment with a group of friends, among them the cellist Emanuel Feuermann. They turned on the radio. Every few minutes a loud voice announced the latest election returns. Matters were taking a surprising twist. The newly emerged Adolf Hitler was winning by a landslide. By three in the morning he had polled about 6,500,000 votes, and it was clear that the Nazis would be the new Reichstag's largest party. Feuermann, usually so gay, left the party suddenly with the words, "It's all over with Germany; all over with Europe."

Bruno Walter had never been particularly concerned with politics. Now he was stubbornly optimistic. Surely the people would awaken in time to the danger of having this half-insane person in office.

Then, in January 1933, when Walter was in New York on a guest conductorship of the New York Philharmonic, word came through that Hitler had been made chancellor of Germany. Still he did not fully grasp the situation. Hitler was in. Well, in time he would be put out. Walter had conducting commitments in Leipzig and Berlin. He was deeply rooted in the artistic life of Germany. It did not even occur to him to cancel his engagements and just stay on in America.

He returned to Germany. When he landed there, the truth broke on him: "An evil magic had turned a familiar world into a strange country."

He went to his Berlin apartment. A telephone call came from the Leipzig Gewandhaus. A faltering voice told him that "certain difficulties" had arisen and would he please come at once. On his arrival in Leipzig he was informed that the Leipzig Nazis were determined to prevent the concert that Thursday on the ground that a concert conducted by a Jew might "endanger public order and security." When he went to the hall, a placard at the entrance briefly announced the performance would not take place. The members of the orchestra greeted him with deep respect as he passed among them.

He returned to Berlin where a Bruno Walter Concert was scheduled for the following Monday. The managers wanted to go through with it. They decided, however, to telephone the Nazi "artistic mediator" first. "We don't wish to prohibit the concert," came an icy voice over the wire, "for we are not interested in getting you out of an awkward predicament or in relieving you of your obligation to pay the orchestra. But if you insist on giving the concert you may be sure that everything in the hall will be smashed to pieces." The voice added, "Herr Walter is politically suspicious."

Walter met his wife outside the building and told her about the call. "You must leave Berlin at once," she said quietly. He had to agree with her. Without even returning to his apartment he started with his elder daughter for Austria. His wife followed shortly after with the younger daughter.

That was in March 1933. The next month Walter, now in Austria, received an invitation to guest conduct the Concertgebouw in Amsterdam. He traveled there, giving Germany a wide berth. As the train drew into the station, he saw an immense crowd in the square. When he appeared they began singing an old Netherlands song of freedom.

During the next five years Walter continued his guest conductorships and his work at Salzburg. In 1936, at sixty years of age, he took upon himself one of the most arduous and responsible musical jobs in all Europe: he became artistic director of the Vienna Opera.

In March 1938 he was again filling a guest conductorship in Amsterdam when another political crisis took place. He had just finished a rehearsal of the Concertgebouw and had gone to his hotel. He turned on the radio and heard the news that Hitler had presented Austria with an ultimatum. Chancellor Schuschnigg offered his resignation, ending with the words, "God save Austria!" Solemn strains of Haydn's Quartet containing the theme of the Austrian national anthem gave way to blaring Prussian military marches. The Austria Walter had loved and worked for had passed away.

One of his daughters who was in Vienna at the time was imprisoned. Later released, she escaped the country. Their flat in Vienna was sealed. Its contents were confiscated and sold at public auction.

The family went to France, where Walter was made a French citizen by a special decree. But within a year he again had to flee Hitler's advance. He sailed with his wife from Genoa on October 31, 1939. Since that time he has been a resident of the United States, and is now a citizen.

The transition had been made less difficult because, as Walter puts it, "All mankind represents my fellow-citizens and I have the good fortune to speak the supernational language of music." In his home in Beverly Hills, California, where he has lived with his elder daughter since the death of his wife, many friends seek him out. Each afternoon he is driven to the ocean for a long, quiet walk along the beach.

In America Walter has been conductor of the Metropolitan Opera for nine seasons and musical adviser to the New York Philharmonic for two. But his greatest influence has been exercised through his wide guest conductorships. He has revealed new beauties in old works. He has introduced new works. His performances, thought out with deep insight, have been artistic events in concert seasons all over the United States. Young conductors have learned much from him.

Leonard Bernstein, in particular, has made a study of Walter's remarkable singing quality. "What can possibly happen," he queries in an article in *Theatre Arts* Magazine, "between the impact of Walter's baton and the sound itself, to determine this sonorous quality?" He decides that it is because Bruno Walter has such authority over his men that he does not need to beat time in the literal sense at all. Thus "the baton is free to mold the phrase, to take its own time between the beats, allowing the phrase to unfold, live its full life, however short, and sing out its meaning." Bernstein believes that this power of Walter's lies in the fact that "he has nothing to prove; he has only the music to make. Because of his singleness of purpose and uncluttered devotion, the battle is half won before he begins to rehearse. There is no barrier between his baton and his player, or—more important—between himself and his baton. Thus whatever communication is possible between one musician and another is free to take place."

But Walter's ability to establish direct communication between himself and his men is only a part of his life's goal. This is to bring great orchestral works to a living state.

Bach has been dead over two hundred years. Mozart saw neither this century nor the last. No one living today has heard any word spoken by Beethoven or Schubert or Schumann. Liszt is a legend, Wagner the man a myth. Mahler, Bartók, Strauss are fading memories. If great and dedicated individuals did not study to get at the message of these composers—archeologists examining caves of the human soul and reconstructing from mere remnants the lives once lived there—we should have only haphazard performances of the *Siegfried Idyll,* hazy approximations of *The Afternoon of a Faun,* garbled versions of the *St. Matthew Passion,* and awkward tries at the Beethoven Ninth.

Bruno Walter is such a great and dedicated person. By devoting his whole life and his great talents to performing the music of composers as the composers meant it to be performed, he has not only clearly defined the boundaries of his calling but has revealed their vast extent. The conductor has the high and noble responsibility of freeing great symphonic and operatic music from the mortal hand of the composer, of making it, like great paintings, the possession of all mankind and of all ages.

PART III

Thumbnail Sketches

In the following miniature biographies, only conducting activities and activities connected with conducting—teaching, playing in orchestras—are mentioned. Their activities as composers, however, have been omitted. Schools which the conductors attended are given, but not their private teachers. Conducting tenures (permanent conductorships) are listed but not guest conductorships.

The following schools, since their names occur so frequently, are given without city designations: Berkshire Music Center (near Lenox, Mass.), Columbia University (New York, N.Y.), Curtis Institute of Music (Philadelphia, Pa.), Eastman School of Music (Rochester, N.Y.), Juilliard School of Music (New York, N.Y.), Peabody Conservatory of Music (Baltimore, Md.). The summer course called L'Ecole Monteux, at Hancock, Maine, is indicated simply by the phrase, "studied with Monteux."

AARON, HENRY, b. New York, N.Y., Sept. 25, 1914. Studied at Juilliard School of Music and with Monteux. He was cond. of WPA music projects and violist in the Metropolitan Opera Orch., 1937–49. He played in the Worcester Music Fest. Orch., 1935–42. In 1935 he became a member of the Chautauqua (N.Y.) Symph. He was asst. cond. of the Buffalo Philh., 1949–52, and since 1955 has been asst. cond. of the Chautauqua Symph.

ABAS, MATHYS, b. The Netherlands, 1924. Studied at Berkshire Music Center and at Univ. of Ill. In 1952 he founded the

Midland (Texas) Symph. He was violinist in the Vancouver Symph. (1953–55). Since 1955 he has been cond. of the Waterloo (Iowa) Symph.

ADAMS, EUGENE, b. Cleveland, Ohio, Aug. 2, 1907. Studied at Cleveland Inst. of Music, Oberlin (Ohio) Cons. of Music, and Univ. of Mich. He was a violinist for four seasons with Cleveland Orch. and eight with the Dallas Symph. He organized the Loraine (Ohio) Symph. and (in 1951) the Cheyenne (Wyo.) Symph., conducting the latter until 1955.

ADLER, KURT HERBERT, b. Vienna, Austria, Apr. 2, 1905. Studied at Vienna Music Acad. and Univ. of Vienna. He conducted at opera houses in Germany, Italy, and Czechoslovakia, 1928–38. He was asst. cond. at Salzburg Music Fest., 1936–37, and was with the Chicago Opera, 1938–43. He has been with the San Francisco Opera since 1943, as gen. dir. since 1953. Since 1949 he has been cond. of the Youth Concerts of the San Francisco Symph. He is chorus master at the Metropolitan Opera.

ADLER, PETER, b. Jablonec, Czechoslovakia, Dec. 2, 1899. Studied at Univ. of Prague. He was musical dir. of the opera house in Jablonec, 1922–24; a cond. of the Brno Opera, 1924–28; cond. of the State Opera in Bremen, 1928–32; dir. of the Ukrainian State Orch., first at Kharkov and then at Kiev, 1933–37. In 1942 he conducted for the New Opera Co., N.Y.C. In 1949 he became musical dir. of the NBC Opera Dept., N.Y.C.

ALDERWICK, EDGAR J., b. 1890. Studied at Syracuse Univ. and Columbia Univ. He founded the Utica (N.Y.) Symph. in 1921 and now conducts the Utica Civic Orch.

ALLERS, FRANZ, b. Carlsbad, Czechoslovakia, Aug. 6, 1905. Studied at the Prague Cons. and the Berlin Hochschule. He was a violinist in the Berlin Philh. He was cond. at the Municipal Theater, Carlsbad, 1926, and cond. at the Municipal Theater at Wupperthal, 1927–33. In 1927 he was asst. at the Bayreuth Fest. In 1938 he conducted the Ballet Russe de Monte Carlo. Since 1945 he has been cond. of Broadway shows (N.Y.C.) and since 1952 cond. of the Dallas (Tex.) State Fair Musical season.

ALLOO, MODESTE, b. Belgium. Studied at Brussels Royal Cons. of Music. For many years he was solo trombonist of the Boston Symph. He was assoc. cond. of the Cincinnati Symph., 1918–22. He conducted the Univ. of Miami Symph., 1942–51, and is on the faculty of Univ. of Miami.

AMFITEATROF, DANIELE, b. St. Petersburg, Russia, Oct. 29, 1901. Studied at St. Cecilia Cons. (Rome). He was artistic dir. of the Genoa and Trieste radio stations, 1929–31; assoc. cond. of the Minneapolis Symph., 1937–38, then became a composer and conductor for motion pictures in Hollywood.

ANDERSON, CLIFFORD, b. Caspar, Cal., Mar. 28, 1904. Studied at Humboldt State Coll. (Cal.), San Francisco State Coll., and Univ. of Cal. He was music educator in schools at Fort Bragg, Gridley, Covelo, and Calistoga. He was concertmaster of the Santa Rosa Symph., 1934–45. Since 1945 he has taught in the Monterey city schools and been cond. of the Monterey County Symph.

ANDERSON, ROBERT B., b. Nome, Alaska, Sept. 23, 1917. Studied at Univ. of Washington. He was a violinist in the Seattle Symph. He helped form the Sno-King Community Orch., made up of residents of districts north of Seattle. Since 1953 he has conducted the Bremerton (Wash.) Symph.

ANDRIE, EUGENE, b. Grand Rapids, Mich. Aug. 23, 1914. Studied at Univ. of Mich. and at Univ. of Wash. He was a violinist in the Grand Rapids Symph., 1931–42. He conducted the West Michigan Youth Orch., 1939–43. Since 1950 he has conducted the Missoula (Mont.) Civic Symph. and the Helena Symph.

ANELLO, JOHN, b. Milwaukee, Nov. 20, 1909. Studied at Univ. of Wisc. and at Wisc. Cons. of Music. He was dir. of the Nat'l Opera Fest., Milwaukee, 1948–49. Since 1948 he has been music dir. of Milwaukee's "Music Under the Stars" series.

ANSERMET, ERNEST, b. Vevey, Switzerland, Nov. 11, 1883. Studied in Switzerland with Denéréaz, Gédalge, Barblan, and Bloch. He conducted in Montreux, 1912–14, and in Geneva, 1915–18. In 1915 he conducted the Diaghilev Russian Ballet on tour. In 1918 he founded and has since conducted the Orchestre de la Suisse Romande, Geneva.

ANTEK, SAMUEL, b. Chicago. Studied at Juilliard School of Music and with Monteux. He was a violinist in the NBC Symph., 1937–54. Since 1947 he has been cond. of the New Jersey Symph., and since 1955 cond. of the Philadelphia Orch. Children's Concerts.

ANTONINI, ALFREDO, b. Nicosia, Italy, May 31, 1901. Studied at Milan Cons. He was organist of Milan Cathedral, 1922, and head of Cons. of Sasseri, Sardinia, 1923–24. He was musical dir. of the N.Y. Folklore Fest. in 1938. In 1941 he conducted the Pan-Amer. Orch. in short-wave programs to So. Amer. Since 1943 he has been musical dir. of CBS.

ARENTSEN, HAROLD W., b. Waseca, Minn., July 28, 1897. Studied at MacPhail Coll. of Music in Minneapolis. He organized the Alexandria (Minn.) Symph. in 1929, and conducted it for twelve years. In 1941 he organized the Oshkosh (Wisc.) Civic Symph. and since then has conducted it and the Civic Chorus.

Since 1940 he has been dir. of music education in the public schools of Oshkosh.

ARMSTRONG, LESLIE H., b. Mount Vernon, Wash., Apr. 23, 1909. Studied at Whitman Coll. and at State Coll. of Wash. He was a music educator in the schools of Dayton, Wash., 1930–36. Since 1936 he has been supervisor of music in the Olympia public schools and since 1946 cond. of the Olympia Symph.

ASEN, SIMON, b. Philadelphia, Pa., Jan. 19, 1911. Studied at Curtis Inst. of Music. He was a violist in the Philadelphia Orch. eight years and in the NBC Symph. four years. In 1946 he became cond. of the Mt. Vernon (N.Y.) Symph., continuing since 1955 as cond. of an outgrowth organization, the Philh. Symph. of Westchester.

ASPER, FRANK W., b. Logan, Utah, Feb. 9, 1892. Studied at Stern Cons. (Berlin), New England Cons., Univ. of Utah, and Chicago Musical Coll. He taught at New England Cons., 1918–20, and directed the Salt Lake City Orpheus Club Chorus, 1922–29. Since 1920 he has been cond. of the McCune School of Music and Art Symph., and since 1924 organist at the Salt Lake Tabernacle.

AUTORI, FRANCO, b. Naples, Italy, Nov. 29, 1903. Studied at Univ. of Naples and gained early experience in opera houses of Italy. In 1928 he became asst. cond. of the Penn. Grand Opera (Philadelphia). He was a member of the Chicago Opera and Ravinia Opera, 1929–32. He conducted the Dallas (Tex.) Sinfonietta, 1932–34. In 1934 he took charge of the Federal Music Project in Buffalo, and in 1936 established the Buffalo Philh. as an independent organization, conducting it until 1945. He was cond. of the Chautauqua Symph., 1944–52. Since 1949 he has been assoc. cond. of the New York Philh.

AVSHALOMOV, JACOB, b. Tsingtao, China, March 28, 1919. Studied at Reed Coll. (Portland, Ore.), and at Eastman School of Music. He taught at Columbia Univ., 1946–54. Since 1954 he has been cond. of the Portland (Ore.) Junior Symph.

BAILEY, WILLIAM H., b. Allentown, Pa. Studied at Pomona Coll. (Cal.) and at Eastman School of Music. He was successively a member (violin) of the Allentown Symph., the Pasadena (Cal.) Civic Orch., and the Burbank Symph. He taught at John B. Stetson Univ., 1936–41. Since 1945 he has been cond. of the Walla Walla (Wash.) Symph. and teacher at Whitman Coll. Cons. of Music.

BAKER, ISRAEL, b. Chicago, Ill., Feb. 11, 1919. He was concertmaster of the Dayton (Ohio) Philh. for two years; then, from 1941, of the All-American Youth Orch.; and from 1945, of the Indianapolis Symph. In 1954 he organized the Alhambra Orch. and in 1956 the Israel Baker Chamber Orch. (Hollywood).

BALABAN, EMANUEL, b. Brooklyn, N.Y., Jan. 27, 1895. Studied at Juilliard School of Music. He was accompanist to concert artists—Zimbalist, Morini—1917–22; assoc. cond. of the Dresden Opera, Germany, 1922–24; head of the opera dept. at Eastman School of Music, 1927–44; musical dir. of the Ballet Russe, 1944–46; cond. of the New Orleans "Pop" Orch., 1947; musical dir. of the United Nations Orch., 1947–49. Since 1946 he has taught at Juilliard School of Music.

BALAZS, FREDERIC, b. Budapest, Hungary. Studied at Royal Acad. of Music in Budapest. In 1939 he became concertmaster of the Budapest Concert Orch. He was cond. of the Wichita Falls (Tex.) Symph., 1948–51. Since 1952 he has been cond. of the Tucson (Ariz.) Symph.

BALES, RICHARD, b. Alexandria, Va., Feb. 3, 1915. Studied at Eastman School of Music and Berkshire Music Center. He was cond. of the Virginia–North Carolina Symph., 1936–38. In the summer of 1947 he was music dir. of the Nat'l Symph. (Washington, D.C.). Since 1943 he has been cond. of the Nat'l Gallery Orch. (Washington, D.C.).

BALLINGER, JAMES S., b. Liberal, Kan., 1925. Studied at Univ. of Wichita and Oberlin (Ohio) Cons. of Music. He was a member (violin and viola) of the Wichita Symph. and the Oberlin Cons. Orch. Since 1951 he has taught at Fort Hays Kansas State Coll. and been dir. of the Fort Hays Coll. Community Orch.

BAMBERGER, CARL, b. Vienna, Austria, Feb. 21, 1902. Studied at Univ. of Vienna. He was opera cond. in Danzig and Darmstadt before coming to the U.S.A. in 1937. He was founder-cond. of the New Choral Group of Manhattan and the Brooklyn Oratorio Soc., 1940–45. Since 1938 he has been dir. of Orchestra and Opera at Mannes Coll. of Music (N.Y.C.). In 1944 he was cond. of the Southern Symph. (Columbia, S.C.). In 1952 he was cond. of the N.Y. City Opera and musical dir. of the Montreal Little Symph.

BAMBOSCHEK, GIUSEPPE, b. Italy, June 12, 1890. He was asst. cond., then casting dir. at the Metropolitan Opera, 1913–29. He was a cond. at the St. Louis Municipal Opera, 1930–32. In 1937 he became cond. of the Philadelphia La Scala Co., and in 1939 its musical dir. Since 1950 he has been artistic dir. of the Philadelphia Grand Opera Co.

BARATI, GEORGE, b. Gyor, Hungary, April 3, 1913. Studied at Franz Liszt Cons. of Music (Budapest) and at Princeton Univ. (N.J.). He was first cellist of the Budapest Symph., 1936–38. He was cond. of the Princeton Ensemble, 1940–43 and organized the Westminster String Quartet. He was a cellist in the San Francisco Symph., 1946–50. Since 1948 he has been musical dir. of the Barati Chamber Orch. (San Francisco), and since 1950 musical dir. of the Honolulu Symph. He organized the Honolulu Little Symph. and the Honolulu Community Chorus.

BARBIROLLI, JOHN, b. London, Dec. 2, 1899. Studied at Trinity Coll. and at Royal Acad. of Music (London). He was a member of the International String Quartet, 1922–27. In 1924 he founded the Barbirolli String Orch. After 1927, he conducted a series of London Symph. and Royal Philh. Soc. concerts and was engaged for several seasons at Covent Garden. He was successively cond. of the Scottish Orch., the Leeds Symph., and 1936–42, of the New York Philh. Since 1943 he has led the Halle Orch. of Manchester, England.

BARERA, ORLANDO, b. Ferrara, Italy, Feb. 6, 1907. Studied at Bologna Cons. In 1940 he became concertmaster of the Havana (Cuba) Philh., and in 1945 of the Kansas City Philh., later becoming its asst. cond. In 1949 he became asst. cond. of the Houston Symph. and conducted Houston's Summer Symph. and its Summertime Light Opera. In 1950 he was cond. of the Baton Rouge Symph. Since 1951 he has been cond. of the El Paso (Tex.) Symph.

BARLOW, HOWARD, b. Plain City, Ohio, May 1, 1892. Studied at Univ. of Colo., at Reed College (Ore.), and at Columbia Univ. In 1923 and 1924 he conducted the American Nat'l Orch. (N.Y.C.). He was musical dir. of CBS, 1927–43, and since 1944 has been cond. of the Voice of Firestone radio (later television) program on NBC.

BARNETT, JOHN M., b. New York, N.Y., Sept. 3, 1917. Studied at Manhattan Cons. and at Mozarteum Acad., Salzburg. He was asst. cond. of the Nat'l Orchestral Assn., 1937–39; cond. of the Stamford (Conn.) Symph., 1939–42; staff cond. of the N.Y. City Symph., 1940–42; cond. of the Phoenix (Ariz.) Symph., 1947–49; and dir. of the Hollywood Bowl, 1953–54. Since 1946 he has been assoc. cond. of the Los Angeles Philh. He is dir. of the Pacific Coast Music Fest.

BARONE, JOSEPH, b. New York, N.Y., May 31, 1910. Studied at Combs Cons. of Music and at Temple Univ. (Philadelphia). In 1939 he organized the Philadelphia Little Symph. and later the New York Little Symph. He became a teacher at Temple Univ. in 1940, and in 1944 dir. of music at the Univ. of Penn. Museum. In 1940 he founded the Philadelphia String Quartet, and in 1941 the Bryn Mawr Cons. of Music. Since 1941 he has headed Harcum Junior Coll. music dept., and been dir. of Monteux's School of Conducting in Hancock, Me. Since 1951 he has directed the Collegium Musicum at Univ. of Penn.

BARRON, ROBERT LOUIS, b. Benton Harbor, Mich., Dec. 7, 1897. Studied at Sherwood Music School (Chicago), at Coll. of the Pacific, and at Mills Coll. He taught violin at Univ. of Ore., 1918–19, and was a member of the Portland (Ore.) Symph., 1919–28. He was dir. of Manning School of Music (San Francisco), 1931–35; and cond. of the Amarillo (Tex.) Philh., 1940–48. Since 1949 he has been cond. of the Arkansas Valley Symph.

BARTH, GEORGE W., b. Tamaqua, Pa., Feb. 18, 1907. Studied at Juilliard School of Music, Columbia Univ., and Univ. of Southern Cal. He was concertmaster successively of the Greenwich (Conn.) Symph., the Wheeling (W.Va.) Symph., and the

Gulf Coast Symph. Since 1938 he has been cond. of Southwestern Louisiana Inst. Symph. (Lafayette, La.).

BARZIN, LEON, b. Brussels, Belgium, Nov. 27, 1900, and came to the U.S.A. at the age of two. Studied violin under Henrotte, Deru, Meergerlin, Ysaÿe. In 1920 he became a violinist in the Nat'l Symph. (N.Y.C.) and between 1921 and 1929 was successively violinist and violist of the N.Y. Philh. In 1929 he became assoc. cond. of the American Orchestral Soc., and the following year musical dir. of the Nat'l Orchestral Assn. (N.Y.C.), a post he has since held. He served as musical dir. successively of the Hartford (Conn.) Symph., 1938–40; of the Ballet Soc., 1947–48; and, after 1948, of the N.Y. City Ballet Co.

BAUER, LEROY. Studied at Milwaukee State Coll. and Northwestern Univ. He has conducted the Kearney (Neb.) Symphony since 1950. He teaches at Nebraska State Teachers Coll.

BEECHAM, SIR THOMAS, b. near Liverpool, England, April 29, 1879. Studied at Oxford Univ. He founded the New Symph. Orch. in London in 1906, introducing new composers to England, among them Frederick Delius. From 1910 he began providing London with exciting opera, with numerous new productions, with fine artists, and with his own well-trained orchestra. In the summer of 1911 he introduced the Russian Ballet to London. In 1928 he made his U.S.A. debut as guest with the N.Y. Philh. In 1932 the present London Philh. was founded under his direction. He guest conducts widely in the U.S.A.

BEHR, JAN, b. Prague, Czechoslovakia, April 1, 1911. Studied at Prague Acad. of Music and Prague Univ. He was a cond. at the German Opera House in Prague, 1930–38. He came to the

U.S.A. in 1946. Since 1951 he has been an asst. cond. at the Metropolitan Opera.

BERENS, FRITZ, b. Vienna, 1907. Studied at Vienna Cons. of Music. After holding positions as coach and asst. cond. in various German and Austrian cities, he came to America in 1939. That year he became musical dir. of the San Francisco Ballet. In 1942 he was asst. cond. with the San Francisco Opera. Since 1950 he has been cond. of the Sacramento Philh.

BERMAN, HARRY, b. Russia and came to the U.S.A. at the age of seven. Studied at Juilliard School of Music. He was principal violist in the New Haven (Conn.) Symph., 1920–53. He has been co-conductor of the New Haven Symph. since 1933, and cond. of its Pop Concerts since their inception in 1945.

BIBO, FRANZ, b. Berlin, Germany. Studied at Berlin Cons. of Music, at Mannes Coll. of Music (N.Y.C.), at New York Univ., at Juilliard School of Music, and with Monteux. He arrived in the U.S.A. in 1946 and from 1950 taught at Mannes. Since 1951 he has been cond. of the City Symph. of New York, and since 1955 on the faculty of Brooklyn Coll.

BITTER, JOHN, b. New York, N.Y. Studied at Curtis Inst. of Music and in Italy and Austria. In 1934 he became cond. of the Jacksonville (Fla.) Symph., and in 1940 of Univ. of Miami Symph., a post which he still holds. (Modeste Alloo served as cond. while Bitter was in the army and a few years thereafter.) He was assoc. cond. of the All-American Youth Orch., 1939–42. He is Dean of Univ. of Miami School of Music.

BLACK, NORMAN. Studied at Curtis Inst. of Music. He conducted over WFIL, Philadelphia, 1940–50. Since 1950 he has been violinist in the Philadelphia Orch. He is cond. of the Arco-Arte Sinfonietta of that city.

BLACKTON, JAY, b. New York, N.Y., 1909. Studied at Inst. of Musical Art and in Berlin and Paris. In 1937 he became asst. cond. of the St. Louis Municipal Opera. He conducted on Broadway and over radio, 1943–50. In 1947 he became cond. of the Delaware Philh.

BLOCH, ALEXANDER, b. Selma, Ala., July 11, 1881. Studied privately. He was cond. of the Central Florida Symph., Winter Park, 1936–43. Since 1950 he has been cond. of the Florida West Coast Symph.

BLOOMFIELD, THEODORE, b. Cleveland, Ohio, June 14, 1923. Studied at Oberlin (Ohio) Cons. of Music, at Juilliard Graduate School (N.Y.C.), and with Monteux. He was apprentice cond. with George Szell and the Cleveland Orch., 1946–47. In 1947 he founded the Cleveland Little Symph. and conducted it until 1952. In 1949 he organized the Civic Opera Workshop of Cleveland. He has guest conducted widely in Europe. In Feb. 1955 he became cond. of the Portland (Ore.) Symph.

BLUMENTHAL, DAVID, b. Hartford, Conn., Aug. 18, 1917. Studied at Julius Hartt School of Music (Hartford), Oberlin Cons. (Ohio), and Columbia Univ. Since 1950 he has been cond. of the Springfield (Mo.) Civic Symph.

BÖHM, KARL, b. Graz, Austria, Aug. 28, 1894. Studied under E. Mandyczewski in Vienna. He conducted at the Graz Opera House, 1919, and at the Munich State Opera, 1921. He was gen. dir. at Darmstadt, 1927, and in Hamburg, 1931. In 1934 he became dir. of the Dresden Opera. He directed the Vienna State Opera,

1943–44. In Feb. 1956 he was guest cond. with the Chicago Symph.

BOMHARD, MORITZ, b. Berlin, Germany, June 19, 1912. Studied at Leipzig Cons., Leipzig Univ., Juilliard School of Music, and Columbia Univ. He conducted Princeton Univ. Orch. In 1946 he organized and toured with "Opera for College." In Louisville (Ky.) he was first dir. of the New Lyric Stage, then, after 1952, dir. of the Kentucky Opera Assn.

BONNEY, MAURICE, b. Maryland, 1923. Studied at Juilliard School of Music. He organized and has since conducted the "Manhattan Symphonette," which became the New Symph. Orch. of New York in 1951. Since 1955 he has been assoc. cond. of the Houston (Tex.) Symph.

BOULT, SIR ADRIAN, b. near Chester, England, April 8, 1889. Studied at Oxford and Leipzig Cons. He taught at Royal Coll. of Music, London, 1919–23. He conducted the Birmingham (Eng.) City Orch., 1924–30. He was dir. of the BBC Symph., 1930–42, after 1942 resigning to devote himself entirely to conducting the BBC Symph. He was knighted in 1937. He was cond. of the London Philh., 1950–1957.

BOUTNIKOFF, IVAN, b. Koupiansk, Russia, Dec. 13, 1893. Studied at Acad. of Music in Kharkov, and with Artur Nikisch (Leipzig). He was cond. of the Symph. Orch. of So. Russia, 1919–20, and of the symph. at Acad. of Music in Athens, Greece, 1922–29. Since 1945, cond. of the Ballet Russe de Monte Carlo.

BOWLES, MICHAEL, b. Riverstown, Ireland, Nov. 30, 1909. Studied at Belvedere Coll. (Dublin) and Nat'l Univ. of Ireland. He formed the first Irish professional full-time symph. and directed its public concerts for six seasons. He was cond. of the New Zealand Nat'l Orch., 1950–53, and of the Indianapolis (Ind.) Philh. Soc., 1956.

BREISACH, PAUL, b. Vienna, June 3, 1896. He was staff cond. at the Nat'l Theater in Mannheim, 1921–24, then asst. cond. of the Vienna Opera, and then of the Berlin municipal and state operas. He came to the U.S.A. in 1939 and has since conducted at the Chicago Civic Opera and, after 1941, at the Metropolitan Opera.

BRICKEN, CARL, b. Shelbyville, Ky., Dec. 28, 1898. Studied at Yale Univ. He taught at Mannes College of Music and Inst. of Musical Art (N.Y.C.). He formed and conducted a symph. orch. at Univ. of Chicago, then became cond. of the symph. at Univ. of Wisc. He was cond. of the Seattle Symph., 1944–48.

BRICO, ANTONIA, b. Holland, June 26, 1902. Studied at Univ. of Cal. and Berlin State Acad. of Music. In 1927 she was a coach at the Bayreuth (Germany) Fest. In 1934 she founded the New York Women's Symph., which in 1938 evolved into the Brico Symph. In Denver (Colo.) she was first cond. of the Denver Philh. Orch., then, after 1947, cond. of the Denver Business-men's Orch.

BRIEFF, FRANK, b. New Haven, Conn., Apr. 19, 1912. Studied at Manhattan (N.Y.) School of Music, at the Amer. Cons. of Music, Fontainebleau, and at Juilliard School of Music. He was violist of the Guilet String Quartet, 1942–48, and in the NBC Symph., 1948–52. He has conducted the New Haven (Conn.) Symph. since 1951. He is cond. of the Bach Aria group (N.Y.C.).

BRINI, BELTRANDO M., b. Plymouth, Mass., May 8, 1907. Studied at Boston Univ. In 1929 he founded the Plymouth Junior

Civic Orch. Since 1950 he has has been cond. of the Plymouth Philh. Orch., since 1951 concertmaster of the Brockton (Mass.) Orchestral Soc., and since 1954 its asst. cond.

BROEKMAN, DAVID, b. Leyden, Holland. Studied at Royal Cons., The Hague. He came to the U.S.A. in 1924 and was a member (violin) of the New York Philh. for two years. He went to Hollywood in 1929 and was employed as dir. of pictures. In New York (after 1950) he conducted a series of orchestral programs in Cooper Union, "Music in the Making." He is a composer-cond. of television programs.

BROUNOFF, ZELMAN, b. Alamogordo, N.M. Studied with Walter Fried and Michael Press. He acts as clinician in Corpus Christi and Dallas schools. Since 1946 he has been asst. concertmaster of the Dallas Symph. and, since 1951, its asst. cond.

BROURMAN, JACQUES, b. Pittsburgh, Pa., April 23, 1931. Studied at Carnegie Inst. of Tech. (Pittsburgh) and at Aspen (Colo.) Music School. He was violinist in the Houston (Tex.) Symph. two seasons. Since 1956 he has been asst. cond. of the New Orleans Philh.

BROWN, H. ARTHUR, b. New York, N.Y., Apr. 8, 1907. Studied at Univ. of Wash., Juilliard Graduate School, and Amer. Cons. of Music, Fountainebleau, France. He conducted the El Paso (Tex.) Symph., 1930–50. In 1948 and 1949 he conducted the New Orleans Summer "Pops" concerts. Since 1948 he has been cond. of the Tulsa (Okla.) Philh.

BROWN, HARRY JOHN, b. Chicago, Ill. Studied at Eastman School of Music and Univ. of Chicago. He organized the Oak Park (Ill.) Junior Symph. He was cond. of the Tri-City Symph.,

Davenport, Iowa, 1949–52. Since 1953 he has been asst. cond. of the Boston Pops Tour Orch.

BUCKLEY, EMERSON, b. New York, N.Y., Apr. 14, 1916. Studied Brooklyn Cons. of Music and Columbia Univ. He was dir. of the Symph. Orch. and Chorus of Palm Beach, Fla., 1938–41; musical dir. of Columbia and San Carlo Opera, 1941–44; musical dir. of WOR and MBS, 1945–54; American musical dir. of the Marquis de Cuevas Grand Ballet, 1950; musical dir. and asst. to the gen. man. of the Grand Opera Fest. sponsored by Univ. of Puerto Rico, 1954 and 1955. From 1950 he was musical dir. of the Miami (Fla.) Opera Guild; from 1954, musical dir. of the Mendelssohn Glee Club (N.Y.C.); and from 1955 cond. of the New York City Opera. He directed the Central City (Colo.) Opera House Assoc. in 1956. In the fall of 1956 he was appointed administrator for the Chicago Theatre Assn.

BUKETOFF, IGOR, b. Hartford, Conn., May 29, 1915. Studied at Univ. of Kan. and Juilliard School of Music. He taught at Juilliard, 1935–45, and Chautauqua (N.Y.) School of Music, 1941–47, and for two seasons conducted the Chautauqua Opera Assoc. He taught at Columbia Univ., 1942–47, then toured, 1947–48, as cond. of Menotti operas. Since 1948 he has been cond. of the Fort Wayne (Ind.) Philh.

BURGIN, RICHARD, b. Warsaw, Poland, Oct. 11, 1892. Studied at Petrograd Cons. of Music. He has been concertmaster of the Leningrad Symph.; the Helsinki (Finland) Symph., 1912–15; the Christiania (Oslo) Philh., 1916–19; and the Stockholm Concert Soc. He was asst. to Leopold Auer, 1916–17. He founded and directed the Burgin Quartet and toured with it, 1916–18. Since 1920 he has been concertmaster of the Boston Symph. He organized the Burgin String Quartet there in 1921. He is assoc. cond.

of the Boston Symph., and, since 1951, cond. of the Portland (Me.) Symph.

BYLER, KENNETH, b. Kansas. Studied at Amer. Cons. of Music (Chicago), Univ. of Mich., and Juilliard School of Music. He founded the Salina-Wesleyan (Kan.) Civic Orch. in 1936. He conducted the Kent State Univ. (Ohio) Orch. and the Kent Civic Orch., 1939–47 with three years out in U.S. Navy. Since 1948 he has conducted the Lawrence Symph. (Appleton, Wisc.) and taught at Lawrence Coll. Since 1950 he has conducted the Badger Symph. (Fond du Lac).

CAMBOURAKIS, NICOS, b. Calymnos Island, Greece, Sept. 7, 1910. Studied at Rostov Cons. of Music (Russia) and Teachers Coll. of Columbia Univ. He was concertmaster of the Trenton (N.J.) Symph. He has taught in Nutley (N.J.) since 1932, been cond. of the Nutley Symph. since 1940 and of the Mountain Lakes Symph. since 1949.

CANTRICK, ROBERT, b. Monroe, Mich., Dec. 8, 1917. Studied at Univ. of Rochester, Harvard Univ., Juilliard School of Music, and Berkshire Music Center. He joined the faculty of Furman Univ. (Greenville, S.C.) in 1946, and in 1948 founded the Greenville Symph., conducting it until 1951. He was apprentice cond. with George Szell and the Cleveland Orch., 1951–52. Since 1952 he has been cond. of Carnegie Inst. of Technology Orch. (Pittsburgh).

CARANO, UGO, b. Naples, Italy, May 20, 1909. Came to the U.S.A. in 1916. Studied at Juilliard School, New York Univ., and Columbia Univ. Since 1939 he has been cond. of the West Hudson (N.J.) Symph.

CARTER, ALAN, b. Greenwich, Conn., July 29, 1904. Studied at Cologne Cons. (Germany). He founded the Westchester Quartette (N.Y.) and the Cremona Quartette (N.Y. City). He organized the Vermont Symph. in 1934, and founded the Composers' Conference and Chamber Music Center in Bennington, Vt., in 1945, both of which he has since directed. He is dir. of the music dept. of Middlebury Coll., Vt.

CAYTING, STANLEY, b. Bangor, Me., June 18, 1898. Studied at Eastman School of Music. He was dir. of music for Univ. of Maine summer session for several years and cond. of Univ. of Maine Symph. He was concertmaster of the Bangor Symph. and cond. of Univ. of Maine Orch., 1922–50. Then he became a member of the Cleveland Symph. Since 1953 he has been cond. of the Bangor Symph. and dir. of the Northern Cons. of Music (Bangor).

CERNY, HAROLD EARL, b. Belle Plaine, Iowa, Nov. 4, 1907. Studied at Iowa State Univ. He was violinist with the Denver Symph., 1930–31. He taught at Univ. of Iowa, 1933–35. Since 1935 he has taught at Nev. State Teachers Coll. and been cond. of the Kearney (Neb.) Symph.

CHAPPLE, STANLEY, b. London, England, Oct. 29, 1900. Studied at London Acad. of Music. In 1929 he became principal of London Acad. of Music. He was a member of the faculty at Berkshire Music Center, 1939–47, and cond. of the St. Louis Philh., 1946–48. He organized and directed the 200-voice St. Louis Civic Chorus. In 1948 he became dir. of Univ. of Wash. School of Music, organized an "Opera Theatre" there, and directed the Univ. Symph. He presented five festivals of contemporary Amer. music on the campus. From 1951 to 1954 he was cond. of the

Seattle Symph., and since 1953 has been cond. of the Tacoma Civic Orch.

CHARDON, YVES, b. Paris, France. Studied at Paris Cons. of Music. He toured southern Europe as cellist. He was assoc. cond. of the Minneapolis Symph., 1944–50. He organized and was cond. of the Florida Symph., 1950–54. He is principal cellist with the Baltimore Symph.

CHARLES, WALTER, b. Jersey City, N.J. Studied at Juilliard School of Music and then took up a career as cellist. During World War II he conducted the Second Air Force Symph. He conducted the Staten Island Symph., 1948–52, and the Plainfield Symph., 1952–54. Since 1955 he has been cond. of the Abilene (Tex.) Symph.

CHÁVEZ, CARLOS, b. Mexico City, Mex., June 13, 1899. Studied with Ponce, Ogazón, and Fuentes. In 1923 he organized and conducted a chamber music orch. in Mexico City. In 1928 he founded the Mexico City Symph., which he conducted till 1948. He was dir. of the Nat'l Cons. of Mexico, 1928–29. In 1929 he founded and directed the Coro del Cons. in Mexico. In 1947 he founded, and until 1952 directed, the Nat'l Inst. of Fine Arts in Mexico. Within this institution he founded the Nat'l Symph. Orch.

CHERKASSKY, PAUL, b. Odessa, Russia. Studied at Imperial Cons. of St. Petersburg. He became concertmaster of the Viipuri Symph. (Finland) and then, at the age of twenty-two, conducted opera for a period in St. Petersburg. Later he was concertmaster of the Helsingfors Symph. and cond. of the Nat'l Opera in Finland. In 1923 he came to the U.S.A. and was a member (violin) of the Boston Symph. until 1952. Since 1944 he has been cond. of the Civic Symph. (Boston).

CHERNIAVSKY, JOSEF, b. Russia. Studied (cello) at Imperial Cons. (St. Petersburg) and in Leipzig (Germany) under Julius Klengel. He toured the U.S.A. with the Zimro Chamber Ensemble and in 1928 became musical dir. of Universal Pictures in Hollywood. Then he entered the radio field. Since 1952 he has been cond. of the Saginaw (Mich.) Civic Symph.

CHRISTIAN, MINAS, b. Wichita, Kan., Apr. 25, 1921. Studied at Univ. of Mich., at Univ. of Wichita, at Juilliard School of Music, and with Monteux. He was violinist in the Kansas City Philh., 1940–42, and subsequently cond. of Univ. of Ark. Symph. Since 1954 he has been cond. of the Evansville (Ind.) Philh.

CHRISTIANSEN, OLAF CHRISTIAN, b. Minneapolis, Aug. 12, 1901. Studied at St. Olaf Coll., Union Seminary, Pacific Luth. Coll., and Allegheny Coll. He taught in various colleges, including Oberlin, 1929–41. Since 1941 he has been chairman of the Dept. of Music at St. Olaf Coll. (Northfield, Minn.), and dir. of the St. Olaf Choir.

CHRISTMANN, ARTHUR, b. New York, N.Y., Oct. 26, 1908. Studied at Juilliard School of Music, at Columbia Univ., and with Monteux. He was first clarinetist, with the Worcester Music Fest. Orch., 1933–42 and with the Chautauqua Symph., 1933–42. He conducted the Yonkers (N.Y.) Symph., 1940–43. He has taught clarinet, since 1934 at Juilliard and since 1952 at Montclair (N.J.) State Teachers Coll. Since 1953 he has been cond. of the Ridgewood (N.J.) Symph. and since 1955 of the Plainfield (N.J.) Symph.

CIMARA, PIETRO, b. Rome, Italy, Nov. 10, 1887. Studied at St. Cecilia Cons. of Music (Rome). He was assoc. cond. of the

Royal Opera (Rome) for seven years, then became accompanist for Luisa Tetrazzini on tour. He was asst. to Toscanini at La Scala (Milan) four years and asst. cond. at the Teatro Colón (Buenos Aires, 1925). Since 1928 he has conducted at the Metropolitan Opera. He was a cond. at the San Francisco Opera, 1938–52.

CLEVA, FAUSTO, b. Trieste, Italy, 1902. Studied at Trieste Cons. From 1919 he was assoc. cond. at the Teatro Carcano in Milan. He was chorus master at the Metropolitan Opera, 1920–42, and assoc. cond. there, 1938–42. Since 1934 he has been a cond. of the Cincinnati Summer Opera, since 1946 of the San Francisco Opera, and since 1950 of the Metropolitan Opera.

CLUYTENS, ANDRE, b. Belgium. He was asst. cond. of the Antwerp Opera and musical dir. of the Lyons, Toulouse, and Bordeaux operas. In 1949 he became cond. of the Nat'l Cons. Orch. in Paris.

COHN, ARTHUR, b. Philadelphia, Pa., Nov. 6, 1910. Studied at Combs Cons. (Philadelphia) and Juilliard Graduate School. He was founder and violinist of the Dorian String Quartet, 1928–33, and of the Stringart Quartet, 1933–38, and cofounder of the Philadelphia Chamber Orch. He was head of the Music Dept. of the Free Library of Philadelphia, 1948–53. Since 1950 he has been cond. of the Germantown (Pa.) Symph.

COHN, WALDO, b. 1910. Studied at Univ. of Cal. In 1944 he founded the Oak Ridge (Tenn.) Symph. and conducted it until 1955, when he went to England to do research.

COLEMAN, ALBERT, b. Paris, France, 1910. He was a member of the Shanghai (China) Symph. He organized a thirty-piece orch. for the New Zealand Broadcasting System (Auckland). In

1945 he founded and has since conducted the Atlanta (Ga.) "pops" summer series.

COMPARETTI, ERMANNO F., b. Italy, May 22, 1909. Studied at Cornell Univ., Univ. of Rome, and Berkshire Music Center. Since 1940 he has taught at Colby Coll. (Waterville, Me.) and been cond. of the Colby Community Symph.

CONTE, JOSEPH, b. Pawtucket, R.I., Nov. 23, 1914. Studied at R.I. Coll. of Education, Univ. of N.H., and Boston Univ. In 1942 he organized the Fort Devens (Mass.) Symph. He is concertmaster of the R.I. Philh. Orch. Since 1955 he has been cond. of the R.I. Philh. Youth Orch.

COOLBAUGH, BLAINE, b. Kansas. Studied at Fort Hays Kansas State Coll. (Kan.) and Univ. of Wyo. He organized the Casper (Wyo.) Civic Symph. in 1947 and has since been its cond. He is supervisor of instrumental music in the public schools of Casper.

COOPER, EMIL, b. Kherson, Russia, Dec. 1, 1880. Studied at Cons. of Odessa; studied conducting under Artur Nikisch. He conducted opera in Kiev and Moscow, and in 1910 became cond. of the Imperial Opera of Russia and of the Imperial Musical Soc. (Moscow). In 1925 he became musical dir. of the Riga Opera. He was cond. of the Chicago Civic Opera, 1929–32, and of the Classical Symph. Concerts at Monte Carlo, 1936–39. In 1941 he conducted at the Chicago Civic Opera and from 1946 to 1950 at the Metropolitan. Since 1951 he has been musical dir. of the Baton Rouge (La.) Civic Symph.

COPPOLA, ANTON, b. New York, N.Y., 1918. Studied at Juilliard School of Music. He was oboist in the Radio City Music Hall Symph., 1936–43. He has been musical dir. of the San Carlo

Opera, the International Opera, and the Connecticut Opera. For four years he was assoc. cond. of the Radio City Music Hall Symph. He has conducted for Broadway musicals and for the Cincinnati Summer Opera.

CORTEZ, MARIO, b. Naples, 1902. Studied at Naples Royal Cons. of Music. He came to the U.S.A. in 1924. He has been a cellist in the New York Philh. since 1929. For two years he conducted the Queens (N.Y.) Symph., and from 1946 to 1950 was one of the conductors of the Carnegie Pop Concerts. He is cond. of the Regina Pacis Symph. (Brooklyn, N.Y.).

CRAFT, ROBERT, b. Kingston, N.Y., Oct. 20, 1923. Studied at Juilliard School of Music and the Berkshire Music Center, and with Monteux. He was cond. of the N.Y. Chamber Art Soc. and the N.Y. Brass and Woodwind Ensemble, 1947–50. He conducted the Los Angeles "Evenings-on-the-Roof," 1950–54. Since 1954 he has conducted the Los Angeles "Monday Evening Concerts" and (summers) at the Ojai Fest. (Cal.).

CRAWFORD, WILFORD B., b. Cameron, Miss., Nov. 1, 1911. Studied at Northwestern Univ. and Juilliard School of Music. Since 1951, he has been cond. of the Dow (Midland, Mich.) Symph.

CRESCENTI, PASQUALE, b. S. Benedetto del Tronto, Italy, Mar. 15, 1895. Studied at San Pietro a Mayella Cons. (Naples), Balatka Cons. (Chicago), and Univ. of Chicago. He conducted the Joliet (Ill.) Symph., 1937–50. Since 1950 he has been cond. of the Joliet Local 37 (A.F. of M.) Symphoniette.

CRONQUIST, ROBERT, b. Chicago, Ill., June 10, 1929. Studied at Arizona State Univ. and Western Reserve Univ. He was a member (horn) of the Phoenix Symph., 1947–49, the Youngstown (Ohio) Orch., 1949–50, and the Canton (Ohio) Symph., 1951–56. Since 1954 he has been musical dir. of the Mansfield (Ohio) Symph.

CURTIS, EDGAR, b. Aberdeen, Scotland, Mar. 11, 1914. Studied at Curtis Inst. of Music and Berkshire Music School. In 1942 he founded the Edgar Curtis String Orch. (Boston). Since 1948 he has been musical dir. of the Albany (N.Y.) Symph. and since 1953 of the Tri-City (Albany, Troy, and Schenectady) Symph., which he founded.

DALVIT, LEWIS, b. Denver, Colo., 1925. Studied at Beloit (Wisc.) Coll. and at Vandercooke (Wisc.) Coll. of Music. In 1955 he organized and has since conducted the Beloit Civic Symph.

DAMIANI, LEO, b. St. Paul, Minn., July 29, 1912. Studied at Univ. of Minn., McPhail School of Music (Minneapolis), and Juilliard School of Music. He was violinist for two years with the Minneapolis Symph. In 1944 he founded the Burbank (Cal.) Symph. and in 1948 the Burbank Youth Symph., both of which he has since conducted. Since 1946 he has taught in California Acad. of Music.

D'ANDREA, FRANK, b. Pittsburgh, Pa., Aug. 9, 1914. Studied at Columbia Univ., Juilliard School of Music, Royal Acad. of Music (London) and Paris Cons. Since 1945 he has been chairman of the music dept., Western Wash. Coll. of Education (Bellingham, Wash.). Since 1949 he has been cond. of the Bellingham Civic Symph., since 1953 of the Vancouver, B.C., Junior Symph. and since 1954 of the New Westminster, B.C., Symph.

DANIEL, ERNO, b. Budapest, Hungary, May 6, 1918. Studied at Royal Acad. of Music (Budapest), and later, 1942–49, taught there. In 1949 he came to the U.S.A., studied at Berkshire Music Center, and taught at Midwestern Univ. (Wichita Falls, Tex.). Since 1952 he has been cond. of the Wichita Falls Symph.

DANIELS, DAVID, b. Warsaw, Poland. Studied in Vienna and Berlin. He came to the U.S.A. in 1914. He helped organize the Wheeling (W.Va.) Symph. and the Parkersburg (W.Va.) Symph. Since 1948 he has been cond. of the Fairmont (W.Va.) Symph.

D'ARTEGA, ALFONSO, b. Mexico, June 5, 1907. Came to the U.S.A. in 1918. He was cond. of the Buffalo Symph. "Pops" concerts, 1948–50, and of the Carnegie (N.Y.C.) "Pops," 1946–50.

DASH, JAMES ALLAN, b. Philadelphia, Pa. Studied at Univ. of Penn., Leipzig Cons., and Basle Cons. He was musical dir. of the Phila. Bach Fest. Soc., 1930–47. In 1946 he became cond. of the Ohio Glee Club. In 1948 he became musical dir. of WBAL, Baltimore.

de ALMEIDA, ANTONIO, b. Paris, France, Jan. 20, 1929. Studied under Alberto Ginastera in Buenos Aires, at Yale School of Music, and at Berkshire Music Center. In 1945 he came to the U.S.A., where he founded and conducted the Mass. Inst. of Technology Symph. (Cambridge). He conducted the (New Haven) "Pocket Symph.," 1947–49.

de CARVALHO, ELEAZAR, b. Iguatu, Brazil, June 28, 1915. Studied at Nat'l School of Music of Univ. of Brazil. He played tuba in the Brazilian Symph. and in 1941 became its asst. cond. Since 1946 he has been on the staff of the Berkshire Music Center.

DEFAUW, DÉSIRÉ, b. Ghent, Belgium, Sept. 5, 1885. Studied at Brussels Royal Cons. and later became its dir. In 1906 he became cond. of the New Symph. Orch. of London. In 1922 he founded Concerts Defauw of Brussels and in 1937 was engaged as cond. of the Nat'l Orch. of Belgium. He was cond. of Les Concerts Symphoniques de Montréal, 1940–43, of the Chicago Symph., 1943–47, then again of Les Concerts Symphoniques de Montréal. Since 1953 he has also been cond. of the Bloomington-Normal (Ill.) Symph., since 1954 of the Grand Rapids (Mich.) Symph., and since 1956 of the Northwestern Univ. Summer Orch.

de FRANK, VINCENT, b. Long Island City, N.Y. Studied at Juilliard School of Music. He played cello in the Nat'l Orchestral Soc., and with the Detroit Symph. He was cond. of the Memphis (Tenn.) Symph., 1945–47. He then was cellist with the St. Louis Symph. for three seasons. Since 1952 he has been cond. of the Memphis Sinfonietta.

DENECKE, HENRY, b. New York, N.Y., Aug. 11, 1914. Trained with the National Orchestral Assn. (N.Y.C.). He was tympanist successively with the Cleveland, Pittsburgh, and Minneapolis symphony orchestras, leaving the latter in 1951. In 1944 he organized and has since conducted the Northwest Sinfonietta (Minneapolis). He conducted the Minneapolis Civic Orch., 1952–54. Since 1953 he has been cond. of the Cedar Rapids (Iowa) Symph.

DENNIS, JOHN, b. Minneapolis, Minn., Apr. 22, 1922. Studied at Chicago Cons. of Music and Univ. of Minnesota. He has taught in the Mankato (Minn.) school system since 1949. Since 1950 he has been cond. of the Mankato Symph.

de RIDDER, ALLARD, b. Dordrecht, Holland, 1887. Studied with Fritz Steinbach and Hermann Abendroth (Cologne). He came to the U.S.A. and was a member of the Los Angeles Philh. in the twenties. He helped re-establish the Vancouver (B.C.) Symph. in 1930, conducting it until 1938. He conducted the Ottawa Philh., 1944–50. He is now a choral cond. and teacher in Vancouver.

de RIMANOCZY, JEAN, b. Vienna, 1904. Studied at Franz Joseph Univ. and Royal Hungarian Acad. of Music. He went to Canada in 1925 and a year later became a member of the Minneapolis Symph. He helped form the Calgary Philh. He is asst. cond. and concertmaster of the Vancouver (B.C.) Symph.

Di BLASI, FRANCESCO. Since 1950 he has been cond. of the Pontiac (Mich.) Symph. and since 1954 musical dir. of the Michigan Opera Co. (Detroit). He is a member of the Detroit Symph.

Di CECCO, MARIO, b. Italy. Studied at New York Univ. In 1936 he founded and has since conducted the Waterbury (Conn.) Civic Orch.

DICKIESON, GEORGE W., b. Brooklyn, N.Y., Feb. 6, 1912. Studied at Cincinnati Cons. of Music and with Monteux. Since 1938 he has been affiliated with the Greensboro (N.C.) Symph., first as concertmaster, then as asst. cond., and since 1950 as cond. Since 1938 he has taught at School of Music of Woman's Coll. of Univ. of N.C.

DICKSON, HARRY ELLIS, b. Cambridge, Mass., Nov. 13, 1908. Studied at New England Cons. of Music, at Berlin Hochschule, and with Monteux. Since 1938 he has been a violinist in the

Boston Symph. He organized the Providence (R.I.) Civic Orch., 1938, and conducted it for seven years. In 1956 he became asst. cond. of the Boston Pops.

DIXON, DEAN, b. New York, N.Y., Jan. 10, 1915. Studied at Inst. of Musical Art, Columbia Univ., and Juilliard Graduate School. He formed the Dean Dixon Symph., 1932–41. In 1940 he led the Nat'l Youth Administration Orch. In 1943 he was musical dir. of the Shoestring Opera Co. (N.Y.C.). In 1944, he organized his own youth orch. in New York.

DUCLOUX, WALTER, b. Switzerland, Apr. 17, 1913. Studied at Univ. of Munich. He conducted the Casino Orch. in Lucerne, 1938–39. He was asst. to Toscanini at the Lucerne Music Fest., 1938–39. In 1939 he came to the U.S.A. He was music dir. of Charles L. Wagner's touring opera, 1940–42. After a period in the army he conducted on radio in Czechoslovakia, 1946–48. Late in 1948 he again became cond. of Wagner's opera co. In 1951 he became musical dir. of the Voice of Amer. and in 1953 head of the Opera Dept. at Univ. of Southern Cal.

DUNCAN, RICHARD, b. Rochester, N.Y., Jan. 15, 1913. Studied at Eastman School of Music and Berkshire Music Center. In 1935 he became head of the violin dept. at Ohio State Univ. and asst. cond. of the Ohio State Symph. In 1937 he reorganized and conducted the Hastings (Neb.) Dime Symph. (Civic Orch.). In 1939 he headed the instrumental and choral depts. at Univ. of Omaha and conducted the Omaha Little Symph., 1939–43. He founded the Omaha Symph. in 1947 and has since conducted it. In 1950 he founded the Omaha Light Opera Co.

ECHÁNIZ, JOSÉ, b. Guanabacoa, Cuba, June 4, 1905. Studied at Falcón Cons. of Music (Havana). In 1927 he made his New

York debut as a pianist and has since toured the country extensively. He became cond. of the Grand Rapids (Mich.) Symph. in 1948, resigning in 1954 to devote himself to piano concerts and to his teaching at Eastman School of Music.

EHRLICH, JULIUS, b. Feb. 3, 1894, Frankfurt-am-Main, Germany. He was musical dir. of "Stadthallen" Symph. Concerts, Hanover, 1923–28, a cond. at the State Opera, Leningrad, 1929–33, and a cond. at the Flemish Opera House, Antwerp, 1934–36. He founded the Milwaukee Symph., 1937, and the Milwaukee Sinfonietta, 1943.

EISENBERG, WALTER, b. Philadelphia, Pa., 1914. Studied (violin) privately and at Juilliard Graduate School (N.Y.C.). In 1947 he became concertmaster of the Denver Symph., and shortly afterward its asst. cond. During the same period he taught at Lamont School of Music of Univ. of Denver and conducted its orchestra. In 1953 he became cond. of the Pueblo (Colo.) Symph., and in 1954 of the Colorado Springs Symph.

ELDER, LEIGH, b. La Crosse, Wisc. Studied at New England Cons. of Music (Boston) and in Europe. Since 1941 he has been cond. of the La Crosse Symph.

ENGEL, LEHMAN, b. Jackson, Miss., Sept. 14, 1910. Studied at Cincinnati Coll., Cincinnati Cons., and Juilliard School of Music. He is known as a composer especially of theater music and as a cond. for stage productions, radio, and television. In 1935 he organized and became dir. of the Madrigal Singers (N.Y.C.).

FACEY, THOMAS. Studied at Cornish School of Music (Seattle), Willamette Univ., and Univ. of Wash. He was a member of the Dallas and Denver symphonies. He is cond. of the Golden Civic Orch., Golden, Colo.

FAIN, SAMUEL S., b. Chicago, Ill., Dec. 25, 1909. Studied at Northwestern Univ., Univ. of Arizona, and Univ. of Southern Cal. He was cond. of the Northwest Civic Symph. (Chicago) 1937–39 and the Tucson (Ariz.) Symph., 1945–50. Since 1946 he has taught at the Univ. of Ariz.

FANTOZZI, WILLIAM, b. Chicago, Ill., May 10, 1896. He played violin in the Chicago Symph. for thirteen years. From 1949 to 1950 he was asst. cond. of the Kansas City Philh.

FARBMAN, HARRY, b. Cincinnati. He formed his own string quartet and became concertmaster of the Nat'l Orchestral Assn. Since 1942 he has been concertmaster and asst. cond. of the St. Louis Symph., and head of the St. Louis String Quartet and Farbman Sinfonietta. Since 1952 he has directed the Springfield (Ill.) Symph. He conducts the Laclede Orch. on a weekly television program in St. Louis.

FELBER, HERMAN, b. in Middle West. He was a member (violin) of the Chicago Symph. for five years—also of the Berkshire String Quartet and the Great Lakes String Quartet. Since 1932 he has been cond. of the Kalamazoo (Mich.) Symph.

FENDLER, EDVARD, b. Leipzig, Germany, Jan. 22, 1902. Studied at Stern Cons. (Berlin). He was dir. of the Kammer-Sinfonie-Orch. (Berlin) 1930–33. Since 1951 he has been cond. of the Mobile (Ala.) Symph.

FENNELL, FREDERICK, b. Cleveland, Ohio, July 2, 1914. Studied at Eastman School of Music, Mozarteum Acad. (Salzburg), and Berkshire Music Center. In 1939 he became a member of the Eastman faculty and cond. of its Little Symph. Since 1945 he has been assoc. cond. of the Eastman School Orch. He is the cond. of the Eastman School Symphonic Wind Ensemble.

FERRERA, DON, b. San Francisco, Cal. He was a violinist in the San Francisco Symph. Since 1955 he has been cond. of the Las Vegas (Nev.) Symph., which he founded.

FETTER, EVERETT, b. Raytown, Mo., May 4, 1908. Studied at Ottawa Univ. (Kans.), at Univ. of Kans., at Juilliard Summer School, and with Monteux. He taught at Ottawa Univ., 1927–42. Since 1946 he has taught at Washburn Univ. (Topeka, Kans.) and been cond. of the Topeka Symph.

FIEDLER, ARTHUR, b. Boston, Mass., Dec. 17, 1894. Studied at Berlin Royal Acad. He was a member of the Boston Symph., 1915–30, first playing the violin, later the viola. In 1924 he organized the Boston Sinfonietta. He organized and began to conduct the Esplanade Concerts in 1929, and since 1930 has been cond. of the Boston "Pops" Orch. He toured the U.S.A. with the Boston "Pops" Tour Orch., 1953 and 1956. He teaches at Boston Univ. and conducts the Cecilia Soc., the MacDowell Club Orch., and the Univ. Glee Club at Providence, R.I.

FINDLAY, FRANCIS M., b. Idaho, Jan. 29, 1894. Studied at New England Cons. of Music, Mozarteum Acad. (Salzburg), and Harvard Univ. He taught at the New England Cons., 1920–50. Since 1950 he has taught at Boston Univ. and been cond. of the Boston Univ. Orch. He is also cond. of the Worcester (Mass.) Symph.

FIORATO, HUGO, b. New York, N.Y., Aug. 28, 1914. Studied at Frankfurt (Germany) Cons., Damrosch School (N.Y.C.), and American School of Applied Music. In 1932 he formed the Estrellita Trio (later called the Gotham Trio). Also from 1932 he was a violinist of the Nat'l Orchestral Assn. and its cond. in the 1956–57 season. Since 1946 he has been affiliated with the

New York City Ballet (earlier called the Ballet Society), first as concertmaster, then as asst. cond., and since 1955 as assoc. cond.

FIORE, ROLAND, b. Jersey City, N.J., Sept. 28, 1923. Studied with Vittorio Giannini (composition) and Tibor Serly (conducting). He was on the conducting staff of the New York City Opera, 1945–47, then for several years was musical dir. for the Schubert theaters. In 1949 he was musical dir. of the Memphis (Tenn.) Open Air Theater, and since 1951 has held this post with the Starlight Theatre, Kansas City, Mo.

FISCHER, IRWIN, b. Iowa City, Iowa, July 5, 1903. Studied at Univ. of Chicago, Amer. Cons. of Music (Chicago), and Mozarteum Acad. (Salzburg). He was cond. of the Nat'l Youth Administration Orch. in Chicago, 1939–42, the South Side Symph., 1942–48, and the Gary (Ind.) Civic Symph., 1949–53, as well as founder of the latter two orchestras. Since 1944 he has been organist of the Chicago Symph., and since 1953 cond. of the Evanston (Ill.) Symph.

FISCHER, MARTIN, b. Sioux City, Iowa. Studied at Morningside Coll. (Sioux City) and Juilliard Graduate School. Since 1948 he has been assoc. cond. of the Rhode Island Philh. and cond. of the Brown Univ. Orch.

FISCHER, RICHARD, b. Chicago, Ill., Aug. 25, 1923. Studied at Eastman School of Music. He has been a violist in the Rochester Philh., the Nat'l Symph., the Pittsburgh Symph., and the Grant Park Symph., Chicago. He has taught at Hastings Coll. (Neb.) and was cond. of the Hastings Civic Symph., 1951–55. Since 1955 he has taught at Eastern N.M. Univ. (Portales, N.M.) and been cond. of the Univ. String Orch.

FISHER, FRANK E., b. Burgettstown, Pa., July 12, 1917. Studied at Ernest Williams School of Music (Brooklyn), Univ. of Mich., and Berkshire Music Center. Since 1946 he has taught at Willamette Univ. and been cond. of the univ. orch. In 1946 he organized and became the cond. of the Salem (Ore.) Community Orch.

FLETCHER, GRANT, b. Hartsburg, Ill., Oct. 25, 1913. Studied at Univ. of Michigan and Eastman School of Music. He has been cond. of the Business Men's Orch. (Springfield, Ill.), the Winthrop (S.C.), Civic Orch., the Rock Hill (S.C.) Civic Orch., the Akron (Ohio) Symph. (which he organized), and the Chicago Musical Coll. Symph. Since 1950 he has been cond. of the Maywood (Ill.) Symph. and the Chicago Symphonietta.

FORESTER, DAVID. A former cond. of the Baton Rouge Symph., he founded the Hollywood Canteen Orch. during World War I. Since 1954 he has been cond. of the San Bernardino Valley (Cal.) Symph.

FORSTAT, MILTON, b. Cleveland, Ohio, 1910. Studied at Bronx (N.Y.C.) House Music School and Juilliard Graduate School. He was a member (cello) of the Nat'l Orchestral Assn. (N.Y.), 1928–31. He taught at the Chautauqua Inst. in 1937. Since 1938 he has been cellist in the New York Philh., and since 1945 cond. of the Westchester (White Plains, N.Y.) Symph.

FOSS, LUKAS, b. Berlin, Germany, Aug. 15, 1922. Studied at French Gymnasium (Berlin), Lycée Pasteur (Paris), Curtis Inst. of Music, Yale Univ., and Berkshire Music Center. He was official pianist with the Boston Symph., 1944–50, and in 1954–55 conducted the UCLA (Los Angeles) Symph. and the Los Angeles Chamber Symph.

FRACHT, J. ALBERT, b. Warsaw, Poland, June 4, 1904. Spent his childhood in Massachusetts. Studied at the Inst. of Musical Art (N.Y.C.) and with Ševčik (Bohemia). Since 1944 he has been cond. of the Charleston (S.C.) Symph., since 1948 music dir. of the Azalea Fest., and since 1951 cond. of the South Carolina Philh.

FREIBURGHAUS, GEORGE E., b. St. Louis, Mo. Studied at Curtis Inst. of Music. He was bass player with the Kansas City Philh., 1942–43, and with the Honolulu Symph., 1944–45. He organized and since 1949 has conducted the Helena (Mont.) Symphonette.

FRICSAY, FERENC, b. Budapest, Hungary, Aug. 9, 1914. Studied at Budapest Acad. of Music. He was cond. of the Philh. Soc. in Szeged, Hungary, 1935–39. He conducted at the 1947 Salzburg Fest. He was musical dir. of the Municipal Opera, Berlin, 1949–52, and cond. of the R.I.A.S. (radio) Orch. there. He was cond. of the Houston (Tex.) Symph., 1954–55.

GAHAN, EDWARD J., b. Fall River, Mass. Studied at New England Cons. He joined the Fall River Symph. as first trumpet in 1937, and since 1950 has been its cond.

GANSZ, GEORGE, b. Philadelphia, Pa., 1924. Studied at Temple Univ., at Univ. of Penn., at Trinity Coll. (London), and with Monteux. He was the cond. of the Lehigh Univ. Fest. Orch., Bethlehem, Pa., 1948–54, and cond. of the Allentown (Pa.) Symphonette, 1948–54. Since 1954 he has been cond. of the Centenary Symph. Orch. and Dir. of Instrumental Music, Centenary Coll., Shreveport, La.

GARDNER, SAMUEL, b. Elizabethgrad, Russia, Aug. 25, 1896. Studied at Inst. of Musical Art (N.Y.C.). He played in the Kneisel

Quartet, 1914–15, and was violinist in the Chicago Symph., 1915–16. He taught at Inst. of Musical Art, 1919–41. He was cond. of the Staten Island (N.Y.) Symph., 1946–47, and of the Brooklyn Coll. Orch., 1953–54.

GASKA, ZIGMONT, b. Elkhart, Ind., Apr. 3, 1908. Studied with Monteux. He was concertmaster of the South Bend (Ind.) Symph. and the Fort Wayne Philh. for seventeen years. In 1939 he organized and conducted the Little Symph. (Mishawaka, Ind.), then organized and for eleven years conducted the South Bend Junior Symph. In 1948 he helped found the Elkhart (Ind.) Symph., which he has since conducted.

GATES, EVERETT, b. Des Moines, Iowa, 1914. Studied at Drake Univ. and Eastman School of Music. He was violist in the Des Moines Symph. Orch., in the Des Moines String Quartet, and (for eight years) in the Oklahoma City Symph. Since 1956 he has been asst. cond. of the Oklahoma City Symph.

GEBERT, ERNST, b. Berlin, Germany, 1910. He held conducting positions with the Berlin Philh., the Berlin State Opera, and the Prague Opera House before coming to the U.S.A. in 1939. In 1943 he headed the opera dept. at Univ. of Wash. In 1940 he became musical dir. of the Seattle Opera. In 1948 he founded the Inglewood (Los Angeles) Symph., which he has since conducted.

GEISLER, LLOYD, b. in Pottstown, Pa., May 30, 1913. Studied at Curtis Inst. of Music. He has been first chair trumpet of the Nat'l Symph. (Washington, D.C.) since 1936. In the summer of 1941 he toured with the All-Amer. Youth Orch. Since 1953 he has occasionally conducted children's concerts of the Nat'l Symph. and the summer series "Under the Stars." He teaches at Catholic Univ. (Wash., D.C.).

GEORGE, GRAHAM, b. Norwich, England, 1912. Studied at Univ. of Toronto, Canadian Coll. of Organists, and Yale Univ. He was cond. of the Queens Symph. (Kingston, Ont.), 1946–52. Since 1946 he has been head of the music dept. of Queen's Univ. and since 1954 cond. of the New Symph. of Kingston and the Kingston Choral Soc.

GERHART, RUSSELL, b. Altoona, Pa., Mar. 26, 1904. Studied at Berkshire Music Center. He developed the Altoona (Pa.) Civic Symph., and conducted it from 1929 to 1951. He conducted the Hagerstown (Md.) Symph., 1937–41; the Bedford (Pa.) Symph., 1940–43; and the Johnstown (Pa.) Municipal Symph., 1946–51. Since 1951 he has been cond. of the St. Louis Philh.

GERKOWSKI, RAYMOND, b. Orwell, Ohio, Mar. 6, 1906. Studied at Cleveland Inst. of Music and Western Reserve Univ. He was a member (cello) of the Cleveland Orch., 1924–39. As dir. of school and community music at Flint, Mich., he conducts the Flint Symph., the Flint Choral Union, and the Flint Civic Opera.

GIGANTE, CHARLES, b. Italy, 1911. He came to the U.S.A. when eight months old. Studied at Eastman School of Music, Berkshire Music Center, and Juilliard School of Music. He was a violinist in the Rochester Philh., and the Nat'l Symph. (Washington, D.C.). He conducted the Eastman School Symph. (Rochester), the Phillips Art Gallery Orch. (Washington, D.C.), and the Rochester Community Orch., 1950–54. Since 1956 he has conducted the Tri-City Symph. serving Davenport (Iowa), Rock Island (Ill.), and Moline (Ill.)

GINSBURG, HENRY T., b. New York, N.Y., Dec. 16, 1892. Studied with Henry Schradieck (N.Y.C.). In 1925 he became concertmaster of the Denver (Colo.) Symph. In 1928 he organized the Denver String Quartet. He teaches at Denver Coll. of Music and at Colo. State Coll. Since 1945 he has been cond. of the Greeley (Colo.) Philh.

GOLDOVSKY, BORIS, b. Moscow, Russia, June 7, 1908. Studied at Moscow Cons., in Berlin, and at Budapest Cons. As a concert pianist he toured Europe and, after 1930, the U.S.A. In 1945 he founded the New England Opera Theater, became its musical dir., and toured with it for several years. He is founder and dir. of the Oglebay Inst. (W.Va.) Opera Workshop.

GOOSSENS, EUGENE, b. London, England, May 26, 1893. Studied at Bruges Cons., Liverpool Coll. of Music, and Royal Coll. of Music (London). He was a violinist in the Queen's Hall Orch. (London). He was cond. at the British Nat'l Opera and the Covent Garden Opera, 1911–15. He was cond. of the Royal Choral Soc., 1917–19, and of the Diaghilev Ballet, 1919–23. He became cond. of the Rochester Philh., 1923–31, and of the Cincinnati Symph., 1931–47. He was cond. of the Sydney (Australia) Symph., 1947–56.

GOULD, MORTON, b. Richmond Hill, N.Y., Dec. 10, 1913. He was staff pianist for Radio City Music Hall and in 1934 became a cond. over WOR. He has toured the U.S.A. with his own concert orchestra and is often heard over the radio.

GREENE, ALLEN, b. Passaic, N.J. Studied at Harvard and Berkshire Music Center. He became a member (French horn) of the Denver (Colo.) Symph. in 1945, and in 1954 its asst. cond.

GROVER, PAUL, b. Ellsworth, Kan., Dec. 17, 1908. Studied at Univ. of Kan., Kan. Wesleyan Univ., and Kan. State Coll. He conducted the Univ. of Dubuque (Iowa) Symph., 1948–51, and since 1951 has led the Ozarks-Clarksville Little Symph. (Clarksville, Ark.).

GUDERYAHN, RICHARD, b. Chicago, Ill., 1904. Studied at Amer. Cons. of Music (Chicago), and with Monteux. He conducted the Youth Orch. at the Amer. Cons., 1925–26; the Central Coll. Orch., Fayette, Mo., 1926–27; and the Augustana Coll. Orch., Sioux Falls, S.D., 1927–52. Since 1952 he has conducted the Town and Gown Symph. in Sioux Falls.

GUIDI, SCIPIONE, b. Venice, Italy. Studied at Milan Cons. of Music. He was concertmaster with the New York Philh. for twelve years, during which time he formed and played in the New York Philh. String Quartet. He was asst. cond. and concertmaster of the St. Louis Symph., 1931–42. Since 1945 he has been cond. of the Glendale (Cal.) Symph.

HAAKER, WILLIAM, b. Albany, N.Y., Mar. 14, 1917. Studied piano and conducting with José Iturbi, and at Eastman School of Music. He conducted the Albany Philh., 1936–40. He taught at Univ. of Ark., 1943–48, and conducted the Ark. State Symph., 1945–47. In 1948 he built up the Virginia Symph. (Richmond, Va.). In 1957 he became cond. of the Syracuse Symph.

HAESLE, LEO M. After serving in World War I, he went to Grand Forks (N.D.). Since 1920 he has been active in its musical life and is the dir. of the Grand Forks Symph.

HAGEN, ERNEST, b. Radcliffe, Iowa, Nov. 23, 1913. Studied at St. Olaf Coll. (Northfield, Minn.) and at Univ. of Iowa. In 1952 he founded the Wartburg (Iowa) Community Symph., which he still conducts.

HALASZ, LASZLO, b. Debrecen, Hungary, June 6, 1905. Studied at Budapest Acad. of Music. He was asst. cond. for the Royal Hungarian Opera, 1929–30; for the Prague Opera, 1930–32; and at Salzburg, 1935–36. He came to the U.S.A. in 1937. He conducted at the Philadelphia Civic Opera, 1938; was dir. of the St. Louis Grand Opera 1939–42; and conducted the Chicago Opera 1941–42. In 1943 he helped form the New York City Opera and was its dir. until 1951. In the fall of 1955 he directed the opera fest. at the Licéo, Barcelona, Spain.

HAMES, EDWYN H., b. Melbourne, Australia, Dec. 29, 1902. Studied at Melbourne Univ., Univ. of Mich., Berkshire Music Center, and Mozarteum Acad. (Salzburg). He founded (1932) and is cond. of the South Bend (Ind.) Symph.; also founded (1951) and conducts the Hillsdale Coll. (Mich.) Symph. He is head of the Music Dept. at Hillsdale Coll.

HANNIKAINEN, TAUNO, b. Finland, Feb. 26, 1896. Studied at Sibelius Acad. (Helsinki). He began his career as a cellist, touring in a trio with his brothers. He came to the U.S.A. in 1938, was cond. of the Duluth Symph., 1942–47, then asst. cond. of the Chicago Symph. He is the cond. of the Helsinki Municipal Orch.

HANSON, HOWARD, b. Wahoo, Neb., Oct. 28, 1896. Studied at Univ. School of Music (Lincoln, Neb.), Inst. of Musical Art (N.Y.C.), Northwestern Univ. (Evanston, Ill.), and American Acad. in Rome. Since 1924 he has been dir. of Eastman School of Music. His compositions have been frequently performed by leading orchestras, guest conducted by himself. In 1924 he inaugurated the American Composers' Concerts, which in yearly festivals in Rochester give public hearings to new American works.

HARE, CLAYTON, b. Ontario, Canada. Studied at Royal Acad. (London). He was a member of the original Boyd Neel Orch. He taught at Mt. Allison Univ. (Sackville, N.B.), 1939–45, and was cond. of the Calgary (Alta., Can.) Symph., 1948–54. Since 1955 he has taught at Univ. of Portland (Ore.), and since 1956 been dean of music there. Since 1955 he has been cond. of the Hood River (Ore.) Symph.

HARSANYI, NICHOLAS, b. Budapest, Hungary. Studied at Royal Hungarian Acad. of Music. He came to the U.S.A. in 1938. He made a world tour as violist with the Lener Quartet, 1945–47. Since 1950 he has conducted the Princeton (N.J.) Symph., and since 1954 taught at Princeton Univ.

HART, WILLIAM SEBASTIAN, b. Baltimore, Md., Oct. 30, 1920. Studied at Peabody Cons. of Music, Johns Hopkins Univ. (Baltimore), and Cal. Golden State Univ. Since 1939 he has taught at Peabody. He has been solo timpanist of the Baltimore Symph. since 1938 and cond. for Baltimore's Bureau of Music since 1947.

HARTH, SIDNEY, b. Cleveland, Ohio, 1925. Studied at Cleveland Inst. of Music. He was a violinist in the Cleveland Orch., summers 1943–47; leader of the Woodstock String Quartet; leader and founder of the Musical Arts Quartet; and concertmaster of the Saidenburg Little Symph. Since 1953 he has been concertmaster of the Louisville Orch., and since 1954 its asst. cond. He is leader of the Louisville String Quartet.

HAWTHORNE, JOSEPH, b. Provincetown, Mass. Studied with Nadia Boulanger on a Damrosch Scholarship, at Juilliard School of Music, and at Princeton Univ. (N.J.). He conducted the Princeton Orch., 1927–30, and the New London (Conn.) Symph., 1943–44. He was asst. cond., 1945–47, then assoc. cond., 1947–49, of the Dallas Symph. He was cond. of the Chattanooga Symph., 1949–55. Since 1955 he has been cond. of the Toledo Symph.

HECK, GEORGE A. J., b. Hartford, Conn., July 6, 1905. Studied at Hartford Cons. of Music and Hillyer Coll., Hartford. From 1934 to 1953 he was a member of the Hartford Symph., first as concertmaster, then as asst. cond., and after 1948 as cond. Since 1945 he has taught at Hartford School of Music and been cond. of the school orchestra and dir. of the Opera Workshop. He is also cond. of the (Hartford) Sphinx Temple Band.

HEERMANN, WALTER, b. Frankfurt, Germany, Feb. 6, 1890. Studied at Goethe Gymnasium in Frankfurt-am-Main. He came to the U.S.A. in 1907, and joined the Cincinnati Symph. as cellist in 1909. After duty as cond. of the U.S. Army Symph. he was again with the Cincinnati Symph., 1919–48. He taught at Cincinnati Coll. of Music, 1917–48; founded the Cincinnati Little Symph. and directed it, 1929–35; and conducted the Springfield (Ohio) Orch., 1946–48. In 1948 he became musical dir. of the Madison (Wisc.) Symph. and Chorus.

HEGYI, JULIUS, b. New York, N.Y., Feb. 2, 1923. Studied at Juilliard School of Music. He joined the Berkshire Quartet, 1945, and founded the Amati Quartet. He was cond. of the Wagner Coll. Symph., Staten Island, N.Y., 1944–46. In 1948 he became concertmaster of the San Antonio Symph., and in 1950 its assoc. cond. He also conducted the San Antonio Little Symph. In 1953 he became cond. of the Abilene Symph., and in 1955 of the Chattanooga (Tenn.) Symph.

HENKEL, JOSEPH, b. Memphis, Tenn., Oct. 26, 1890. Studied privately. He was a violinist with the Blüthner Orch. (Berlin). He was cond. of the Memphis Symph., 1922–25, and assoc. cond. of the Houston Symph., 1939–48. Since 1942 he has taught at the Univ. of Houston and conducted the Univ. Symph.

HERBERT, WALTER. He was dir. of the New Orleans opera for eleven years, and is now artistic dir. of the Houston (Tex.) Grand Opera Assoc.

HERRMANN, BERNARD, b. New York, N.Y., 1911. Studied at New York Univ. and at Juilliard Graduate School. He organized the New Chamber Orch., 1931, which gave concerts in New York City and at the Library of Congress. In 1934 he joined CBS and in 1938 became staff cond.

HERZ, HERMANN, b. Munich, Germany, June 20, 1908. Studied at Munich State Acad. of Music. He was asst. cond. of the Munich State Opera, then, for two years, of the Municipal Theater of St. Gallen, Switzerland. He conducted symphony and opera in Johannesburg, So. Africa, 1936–47, before coming to the U.S.A. in 1948. That summer he taught in the Berkshire Music Center. Since 1950 he has been cond. of the Duluth (Minn.) Symph.

HICKS, ALFRED, b. Keokuk, Iowa, Feb. 3, 1898. Studied at Drake Univ. He was English hornist with the St. Louis Symph., 1926–47, and cond. of the St. Louis Philh., 1930–43. Since 1943 he has taught at the St. Louis Inst. of Music.

HOBDAY, GEOFFREY, b. Birmingham, England, 1912. Studied in Rydal (England). He became musical dir. of the Birmingham

Operatic Soc., 1934. After World War II—he was an officer in the British Army—he toured England and Wales with his own Universal Symph. He conducted on the Continent, 1948–52, and in 1953 became musical dir. of the Fort Worth Civic Opera Assn. and dir. of the Opera Workshop at Texas Christian Univ. In 1954 he became cond. of the Charleston (W.Va.) Symph.

HODGE, LESLIE, b. Albany, Australia. Studied at Cons. of Music at Univ. of Melbourne. He conducted the Sacramento (Cal.) Municipal Symph., the Bay Region Federal Symph., and the Portland (Ore.) Philh. In 1941 he founded the Guadalajara (Mex.) Symph., and in 1945 became its musical dir. In 1950 he was cond. of the San Diego (Cal.) Philh. Since 1952 he has been cond. of the Phoenix (Ariz.) Symph.

HOFFMAN, IRWIN, b. New York, N.Y., 1924. Studied at Juilliard School of Music. He was musical dir. for the Martha Graham Dance Co., 1949–50. He conducted the Yonkers Philh., the Bronx Symph., and the Westchester Chamber Orch. before becoming cond. of the Vancouver Symph. in 1952.

HOLLI, MATTI, b. Tampere, Finland, Dec. 12, 1916. Studied at Ursuline School of Music (Windsor, Can.), at Toronto Cons., and at Detroit Cons. Since 1936 he has conducted the Holli Orch., and since 1946 the Windsor Symph.

HOLTER, RALPH B., b. Minneapolis, Minn. Studied at State Teachers Coll., St. Cloud, Minn., Univ. of Minn., and MacPhail Coll. of Music, Minneapolis. He was concertmaster of the Oshkosh (Wisc.) Civic Symph. four years, then concertmaster of the Green Bay (Wisc.) Symphonette, 1947–52. Since 1952 he has been cond. of the Green Bay Symphonette.

HURST, GEORGE, b. Edinburgh, Scotland, May 20, 1926. Studied at Royal Cons. of Music, Toronto, and with Monteux. He conducted the Royal Cons. Little Symph. and the Royal Cons. String Orch. He left Canada in 1947 to teach at Peabody Cons. In 1949 he became cond. of the York (Pa.) Symph., and in 1951 of the Peabody Cons. Orch. He resigned from his engagements in the U.S.A. in 1955 to become asst. cond. of the London Philh. under Sir Adrian Boult.

HUTCHINS, GUY, b. Spartanburg, S.C., Mar. 12, 1905. Studied at Wofford Coll. (Spartanburg), Clemson Coll., and Curtis Inst. of Music. He was cond. of the Spartanburg Symph., 1933–35, the Greenville Symph., 1938–40, and the Charlotte Symph., 1945–48.

INSANA, SILVIO, b. Italy. Studied there, and started conducting ballet and opera. He is regularly a cond. of Grant Park summer concerts (Chicago), and of Chicago Park District Opera.

IRWIN, GEORGE, b. Quincy, Ill., May 2, 1921. Studied at Univ. of Mich. and under Vladimir Bakaleinikoff. Since 1946 he has been musical dir. of the Quincy Chamber Music Ensemble, and since 1948 cond. of the Quincy Symph., which he founded.

ITURBI, JOSÉ, b. Valencia, Spain, Nov. 28, 1895. Studied at Valencia Cons. and Paris Cons. He has appeared as piano soloist with leading orchestras both in Europe and America, often playing his own compositions. In 1937 he was co-conductor with Ormandy of the Phila. Orch. on its spring tour. He was cond. of the Rochester Philh., 1935–47, and a teacher during the same period at Eastman School of Music.

IULA, ROBERT P. b. Baltimore, Md. Studied at Peabody Inst. of Music. In 1928 he organized and conducted the Park Little

Symph. (Baltimore). In 1932 he was cond. of the Civic Summer Symph. at Carlin's Park. In 1939 he organized the Baltimore Stadium Civic Summer Symph.

JAFFE, CHARLES. Studied at Curtis Inst. of Music. He was a member of the Curtis String Quartet and taught at Curtis. He was a violinist in the NBC Symph. under Toscanini. Since 1954 he has been cond. of the Symph. Soc. of Long Island (N.Y.).

JANIEC, HENRY, b. Passaic, N.J., Nov. 21, 1929. Studied at Oberlin (Ohio) Cons. of Music, and was founder and cond. of the Oberlin Repertoire Orch. He conducted at the Berkshire Music Center, 1952–55. Since 1952 he has been cond. of the Spartanburg (S.C.) Symph.

JANSEN, GEORGE, b. New York, N.Y. Studied at Juilliard School of Music and Columbia Univ. He was first trumpet of the Nat'l Orchestral Assn. (N.Y.C.). He is dir. of the Loyola Univ. (New Orleans, La.) band, and founder and dir. of its Brass Ensemble. Since 1946 he has been a member of the New Orleans Philh. and of the Opera House Assn. Orch. there. Since 1954 he has been a cond. of the Crescent City Pops Concerts (New Orleans).

JANSSEN, WERNER, b. New York, N.Y., 1899. Studied at Phillips Exeter Acad. and Dartmouth Coll. He was a regular cond. of the New York Philh., 1934–35, and cond. of the Baltimore Symph., 1938–40.

JELESNIK, EUGENE, b. Russia. Studied in Budapest and Germany. After radio positions in New York City he went to Salt Lake City in 1945. For nine years he was dir. of radio station KDYL there. Since 1954 he has been cond. of the Salt Lake City "Pops" Orch., which he founded.

JELÍNEK, OTTO, b. Chicago, Ill., May 26, 1910. Studied at Chicago Acad. of Music, De Paul Univ. (Chicago), and Northwestern Univ. (Evanston, Ind.) He conducted the Waterloo (Iowa) Symph., 1947–55. Since 1947 he has been a violinist in the Grant Park (Chicago) Symph.

JENKINS, NEWELL, b. New Haven, Conn., Feb. 8, 1915. Studied with Carl Orff in Germany, at Yale School of Music (New Haven), and with the Nat'l Orchestra Assn. (N.Y.C.) He conducted concerts of the Bologna Chamber Orch. Since 1950 he has been cond. of Piccola Accademia (Florence, Italy).

JENSEN, ALLEN, b. Provo, Utah, Aug. 29, 1923. Studied at Brigham Young Univ. and Eastman School of Music. He was a flutist with the Rochester Philh., 1944–45, and with the Indianapolis Symph., 1945–46. Since 1947 he has been cond. of the Intermountain Symph. (Provo).

JOHANOS, DONALD, b. Cedar Rapids, Iowa, Feb. 10, 1928. Studied at Eastman School of Music, and was for several years a violinist in the Rochester Philh. Since 1953 he has been cond. of the Altoona (Pa.) Symph., and since 1955 of the Johnstown (Pa.) Symph.

JOHNS, CONSTANTINE, b. Europe. He began his conducting career in Cape Girardeau, Mo., where at the age of eighteen he organized the Cape Girardeau Little Symph. He organized the Springfield (Ill.) Little Symph., and conducted it, 1947–52. He taught at Wittenberg Coll., Springfield, Ohio, 1953–54, and since 1954 has taught at State Teachers Coll., West Chester, Pa. He conducts the Coll. Sinfonietta.

JOHNSON, ALBERT C., b. Hendersonville, N.C., Feb. 9, 1926. Studied at Univ. of Mich. and Univ. of N.C. He was assoc. cond.

of the Florence (S.C.) Civic Orch., 1952–54, and since 1954 has been its musical dir.

JONES, IFOR, b. Merthyr Tydfil, South Wales, Jan. 23, 1900. Entered Royal Acad. of Music, 1920, and became asst. prof. there, 1925. In 1926 he became asst. cond. of the British Nat'l Opera. In 1927 he toured the U.S.A. as solo organist, and the following year joined the faculty of Rutgers Univ. (New Brunswick, N.J.). In 1930 he founded the Handel Choir of Westfield, N.J. Since 1938 he has directed the Bach Choir of Bethlehem, Pa., in its May festivals, and since 1942 has taught at Peabody Cons. of Music.

JONES, J. RANDOLPH, b. Kershaw, S.C., Feb. 26, 1910. Studied at Richmond Cons. of Music and Juilliard School of Music. Since 1939 he has been cond. of the Jersey City (N.J.) Philh.

JONES, L. BRUCE, b. Aurora, Ill., Oct. 11, 1905. Studied at Northeast Missouri State Teachers Coll., Univ. of Ill., and George Peabody Teachers Coll. He was cond., 1942–43, of the Arkansas State Symph. He is head of the Dept. of Music Education at Louisiana State Univ.

JONES, LAURIS L., b. Visalia, Cal., Nov. 30, 1917. Studied at San José State Coll. and Columbia Univ. In 1947 he became cond. of the Visalia Civic Chorus and assoc. cond. of the Pasadena Orch. Since 1954 he has been cond. of the Santa Barbara (Cal.) Symph.

KASH, EUGENE, b. Toronto, Ont., Canada. Studied at Curtis Inst. of Music and at Vienna State Acad. He was concertmaster of the Toronto Prom Orch. for two seasons. In 1944 he became concertmaster of the Ottawa Philh., and in 1950 its cond.

KATIMS, MILTON, b. Brooklyn, N.Y., June 24, 1909. Studied Columbia Univ. In 1934 he became asst. cond. of the Nat'l Orchestral Assn. (N.Y.C.). In 1935 he was appointed to MBS as solo viola and cond., and later became asst. cond. of Wallenstein's Sinfonietta (WOR). From 1943 he was violist in the NBC Symph. From 1947 he occasionally conducted the NBC Symph. In 1952 he took the Buffalo Philh. on tour. He was on the faculty of Juilliard School of Music, 1946–54. Since 1954 he has been cond. of the Seattle (Wash.) Symph.

KATZ, DAVID, b. Mishawaka, Ind., June 28, 1924. Studied at Juilliard School of Music and Columbia Univ. In 1953 he founded the Queens (N.Y.C.) Symph. which he has since conducted.

KATZ, PAUL, b. New York, N.Y., Nov. 2, 1907. Studied with Heermann, Ševčik, Ysaÿe, Auer, and Poliakin. He played in the Cleveland and Cincinnati symphonies. Since 1933 he has been cond. of the Dayton (Ohio) Philh., and since 1944 a member of the faculty of Cincinnati Cons. and cond. of the Cons. Orch.

KAUFMANN, WALTER, b. Carlsbad, Czechoslovakia, Apr. 1, 1907. Studied at Univ. of Prague, and with Franz Schreker at State Coll. of Music in Berlin. He was music dir. at the All-India Radio (Bombay), 1938–46; headed the piano dept. at Halifax Cons. of Music (N.S.), 1947; conducted the Winnipeg Symph., 1948–57; and since 1957 has taught and conducted at the Univ. of Ind.

KELLER, LEONARD, b. Chicago, Ill., Oct. 6, 1909. Studied at Cons. of Music, Chicago, Univ. of Wisc., and Juilliard School of Music. Since 1945 he has taught at the Metropolitan School of Music (Chicago), and since 1949 been cond. of the Chicago Woman's Symph.

KELLEY, CHAUNCEY, b. Pittsburgh, Pa., Sept. 23, 1915. Studied at Fine Arts Coll., Carnegie Inst. of Technology (Pittsburgh) and Juilliard Graduate School. He was oboist with the Pittsburgh Symph. and with the NBC Symph. He was asst. cond. of the Pittsburgh Summer Pops Orch. In 1953 he founded and has since conducted the Savannah (Ga.) Symph.

KEMPE, RUDOLF, b. near Dresden, Germany, 1910. Studied at Orchestra School of the Saxon State Chorus. He was first oboist in the Gewandhaus Orch. (Leipzig), and was cond. of the Leipzig Opera, then cond. at Chemnitz and Weimar. In 1949 he became Gen. Musical Dir. at Dresden, and in 1952 at Munich. He made his debut as Metropolitan Opera cond. on Jan. 26, 1955.

KESNAR, MAURITS, b. Amsterdam, Holland, 1900. Studied at Amsterdam Cons., Berlin High School of Music, and Univ. of Iowa. He came to the U.S.A. in 1923 after being violinist in the Amsterdam Concertgebouw Orch. In 1935 he founded the Enid (Okla.) Symph. and in 1948 the Southern Illinois Symph. of Carbondale, which he still conducts.

KING, DANA M. Studied at Ohio Univ. (Athens). He taught at Bucknell Univ. (Lewisburg, Pa.), at Univ. of Penn. and, since 1950, at Georgia Teachers Coll. (Collegeboro). He became trombonist in the Savannah Symph. in 1953 and in 1956 was appointed its asst. cond.

KITZINGER, G. CHESTER, b. Columbus, Ind., May 1, 1894. Studied at Metropolitan School of Music (Indianapolis) and Cincinnati Coll. of Music. In 1922 he founded the Columbus (Ind.) Symph. and has since conducted it.

KLEMPERER, OTTO, b. Breslau, Germany, May 14, 1885. Studied at Frankfurt Cons., then in Berlin. He became a cond.

at the Prague German Opera House, 1907. After conducting at the operas of Hamburg, Bremen, Strasbourg, Cologne, and Wiesbaden, he became first cond. at the Berlin State Opera, 1927, a position he held until he left Germany in 1933. He conducted the Los Angeles Philh., 1933–39, and again, 1940–41. He is now guest conductor on European podiums.

KLETZKI, PAUL, b. Lodz, Poland, Mar. 21, 1900. He was a member of the Lodz Philh., 1914–19. He has guest conducted widely, at first confining himself to his own compositions. He is one of the regular conductors at the Lucerne Fest. In 1953 he conducted some twenty concerts with the Israel Philh.

KNAPPERTSBUSCH, HANS, b. Elberfeld, Germany, Mar. 12, 1888. Studied at Cologne Cons. He was dir. of opera at Elberfeld, 1913–18; Leipzig, 1918; and Dessau 1919–21; and was gen. man. of the Munich Opera, 1922–36. In 1936 he conducted the Vienna Philh. and in 1937 the Vienna State Opera. Since 1951 he has directed at Bayreuth.

KOLAR, VICTOR, b. Budapest, Hungary, Feb. 12, 1888. Studied at Prague Cons. of Music with Ševčik and Dvořák. He came to the U.S.A. in 1904 and became asst. cond. of the Pittsburgh Symph. and later of the New York Symph. Next, for twenty-five years, he was asst. cond. of the Detroit Symph. He is a teacher at Inst. of Musical Art in Detroit.

KOLBERG, HUGO, b. Warsaw, Poland. He became concertmaster of the Philh. Orch. of Oslo, Norway, at the age of eighteen, and soon after concertmaster of the Berlin Philh. After coming to the U.S.A. he became concertmaster of the Pittsburgh Symph., then held the same post in the Cleveland Orch., the Metropolitan Opera Orch., and, since 1955, the Chicago Grant Park Symph.

Since 1951 he has been cond. of the West Shore Symph., serving several communities in southwest Michigan.

KONNERTH, FRANK J., b. Bucharest, Roumania. Studied at Inst. of Musical Art (N.Y.C.) and Columbia Univ. He was first violinist of the Brooklyn Symph. Since 1934 he has been cond. of the Peekskill (N.Y.) Civic Orch. (which he founded), and dir. of the annual music fest. of the Peekskill city schools.

KOPP, LEO, b. Budapest, Hungary, Oct. 7, 1906. He conducted in German opera houses, 1926–30; then came to the U.S.A., where he conducted for the Chicago Opera, 1930–42. He has conducted at the Grant Park series since 1935, and for the St. Paul Civic Opera and "Pops" since 1938. Since 1945 he has been cond. of the Lincoln (Neb.) Symph., and since 1946 a teacher at Pacific Music Camp (Cal.).

KORN, PETER JONA, b. Berlin, Germany, 1922. He came to the U.S.A. in 1941. He founded in 1948, and has since conducted, the New Orch. of Los Angeles.

KORN, RICHARD, b. New York, N.Y., 1908. Studied at Princeton Univ. and Yale Law School; studied conducting with Koussevitzky, at Juilliard Graduate School, and with Nat'l Orchestral Assn. In 1941 he formed his own orchestra. In 1949 he was asst. cond. of the Brooklyn Symph. and cond. of the Memphis Symph. In 1951 he conducted the Baton Rouge (La.) Symph., and in 1955 was asst. cond. of the N.Y. City Center Opera.

KOZMA, TIBOR, b. Budapest, Hungary. Studied at Budapest Music Acad. and at School of the Saxon State Orch. In 1936 he became cond. of the Municipal Theater in Troppau (Czechoslovakia), then in Bruenn. He came to the U.S.A. in 1941, and joined the staff of the Metropolitan Opera in 1948. He was appointed assoc. cond. there in 1951.

KRAUSZ, LASZLO, b. Hungary. He is a violist with the Cleveland Orch., cond. since 1951 of the Cleveland Chamber Orch., and cond. since 1955 of the Akron (Ohio) Symph.

KRITZ, KARL, b. Vienna, Austria, 1906. Studied at Vienna State Acad. of Music, 1927. He was chief cond. of opera and philh. concerts in Nuremberg-Furth, 1933–35, and assoc. cond. at the Berlin State Opera, 1935–37. He was dir. of the Connecticut Opera Co., 1937; of the Cincinnati Summer Opera, 1938–45. He was assoc. cond. of the San Francisco Opera, 1942–55, and of the Metropolitan Opera, 1943–48. From 1949 to 1953 he was gen. dir. of the Fort Worth Civic Opera Assn., and in the summers of 1941, '46, '47, and '48 of the Central City (Colo.) Opera. Since 1948 he has been dir. of the Pittsburgh Civic Light Opera, and since 1953 assoc. cond. of the Pittsburgh Symph.

KRUEGER, JOHN H., b. Benton, Wisc., Mar. 22, 1922. Studied at Cincinnati Cons. of Music, Univ. of Cincinnati, and Colo. Coll. He was a trombonist in the Cincinnati Symph. and in four community orchestras. He directed the Oak Ridge Community Chorus, 1949–51. In 1951 he founded, and has since conducted, the Youngstown (Ohio) Philh. Orch.

KRUEGER, KARL, b. Atchison, Kan., Jan. 19, 1894. Studied at Vienna Univ., Heidelberg Univ., and Univ. of Kan. He was asst. cond. at the Vienna State Opera, 1919–24, and cond. of the Seattle Symph., 1926–32, of the Kansas City Philh., 1933–42, and of the Detroit Symph., 1943–49.

KRUGER, HARRY, b. Atlanta, Ga., July 20, 1929. Studied at New England Cons. (Boston) and with Monteux. He played flute with the Atlanta Symph., 1946–49. He was cond. of the Cambridge Chamber Orch., the New England Cons. Orch., and the Arlington (Mass.) Philh. and Chorus. He is cond. of the Kruger Sinfonietta (Atlanta). Since 1955 he has been asst. cond. of the Atlanta Symph.

KRUGER, RUDOLF, b. Berlin, Germany, 1917. Studied at Vienna State Acad. of Music. In 1939 he came to the U.S.A. as asst. cond. of the Southern Symph. and the Columbia (S.C.) Choral Soc. In 1942 he became asst. cond. of the New Orleans Symph., and in 1950 cond. of the New Orleans Light Opera. Since 1955 he has been gen. dir. of the Fort Worth Civic Opera and dir. of the Opera Workshop at Texas Christian Univ.

KUBELIK, RAFAEL, b. Brno, Czechoslovakia, June 29, 1914. Studied at Prague Cons. He served as piano accompanist and orchestra conductor to his father (Jan Kubelik) in tours of Europe, 1934–35. He led the Czech Philh., 1936–48, with two years' interruption, 1939–41, when he was musical dir. of the Brno Opera. He was cond. of the Chicago Symph., 1950–53. In the winter of 1954 he toured the U.S.A. as one of the conductors of the Concertgebouw Orch. of Amsterdam. Since 1955 he has been musical dir. of the Royal Opera House, Covent Garden, London.

KUCINSKI, LEO, b. Warsaw, Poland, Jan. 29, 1904. Studied at Warsaw Cons. of Music, Oberlin Coll. (Ohio), Cleveland Inst. of Music, and Juilliard Graduate School. He was cond. of the Lincoln (Neb.) Symph., 1934–42. Since 1935 he has been cond. of the Sioux City (Iowa) Symph.

KURINSKY, ARPAD, b. Hungary, May 2, 1898. Came to the U.S.A. in 1904. Studied at Univ. of Akron (Ohio), Western Reserve Univ., and Cleveland Inst. of Music. He conducted the

Cuyahoga Falls (Ohio) Symph., 1931–34, and the Cleveland Civic Symph., 1938–41. Since 1950 he has been cond. of the Kingsport (Tenn.) Symph.

KURKEWICZ, WALTER, b. Newark, N.J., Jan. 28, 1901. He was violinist with the Newark Symph. He has been cond. of the Bloomfield (N.J.) Symph. since 1932 and of the Bloomfield Civic Chorus since 1934.

KURTZ, EFREM, b. St. Petersburg, Russia, Nov. 7, 1900. Studied at St. Petersburg Cons. and Stern Cons. of Music (Berlin). In 1924 he became cond. of the Stuttgart Philh., and in 1927 toured as cond. of Pavlova's ballet company. He was cond. of the Ballet Russe de Monte Carlo, 1929–38. He was cond. of the Kansas City Philh., 1945–48, and of the Houston Symph., 1948–54. In 1955 he became cond. of the Liverpool (England) Philh.

KURZWEIL, FREDRIC, b. Vienna, Austria, Aug. 20, 1912. Studied Vienna Cons. of Music. He was appointed a cond. of the St. Louis Grand Opera in 1941; directed the Philadelphia Opera Chorus, 1942–43; and after a period in the army, 1943–46, was appointed (1947) to the conducting staff of the City Center Opera (N.Y.C.). Also in 1947, he founded and conducted the Fine Art Symph. (N.Y.C.). Since 1956 he has been musical dir. of the Mobile (Ala.) Opera Guild. He teaches at New York Univ., New York Coll. of Music, and Queens Coll.

LABELLA, PETER, b. Port Chester, N.Y., June 9, 1921. Studied at Eastman School of Music, Berkshire Music Center, Columbia Univ., and Chicago Musical Coll. In 1948 he was appointed dir. of orchestras at Joliet (Ill.) Township High School. In 1949 he organized and has since conducted the Joliet Junior Coll.–Community Little Symph.

LA MARCHINA, ROBERT, b. New York, N.Y., 1928. He was cellist in the NBC Symph., 1944–46. Since 1946 he has been principal cellist with the Los Angeles Philh., and since 1955 musical dir. of the Opera Theatre of Los Angeles.

LANDAU, SIEGFRIED, b. Berlin, Germany, Sept. 4, 1921. Studied at Stern Cons. of Music, at Klindworth-Scharwenka Cons., at Trinity Coll. of Music (London), at the Mannes College of Music (N.Y.C.), and with Monteux. Since 1944 he has headed the orchestra and opera departments of the New York Coll. of Music, and since 1955 has been cond. of the Brooklyn Philharmonia.

LANE, LOUIS, b. Eagle Pass, Tex., Dec. 25, 1923. Studied at Univ. of Tex., Eastman School of Music, and Berkshire Music Center. He was an apprentice cond. (under George Szell) of the Cleveland Orch., 1947–49, then became pianist, celesta player, and organist of the orchestra. Since 1949 he has been cond. of the Canton (Ohio) Symph., since 1955 of the Cleveland Summer Orch. ("pops" series), and since 1956 asst. cond. of the Cleveland Orch.

LANGE, ARTHUR, b. Philadelphia, Pa., Apr. 16, 1889. He began his career in 1905 as a pianist and arranger. He was music dir. for MGM, 1929–31, for Twentieth Century–Fox, 1932–38, and for Internat'l Pictures, 1945. In 1947 he organized and has since conducted the Santa Monica (Cal.) Symph.

LANGE, HANS, b. Constantinople, Turkey, Feb. 17, 1884. Studied violin at Prague Cons. He was concertmaster in the Frankfurt Opera Orch. and the Museum Concerts Orch., 1905–20. He was a member of the New York Philh., 1921–26, then its asst. cond., 1926–34. He was assoc. cond. of the Chicago Orch., 1936–45. He organized the Chicago Chamber Orch. and the St. Louis

Little Symph. He directed the Friends of Music Orch. in Toledo, 1946–49. Since 1950 he has been cond. of the Albuquerque (N.M.) Civic Symph. and the Santa Fe Sinfonietta and Choral Soc.

LANNING, VAN LIER, b. Philadelphia, Pa., Nov. 30, 1912. Studied at Ithaca Coll. and Curtis Inst. of Music. He conducted the Washington (D.C.) Sinfonietta, 1939–45; the Arlington (Va.) Civic Symph., 1945–49; and the Jacksonville (Fla.) Symph., 1949–52. In 1952 he re-established the orchestra in Atlantic City, N.J. In 1955 he became cond. of the Wilmington (Del.) Symph.

LEHMANN, OTTO, b. Munich, Germany, July 4, 1908. Studied at Munich State Acad. of Music and at Salzburg Mozarteum. In 1932–33 he was asst. cond. at the Municipal Opera in Kaiserslautern. He was assoc. cond. of the Municipal Opera at Zurich, 1934–36. Coming to the U.S.A. in Dec., 1937, he conducted opera here: Boston Grand Opera, 1945; San Carlo Opera, 1947; Internat'l Opera, 1947; Cincinnati Summer Opera, 1950; San Antonio Grand Opera Fest. 1950, '51.

LEIDE, ENRICO, b. Turin, Italy, 1897. Studied at conservatories of Milan and Bologna and at French Univ. (Grenoble). Coming to the U.S.A., he conducted an orchestra in Atlanta, Ga., in the late twenties. After the war he returned to Italy for operatic commitments. Since 1950 he has conducted an orchestra organized by A.F. of M. Local 802 (N.Y.C.), called first "The Old Timers Symph.," then "The American Symph."

LE JEUNE, FRANK F., b. Canada, 1932. Studied at Northwestern Univ. (Evanston, Ill.). He was a cellist in the Indianapolis Symph. and is now a cellist in the Duluth Symph. Since 1952 he has been cond. of the Gogebic Range Symphonette, Ironwood, Mich.

LERT, RICHARD, b. Mannheim, Germany. He became gen. musical dir. of the opera, symphony and conservatory in Mannheim, and later of the State Opera in Berlin. In 1935 he conducted the first Pasadena (Cal.) Music Fest. Since 1936 he has been cond. of the Pasadena Symph. and the Pasadena Civic Chorus.

LEVENSON, HARRY, b. New York, N.Y., Mar. 21, 1905. Studied at Paris Cons., at Harvard Summer School, and with Monteux. He was cond. of the Russian Ballet and violinist in the Paris Symph., 1931–33. He was concertmaster of the Worcester Philh., 1933–36, and of the Worcester Sinfonietta, 1936–41. He conducted the Worcester County Light Opera Club. In 1947 he founded the Worcester Youth Orch. and the Worcester Little Symph., and continued as cond. of the latter on its reorganization as the Worcester Orch. in 1955.

LEVIN, SYLVAN, b. Baltimore, Md., May 2, 1903. Studied at Peabody Cons. of Music and Curtis Inst. of Music. In 1929 he became asst. to Stokowski (Philadelphia Orch. cond.) and in 1933 assoc. cond. He organized and conducted the York (Pa.) Symph. He organized, together with David Hocker, the Philadelphia Opera Co., and for six years served as its dir. He was musical dir. of WOR-Mutual, 1944–53.

LEVINE, JOSEPH, b. Philadelphia, Pa., 1910. Studied at Curtis Inst. of Music. While still at Curtis he was asst. cond. of the Philadelphia Grand Opera. On graduation, he became a member of the Curtis staff. He was official pianist of the Philadelphia Orch. and of the Robin Hood Dell Orch. After his discharge from the Army Air Force in 1945, he founded the Chamber Opera Soc. and acted as musical dir. of the Co-Opera Co. (Philadelphia). From 1946 to 1950 he served as accompanist to Joseph Szigeti. Since 1950 he has been musical dir. of the Ballet Theatre.

LEVINE, MAURICE, b. New Haven, Conn., Jan. 11, 1918. Studied at Yale Univ. School of Music. After a period in the U.S. Army, 1942–46, he was appointed musical dir. of Weill's *Lost in the Stars,* and has since directed many other Broadway productions.

LEVITE, MYRON, b. Kirov, Russia, Oct. 13, 1914. Studied at Juilliard School of Music, at New York Univ., at Virginia Polytechnic Inst., at Yale Univ., and in the Nat'l Orchestral Assn. He was cond. of the Doctors' Symph., 1940–42. Since 1930 he has been cond. of the YMHA Symph. (N.Y.C.).

LIPKIN, ARTHUR BENNETT, b. London, England, 1907. Came to the U.S.A. in 1926. For twenty years he was a violinist in the Philadelphia Orch. and leader of the Philadelphia String Quartet. He was also cofounder and cond. of the Main Line Symph. and the Germantown Symph. (Philadelphia). In 1949 he organized, and has since conducted, the Birmingham (Ala.) Symph.

MacMILLAN, SIR ERNEST, b. Mimico, Ont., Canada, Aug. 18, 1893. Studied at Oxford Univ. and Univ. of Toronto. He toured the U.S.A. as organist. He was principal of the Toronto Cons. of Music, 1926–42, and cond. of the Toronto Symph., 1931–56.

MACY, WILLIAM K., b. Manilla, Ind., Dec. 12, 1916. Studied at Westminster Choir Coll., Columbia Univ., and Univ. of Wisc. He was choral dir. for Iowa State Teachers Coll. Symph., 1953–55. Since 1955 he has been cond. of the Univ. of Nevada Community Symph.

MADEIRA, FRANCIS, b. Jenkintown, Pa., Feb. 21, 1917. Studied at Juilliard Graduate School and with Monteux. He was a member of the Chautauqua Symph., summer 1943. He conducted the Brown-Pembroke Orch. at Brown Univ. (Providence, R.I.), 1943–47, and has been cond. of the Rhode Island Philh. since its founding in Aug. 1945.

MAGANINI, QUINTO, b. Fairfield, Cal., Nov. 30, 1897. He was flutist with the San Francisco Symph., then became a member of the New York Symph. He conducted the New York Sinfonietta and founded (1932) the Maganini Chamber Orch. Since 1939 he has been the regular cond. of the Norwalk (Conn.) Symph., and since 1953 pres. of American Schools of Music and Art at Fontainebleau, France.

MAHLER, FRITZ, b. Vienna, Austria, July 16, 1902. Studied at Univ. of Vienna and Acad. of Music in Vienna. He conducted in opera houses in Mannheim and Berlin, then was cond. of the Copenhagen Symph., 1930–36. He has conducted the Bridgeport (Conn.) Symph., the Philadelphia Civic Symph., and the Greenwich (Conn.) Orch. He was musical dir. of the Philadelphia La Scala Opera, 1937–40, and of the Charles Wagner Opera, 1945–47. He taught at Juilliard Summer School, 1939–50. He was dir. of music of the Nat'l Youth Administration in N.Y.C., 1940–41, and conducted the Erie (Pa.) Philh., 1947–53. Since 1953 he has been cond. of the Hartford (Conn.) Symph.

MAIRS, G. DONALD, b. Scotia, N.Y., 1911. Studied at Ithaca Coll. and Univ. of Mich. For eighteen years he was supervisor of music in the New Jersey public schools. Since 1949 he has been the cond. of the Teaneck (N.J.) Symph.

MALKO, NICOLAI, b. Brailov, Ukraine. Studied at St. Petersburg Cons. of Music under Rimsky-Korsakov, Liadov, Glazounov, and Tcherepnin, and in Germany under Felix Mottl. While still a student he conducted the ballet of the Marinsky Theater in St. Petersburg. For a while he was musical dir. of the Leningrad Philh. After he left Russia in 1929, he organized conducting courses in Prague and Copenhagen, and taught at the Salzburg Mozarteum Acad. Later in Amer. he lectured at Mills Coll., Cal., De Pauw Univ., Chicago, and other colleges. The year 1955 marked his twenty-fifth jubilee with the Danish State Radio Symph. His first appearance in the U.S.A. was as guest cond. of the Boston Symph. in 1940. Since 1945 he has been the resident cond. of the Grant Park Symph. in Chicago, and since 1956 of the Sydney (Australia) Symph. He is principal cond. and musical adviser of the Yorkshire Symph. (Leeds, England).

MANTANI, WALTER, b. New York, N.Y., 1918. Studied at Juilliard School of Music. He conducted the North Jersey Symph., 1940–42; the Stevens Inst. of Technology Symph. (Hoboken, N.J.), 1941–52; the New York Junior Symph., 1947–50; and the Young People's Orch. Soc. (N.Y.C.), 1952–53. Since 1953 he has been cond. of the Midland (Tex.) Symph., since 1954 of the Odessa (Tex.) Symph.

MANUSEVITCH, VICTOR E., b. Alexandrovsk, Russia, July 16, 1906. Studied at Petrograd Cons. of Music, Berlin Cons. of Music, and Boston Univ. While in the army, 1942–44 he organized and conducted a symph. in Orlando, Fla. Since 1944 he has been a violinist in the Boston Symph., and since 1947 cond. of the Cecilia Soc. Chorus (Boston).

MARKEVITCH, IGOR, b. Kiev, Russia, July 27, 1912. Studied with Alfred Cortot, Nadia Boulanger, and Herman Scherchen. Since 1948 he has been dir. of the Internat'l Course in Conducting at the Mozarteum, Salzburg. Since 1955 he has guest conducted widely in the U.S.A.

MATESKY, RALPH, b. New York, N.Y., Jan. 4, 1913. Studied at Juilliard School of Music, Columbia Univ., and Univ. of Southern Cal. He was a violinist with the Los Angeles "Pops" Concert Orch., 1940–41. Since 1947 he has been cond. of the Compton (Cal.) Civic Symph.

MATTERN, DAVID, b. Colfax, Iowa, Dec. 11, 1890. Studied at Bush Temple Cons. of Music (Chicago), Chicago Cons. of Music, Cornell Univ., Eastman School of Music, and Univ. of Mich. He taught at Bush Temple Cons., 1906–11, Cornell, summers 1915–20, West Chester (Pa.) State Teachers Coll., summers 1922–25, and Eastman School of Music, 1921–26. He was supervisor of music in schools at Grand Rapids, Mich., 1926–29. Since 1929 he has been music education head at Univ. of Mich., and since 1945 cond. of the Univ. of Mich. Extension Orch. (Detroit).

MAXWELL, OTIS G., b. Cleveland, Ohio, Mar. 25, 1900. He was violinist in the Akron (Ohio) Symph. and the Canton (Ohio) Symph. In 1950 he organized, and has since conducted, the Akron Symphonette.

MAZER, HENRY, b. Pittsburgh, Pa., 1919. Studied with Monteux. In 1940 he organized the Pittsburgh Sinfonietta. In 1945 he was apprentice cond. with the Pittsburgh Symph. Since 1948 he has been musical dir. of the Wheeling (W.Va.) Symph.

McARTHUR, EDWIN, b. Denver, Colo., Sept. 24, 1907. Studied in Denver and New York. After 1935 he was accompanist for Kirsten Flagstad for several years. In 1939 he conducted the San Francisco Opera. Since 1945 he has been dir. of the St. Louis Municipal Opera, and since 1950 cond. of the Harrisburg (Pa.) Symph.

McDERMOTT, WILLIAM, b. Valparaiso, Chile, 1906. Studied at Nat'l Cons. of Chile and Royal Acad. of London. He was a violinist in the Nat'l Symph. of Chile, 1932–38; in the London Philh., 1938–39; and in the BBC Empire Orch., 1938–39. He toured So. and No. Amer. as cond. and piano soloist of the Ballet Russe, 1944–47. He has been asst. cond. of the New Orleans Philh. since 1955.

MIDDLETON, POWELL, b. Norristown, Pa., May 20, 1904. He has taught at West Chester (Pa.) State Teachers Coll. since 1935 and conducts the coll. symph. He was cond. of the Choral Art Soc. of Reading, 1940–48. Since 1952 he has been cond. of the Columbia (Pa.) Symph.

MILLER, FRANK, b. Baltimore, Md., Mar. 5, 1912. Studied at Peabody Cons. of Music and Curtis Inst. of Music. He was cellist in the Philadelphia Orch., 1930–35; and cellist and later asst. cond. of the Minneapolis Symph., 1935–39. He was first cellist in the NBC Symph., 1939–54. For two years he conducted the Hempstead (L.I.) Community Orch., which he organized, and for one year the Great Neck (L.I.) Symph., 1953–54. Since 1954 he has been cond. of the Florida Symph.

MILLER, KARL, b. Kaukauna, Wis., 1922. Studied at Univ. of Wis. In 1951 he organized, and has since conducted, the Manitowoc (Wis.) Civic Symph.

MILLS, ALVIN, b. Chicago, Ill., Feb. 2, 1922. Studied at Univ. of Southern Cal., at Univ. of Cal., and with Monteux. He was first violinist in the Kansas City Philh. and the Hollywood Bowl orch. In 1949 he organized the Lompoc (Cal.) Symph.; in 1953, the Brentwood (Cal.) Symph.; and in 1954, the Brentwood Junior Symph., all of which he still conducts.

MINOT, BRYANT. In 1946 he reorganized the New Rochelle (N.Y.) Symph., and has since conducted it. He teaches instrumental music in the New Rochelle public schools.

MOECK, WALTER, b. Milwaukee, Wis. Studied at Eastman School of Music and Univ. of Iowa. He taught at Univ. of Iowa and at Univ. of Ala., conducting the orchestra in the latter. Since 1956 he has been cond. of the Alabama Pops Orch. (Birmingham). He is first trumpet and asst. cond. of the Birmingham Symph.

MOFFATT, CHESTER B. He is dir. of music education in the Springfield (Mo.) public schools, and since 1955 has been cond. of the Springfield Symph.

MOREL, JEAN, b. Abbeville, France. After conducting at the Opéra Comique in Paris he became dir. of the Symphony Orchestra of Paris with which he toured So. Amer. He conducted the New York City Symph. and the National Opera in Mexico City. He conducted at the New York City Center, 1944–52. In 1955 he conducted at the San Francisco Opera. In 1956 he again was cond. at the New York City Center, and became cond. at the Metropolitan Opera. He teaches at Juilliard School of Music.

MORESCO, CARLO, b. Genoa, Italy, May 20, 1905. He conducted at the Teatro Carlo Felice di Genoa, 1923–24. He toured So. Amer. as conductor, 1924–25. In 1949–50 he headed a government-sponsored company in Venezuela. In the U.S.A. since 1949, he has conducted the La Scala Opera (Philadelphia); the Delaware Philh. and Grand Opera; the Cosmopolitan Opera Assn. (San Francisco); the Cincinnati Summer Opera; the Grand Opera Assn. (Hartford, Conn.); the San Carlo Opera (Washington, D.C.); and the Pro Arte of Havana (Cuba).

MORGENSTERN, SAM, b. Louisville, Ky., Sept. 1907. Studied at Univ. of Cincinnati, Cincinnati Cons. of Music, and Juilliard School of Music. He was apprentice cond. with the Metropolitan Opera, 1952–53. He has been musical dir. of the Lemonade Opera (N.Y.C.), 1947–49; assoc. dir., New Friends of Music (N.Y.C.), 1951–52; choral dir. and teacher at Mannes Coll. of Music, 1949–55; and cond. of the New Chamber Orch., Philadelphia, 1954–55. Author of *Composers on Music* (Pantheon Books, 1957).

MORRISSEY, GIBSON, b. Bluefield, W.Va., Jan. 1, 1918. Studied at Juilliard School of Music, Columbia Univ., and Berkshire Music Center. In 1945–46, on the invitation of the Dept. of State, he made a good-will tour of Yugoslavia. In May, 1951, he conducted the Salzburg Mozarteum Orch. In 1952 he helped found, and has since conducted, the Roanoke (Va.) Symph.

MUCCINI, CORRADO, b. Livorno, Italy, Feb. 19, 1899. Studied at Rossini Cons. (Pesaro) and Inst. of Sacred Music (Rome). He acted as asst. cond. at opera houses in Genoa, 1929; Rome, 1930–40; Verona, 1936–37; and Milan, 1921–42; and cond. in Rome, 1944–46, and Brazil, 1946–54. He was asst. cond. at the San Francisco Opera, 1950–55, and at the Lyric Theatre, Chicago, 1954. In 1955 he became asst. cond. at the Cincinnati Opera and at the Metropolitan Opera.

MURRAY, EARL, b. San Francisco, Cal., 1926. Studied at Univ. of Cal. and with Monteux. In 1942 he became a member of the San Francisco Symph., in 1951 its rehearsal cond., in 1953 its asst. cond., and in 1955 its assoc. cond. Since 1952 he has been musical dir. of the San Francisco Ballet, and since 1954 head of the orch. and opera depts. at San Francisco State Coll.

NEE, THOMAS, b. Evanston, Ill., 1920. Studied at Univ. of Minn., Hamline Univ. (St. Paul, Minn.), Berkshire Music Center and

Univ. of Vienna. He taught at Hamline Univ., 1947–56. He conducted the St. Paul Opera Workshop, 1948–51, and was asst. cond. of the St. Paul Civic Orch. Since 1954 he has been cond. of the Minneapolis Civic Orch.

NEEL, BOYD, b. England, July 19, 1905. Studied at Dartmouth Naval Coll. and Caius Coll., Cambridge (England). In 1933 he founded the Boyd Neel Orch. and toured Europe with it, appearing at the Salzburg Fest. in 1937. He conducted the Sadler's Wells Opera, 1945–47. In 1947 he took his orchestra to Australia, and again toured Europe with it, 1948–54. In 1953 he became dean of Royal Cons. of Music (Toronto), and in 1954 cond. of the Hart House Orch. (Toronto). In 1955 he became principal cond. for the annual Fest. of Music at Stratford, Ont.

NEWBURGER, NATHAN, b. Providence, R.I., Dec. 29, 1903. Studied at New England Cons. of Music and Harvard Univ. In 1949 he organized, and has since conducted, the New Providence Symph.

NEWTON, HAROLD, b. Chicago, Ill., Oct. 10, 1906. Studied at Chicago Cons. of Music. He taught there, 1930–35; at Univ. of Kansas City, 1936–39; at Kansas City Cons. of Music, 1939–44; at Cottey Coll., 1941–43; and at Northwestern Univ., 1948–55. He has been a violist in the Chicago Symph., NBC Symph., New York City Center, Kansas City Philh., and Little Symph. of Chicago. Since 1949 he has been cond. of the Kenosha (Wis.) Symph., and since 1953 of the Twin City Symph. (Benton Harbor and St. Joseph, Mich.).

NIEMI, ALLAN L., b. St. Paul, Minn., June 16, 1918. Studied at Univ. of Minn. and Columbia Univ. Since 1949 he has headed the music dept. of Northern Mich. Coll., directed the Northern

Community Symph., and led the Northern String Ensemble (Marquette, Mich.).

NIES-BERGER, EDOUARD, b. Strasbourg, France. Studied at Municipal Cons. of Music, Strasbourg and in Milan, Salzburg, and Vienna. He was cond. of the Brooklyn Oratorio Soc. He organized the Richmond (Va.) Training Orch. Since 1947 he has been cond. of the Nies-Berger Chamber Orch., New York.

NORMAN, VICTOR, b. Oslo, Norway, Nov. 14, 1905. Studied at Copenhagen Royal Cons., Mozarteum Acad. (Salzburg), Ecole Normale de Musique (Paris), and Univ. of Conn. He has conducted the Copenhagen Royal Cons. Orch., 1932–33; the Danish State Radio, 1933–36; the Glyndebourne (England) Opera Fest., 1933–36; the Naumburg Memorial Concerts (N.Y.C.); the Eastern Conn. Symph.; and the Norman Chamber Orch. He developed the New London (Conn.) Symph., 1941; which, merged with the Willimantic Symph., 1947, became known as the Eastern Conn. Symph.

NOYES, FRANK, b. Prophetstown, Ill., Aug. 18, 1901. Studied at Curtis Inst. of Music and with Monteux. He founded the Hastings (Neb.) Symph. He teaches at Hastings Univ., and at Drake (Iowa) Univ., and since 1937 has developed the latter's orch. into the Drake–Des Moines Symph.

ORNER, GEORGE, b. New York, N.Y. Studied at N.Y. Coll. of Music. He was violinist in the Mannes String Quartet and the New York Symph. under Arnold Volpe. In 1923 he helped organize the Jacksonville (Fla.) Coll. of Music, served thirty-two years as its pres., and now heads its violin dept. and is chairman of the board of directors. In 1922 he organized the Friday Musicale Junior Symph. (Jacksonville), which in 1928 became the Friday

Musicale (adult) Symph. In 1936 he organized, and has since directed, the Jacksonville Philh. Orch.

PACINI, RENATO, b. Utica, N.Y., Dec. 4, 1912. Studied at Royal Acad. of Saint Cecilia (Rome), and New England Cons. of Music (Boston). He was concertmaster of the New England Cons. Orch., 1932–35; asst. concertmaster of the People's Symph. of Boston, 1932–35; and concertmaster of the State Symph., 1934–38. In 1947 he organized the Teen Sinfonietta (Indianapolis) and the Indianapolis Alumni Orch., and conducted both until 1952. In 1938 he became asst. concertmaster of the Indianapolis Symph., and in 1955 its assoc. cond.

PAGE, WILLIS, b. Rochester, N.Y., Sept. 18, 1918. Studied at Eastman School of Music and with Monteux. He was first-desk double-bass in the Boston Symph. and the Boston Pops, 1940–55, and taught at the Julius Hartt School of Music, 1949–54. In 1949 he organized and conducted the Page Chorale, and in 1952 the Little Symph. of Boston. In 1953 he became musical dir. of the New Orch. Soc. of Boston. Since 1955 he has been assoc. cond. of the Buffalo Philh.

PALES, MARX J., b. Cleveland, Ohio, Dec. 27, 1923. Studied at Baldwin-Wallace Coll. Cons. (Berea, O.), Columbia Univ., and Juilliard School of Music. From 1948 he taught at the Univ. of Ark. He organized (and still conducts) the Univ. of Ark.–Fayetteville Symph., the Fayetteville Youth Orch., and the Fayetteville Symph. Soc.

PARANOV, MOSHE, b. Hartford, Conn., 1895. Studied piano with Julius Hartt and Harold Bauer and theory and composition with Ernest Bloch and Rubin Goldmark. In 1920 he was cofounder with Julius Hartt of the Julius Hartt School of Music, was its assoc. dir. until 1932, then its dean until 1938, when he became dir. of the Julius Hartt Music Foundation. He directs the Hartt Opera Guild. He conducted the Hartford Symph., 1947–53. Since 1954, musical dir. of the Brockton (Mass.) Orch.

PARKES, ROGER, b. Buffalo, N.Y. Studied at Eastman School of Music and later taught there. He became musical dir. of the Buffalo Broadcasting Corp. and asst. cond. of the Buffalo Philh. Since 1947 he has been cond. of the Battle Creek (Mich.) Symph.

PELLETIER, WILFRID, b. Province of Quebec, Canada, June 20, 1896. Studied with Philipp, Rousseau, Widor, and Bellaigue. While still in his teens he acted as asst. cond. of the Montreal Opera Co. He became asst. cond. at the Metropolitan Opera House in 1915 and a full cond. in 1922. He became cond. at the Ravinia Opera and the San Francisco Opera, 1921–31. He was musical dir. of the "Roses and Drums" program, 1934–38. In 1935 he became musical dir. of the "Metropolitan Opera Auditions of the Air." He formed the Montreal Fest. Orch., the Bach-Beethoven Fest., and Concerts Symphoniques, all in Montreal. In 1942 he was instrumental in establishing the Cons. of Montreal, and was named its dir. In 1943 he established and became dir. of a Cons. of Music in Quebec. Since 1951 he has been cond. of the L'Orchestre Symphonique de Québec.

PENNINGTON, JOHN, b. England. He was concertmaster and asst. cond. in the Royal Philh. (London), a member of the London String Quartet, and cond. of the orch. that accompanied Pavlova. He is cond. for the Fairfield County (Conn.) Symph. Soc. Youth Concerts, held in Bridgeport.

PERKINS, GEORGE, b., Lakeland, Fla., Sept. 16, 1923. Studied at Eastman School of Music and with Monteux. He organized and conducted the Yakima Valley (Wash.) Symph., 1947–48. Since 1952 he has headed the music dept. at Northwest Community Coll., Univ. of Wyo. (Powell), and since 1955 been cond. of the Billings (Mont.) Symph. Orch.

PERLEA, JONEL, b. Ograda, Roumania, Dec. 13, 1901. Studied at Cons. of Leipzig and was asst. cond. at the Leipzig Opera. In 1930 he became dir. of the Royal Opera in Bucharest. He came to the U.S.A. in Dec., 1949, and conducted at the Metropolitan Opera, at the San Francisco Opera, and at the San Antonio Grand Opera Fest. Since 1955 he has been musical dir. of the Connecticut Symph. He is head of the orchestra dept. of the Manhattan School of Music.

PETERSON, LaVERNE RAY, b. in Waupaca, Wis., Nov. 9, 1903. Studied at Univ. of Wis. and with Monteux. He was cond. of the Wausaw (Wis.) Symph., 1943–55. He was musical dir. of radio station WSAU, 1939–47. He is a composer and was founder and first pres. of the Wisconsin Composers' League.

PFOHL, JAMES CHRISTIAN, b. Winston-Salem, N.C., Sept. 17, 1912. Studied at Univ. of N.C., 1930–31, Univ. of Mich., 1939, and Cincinnati Cons. of Music. He was dir. of the music dept. at Queens Coll., Charlotte, N.C., for eight years. He founded and conducted, 1944–46, the Mint Museum of Art Orch. (Charlotte). In 1936 he founded, and has since directed, the Transylvania Music Camp; and has directed the Charlotte Symph. since 1949, the Charlotte Opera Assn. since 1950, and the Jacksonville (Fla.) Symph. since 1952.

PHILLIPS, CLAUDE, b. Woonsocket, R.I., Jan. 25, 1888. He conducted the "Now and Then Orch.," 1913–16. In 1920 he started public school instrumental music in Beverly, Mass., and later became supervisor of school music there. He conducted the Read Fund–Harmonic Hour winter series of the Salem Philh., 1943–56.

PIASECKI, WALTER, b. Jersey City, N.J., Apr. 10, 1916. Studied at Cummington (Mass.) School, Juilliard School of Music, and David Mannes School (N.Y.C.). He and his wife (Virginia Fox) made three transcontinental tours giving chamber music recitals (cello and flute). He conducted the Staten Island (N.Y.) Orch., 1948–52. Since 1952 he has been cond. of the Plainfield (N.J.) Symph.

PIASTRO, MISHEL, b. Russia. Studied at Petrograd Cons. of Music. He came to the U.S.A. in 1921 and was violin soloist with major orchestras. He was concertmaster and asst. cond. with the San Francisco Symph., 1926–30. In 1931–40 he was concertmaster, and later assoc. cond., of the New York Philh. Symph. under Toscanini. Since 1941 he has been cond. of the Longines Symphonette broadcast over WNBC.

POOLE, VALTER, b. Pooleville, Okla., Feb. 6, 1903. Studied at New England Cons. of Music (Boston) and Paris Cons. In 1927 he became a violinist in the Detroit Symph. and in 1945 its assoc. cond. He is assoc. prof. of music at Wayne Univ. (Detroit), and conducts the Wayne Orch. and the Wayne Ensemble.

PREVES, MILTON, b. Cleveland, Ohio, June 18, 1909. Since 1934 he has been a violist in the Chicago Symph.—since 1939, principal of the section. Since 1948 he has been cond. of the North Side Symph., and since 1955 cond. of the Oak Park–River Forest Symph.

PREVITALI, FERNANDO, b. Adria, Italy, Feb. 16, 1907. Studied at Giuseppi Verdi Cons., Turin. In 1936 he became cond. of the

Rome Radio Symph. Since 1953 he has been artistic dir. of the St. Cecilia Acad., Rome. Since 1956 he has guest conducted widely in the U.S.A.

RAAB, EMIL. Studied at Univ. of Mich. Since 1949 he has taught on its faculty and been violinist in its Stanley Quartet in residence. Since 1955 he has been cond. of the Jackson (Mich.) Symph.

RACHLIN, EZRA, b. Los Angeles, Cal., Dec. 5, 1916. Studied in Berlin and at Curtis School of Music, where he later taught. He concertized throughout the U.S.A. as pianist. He was assoc. cond., then cond., of the Philadelphia Opera Co., 1942–44. In 1945 he organized and directed the Memphis Open Air Theatre. Since 1947 he has been cond. of the Austin (Tex.) Symph.

RAISIS, ANTHONY, b. Lawrence, Mass., 1915. Studied at State Teachers Coll. (Lowell, Mass.), New York Univ., Columbia Univ., and Univ. of Ill. He was violinist in the Birmingham Civic Symph. and cond. of the Birmingham Symph. Youth Orch., 1950–53. Since 1955 he has been cond. of the Oak Ridge (Tenn.) Symph.

REICHENFELD, EUGENE, b. Budapest, Hungary, Aug. 15, 1911. Studied at Duquesne Univ. (Pittsburgh, Pa.). He organized and led the Westinghouse Center Symph., Duquesne, Pa., 1941–48. He taught at Duquesne Univ., 1947–48. Since 1948 he has been cond. of the Wilkinsburg (Pa.) Civic Symph.

REINERS, RUDOLPH, b. Chicago, Ill., 1901. Studied in Berlin and at Chicago Musical Coll., where he later taught. In 1926 he became violinist in the Chicago Symph. He founded and conducted the North Side Symph. (Chicago) for eight years. He led the Gary (Ind.) Symph. and the Waukegan (Ill.) Symph. In

1945 he organized the Chicago String Ensemble and in 1954 the Chicago "Pops." Since 1947 he has been cond. of the Peoria (Ill.) Civic Symph.

RESCIGNO, NICOLA, b. New York, N.Y. Studied at Univ. of Rome and Columbia Univ. He conducted a transcontinental tour for the San Carlo Opera, and was musical dir. of the Connecticut Grand Opera Assn. He has conducted at the Cincinnati Summer Opera and the Chicago Opera Company. In 1956 he was artistic dir. of the Chicago Lyric Theatre.

RINGWALL, RUDOLPH, b. Bangor, Me., Mar. 19, 1891. Studied at New England Cons. (Boston), 1909–13, and taught there, 1917–20. He joined the Innisfail String Quartet in San Francisco in 1915. He was a violinist in the Boston Symph. for five years, and in the Nat'l Symph. of New York, 1920–21. In 1926 he became asst. cond. of the Cleveland Orch. and in 1934 its assoc. cond., a post he held until his retirement in 1956.

ROBERTSON, JAMES, P., b. Paola, Kan., Aug. 23, 1909. Studied at Drury Coll. (Springfield, Mo.), at Columbia Univ., at Juilliard School of Music, and with Monteux. In 1934 he organized the Springfield Civic Symph., which he conducted for fourteen years. In 1949 he became head of the orchestra dept. at Univ. of Wichita Kan. and cond. of the Hutchinson (Kan.) Symph. Since 1949 he has been cond. of the Wichita (Kan.) Symph. In 1955 he received a Rockefeller Grant for three years of study.

RODZINSKI, ARTUR, b. Spalato, Dalmatia, Austria-Hungary, Jan. 2, 1894. Studied at Vienna Univ. and Vienna Musical Acad. He was coach and later a cond. of the Lwow Opera. He spent four years at the Warsaw Opera House. Leopold Stokowski saw him conduct there and invited him to the U.S.A. After arriving in

this country in 1926, he served as asst. cond. of the Philadelphia
Orch. for three years, then as cond. of the Los Angeles Phil., 1929–
33, and of the Cleveland Orch., 1933–43. He was a cond. of the
NBC, 1937–38. He conducted the New York Philh., 1943–47, and
the Chicago Symph., 1947–48.

ROLLER, A. CLYDE, b. Rogersville, Mo., Oct. 13, 1914. Studied
at Oklahoma City Univ., Eastman School of Music, and Berkshire Music Center. He was solo oboist of the Oklahoma City
Symph., then, 1937–39, its asst. cond. He was solo oboist with
the Birmingham (Ala.) Symph., 1940–42, and cond. of the Southern Methodist Univ. Orch., 1947–48. Since 1948 he has been cond.
of the Amarillo (Tex.) Symph.

RONCONE, EDWARD, b. Pennsylvania. Studied at Carnegie
Inst., Pittsburgh, and at the Berkshire Music Center. He was cond.
of the Pittsburgh Savoyards Opera, 1947–48. Since 1949 he has
been cond. of the Butler (Pa.) Symph.

ROSENSTOCK, JOSEPH, b. Cracow, Poland, Jan. 27, 1895.
Studied at Vienna Acad. of Music and Univ. of Vienna. He was
cond. at the State Opera in Stuttgart, 1921–22; musical dir. of
the opera and symph. in Darmstadt, 1922–27; cond. at the Wiesbaden State Opera, 1927–29; musical dir. at the Mannheim Nat'l
Theater, 1930–33; and cond. of the Jewish Cultural Assn. in
Berlin, 1933–36. He conducted the Nippon Philh. (Japan),
1936–41 and 1945–46. In 1948 he became cond. of the City Center
Opera (N.Y.C.), a post he held until 1955, when he again became cond. of the Nippon Philh.

ROSENTHAL, MANUEL, b. Paris, France, June 18, 1904. He
was asst. cond. of the Orch. Nat'l of the Radiodiffusion Française
(Paris), 1935, and its cond., 1944–46. He was cond. of the Seattle
(Wash.) Symph., 1949–52.

ROSEVEAR, ROBERT A., b. Bloomfield, N.J., 1915. Studied at Cornell Univ. and Eastman School of Music. He was first horn with the Toronto (Ont.) Philh., the Toronto Symph., and the CBC Symph. He is assoc. prof. of musical education at Univ. of Toronto. He is a cond. of the Univ. of Toronto Symph.

ROSS, HUGH, b. Langport, England, Aug. 21, 1898. Studied at Royal Coll. of Music (London) and at Oxford Univ. He conducted his own orch. and chorus in Winnipeg, Canada, in the twenties. Since 1927 he has been conductor of the Schola Cantorum (N.Y.) and since 1941 head of the choral dept. at Berkshire Fest. (Tanglewood).

RUDEL, JULIUS, b. Vienna, Austria, 1921. Studied at Vienna Acad. of Music and Mannes College of Music (N.Y.C.). He was dir. of the Third Street Music School Settlement and cond. of its senior orchestra, 1945–52. In 1954 and 1955 he conducted musicals at Cape Cod Melody Tent (Mass.). He has been a cond. at the New York City Opera since 1944, its man. dir. since 1957.

RUDOLF, MAX, b. Frankfurt-am-Main, Germany, June 15, 1902. Studied at Univ. of Frankfurt and Hoch Cons. of Music. He was cond. of the opera houses of Freiburg, Darmstadt, Prague, and Göteborg, 1922–40. Since 1945 he has been a member of the staff of the Metropolitan Opera, and since 1950 artistic administrator. He conducted at the Cincinnati Summer Opera, summer 1948.

RUDOLF, ROBERT C., b. Wyo. Studied at Univ. of Wash. (Seattle). He conducted the Holy Names Acad. Orch., 1954–55. He organized an orchestra of players from Sheridan, Big Horn, and Buffalo (Wyo.), 1953–54, and in 1956 formed an orchestra in Little Rock (Ark.), which he has since conducted.

RUSSELL, MYRON, E., b. Stafford, Kan., Oct. 18, 1904. Studied at Kansas State Coll., Eastman School of Music, and Univ. of Mich. He was a member of the Chicago Civic Orch., 1924–26, and of the St. Louis Symph., 1927–28. He taught at Kansas State Coll., 1928–29, and at the Univ. of Mich., 1947–48. Since 1949 he has been dir. of Iowa State Teachers Coll. Symph., and since 1951 head of its dept. of music.

RUSSELL, THEODORE, b. Kirksville, Mo., Feb. 7, 1911. Studied at Northeast Mo. State Teachers Coll. (Kirksville) and Northwestern Univ. (Evanston, Ill.). Since 1944 he has been cond. of the Jackson (Miss.) Symph.

SABATA, VICTOR de, b. Trieste, Italy, Apr. 10, 1892. Studied at Milan Cons. He directed the Monte Carlo Opera, then conducted at La Scala in Milan for twenty years. He first came to the U.S.A. in 1927 as guest conductor, and has since periodically visited this country.

SABATINI, GUGLIELMO, b. Casalanguida, Italy, May 19, 1902. Came to the U.S.A. in 1914. Conducted the Philadelphia Civic Orch., 1935, and the Pennsylvania Symph., 1940. Since 1937 he has been cond. of the Trenton (N.J.) Symph.

SACKSON, DAVID, b. New York, N.Y., May 17, 1912. Studied at Inst. of Musical Art (N.Y.C.). In 1933 he became a member of the Gordon String Quartet and in 1940 musical dir. of the Charleston (S.C.) String Symph. (later the Charleston Symph.). After service in World War II, he conducted for Broadway musicals. In 1955 he formed the Phoenix Chamber Orch. (N.Y.C.) and conducted it and the New York City Symph. Workshop, made up of members of orchestras of Broadway shows.

SAIDENBERG, DANIEL, b. Winnipeg, Canada, Oct. 12, 1906. Studied at Paris Cons. of Music and Juilliard Graduate School of Music. He was solo cellist of the Philadelphia Orch., 1925–29, then of the Chicago Symph., 1930–37. He was head of the cello dept. of Chicago Musical Coll., 1933–37. In 1941 he formed the Saidenberg Little Symph. (N.Y.C.). In 1944 he helped found the Connecticut Symph. (Bridgeport) and conducted it until 1955.

SAMPLE, JAMES, b. Minneapolis, Minn., Oct. 8, 1910. Studied at Mozarteum Acad. (Salzburg) and at L'Ecole des Chefs, Paris. He studied conducting with Verbrugghen, Paumgartner, and Monteux. He organized the Little Symph. of Minneapolis, 1931–33, and developed musical units in Southern Cal., 1937–41. He was asst. to Wilfrid Pelletier at the Metropolitan Opera, 1942–43; was at the New York City Center, 1943–45; was assoc. cond. of the San Francisco Symph. on tour, 1947; and was cond. of the San Bernardino Symph. and the Hollywood Chamber Orch., 1947–49. In 1949 he became cond. of the Portland (Ore.) Symph. In 1953 he became musical dir. of the Erie (Pa.) Philh.

SAMUEL, GERARD, b. Bonn, Germany, 1924. Came to the U.S.A. in 1939. Studied at Eastman School of Music, Yale School of Music, and Berkshire Music Center. He was a violinist with the Rochester Philh. Since 1949 he has been asst. cond. of the Minneapolis Symph. In that time he has founded the Collegium Musicum and become musical dir. and cond. of the Cecilian Singers, musical dir. of the Minneapolis Civic Opera Assn., and musical and educational dir. of the New Friends of Chamber Music.

SAN JUAN, PEDRO, b. Spain. Studied at Nat'l Cons. of Madrid and Schola Cantorum (Paris). He founded the Havana (Cuba)

Philh., and is at present its honorary cond. He is the cond. of the Greenville (S.C.) Symph.

SARGENT, SIR MALCOLM, b. Stamford, Lincolnshire, England, April 29, 1895. Studied at Royal Coll. of London and thereafter took several posts as organist. He conducted his *Impressions on a Windy Day* at a Promenade Concert in London and therewith decided to become a cond. He led the Halle Orch., 1939–43, and the Liverpool Philh., 1942–48. In 1947 he was knighted, and the same year became cond. of the London Promenade Concerts. In 1950 he became musical dir. of BBC (London).

SCHEER, LEO, b. Jersey City, N.J., Oct. 2, 1909. Studied with Monteux and Altschuler. He was cond. of the Federal (WPA) Symph. of San Diego two years; assoc. cond. of the San Diego Symph. four years; cond. of the San Diego Opera three years, of the San Diego Youth Symph. seven years, and of the Eagle Rock Civic Symph. of Los Angeles two years. He is asst. cond. of the Kansas City Philh. and cond. of the orchestra's "Pretzel" concerts.

SCHENKMAN, EDGAR, b. New Market, N.J., May 9, 1908. Studied at Juilliard School of Music and later taught there and was cond. of the Juilliard Orch. He has been cond. of the Chautauqua (N.Y.) Opera and of the Toledo Friends of Music Orch., 1943–46. Since 1948 he has conducted the Norfolk (Va.) Symph., and since 1950 has been dir. of the Virginia Music Fest. In 1952 he founded the summer school of music at Mary Washington Coll. of the Univ. of Va.

SCHERCHEN, HERMANN, b. Berlin, Germany, June 21, 1891. He played with the Berlin Blüthner Orch., 1907–10, then with the Berlin Philh. He began conducting at Riga in 1914, then in the twenties conducted at Leipzig and Frankfurt, and in the early thirties in Königsberg. He left Germany in 1935 and has since made his home in Zurich, Switzerland.

SCHERMAN, THOMAS. Studied at the Mannes College of Music (N.Y.C.). He was engaged on MBS, 1946, where he originated the "Let's Go to the Opera" program. In 1947 he organized the Little Orch. Soc. of N.Y.C. and has since been its cond. In 1954 he organized the Music-Appreciation Record Club and became its musical dir.

SCHICK, GEORGE, b. Prague, Czechoslovakia, April 5, 1908. Studied at the Prague Cons. In 1927 he became asst. cond. of the Prague Opera. He came to the U.S.A. in 1939 as coach and dir. of Risë Stevens. In 1943 he became musical dir. of the San Carlo Opera, and dir. of New York's Center Theatre Opera and of Chicago's summer opera fest. at Soldier's Field. In 1944 he toured as cond. with the Baccaloni Opera Co. and the Ballet Internationale of New York. In 1946 he directed the Miami Opera Guild. He was musical dir. of the Little Symph. of Montreal, 1948–50, and assoc. cond. of the Chicago Symph., 1950–56.

SCHIPPERS, THOMAS, b. Kalamazoo, Mich., Mar. 9, 1930. In 1949 and 1954 he conducted Menotti operas in New York. In 1952 he was appointed a cond. of the New York City Center Opera. In 1955 he became a cond. at the Metropolitan Opera.

SCHOEDER, WALTER, b. Paterson, N.J., 1917. Studied at Vienna State Acad. of Music and Juilliard School of Music. He was successively cellist and assoc. cond. of the Paterson (N.J.) Symph. and, since 1947, its cond.

SCHOLZ, ROBERT, b. Steyr, Austria, Oct. 16, 1902. Studied at the Mozarteum in Salzburg, and in 1924 became a member of its faculty. He was the cond. of the Henry Street Settlement in New York, 1938–56. Since 1952 he has been cond. of the Amer. Chamber Orch., N.Y.

SCHULTE, FREDERICK, b. Racine, Wis., 1881. Since 1921 he has taught in public schools in Racine. He is music consultant to the city's six junior and senior high schools and has charge of instrumental music in the fourteen elementary schools. In 1930 he organized the Little Symph. and developed it into the present Racine Symph.

SCHULTE, KARL, b. Racine, Wis. Studied at Chicago Music Coll. and later taught there. He was a violinist in the Milwaukee Symph., and in the Chicago Symph., 1917–22. In 1921 he organized the Little Symph. of Chicago and became its assoc. cond. Since 1947 he has been musical dir. of the West Suburban Symph. (La Grange, Ill.).

SCHWARTZ, WILL, b. New York, N.Y., Sept. 23, 1923. Studied at Juilliard School of Music and Columbia Univ. During World War II he was appointed musical dir. of Special Programs on army radio station in Pilsen, Czechoslovakia. In 1949 he founded, and has since conducted, the Fort Collins (Colo.) Symph. In 1955 he was appointed musical dir. of the Cheyenne (Wyo.) Symph. and Choral Soc.

SECUNDA, SHOLOM, b. Russia, 1894. Studied at Columbia Univ. and Inst. of Musical Art (N.Y.C.). In summers he conducts an orchestra of symphonic proportions at the Concord Hotel, Kiamesha, N.Y.

SEE, ORLEY, b. Galion, Ohio. Studied at Denison Univ. (Ohio), and later taught there and conducted its orchestra. He was violinist in the Cincinnati Symph. and the San Francisco Symph. In 1934 he organized, and has since conducted, the Oakland (Cal.) Symph.

SEVITZKY, FABIEN, b. Vyshnii Volochek, Russia, Sept. 30, 1893. Studied at St. Petersburg Cons. He became a member of the Moscow Imperial Theater Orch. In 1915 he toured Russia as a double-bass virtuoso. Leaving Russia in 1922, he became a member of the Warsaw Philh. He made a tour of So. Amer. and Mexico, and in 1923 became a member of the Philadelphia Orch. In 1925 he organized the Philadelphia Chamber String Sinfonietta and led it until 1930, when he went to Boston. There he became cond. of the Metropolitan Theater Symph. and of the Boston People's Symph. He was cond. of the Indianapolis Symph., 1936–56.

SHANET, HOWARD, b. Brooklyn, N.Y., Nov. 9, 1918. Studied at Berkshire Music Center and Columbia Univ., and was first cellist of the Univ. Orch. In 1941 he was appointed to the faculty of Hunter Coll. In 1947 he became asst. cond. of the New York City Symph., and in 1949 a member of the Berkshire Music Center faculty. He accompanied Koussevitzky on his world tour with the Boston Symph., 1950. He was cond. of the Huntington (W.Va.) Symph., 1951–53. Since 1953 he has been cond. of the Columbia Univ. Orch. and an asst. prof. of music there.

SHAW, ROBERT, b. Red Bluff, Cal., April 30, 1916. Studied at Pomona Coll. In 1941 he organized the Collegiate Chorale (N.Y.C.), which he conducted until 1954. He was choral dir. at the Berkshire Music Center, 1942–45, and at Juilliard School of Music, 1946–50. In 1948 he organized the Robert Shaw Chorale (N.Y.C.). He has led the San Diego Symph. in summer concerts since 1953. Since 1956 he has been assoc. cond. of the Cleveland Orch.

SHENAUT, JOHN, b. Galesburg, Ill. Studied at Knox Coll. Cons. of Music (Galesburg), at Amer. Cons. of Music (Chicago), at Univ. of Mich., and with Monteux. He was a violinist with the Chicago Civic Orch., the Sioux City (Iowa) Symph., and the Alexandria (La.) Military Symph. After conducting a naval band in World War II he spent four years building a college-community orchestra at Louisiana State Normal Coll. (Natchitoches, La.). In 1948 he organized and became cond. of the Shreveport (La.) Symph.

SIEGL, HENRY, b. Detroit, Mich. Studied at Curtis Inst. of Music. In fifteen years' residence in Detroit he was concertmaster of the Michigan Theater Orch. and a member of other musical groups. He was concertmaster of the Orquestra Sinfónica Brasileiro (Rio de Janiero), 1946–47, and a violinist of the NBC Symph., 1947–52. He was concertmaster of the New York City Ballet Orch. and the Knickerbocker Chamber Players. He was a member of the Saidenberg Sinfonietta, the Galimir Quartet, the Guilet Quartet, and the Symph. of the Air. Since 1956 he has been concertmaster and asst. cond. of the Seattle (Wash.) Symph.

SIEGMEISTER, ELIE, b. New York, N.Y., Jan. 15, 1909. Studied at Juilliard Graduate School. For five years he toured with the American Ballad Singers, which he had organized. He conducted his own musical, *Sing Out, Sweet Land,* on Broadway. He is cond. of the Hofstra Symph. (Hempstead, N.Y.).

SILVA, MANLIO, b. Chiavari, Italy, Nov. 4, 1893. He was violinist in the Municipal Opera Orch. (Chiavari). The Little Symph. that he organized in 1926 in Stockton (Cal.) grew into the Stockton Symph., which he still conducts.

SINGER, EUGENE JOSÉ, b. Rumania. Studied in Germany. In 1949 he organized the Clarksburg (W.Va.) Symph. and conducted it for three years. In 1954 he became a violinist in the Dallas (Tex.) Symph.

SINGER, JACQUES, b. Przemyśl, Poland, 1913. He came to the U.S.A. in 1921. Studied at Curtis Inst. of Music and Juilliard School of Music. At eighteen he became a member of the Philadelphia Orch. He was cond. of the Dallas Symph., 1938–42, and was musical dir. of the New Orleans Summer Concerts, 1946. He was musical dir. of the Vancouver Symph., 1947–51. In 1952 he conducted Broadway shows. Since 1954 he has been cond. of the Corpus Christi (Tex.) Symph.

SIRPO, BORIS, b. Finland. He was founder and dir. of Cons. of Viipuri. He came to the U.S.A. in 1940. In 1946 he founded the Portland (Ore.) Chamber Orch. Since 1950 he has been the cond. of the Hood River (Ore.) Music Fest. In 1953 he formed the "All-Girl" Ensemble in Portland.

SMALLENS, ALEXANDER, b. St. Petersburg, Russia, Jan. 1, 1889. Came to New York in 1890. Studied at City Coll., Inst. of Musical Art, and Paris Cons. He was successively asst. cond. at the Boston Opera, 1911–14; its cond., 1915–17; cond. with the Pavlova Ballet on a So. Amer. tour, 1917–19; with the Chicago Opera, 1919–22; with the Philadelphia Civic Opera Co., 1924–31; and asst. cond. of the Philadelphia Orch., 1927–34. During the season of 1934–35 he was co-cond. with Fritz Reiner of opera in cooperation with the Philadelphia Orch. He conducted the Ballet Theatre for several seasons. He was musical dir. at Radio City Music Hall (N.Y.C.), 1947–50.

SMITH, WILLIAM R., b. Haddon Heights, N.J., May 27, 1924. Studied at Univ. of Penn. and taught there, 1944–46. He founded the Philadelphia Orch. Chorus and directed the Youth Orch. of Philadelphia for three seasons. He is cond. of the orchestra of

Curtis Inst. of Music. Since 1952 he has been asst. to Eugene Ormandy, and since 1956 asst. cond. of the Philadelphia Orch.

SOKOLOFF, NIKOLAI, b. Kiev, Russia, May 28, 1886. He came to the U.S.A. when he was twelve. Studied at Yale Univ. School of Music. He was violinist with the Boston Symph., 1904–7. After being concertmaster of the Russian Symph. in New York for five years, he went to the Pacific Coast and became cond. of the San Francisco Philh. He was musical dir. of the Cleveland Orch., 1918–33; dir. of the Federal Music Project, WPA, 1935–39; and cond. of the Seattle Symph., 1938–40. In 1942 he formed the Musical Arts Soc. of La Jolla, Cal., which he still conducts.

SOLTI, GEORG, b. Budapest, Hungary, 1912. Studied at Budapest High School for Music. He was cond. of the State Opera in Budapest, 1932–39, then guest cond. and later gen. musical dir. of the State Opera in Munich, 1945–52. Since 1952 he has been gen. musical dir. of the Frankfurt Opera and the Frankfurt Museum Symph. In 1953 he was a cond. of the San Francisco Opera, and in 1956–57 of the Opera Theatre Assn., Chicago.

SOMOHANO, ARTURO, b. San Juan, Puerto Rico, 1910. Studied at the Academia Católica in San Juan. In the early fifties he founded his own concert orchestra which, as the Puerto Rico Concert Orch., has over fifty members.

SORANTIN, ERIC, b. Vienna, Austria, 1905. Studied at Vienna State Acad. of Music, Vienna Univ., and Vanderbilt Univ. He came to the U.S.A. in 1924 and appeared with major orchestras as violin soloist. In 1936 he reorganized the Chicago Little Philh. and toured with it for seven seasons. In 1941 he founded the San Antonio Chamber Music Soc. and was musical dir. of the San Antonio (summer) Civic Opera for several seasons. In 1950 he founded the San Angelo Symph., which he still directs, and in 1953 formed the San Antonio Community Orch.

SPEAR, LLOYD, b. Windom, Kan., Sept. 15, 1917. Studied at Bethany Coll., Lindsborg, Kan. and Chicago Cons. of Music. Since 1947 he has been cond. of the Bethany Symph., since 1948 dean of the school of fine arts, and since 1956 cond. of the Lindsborg Messiah chorus.

STAFFANSON, ROBERT L., b. Sidney, Mont., Nov. 11, 1921. Studied at Montana State Univ. School of Music (Missoula) and served as asst. cond. of the Univ. Symph. In Jan. 1951 he organized the Billings (Mont.) Symph., which he conducted until 1955, when he became musical dir. of the Springfield (Mass.) Symph.

STANGER, RUSSELL, b. Arlington, Mass., May 8, 1924. Studied at New England Cons. of Music. In 1950 he was appointed musical dir. of the Harvard-Radcliffe Orch., a position he still holds. In 1952 he was musical asst. at the Fest. of Creative Arts at Brandeis Univ., Waltham, Mass. In 1953 he was engaged as cond. of Boston's Cecilia Soc. for its tour of France. In 1954 he was appointed musical dir. of the Pioneer Valley Symph. (Greenfield, Mass.).

STANLEY, LEONARD G., b. West Troy, N.Y., Dec. 18, 1871. Studied at Union Coll. (Schenectady, N.Y.). He started the Empire Orch. in Albany in 1902 and is still its cond. He was asst. cond. of the Albany Symph. for seventeen years.

STARK, ETHEL, b. Montreal, Canada. Studied at McGill Cons. of Music (Montreal) and Curtis Inst. of Music. She teaches violin at Provincial Cons. de Musique in Montreal. Since 1939 she has been cond. of the Montreal Women's Symph. as well as the Ethel

Stark Symphonietta. The Montreal Women's Symph. under her baton was the first Canadian orchestra to perform in Carnegie Hall, this in 1947.

STEFAN, ANTHONY R., b. Budapest, Hungary, 1903. Studied at Royal Coll. of Music (Budapest). He has taught violin at the Schenectady (N.Y.) Cons. of Music since 1928, and since 1933 has been successively concertmaster 1933–39 and cond. of the Schenectady Symph.

STEIN, LEON, b. Chicago, Ill., Sept. 18, 1910. Studied at American Cons., Crane Junior Coll., and De Paul Univ. (Chicago). He has taught at De Paul since 1931, and since 1951 has been dir. of the graduate division. Since 1946 he has conducted the Community Symph. of Chicago.

STEINDEL, MAX, b. Munich-Gladbach, Germany. Studied at Royal Cons. of Music (Stuttgart). He was principal cellist with the Seattle Symph., 1908–11. He toured the U.S.A. as part of a trio, 1914–17. He was cellist with the St. Louis Symph., 1912–1914 and 1918–46. Since 1946 he has been personnel manager of the St. Louis Symph. In 1921 he organized his own concert orch. Since 1934 he has been resident cond. of the Little Symph. Assoc. (Summer Symph.) of St. Louis.

STEINER, GEORGE, b. Baltimore, Md., May 17, 1918. Studied at Johns Hopkins Univ. and Peabody Cons. He has taught at Peabody, George Washington Univ., and Catholic Univ., all in or near Washington, D.C. He is asst. prof. of music at Amer. Univ. and at Univ. of Maryland, asst. concertmaster of the Nat'l Symph., and concertmaster of the Nat'l Gallery of Art Orch. He conducts the Amer. Univ. Orch.

STEWART, REGINALD, b. Edinburgh, Scotland, April 20, 1902. Studied at Gillespie School and St. Mary's Coll. (Edinburgh). In the twenties he became cond. of the Canadian Operatic Soc. (Toronto); dir. of music at Hart House, Univ. of Toronto; and pianist of the Hambourg Trio. In 1930 he conducted the London Symph. during the Celebrity Series at Albert Hall. In 1934 he inaugurated the symph. concerts of the Toronto Philh. and conducted them for seven years. In 1941 he became dir. of Peabody Cons. of Music and in 1942 cond. of the Baltimore Symph., relinquishing the latter post in 1952.

STIEDRY, FRITZ, b. Germany. He was successively coach in the Dresden Opera, a cond. at the Berlin Municipal Opera, and a cond. of the Vienna Opera. Subsequently he was musical dir. of the Leningrad Symph. He arrived in this country in 1937 and for four years conducted the newly founded Orch. of the New Friends of Music. Since 1946 he has been a cond. at the Metropolitan Opera.

STONE, THOMPSON, b. Boston. Studied at Harvard, at Boston Univ., and abroad. He was cond. of the People's Symph. (Boston) for three years, and cond. of the Fine Arts Fest., Univ. of Iowa, for eleven years. Since 1944 he has headed the music dept. of Tufts Coll. (Medford, Mass.), and since 1926 been musical dir. of the Boston Handel and Haydn Soc.

STRASFOGEL, IGNACE, b. Warsaw, Poland, 1909. Studied at Hochschule für Musik (Berlin). He was accompanist to Joseph Szigeti on a world tour, 1927–28. In 1930 he was appointed asst. cond. of the Berlin State Opera. In 1933 he came to the U.S.A. He was official pianist, 1935–44, and asst. cond., 1944–45, of the New York Philh. Symph. In 1951 he became musical dir. of WABF (N.Y.C.). Also he conducted Broadway shows and, for several years, the New York Doctors' Orchestral Soc. Since 1951 he has been an asst. cond. at the Metropolitan Opera.

STRAUSS, PAUL, b. Chicago. Studied at Northwestern Univ. Conducted WPA orchestras in Lansing, Mich., and Brooklyn, N.Y. In 1946 he was asst. cond. to Mitropoulos at Robin Hood Dell (Philadelphia), and in the fall of that year was cond. of the Ballet Russe de Monte Carlo, a post he held for six years.

STRESEMANN, WOLFGANG, b. Dresden, Germany, July 20, 1904. He came to the U.S.A. in 1939 and joined the Nat'l Orchestral Assn. (N.Y.C.), first as conducting member, then as asst. cond. In 1944 he became a teacher at Westminster Choir Coll. (Princeton, N.J.) and cond. of the Westminster Orch. He was music editor of the N.Y. *Staatszeitung,* 1945–49, then musical dir. of the Toledo (Ohio) Orch., 1949–55. In 1956 he was appointed general manager of the Radio Symph. Orch. of West Berlin.

STRICKLAND, WILLIAM, b. Defiance, Ohio, Jan. 25, 1914. He founded and conducted the Nat'l Youth Administration Sinfonietta in New York, 1940, and organized and became cond. of the Nashville (Tenn.) Symph., 1946. He taught at Juilliard Summer School, 1948–49, and at the Opera School of Mozarteum Acad., Salzburg, 1953–54. In 1955 he became musical dir. of the Oratorio Soc. of New York.

STUBBLEFIELD, PHILIP, b. Rutherford, Tenn., June 23, 1913. Studied at Miss. State Coll. and Univ. of Southern Cal. He taught in high schools of California for six years and in Shashta Junior Coll. (Redding, Cal.) for five. Since 1950, cond. of Shashta Symph.

STULBERG, JULIUS, b. Poland, June 2, 1913. Came to the U.S.A. at seven years of age. Studied at Michigan State Coll. He was concertmaster of the Lansing Civic Symph. He has been cond.

of the Kalamazoo (Mich.) Junior Symph. since 1943, and of the Western Michigan Coll. of Education (Kalamazoo) Symph. since 1945.

SUSSKIND, WALTER, b. Czechoslovakia, 1908. He became asst. cond. at the Prague Opera House at the age of twenty. He conducted the Scottish Orch., 1946–50, the Scottish Nat'l Orch., 1950–52, and the Victoria Symph., Melbourne, Australia, 1952–55. In 1956 he became cond. of the Toronto (Canada) Symph.

SWAN, VIRL M., b. Sidney, Neb., May, 1910. Studied at Coll. of the Pacific, Stockton, Cal. In the early forties, he organized and directed the Tuolumne County Symph. In 1945 he became supervisor of instrumental music in the Vallejo (Cal.) unified school district. He played French horn in the Vallejo Symph., and became its conductor in 1949.

TAUSSIG, WALTER, b. Vienna, Austria, Feb. 9, 1908. Studied at Vienna State Acad. of Music. He was asst. at the Theater an der Wien and at the People's Opera, 1933–36. He has been on the staffs of the New Opera Co. (N.Y.C.), the Montreal Opera, and the Chicago Opera, and has conducted Broadway productions. He was asst. cond. with the San Francisco Opera in 1947, '48 and '49. He was assoc. musical dir. with the Central City Opera House, 1950–54. Since 1949 he has been assoc. chorus master and cond. with the Metropolitan Opera.

TAYLOR, GUY, b. Anniston, Ala., Dec. 25, 1919. Studied at Birmingham Cons. of Music and at Juilliard School of Music. He was cond. of the Birmingham Nat'l Youth Assn. Symph., 1938–41. He was cond. of the Springfield (Ohio) Symph., 1948–51. In 1951 he became musical dir. of the Nashville (Tenn.) Symph. Assoc. He is cond. of the Nashville Symphonette, the Nashville Choral Soc., and the Nashville Summer Symph.

THOMPSON, LEON E., b. Portsmouth, Va., Aug. 1, 1928. Studied at Va. State Coll., at Ohio State Univ., at Eastman School of Music, and with Monteux, Szell, and Fournet. He is the cond. of the W.Va. State Coll. (Institute, W.Va.) Little Symph.

TILLERY, HUBERT, b. Richmond, Va., Nov. 27, 1920. Studied at Washington Univ. (St. Louis), at Cincinnati Cons., and with Monteux. Since 1949 he has been cond. of the Petersburg (Va.) Little Symph.

TORNO, LAURENT. He was flutist with the St. Louis Symph., and cond. of the St. Louis Philh. for two years and of the St. Louis Women's Symph. for ten years. Since 1950 he has been cond. of the Kirkwood (Mo.) Symph.

TOTH, ANDOR, b. New York, N.Y. Studied under Edgar Schenkman and Hans Letz. He was concertmaster with the Ballet Theatre Orch., asst. concertmaster with the Cleveland Orch., and cond. of the Cleveland Little Symph. He was assoc. cond. of the Houston (Tex.) Symph. until 1955, when he became a member of the faculty of Oberlin (Ohio) Cons.

TROMBLEY, GEORGE, b. Saginaw, Mich., Oct. 27, 1884. Studied at Michigan Cons. of Music (Detroit). In 1921 he helped form the Kalamazoo Symph., and in 1925 founded the Kalamazoo Cons. of Music and Associated Arts. In 1926 he went to California and founded the Santa Rosa Symph., which he still conducts.

UNGER, HEINZ, b. Germany, Dec. 14, 1895. Studied at Univ. of Berlin, Univ. of Munich, and Cons. of Berlin. He conducted the Northern Philh. Orch. (Leeds, Yorkshire). Since 1952 he has conducted the York Concert Society (Toronto).

VAN den BURG, WILLIAM, b. The Hague, Holland, 1901. Studied at Royal Conservatorium (cello) and at Ecole-Normale de Musique, Paris. He was cellist in the San Francisco Symph., 1925–26, and solo cellist with the Philadelphia Orch., 1926–35. During this period he studied conducting under Fritz Reiner at Curtis Inst. He was solo cellist and assoc. cond. of the San Francisco Orch., 1935; organized the Sacramento and the San Jose orchestras; and conducted the San Francisco Nat'l Youth Orch. He was first-chair cellist and asst. cond. of the Los Angeles Philh., 1950–53. In 1935 he organized the Los Angeles Doctors' Symph. and the Los Angeles Civic Orch., which he still leads.

VAN VACTOR, DAVID, b. Plymouth, Ind., May 8, 1906. Studied at Northwestern Univ., Vienna Acad., Ecole-Normale, and Paris Cons. In 1941 he toured Mexico, Central and So. Amer. with the American Wind Quintet. He was flutist in the Chicago Symph., 1931–43, and in the Kansas City Phil., 1943–45. He was asst. cond. of the Kansas City Philh., 1943–45, and cond. of Allied Arts Orch., Kansas City, 1946–47. Since 1947 he has been cond. of the Knoxville (Tenn.) Symph. and head of the Dept. of Fine Arts at the Univ. of Tenn.

VIANELLO, HUGO, b. New York, N.Y., Jan. 16, 1926. Studied at Manhattan School of Music (N.Y.C.) and Adelphi Coll. (Garden City, N.Y.). He was violist with the Nat'l Orchestral Assn., 1951–52, the Minneapolis Symph., 1952–54, and the Knickerbocker Chamber Players. He was asst. cond. of the Center Symph. (N.Y.C.) and of the Mahopac (N.Y.) music fest. He was asst. cond. of the Oklahoma City Symph., 1954–56.

VON der HEIDE, HENRY, b. Grand Rapids, Minn., Aug. 3, 1921. Studied at Univ. of Minnesota and Univ. of Idaho. He conducted the Owatonna (Minn.) Symph. for four years. Since 1949 he has been cond. of the Boise (Idaho) Civic Symph.

VON KARAJAN, HERBERT, b. Salzburg, Austria, Apr. 5, 1908. Studied at Ulm and in Vienna. He became cond. in the Opera in Ulm in 1934 and dir. of the Opera in Aachen in 1935. During World War II he was dir. of the Berlin State Orch. In 1946 he conducted the Vienna Philh. Since 1949 he has been a concert dir. of the Viennese Friends of Music Soc. In 1954 and 1955 he toured the U.S.A. as cond. of the Berlin Philh. and as cond. of the Philharmonia Orch. of London. Since 1956 he has been artistic dir. of the Vienna State Opera, and since 1957 of the Salzburg Fest.

VOORHEES, DONALD, b. Allentown, Pa., 1903. Studied under Dr. J. Fred Wolle. In 1920 he began conducting theater orchestras on Broadway and in 1927 entered radio work. In 1937 he became house cond. with Howard Barlow of CBS. In 1940 he became cond. of the Bell Telephone Hour Orch. Since 1951 he has conducted the Allentown (Pa.) Symph.

VRIONIDES, CHRISTOS, b. Crete, Greece, Jan. 12, 1894. Studied at Odeon, Athens, Juilliard School of Music, David Mannes School of Music. He conducted the Nassau-Suffolk Federal Orch., 1935–41. In 1942 he organized the Brunswick (Ga.) Little Symph. Since 1946 he has conducted the Town of Babylon (N.Y.) Symph., and since 1954 has taught at the Greek Theological Seminary in Brookline, Mass., where he has presented concerts with the seminary choir.

VYNER, LOUIS, b. Pittsburgh, Pa., May 30, 1910. Studied at Curtis Inst. of Music. He was asst. cond. of the Philadelphia Grand Opera Co., 1929–32, head of the orchestra dept. of the Wilmington (Del.) Music School, 1930–33, and musical dir. of the York (Pa.)

Symph., 1934-48. In 1940 he became musical dir. of the Nat'l Youth Orch. of Philadelphia, and in 1947 founded and has since been musical dir. of the Lancaster (Pa.) Symph. Since 1949 he has conducted the Reading (Pa.) Symph.

WAGNER, JOSEPH FREDERICK, b. Springfield, Mass., Jan. 9, 1900. Studied at New England Cons., at Boston Univ., and with Monteux. He was asst. dir. of music in the Boston public schools, 1923-44; and taught at Boston Univ. Coll. of Music, 1929-40; at Rutgers Univ., summers, 1928-30; at Univ. of Okla., summer, 1938; at Hunter Coll., N.Y.C., 1945-46; and at Brooklyn Coll., 1945-47. He founded and conducted the Boston Civic Symph., 1925-44; the summer series of the Buffalo Philh., 1945; the St. Paul (Minn.) Pop Concerts, 1947-48; the Duluth Symph., 1947-50; and the Orquesta Sinfónica Nacional de Costa Rica, 1950-54.

WALDO, MAXIM, b. New York, N.Y., Apr. 24, 1907. Studied at Teachers' Coll., Columbia Univ.; at Inst. of Musical Art (N.Y.C.); and with Monteux. After tenures as solo oboist in various orchestras, he conducted successively (in N.Y.C.) the Grand Street Settlement Symph., the Tremont Symph., the Washington Heights Symph., the Jewish Community House Symph., the Gotham Orchestral Soc., and (since 1955) the New York Doctors' Orchestral Soc.

WAXMAN, FRANZ, b. Germany. Studied in Dresden and Berlin. He came to the U.S.A. in 1934. In 1947 he founded the Los Angeles Music Fest. and has since been its musical dir.

WEBER, HENRY, b. Berlin, Germany, Dec. 9, 1900, the son of Amer. parents. Studied at Imperial Academy of Music, Vienna. He directed the Chicago Civic Opera, 1924-29, then conducted at the Florence (Italy) Opera, and in 1933 became dir. of the

Chicago City Opera. He was staff producer and cond. at NBC, 1933–34, and gen. dir. of the Chicago Opera, 1938–41. Since 1934 he has been dir. of music and cond. of WGN, Chicago. He has served for many years as gen. dir. of the Annual Chicagoland Music Fest.

WEBER, JOHN ROY, b. Fond du Lac, Wis. He founded the Hollywood (Cal.) Symph. as an outgrowth of the Hollywood Canteen Symph. Since 1950 he has conducted this group, known as the Hollywood Pops Orch., in summer "Twilight Concerts."

WEBER, MILTON, b. Graz, Austria, May 30, 1910. Studied violin and conducting at Graz Cons. of Music, at Acad. of Vienna, at Univ. of Mich., and with Monteux. He came to the U.S.A. in 1941. In 1946 he conducted the Milwaukee Chamber Opera. Since 1947 he has been music instructor at Carroll Coll. (Waukesha, Wis.) and cond. of the Badger Symph., the Waukesha Symph., and the Waukesha Opera Guild.

WEDDLE, FRANKLYN S., b. near Bantry, N.D., Aug. 24, 1905. Studied at Univ. of Iowa, Northwestern Univ., Univ. of Mich., and Berkshire Music Center. In the 1930's he helped launch the Flint (Mich.) Little Symph. He was clarinetist with the Flint Symph., 1931–34. In 1934 he founded, and has since conducted, the Independence (Mo.) Symph.

WEICHER, JOHN, b. Chicago, Ill., Mar. 29, 1904. Studied at Prague Cons. of Music. He became violinist in the Cleveland Orch. in 1921 and in the Chicago Symph. in 1923. In 1928 he became concertmaster of the Seattle Symph., and in 1929 asst. concertmaster of the Chicago Symph. In 1930 he organized the Philharmonic String Quartet. Since 1937 he has been concertmaster of the Chicago Symph. He conducted the Civic Orch. of

Chicago, 1946–47, and was reappointed to the post in 1955. He conducts the young people's concerts of the Chicago Symph.

WEISSMANN, FRIEDER, b. Germany. Studied at Univ. of Heidelberg and Univ. of Munich. He conducted in Münster and Königsberg opera houses. In 1931 he became cond. of the Berlin Symph. and led it till it merged with the Berlin Philh. in 1933. From 1933 to 1940 he was annual guest cond. of the Amsterdam Concertgebouw Orch. and presented opera on Holland's radio station AVRO. Since 1943 he has been cond. of the Scranton (Pa.) Philh., and since 1950 of the Havana (Cuba) Philh.

WERNER, EDUARD, b. Vienna, 1891. For many years he was a cond. in motion pictures. He conducts the Detroit Symph. once annually. Since 1951 he has been pres. of the Detroit local of the Amer. Fed. of Musicians.

WHALLON, EVAN, b. Akron, Ind. Studied at Eastman School of Music, and with Monteux. He conducted Menotti's *The Consul* four months in N.Y.C. and on its Amer. tour, 1950. Since 1951 he has been cond. of the Springfield (Ohio) Symph., and since 1956 of the Columbus (Ohio) Symph.

WHELAN, HAROLD PAUL. Studied at Univ. of Washington, at Northwestern Univ., and with Monteux. In 1945 he organized the Spokane (Wash.) Philh., which he has since conducted.

WHITE, PAUL, b. Bangor, Me., Aug. 22, 1895. Studied at New England Cons. of Music. He played violin in the Bangor Symph. at twelve years of age. He was violinist in the Cincinnati Symph., 1918–21, then taught at New England Cons. He was asst. cond. of the Eastman Theatre Orch., Rochester, 1923–31. Since 1928 he has taught at Eastman School of Music. He was assoc. cond. of the Rochester Civic Orch., 1929–53, then became its regular cond. He also conducts the Rochester Little Symph. and the Eastman School of Music Senior Symph.

WILLSON, MEREDITH, b. Mason City, Iowa, May 18, 1902. Studied at Inst. of Musical Art. He was flutist in the New York Phil., 1924–29. He has been musical dir. and cond. of several nat'l NBC network programs. He conducts summer school music festivals throughout the country.

WILSON, GILBERT E., b. Girard, Ohio, June 10, 1914. Studied with Carmen Ficocelli (Youngstown, Ohio). He was a violinist in the Youngstown Civic Orch. Since 1949 he has been on the teaching staff of Knox Coll. (Galesburg, Ill.) and cond. of the Knox-Galesburg Symph.

WILSON, THOMAS, b. Green Hill, Ind., Oct. 1, 1918. Studied at Central Normal Coll., Danville, Ill., Univ. of Mich., and Berkshire Music Center. In the late 1930's he taught at Central Normal Coll. and formed the Hoosier Symph. and Chorale. In 1950 he toured Denmark, Norway, and Sweden as asst. cond. of the Scandinavian Symph. of Detroit. In 1951 he formed, and has since conducted, the Lafayette (Ind.) Symph.

WILTSE, LYMAN, b. Perry, Iowa, May 7, 1899. He conducted theater orchestras from the age of fifteen. Studied at Drake Cons. (now called Northwestern Univ. School of Music) and Cincinnati Cons. of Music. He became dir. of music at Univ. of Tampa, Fla., in 1938. He has conducted the Tampa Philh. since its founding in 1947. He assisted in founding the Florida West Coast Symph., and conducted it in 1948. He organized the Tampa Philh. Chorus in 1952.

WINCENC, JOSEPH, b. Buffalo, N.Y., Oct. 16, 1915. Studied at Oberlin Cons., 1932–37, State Cons. of Music, Prague, Czechoslovakia, Columbia Univ., and Berkshire Music Center. He was a member of the Buffalo Philh., 1938–41, and from 1940 its concertmaster. He organized and conducted the Business and Professional Men's Symph. in Buffalo. He was a member of the Chautauqua Symph., 1939–43. In 1946 he organized, and has since conducted, the Amherst Symph. (Snyder, N.Y.). He conducted the Buffalo Opera Workshop, 1951–54. Since Jan. 1950 he has been cond. of the Orchard Park (N.Y.) Symph.

WINDINGSTAD, OLE, b. Sandefjord, Norway, May 18, 1886. In 1906 he came to New York and conducted the Norwegian "Skald" choral soc. In 1923 he conducted several concerts of the Philh. Soc. of Oslo. Cond. of New Orleans Symph., 1941–44.

WIRTH, CARL ANTON, b. Rochester, N.Y., Jan. 24, 1912. Studied at Eastman School of Music. He taught at Iowa State Coll. and conducted the Iowa State Teachers Coll. Symph., 1935–48. In 1949 he organized the Twin City (St. Joseph and Benton Harbor, Mich.) Symph., and conducted it until 1952. Since 1953 he has been cond. of the Rochester (N.Y.) Community Orch.

WISHNOW, EMANUEL, b. England, 1910. Came to the U.S.A. in his early youth. Studied violin with Stearns, Molzer, and Gordon, and conducting with Monteux. He was concertmaster of the Lincoln Symph., 1936–50. He conducted the Omaha Symph, 1951–53. Since 1939 he has headed Univ. of Neb. string dept., and since 1941 has been cond. of the Univ. of Neb. Symph.

WOESSNER, JULIUS, b. Lourach-Baden, Germany, Feb. 9, 1893. Studied privately. In 1925 he organized and became cond. of the Lowell (Mass.) Philh.

WORLEY, JOHN C., b. Waltham, Mass., Sept. 2, 1919. Studied clarinet with Rudolph Toll and George Wain, and conducting with Monteux. He was clarinetist in the Columbus (Ohio) Philh., 1942–45; the Norwalk (Conn.) Symph., the Connecticut Symph., and the Connecticut "Pops," 1947–52. He was supervisor of music in the public schools of New Canaan (Conn.), 1945–49. In 1953 he re-formed the Oneonta (N.Y.) Community Symph., which he has since conducted. He teaches at N.Y. State Coll. for Teachers, Oneonta.

YARBOROUGH, WILLIAM, b. Wilmington, N.C., Jan. 3, 1924. Studied at Peabody Cons., Univ. of So. Cal., Univ. of Chicago, Chicago Musical Coll., Indiana Univ., and Berkshire Music Center. He was cond. of the American Symph., Paris, 1945; of the Augusta (Ga.) Symph., 1947; and of the Richmond (Va.) Philh., 1949. Since 1953 he had been cond. of the Purdue Univ. (Lafayette, Ind.) Symph.

ZACK, ARTHUR, b. Vilna, Russia, Jan. 24, 1900. Studied at Inst. of Musical Art. and at Fontainebleau School of Music (France). He was a cellist with the New York Symph., 1917–18, with the Nat'l Symph. (N.Y.C.), 1918–19, and with the Cincinnati Symph., 1927–35. He founded and conducted the Cincinnati Civic Orch., 1929–35. In 1936 he founded the New Orleans Civic Symph., precursor of the present orchestra, and conducted it until 1941. He was cond. of the Gary (Ind.) Civic Symph., 1941–45. Since 1943 he has been cond. of the Rockford (Ill.) Symph.

ZIPPER, HERBERT, b. Vienna. Studied at Vienna State Acad. of Music and Univ. of Vienna. He conducted the Düsseldorf City Music Soc., 1931–33. In 1933 he helped organize the Vienna Concert Orch. After 1939 he conducted the Manila (Philippines) Symph. and headed the Acad. of Music there. In 1946 he came to the U.S.A. He taught at the New School for Social Research in New York, 1947–55, and was musical dir. of the Brooklyn Symph., 1949–51. Since 1951 he has conducted annual summer music fests. of the Manila Symph., and since 1955 the Business Men's Orch. of Chicago.

INDEX

NOTE: See also Thumbnail Sketches for conductors not entered in index.

Index

NOTE: See also Thumbnail Sketches for conductors not entered in index.

Index

Index

NOTE: See also Thumbnail Sketches for conductors not entered in index.

Index

Index

NOTE: See also Thumbnail Sketches for conductors not entered in index.

Index

Index

NOTE: See also Thumbnail Sketches for conductors not entered in index.

Index

NOTE: See also Thumbnail Sketches for conductors not entered in index.

Index

Index

NOTE: See also Thumbnail Sketches for conductors not entered in index.

Index

Index

Walter, Bruno, 10, 32, 42, 100, 238, 260-62, 280-91
  Berlin Opera, 283-84, 286-87
  Mahler influence, 282, 284-86
  musical education, 280-81
  Nazi regime, 287-90
  Vienna Opera, 284-85
Wartburg Community Symphony, 331
Waterbury Civic Orchestra, 320
Waterloo Symphony, 295, 339
Waukegan Symphony, 364
Waukesha Symphony, 386
Wausaw Symphony, 362
Wayne Orchestra, 363
Weill, Kurt, 8, 12
Weiner, Leo, 48, 172
Weingartner, Felix, 100, 113-14, 217, 238
West Hudson Symphony, 310
West Michigan Youth Orchestra, 297
West Shore Symphony, 344
West Side Story, The, 37
West Virginia State College Little Symphony, 382
Westchester Philharmonic Symphony, 298
Westchester Symphony, 326
Western Michigan College of Education Symphony, 381
Westminster Orchestra, 380
Wheeling Symphony, 318, 354
White, Paul, 20
Whitney, Robert, 248-56
  Concerto Grosso, 250
  Louisville Orchestra conductorship, 250-56
  Louisville Plan, 251-52
  modern music encouragement, 248-49, 253
  musical education, 250
Wichita Falls Symphony, 299, 318
Wichita Symphony, 365
Wilkinsburg Civic Symphony, 364

Willimantic Symphony, 359
Wilmington Symphony, 349
Windsor Symphony, 336
Winnipeg Symphony, 341
Woman's Symphony of Chicago, 196
Wonderful Town, 37
Woolett, Wilfred, 37, 201
WOR, 82, 231-32, 277
Worcester Festival, 43
Worcester Orchestra, 324, 350
Works Progress Administration, 22, 34, 100, 194-97, 212, 224, 230, 232, 376
World War I, 67, 139, 163, 166, 208, 269
World War II, 18, 31, 77, 115, 126, 165, 240, 246

xylophone, 38

Yakima Valley Symphony, 362
YMHA Symphony, 351
Yonkers Symphony, 313
York Concert Society, 382
York Symphony, 337, 350, 384
Young, Brigham, 15
Young People's Orchestra Society, 353
Young People's Record Guild, 87
Youngstown Philharmonic, 345
youth:
  attitude toward conductor, 222-23
  broadcasting for, 94, 197
  concerts for, 45, 205, 212, 219, 226-27, 230
  projects for, 38, 80, 124, 253, 278
  school music, 94, 202-3
youth orchestras (*see also* All-American Youth Orchestra), 45, 203, 205, 224-25
Ysaÿe, Eugène, 176

Zechiel, Ernest, 42
Zemlinsky, Alexander von, 209

NOTE: See also Thumbnail Sketches for conductors not entered in index.

About the Author

HOPE STODDARD was born in New Bedford, Massachusetts, and her childhood was given over, at least in after-school hours, to the study of the violin and to engaging in family quartet practice. During her adolescence she trained in other branches of music, first at the Indianapolis Conservatory of Music, then at the Institute of Musical Art (now the Juilliard School of Music), and finally at the University of Michigan. While at the university she was a violinist in a theater orchestra. Along with her musical activities, she majored in journalism. After graduation, she taught English in the Berlitz School system, one year in Copenhagen, Denmark, one year in Hamburg, Germany, and one year in New York City. She also taught the violin for a brief period. In recent years she has been engaged in editorial work on music magazines, first on the staff of *Etude—the Music Magazine,* and, since 1942, as associate editor of the *International Musician.*

Symphony Conductors of the U.S.A. is in a sense a sequel to her book *From These Comes Music: Instruments of the Band and Orchestra,* published in 1952. After writing the earlier book, she realized she had not dealt with the most important instrument of all, the symphony orchestra and its "player," the conductor. The present volume, she hopes, will make good this omission.